MIND *vs.* MONEY

MIND *vs.* MONEY

The War between
Intellectuals and Capitalism

Alan S. Kahan

Transaction Publishers
New Brunswick (U.S.A.) and London (U.K.)

Library of Congress Catalog Number: 2009038143
ISBN: 978-1-4128-1063-0
Printed in the United States of America

Library of Congress Cataloging-in-Publication Data

Kahan, Alan S.
  Mind vs. money : the war between intellectuals and capitalism / Alan S. Kahan.
      p. cm.
  Includes index.
  ISBN 978-1-4128-1063-0
    1. Capitalism. 2. Intellectuals. I. Title. II. Title: Mind versus money.

HB501.K224 2009
330.12'2--dc22

                                                    2009038143

Contents

Part II: Intellectuals and their Discontents: The Nineteenth Century (1850-1914)

Part III: Triumphs and Tragedies of the Anti-Capitalist Spirit: The Twentieth Century (1914-2001)

Acknowledgments

In writing this book I have often benefitted from the kindness of strangers and of friends. I owe thanks to the Earhart Foundation for a summer research grant that allowed the project to begin, and to Florida International University for granting me a year's leave in which to pursue it. I received valuable comments and advice from many more people than can be mentioned here, but among them must be singled out Nicholas Capaldi, Farley Chase, Henry C. Clark, Aurelian Craiutu, John Hellman, Irving Louis Horowitz, Robert Johnson, Jonathan B. Imber, Kenneth Lipartito, Aurora Morcillo, Filippo Sabetti, and Richard Whatmore. To all of them my thanks. All responsibility for the remaining errors in their fields of expertise is my own. Above all I wish to thank my family, who have been living with this project for more years than I care to count.

Part I

Mind vs. Money

1

The Ivory Tower at War

Mind vs. Money

For over 150 years, Western intellectuals have been at war with capitalism. The consequences have often been disastrous for all concerned. It is time the world realized it was at war. It is long past time for a truce.

The German philosopher Hegel said that the owl of wisdom only flies after sunset. By this he meant that we only really understand events, even ones that last a long time, when they are over. The hostility of a considerable portion of the Western intellectual elite towards capitalism has been a constant factor in modern history, sometimes with disastrous results, yet somehow escaped notice. But when an ongoing conflict lasts 150 years, we ought to be able to recognize it.

For the past 150 years, numerous Western intellectuals have trumpeted their contempt for capitalism and capitalists. They have written novels, plays, and manifestos to demonstrate the evils of the economic system in which they live. Dislike and contempt for the "bourgeoisie," for the middle classes, for industry and commerce have been prominent among leading Western writers and artists. They have been expressed by personalities as diverse as Gustave Flaubert and Karl Marx, T. S. Eliot and Friedrich Nietzsche, Ezra Pound and Pablo Picasso. It would not be hard to add another hundred famous names to this list, from Matthew Arnold to Emile Zola, and many will be found in the following chapters. Not all Western intellectuals have hated capitalism, probably not even the majority—no one has ever counted how many intellectuals there are, let alone polled them. But it is certain that a great number, and those not the least influential, have felt this way.

Such intellectuals have expressed their rejection of capitalism through participation in many different movements, including nationalism, anti-

3

Semitism, socialism, fascism, communism, and the counterculture. Anti-capitalism continues to take new forms today. The anti-globalization, Green, communitarian, and New Age movements are examples. Intellectuals have given all of them strength, legitimacy and leadership they would otherwise have lacked. What unites the radical intellectuals of the nineteenth century, the communist and fascist sympathizers of the twentieth, and the anti-globalization protestors of the twenty-first, along with many other intellectuals, is their rejection of capitalism. The more thoroughly one is an intellectual, the more likely one is to be thoroughly opposed to capitalism.

Capitalism puts many intellectuals into permanent opposition. Only the form of that opposition varies. Not all intellectuals who reject capitalism have an alternative in mind. Just as many people regard their system of government as illegitimate without having more than a hazy idea of a better one, so many intellectuals regard capitalism as illegitimate without necessarily favoring socialism or having another replacement ready to hand. One can criticize human faults without knowing how to eliminate them. Intellectuals who reject capitalism are often in this position. It does not make their criticism any less harsh.

In the days of communism and fascism, the war between mind and money was fought with deadly weapons. Millions of people died as a result, in concentration camps, gulags, and famines. They may again, unless we learn a better way to deal with the conflict. For the moment, however, mind has turned to a different kind of weapon in its perennial struggle against money. Now the war between mind and money is mostly fought as a struggle over culture and lifestyle. Culture wars are preferable to shooting wars. But even if we are lucky, and the war between mind and money remains a cultural cold war, we will still pay a high price for the conflict. Today, one of the deepest divides in Western culture is between those who despise and distrust business and those who can't understand why they do. Throughout the Western world, societies remain divided between those who practice capitalism and those who condemn it. We talk past each other, and then complain that we can't find common ground. Intellectuals and businessmen live in mutual incomprehension. In myriad forms, on myriad fronts, the battle between mind and money goes on, as it has for the last 150 years. The war between mind and money is the great unresolved conflict of modern Western society. Its death toll has been high, and may yet go higher. To have a hope of ending it, we must first understand it.

Why do so many intellectuals hate capitalism? What is wrong with it? To many intellectuals, the answers to these questions are so obvious that they are not worth asking. The reasons they feel this way are part of their very identity. They derive from the role intellectuals play in modern societies, and from the historical traditions that inspire them. Intellectuals' identity, their social situation, and their history are the point of departure for their assaults on capitalism.

By "capitalism," for which I will occasionally substitute the less politically-charged term "commercial society," I mean the sum total of a way of organizing economic production, and the people, technology and values most closely associated with that form of production. To put it another way, capitalism equals a free market economy + modern technologies + the middle classes + the set of values and attitudes associated with them. Typical anti-capitalist intellectuals may not attack all aspects of capitalism, but they reject at least one, and often more. They may wish to abolish private property, or preserve it while abolishing big business and modern technology. They may make big-time stock speculators or small-town shopkeepers the chief targets of their wrath, or regard both as slaves of Mammon. Sometimes intellectuals want to replace capitalism with something else. Sometimes they disdain capitalists while being resigned to the system. There is a broad spectrum of intellectual opposition to capitalism. It varies in both kind and intensity, but it is always there. Many intellectuals don't like capitalism. They almost never have. They never will. Sometimes they find an audience.

Does this constitute a war? Sometimes it kills people, sometimes not. Sometimes capitalism is for a time overturned—mostly not. The intensity of the conflict rises and falls over time, as does the intensity of intellectuals' anti-capitalist sentiments. Those intellectuals most violently opposed to capitalism are usually a minority of those who disdain capitalists. Some may wish to quibble over whether "war" is the right word for a perennial conflict waged more often with insults than with guns. None can dispute the conflict's existence, duration, and importance. It is all part of the same struggle, that of mind vs. money.

Who Are the "Intellectuals"?

To understand intellectuals' hostility towards capitalism, we must understand who "intellectuals" are. Responding to a similar question about how to define a notoriously slippery term, a justice of the United States Supreme Court once said that while he couldn't define pornography, he knew it when he saw it. It is not hard to identify intellectuals this way, but an understanding of the conflict between mind and money requires a more lengthy analysis of what makes an intellectual and how intellectuals fit, or don't fit, into modern society.

What is an intellectual? How do you recognize one? A short answer is that the modern intelligentsia is composed of academia plus bohemia, that is, of professors, writers, and artists. But this answer, while short and simple, is also vague, and, strictly speaking, inaccurate. Many professors, writers, and artists are not intellectuals, while many people outside these professions are. An English professor is more likely to be an intellectual than is a plumber or an accountant, but not all English professors are intellectuals, and some intellectuals are plumbers.

There are three ways to distinguish intellectuals that together give us insight into why intellectuals dislike capitalism—the social, the linguistic, and the moral. The social signs like occupation and education are the ones that first strike the eye, although they are less important than the kind of language a person uses, and above all the kinds of moral attitude they have.

Socially, intellectuals can often be distinguished by their occupations and their education. The occupations intellectuals practice have changed over time. In the nineteenth century, bohemia, that is, independent writers and artists, novelists and journalists and poets, made up a much larger portion of the intellectual class than did academia. Until the late nineteenth century there were very few professors, even in Europe. In 1860, England, France, and Germany could count fewer than 3,500 university faculty among them, versus more than 10,000 writers and editors. By comparison, in 2004 there were 1.6 *million* "post-secondary teachers" in the United States versus about 320,000 "writers and editors." The change in proportion, as well as in number, has been enormous. A twenty-first-century list of professions in which American and European intellectuals congregate would include professors of humanities and the social sciences, now the largest single group, along with other concentrations in media, publishing, non-profit work, some church organizations, and writers and critics. It is above all the elites of these professions who are most likely to be intellectuals—and correspondingly most likely to be opposed to capitalism.[1]

One thing that hasn't changed from the nineteenth century to the present is what intellectuals *don't* do for a living. They are not part of the business world. As a general rule the more distant from the process of production and trade, and the more permanent this isolation, the more willing a social group is to be radically anti-capitalist. This is why intellectuals have often been more hostile to capitalism than people who work on the assembly line.

The other social marker for intellectuals, along with occupation, is education. One thing intellectuals have had in common throughout history is an advanced education. Bohemians may drop out of college, but one way or another they have learned what they need outside the classroom. Through their education, intellectuals have attained a mastery of certain cultural values, acquired a cultural capital. But intellectuals are not an *economic* class. Like medieval nobles, intellectuals derive their identity from their status, not their money. Their education is a crucial part of how they get their status. Over the course of the twentieth century, this status has increasingly required academic proof in the form of a college degree, and increasingly an advanced degree (bohemians partly excepted). Proving one's educational pedigree has replaced proving one's noble ancestry.[2]

What matters most, however, is not the degree, it is the kind of education received. Before 1914, a high school diploma of the correct kind, involving lots of study of Greek and Latin, was often all the formal education many intellectuals had. Today, the vast majority of people with college degrees are not intellectuals, because they do not have the right *kind* of education. The kind of education necessary to make an intellectual has always been centered around the liberal arts. As etymologists love to repeat, "liberal" derives from the Latin *liber*, "free," and the liberal arts are those subjects suitable for a free person to study. In the ancient world a free person, unlike a slave, was presumed to be someone who did not need to work for a living, and thus the subjects included in a liberal education had no direct professional purpose. The canonical texts from the Greco-Roman world that were the basis for advanced education through World War I were anything but friendly to commerce. The divorce between elite education and business is of long standing in Western society.

Advanced education has always been a necessary, never a sufficient qualification for being an intellectual. Education and occupation need to be supplemented by more intimate traits, such as language and attitudes, before we identify someone as an intellectual. Indeed, intellectuals betray themselves well before an observer has had time to learn what they do for a living or whether they have a Ph.D. By and large, when you see one, hear one, or read one, you know one. Modern Western intellectuals use a common language that distinguishes them from non-intellectuals.

Intellectuals, whether they speak English, French, or German, use a special kind of language: careful critical discourse (CCD). In CCD, if you say something, you must be prepared to prove it by giving reasons, not by appeals to higher authority. For an intellectual, nothing can be justified simply by an appeal to authority or tradition. True, it gives weight to an intellectual's argument to quote Plato or Kant in its favor. But CCD never considers an authority beyond challenge—in principle anything and anyone is subject to being corrected.[3] You can never say something "just because it's my opinion." In the language of CCD, you are only entitled to have an opinion if you can justify it. This is democratic in one sense, but aristocratic in another, since not everyone is capable of making the kind of argument careful critical discourse requires, and those who can't don't get to vote: "Intellectuals have long believed that those who know the rule, who know the theory by which they act, are superior because they lead an 'examined' life...." If you don't talk right, intellectuals will look down on you because you are not using CCD to justify your actions or beliefs. This is another way in which modern intellectuals form a kind of aristocracy. In return, intellectuals are often disdained as "highbrows" by those who find CCD alien and alienating. This linguistic divide is one source of the hostility between mind and money.[4]

If one thinks of intellectuals as the people who use this kind of language, the people who follow the rules of this game, one can see how certain groups stand at the fuzzy periphery of the intelligentsia, for example clergy who refer to revelation as unchallengeable authority—although the meaning of revealed scripture may remain open to debate following the rules of careful critical discourse. The more fundamentalist the clergy, the less they believe interpretation is open to debate, the less chance there is that they are intellectuals. Another way in which CCD distinguishes the intellectual from the generic clergyman or teacher is that its critical function is dedicated to creating *new* truths, and new language, not just passing on old traditions. Part of being an intellectual in the modern world is to aspire to originality. Both because of their bias in favor of innovation, and because of their willingness to criticize old ways of doing things, intellectuals can be very useful in capitalist society.[5]

Are scientists or engineers intellectuals? They certainly want to make new discoveries, but in a sense much of science and technology does not use critical language in ordinary circumstances, and thus it is sometimes unclear whether they are intellectuals. Scientists generally agree about so many things that for them there are large areas that are effectively beyond debate. On the other hand, when experiments give unexpected results, scientists use critical discourse to resolve their problems. Perhaps because they use critical discourse relatively rarely, scientists and technicians are the intellectuals least likely to be hostile to capitalism, basically because they are the least intellectual of intellectuals. Which is not to deny that many of those engaged in "basic research" look down on those who work in "applied" fields, partly because of the association of applied science with commerce.[6]

But the most important part of what makes intellectuals are not their jobs, the universities they attend, or even the way they talk. It is something deeper. The nineteenth-century American psychologist and philosopher William James contrasted businessmen and intellectuals as "men who *have*" and "men who *are*." Beyond the anti-commercial prejudice he expressed (James doesn't think businessmen are anything but their money), he is right that intellectuals are people who are recognized for their internal qualities. The external signs are never sufficient. It is the attitude that makes the intellectual. All intellectuals have a bohemian attitude. They all like to use the moral voice, though some speak very quietly.[7]

What is a bohemian attitude? Both academics and other intellectuals possess it. It is based on pride in independence and autonomy. Autonomy is a crucial value for intellectuals, who need to be as free and independent as possible in order to speak the language of critical discourse, free from interference by authority.[8] This means not just freedom from interference by political or religious authority, but freedom from the authority of the marketplace. Indeed, as freedom from political and religious restraint became increasingly common in Western societies, freedom from the demands and desires of the vulgar crowd who make up the marketplace has seemed to many intellectuals of ever-greater importance.

Western intellectuals place great emphasis on their own autonomy and independence. Avant-garde artists take pride in their lack of affiliation with anything, and they look down on all "establishment" institutions—including universities. They are the most autonomous of all intellectuals, the most independent. Tenured professors feel autonomous even when they are employed by large corporations (universities). The value they place on autonomy is the real reason academics are so attached to the idea of tenure—it is necessary to their self-image as autonomous agents. Tenure means autonomy. Without tenure, they would find it harder to be intellectuals.

Intellectuals' emphasis on autonomy and independence sometimes takes on external forms, e.g., long hair, unusual dress, etc. Among intellectuals, the externals of lifestyle help separate academia from bohemia. Despite their fundamental kinship, academic intellectuals do not always get along with bohemian intellectuals, and relations between the two fractions of the intelligentsia have often been strained. The bohemian rejects the outward forms of life typical of capitalism in favor of lifestyles more in keeping with a stress on autonomy and individuality. The bohemian fraction of the intelligentsia insists on the external display of its values, whereas the academic wing is more discreet. Bohemians sometimes upset both academic intellectuals and the bourgeoisie with their ways. For bohemians, all forms of experimental living, sexual, communal, primitive, etc., are weapons in the struggle against capitalism. These methods derive from the stress on autonomy and independence common to all intellectuals, and as a result they often get some sympathy from shorthaired academics.

The bohemian attitude leaves little room for recognition of how a life within capitalist society could possibly be worthwhile. From the beginning of modern bohemia in the 1830s, artists used the word "bourgeois" as a term of abuse, the most insulting in their vocabulary. It meant "slave." This attitude is epitomized by the French poet, Surrealist, and later Communist, Louis Aragon: "Ah, bankers, students, workers, officials, servants, you are the cock-suckers of the useful, the masturbators of necessity. I shall never work. My hands are pure." This is extreme. However, even the most externally conformist intellectuals share the bohemian attitude to some degree. They insist on their autonomy and independence.[9]

Bohemia's aura is always hovering somewhere near the back of the academic's two-car garage, at least in her imagination. Intellectuals have to float free, or they aren't intellectuals. Karl Mannheim, a very short-haired, clean-shaven Hungarian/German sociologist, defined the essence of being an intellectual as enjoying a "free-floating" social position, unattached to any social group. Mannheim used this free-floating status to claim that intellectuals should act as the arbiters of all social conflicts, since they alone could see beyond narrow class interests. Most real bohemians are more free-floating than the academic Mannheim—they would rather ridicule society than rule it.[10]

The bohemian attitude is at the root of much intellectual opposition to middle-class lifestyles. For example, most intellectuals think that being employed by a large corporation (without tenure) must be a terrible thing. The corporate employee is unable to maintain the attitude of autonomy necessary to being an intellectual—or so many intellectuals think. Intellectuals cannot comprehend how anyone could possibly accept such a life. Middle management is their nightmare. They have nothing but contempt for those who in their view have surrendered their autonomy, who have "sold out," words commonly employed both by artists and academics for those who enter the business world. Intellectuals project their own need for workplace autonomy onto others. To be employed by a large corporation is to be less than fully autonomous, hence less than fully able to speak the language of critical discourse, hence less than fully rational, hence transformed into a "thing," hence "alienated." If the intellectual reserves his contempt for the Harvard graduate who chooses an alienated life because it pays well, he reserves his compassion for the poor man who has no real choice but to take a job on an assembly line or in a supermarket. Intellectuals typically claim that these proletarians are alienated and oppressed because they lack professional autonomy, that capitalism is the source of this oppression, and that the proletariat should make a revolution against it. Their bohemian attitude makes ordinary life in capitalist society *unintelligible* from intellectuals' perspective. It can only be understood as the result of oppression, stupidity, or a profound spiritual flaw.

A revealing historical analogy can be drawn between intellectuals and the Catholic clergy. One might think of the academic and bohemian wings of the intelligentsia as the modern equivalents of the regular and secular clergy of medieval times. Regular clergy (professors, other intellectuals with settled professions) are those who follow the "rules" of monastic life, that is have fixed positions and wear appropriate clothing. Secular clergy (independent writers, self-employed journalists, artists) are out wandering, in the world but not of it.[11] Some look the part, others don't. There is no sharp frontier line. Bohemia is academia's most distant province, not a separate country—the academic is a bohemian with a steady job. To continue the analogy between modern intellectuals and the Catholic clergy, being an intellectual demands a certain voluntary isolation from "the world." Both the academic and bohemian wings of the intelligentsia take care to physically separate themselves from the bourgeoisie. The academic works in his Ivory Tower. He inhabits a college that is physically and psychologically isolated from what students and professors often call "the real world." The campus is the direct spiritual descendant of the cloister.

The bohemian, whether Parisian artist, London musician, or San Francisco hippy, lives in a bohemia, a neighborhood like Montmartre or Soho or Haight-Ashbury that may not be populated entirely by intellectuals (there usually aren't enough), but rarely includes many middle-class types. This physical isolation from capitalism, and the sense of autonomy that goes with it, gives bohemians something in common with the medieval monks and nuns who also renounced the world, although modern bohemians keep at most the vow of poverty, not the vows of chastity and obedience. But even their sexual mores have something in common with those of the Catholic clergy—they don't get married. Nineteenth-century bohemians renounced the practice of marriage well before it declined throughout society. In the early twentieth century the arch-intellectual Julien Benda was so impressed by clerical habits in this respect that he thought all intellectuals should remain unmarried (although he eventually gave in at the age of 80). Marriage was bourgeois, and had a deleterious effect on one's intellectual and financial independence.[12]

Intellectuals' resemblance to a clergy is increased when one considers a final aspect of the defining moral core of intellectuals. Along with their profession, their education, their language, and their bohemian attitude, intellectuals see themselves as the moral conscience of society.[13] They may be the conscience of a class, an ethnic group, a nation, a world or an era, depending on the inspiration of the moment, but all intellectuals are to some extent "public moralists." They like to see themselves as the world's conscience, the "unacknowledged legislators of the world," as the English poet Shelley put it. It is this attribute that makes professors feel entitled to despise stockbrokers, and obligated to condemn child labor.[14]

The moral tone is one of the identifying marks of the intelligentsia. Whether intellectuals are on the left or the right, whether they hate capitalism or love it, they all use the moral voice. Appropriately, it has been suggested the word "intellectual" was first coined at the end of the nineteenth century during the Dreyfus Affair in France, when many prominent artists and scholars took moral stands (on both sides) about Captain Dreyfus, a Jew wrongfully accused of being a German spy.[15] But Western intellectuals have always adopted the tone of moral critics.

Intellectuals see themselves as people with a moral role to play. They play it, of course, in a characteristically intellectual way, following the rules of critical language. They use CCD to morally condemn capitalism. While intellectuals often violently disagree among themselves about values, they commonly appeal to a moral order against the moral cacophony of the marketplace. It is hard to imagine a more clerical role than this, albeit performed (usually) without benefit of scripture. Modern intellectuals have inherited the clergy's role as moral critics. The passion intellectuals put into their moral function is a religious fervor. But unlike the clergy, their basis for criticism is ambiguous, and doubly so: Their vocation is not universally recognized, and they have no revelation to appeal to. Instead they appeal to logic of their own creation, backed by no greater and no less an authority than reason. Intellectuals are a pseudo-clergy.

Such a class is likely to be critical of any society. To a limited extent, therefore, intellectuals' criticism of capitalism is simply criticism of the society they happen to live in. But intellectuals are especially likely to criticize capitalist society, and to do so especially harshly. This is partly because of the Western educational tradition, but it is still more because the attitudes and values that make up an intellectual's identity conflict with capitalism. However, to understand what has made intellectuals into a permanently alienated elite, it is not enough to understand who intellectuals are. Their identity must be placed in its social context.

An Accidental Aristocracy

Democratic society is based on equality. Intellectuals stick out from democratic society like a sore thumb. They are different—even when they hate to be. However much they identify themselves with the people around them, they are not the same. Their feeling of autonomy sets them apart from others. Their education provides their pedigree, and their lifestyle, whether academic or bohemian, separates them from the middle classes—not necessarily very far, but far enough. They occupy a social position that other groups in democratic society cannot easily attain, no matter how much money they make. No intellectual has ever been foolish enough to prophesy that the majority of people will ever become intellectuals. Intellectuals' education, language, and bohemian attitude are genuinely aristocratic traits that they cannot give up, no matter how much they might want to. Despite the intellectual's allegiance to democratic values, he is always part of a small, elite minority. He is an aristocrat.[16]

However, intellectuals are the first accidental aristocracy in the history of the world. Their status does not come from conquest, inheritance, or any deliberate imposition of their superiority over others. It is not formally acknowledged. Yet it exists. Because intellectuals are an accidental aristocracy, created and reproduced by a democratic society, their social and psychological situation is particularly complicated. They are both alien to democracy and democracy's leading partisans. Their criticism of capitalism is shaped by both these traits.

Intellectuals adopt some aristocratic attitudes hostile to democratic society and capitalism. They look down on people who don't speak their language of careful critical discourse—the majority. They look down on people who accept too many limits on their autonomy—such people are alienated, bourgeois, slaves—but these people are most of the workforce. In a democratic society, the chief way people have of distinguishing themselves is by their wealth. From this comes democratic society's constant preoccupation with making money. Intellectuals look down on people who work for money—and that is what capitalism is all about. Further, intellectuals do not accept that since all people must work for their bread, all work is morally equal. Intellectuals are a hard-working bunch for the most part (it is not easy to write a novel or a Ph.D. thesis), and they consider work a virtue. But not all work. Intellectuals have an aristocratic contempt for work whose chief motivation is profit, and for those who choose to perform that work, although they may exempt the poor and uneducated from their contempt, as people with no choice. Few intellectuals will admit in public that they are even partly motivated to do what they do for mere pay. They say that if they cared about money, they'd be lawyers.[17]

The aristocratic attitude intellectuals take towards doing something for money is especially important. It is at the center of the clash between capitalism and intellectuals. Once people make the democratic assumption that working is honorable and that work is always motivated, at least in part, by pay, "the huge gap that formerly separated the various occupations in aristocratic societies disappears." It is precisely because intellectuals do not accept these democratic assumptions about work that there is an aristocratic difference between them and everyone else. This difference is a point of departure for intellectuals' contempt for capitalism. It is one reason why poets and professors despise stockbrokers and businessmen. Groups defined primarily by their status, their non-economic identity, like aristocrats and intellectuals, look down on money-making and especially on entrepreneurship. It is impossible for them to accept doing business as a legitimate way for people to spend their lives. This is why intellectuals are fundamentally hostile to a bourgeois lifestyle.[18]

But intellectuals are not an aristocracy. Intellectuals cannot be a real aristocracy because they live in a democratic society that assumes everyone is equal. Even though they are a permanent minority with aristocratic traits, they are not true aristocrats. Their aristocratic status is an accident. Just as they are a pseudo-clergy, intellectuals are a pseudo-aristocracy. This shapes their hostility to capitalism in three ways. First, intellectuals feel isolated from the masses by all the things that make them different. A real aristocracy wouldn't care (and wouldn't *be* isolated), but intellectuals hate this. Second, as a pseudo-aristocracy, intellectuals have a hard time achieving a sense of class consciousness. They cannot openly claim to lead society like an aristocracy should, not just because society wouldn't let them, but because they don't feel they have a right to lead it. After all, they believe in equality too. Finally, this difficult social position leads many intellectuals to suffer all kinds of painful psychological difficulties, from megalomania to self-hatred.

Many intellectuals think there is a simple way to solve *all* these problems, and more: Revolution. The Polish writer Czeslaw Milosz suggested that revolution is attractive to intellectuals because it is the only way they can join the rest of society and overcome their isolation. In a revolution, intellectuals' hostility to capitalism takes on a democratic appearance. During revolutions intellectuals, even though they are a minority, can attack capitalism on behalf of the majority. Their need to identify with a larger group makes an important psychological contribution to anti-capitalism among intellectuals. It helps make them into revolutionaries.

But unless there is a revolution going on, many intellectuals feel isolated. They long for ties with "the people." If only they had them, what miracles could they not produce? "We lack a lever, the earth slips out from under our feet. The support is missing for all of us, literary men and scribblers that we are. What good does it do? To what needs does all this language respond? There is no link between us and the crowd.—Too bad for the crowd, but too bad for us, above all," wrote the great French novelist Gustave Flaubert.[19] Real aristocrats are linked with those above and below them in a thousand ways, but intellectuals, mere pseudo-aristocrats, are not. So the inhabitants of the Ivory Tower bemoan their own isolation and alienation. Attempting to escape from their Towers, they write paeans to the simple life and the simple people (not Flaubert—he was much too aristocratic). Often they wish they really were "authentic" proletarians or peasants or members of oppressed racial minorities: "Up to now there has only been one category of person who sometimes argues that a pair of boots is worth more than Shakespeare: writers. Exclusively. And there was even one of them, one of the greatest, who put down his pen and set himself to making boots: Tolstoy."[20] The white American novelist Norman Mailer liked to imagine himself a "nigger." Intellectuals romanticize the masses to whom they do not belong. At the extreme, like Mailer, they envy them. There is an element of self-hatred motivating intellectuals' hostility to capitalism. They often really wish they weren't aristocrats in so many ways. But they can't help it. You can give your money to the poor, but you can't give your education to the underprivileged (although you can imitate the way they talk). Nothing short of suicide can prevent intellectuals from being aristocrats. Their situation, while accidental, is inevitable. As a result, many feel torn between an aristocratic sense of their own superiority and a desperate desire to be like everyone else. Or rather, like everyone else except the bourgeoisie. So, in order to pretend they are like other people, they attack those who stick out above the masses—like the rich. They can do this by supporting reforms, but there is much more psychological satisfaction to be found in revolution.

After a while, however, intellectuals tend to leave whatever party they join. Bohemia, homeland of rampant individualism, is not fertile territory for the development of enduring loyalties. For individual intellectuals the need for commitment can sometimes triumph, as in the case of some well-known communist intellectuals. But more often intellectuals become disillusioned. They have a hard time making durable connections with other groups. Even if the revolution succeeds in taking power, afterwards the intellectuals go back to being pseudo-aristocrats. Stalin chased them out of the party in Russia, and Mao did the same in China. But the harm had been done.

It is a consequence of the accidental nature of their role that intellectuals make their revolutions in someone else's name. Intellectuals are part of democratic society, and thus find it difficult to claim privileges for themselves. In an aristocratic society, class consciousness is natural to every social group. In democratic society, class consciousness is much harder to come by, as socialists everywhere have learned (democratic societies contain classes, but aristocratic societies are defined by them). Even when it exists, class consciousness in democratic society is much weaker than in aristocratic society. Its functions are largely usurped by national/ethnic identifications, which intellectuals (and others) often adopt in preference to a developed consciousness of themselves as a class. When intellectuals lead a revolution or a reform, they do not do so in the name of their own interests, but always in the name of some group with whom they identify themselves—the proletariat, the nation, the Third World.

Intellectuals hide behind egalitarian masks because they are afraid of letting others see that their face looks different. This is a psychologically difficult position. Intellectuals' position as a pseudo-aristocracy has other psychological consequences, too. Their self-esteem is boosted by "the self-regard which comes from preoccupation and contact with the most vital facts of human and cosmic existence, and the implied attitude of derogation towards those who act in more mundane or more routine capacities." On the other hand, intellectuals are also capable of an unusual degree of self-abasement. The Czech novelist Milan Kundera put it this way: "The intellectual is the person who doubts. He doubts nothing with so much verve as himself.... There exists a sort of masochism of intellectuals. With delight, they say that those who steal their freedom are right." The classic example is communist intellectuals abasing themselves in submission to party discipline, while asserting themselves against bourgeois society. The self-abasement of some intellectuals comes from their need to belong to a larger whole from which they feel excluded, as well as from their awkward social position and weak group consciousness. Victor Brombert, in his study of French intellectuals, found that politically engaged intellectuals often had enormous self-hatred and a strong death wish. The origin of their attraction to Marxism often lay in a sense of humility with regard to the proletariat and a need to save their souls by sharing the lower classes' suffering.[21]

These psychological traits—self-abasement/self-esteem, guilt at being different, a desire to connect with a bigger group—are not found in every individual intellectual, or perhaps even most. But they contribute greatly to the fervor with which many intellectuals wage war against capitalism, because intellectuals blame them on capitalism. This arms their anti-capitalism with the enthusiasm usually reserved for religion. Intellectuals' psychology gives their anti-capitalism its messianic tinge, and makes it into a religion. By overcoming capitalism, intellectuals' problems as individuals and those of the whole world can be simultaneously overcome. Fighting capitalism has given ultimate meaning to the lives of many intellectuals. Indeed, anti-capitalism is the most widespread and widely practiced spiritual commitment among intellectuals.

As a source of ultimate meaning and a means of resolving psychological problems, anti-capitalism becomes a religion, but it is a religion usually described in secular terms. Such a secular religion may be something like communism or ecologism, but more broadly it refers to the moral role intellectuals play and the intensity with which they play it. Intellectuals bring prophetic fervor to their pronouncements on politics and socio-economic policy. Simultaneously aristocrats and clerics, they aim to "*reunite... power and goodness.*" It is their mission as a pseudo-clergy to bring their moral voice to bear on capitalism's moral failings, and their duty as pseudo-aristocrats to lead the people on a better path. Intellectuals want to be rationally critical yet morally exalted. Thus they manufacture ersatz religions that combine rationality and romance, such as the myth of revolution. Alas, intellectuals' myths have proven as murderous as those of any fundamentalism.[22]

For the past 150 years, intellectuals' position in democratic society has led them to reject capitalism far more often than any other social group in Western civilization. Their identity and social situation has made them a permanently alienated elite. Maybe the solution to all the trouble they've caused is as simple as most of the remedies they have proposed for capitalism. Maybe we should just get rid of them.

The First Thing We Do, Let's Get Rid of All the Intellectuals?[23]

Since intellectuals don't like capitalism, why does capitalism put up with them? Why should a capitalist society tolerate this revolutionary clergy, this pseudo-aristocracy, with all its conflicts and complexes? Because it finds them useful, and because in any case they are its inevitable by-product.

The formation of modern capitalism and the creation of an independent class of intellectuals seem to have occurred more or less simultaneously, in the eighteenth and early nineteenth centuries (see chapter 3). Born at the same moment, their early alliance against common enemies—feudalism, the Church, tradition—soon turned into a bitter quarrel, as is often the case with siblings. But intellectuals' contributions to capitalism did not end with their quarrel. When modern capitalism was taking shape, intellectuals contributed greatly to it, and they continue to contribute to it today, like it or not, and whether they intend to or not.

Capitalism depends on innovation, and while intellectuals don't have a monopoly on innovation, they are an important source of it. Their independence, and their careful critical language, make them a prime source of new ideas and of questioning old ones. A class of critics is a nuisance, but it is a useful nuisance. This is especially true when it comes to science and technical innovation. However, intellectuals' contribution to capitalism is not just a matter of technical and scientific innovation. It is also a question of the moral and political contributions intellectuals have made and continue to make to capitalism, willy-nilly.

For example, intellectuals helped instigate the tremendous increase in religious tolerance in the West, which contributed enormously to the development of Western capitalism. If Catholics couldn't do business with Protestants, and Jews couldn't do most kinds of business at all, where would the Western economy be? More directly, intellectuals created the revolution in attitudes towards commerce and industry that, briefly but crucially, helped eighteenth-century capitalism become respectable (see chapter 3). Capitalism is further indebted to intellectuals for their role in destroying traditional economic and political forms that hinder it. Their critical language, their rejection of traditional authority, help create free markets, and their insistence on information being made available to the public makes it available to business. From the Enlightenment to the New Deal to the environmental movement, intellectuals have stimulated reforms that strengthened capitalism. Capitalist society cannot do without intellectuals because it depends on their critical thinking.

Perhaps above all, capitalism owes to intellectuals the moral *criticism* which has resulted in a socio-economic system strong enough to withstand all the assaults that intellectuals and others have mustered against it. Capitalism needs the intellectual to bring other standards of judgment than its own to bear on the problems a capitalist society faces—it needs their moral voice. Capitalism encourages certain virtues, like prudence. It teaches us lying and cheating are bad policy. But people need other moral standards alongside enlightened self-interest. This is one use for a class of aristocratic, alienated preachers—every society needs someone with a moral voice, and a secular society has nowhere else to turn for one. So much the better if the voices don't agree with each other, as intellectuals typically don't. Competition is good.

Even if capitalism didn't need intellectuals for their positive contributions, the increasing demand for educated workers would create an ever-increasing number of them. At the most practical level, capitalism needs intellectuals to train its technicians and experts in the universities. Although full-fledged intellectuals, as opposed to technicians and experts, are unintended by-products of education in a technology-based economy, they are an inevitable one. Nevertheless, mind and money struggle over how many intellectuals should be produced. The struggle between mind and money over whether the university is intended to train experts or intellectuals has been behind many battles over the reform of higher education. In the early twentieth century the German sociologist Max Weber realized that "behind all the present discussions of the foundations of the educational system, the struggle of the 'specialist type of man' against the older type of 'cultivated man' is hidden at some decisive point...." It is at the root of academics' resistance to curriculums that emphasize vocational training.[24]

Capitalism tries to fight back against its intellectual critics by destroying the educational system that produces them. It cannot simply destroy the universities, but it can try to limit the education universities offer to what is necessary for producing bureaucrats and experts, rather than intellectuals. It mostly succeeds, but there are exceptions. If there weren't, capitalism would be forced to create them, because it does need intellectuals. The result is that "unlike any other type of society, capitalism inevitably and by virtue of the very logic of its civilisation creates, educates and subsidizes a vested interest in social unrest," intellectuals. Intellectuals, like the poor, will always be with us. Or perhaps the intelligentsia will outlast the poor. One can foresee a time when capitalism will abolish poverty as Jesus knew it, but capitalism is doomed to keep rearing these wolves at its breast. Nothing it can do will change them into lambs (turning wolves into lambs requires an Apocalypse first), and in any case capitalism needs these wolves.[25]

The argument that capitalist society requires intellectuals and cannot afford to get rid of them does much to explain why capitalist society has preserved and reproduced this hostile element in ever-greater numbers. The intellectuals thus created cannot be silenced by a capitalist society except at an unacceptable cost. The result? Capitalism creates an intellectual class that detests it. This means that the conflict between mind and money will be with us forever, or at least as long as capitalism shall last. This is not a bad thing. It is a paradox of history that, unintentionally or even against their will, intellectual critics of capitalism have helped improve it. Intellectuals would do an even better job of improving capitalism, at much less cost in blood and tears, if they were persuaded that capitalism was worth keeping. Capitalism's, and civilization's, fate may depend upon persuading them. Western history since World War I has been the story of one hair's-breadth escape from disaster after another, when capitalism, by the skin of its teeth, has held off the assaults of communism, fascism, the counterculture, and other movements many intellectuals have supported against it, while so far avoiding nuclear catastrophe. The purpose of this book is to explain how this often-deadly class war between mind and money can be limited. The conflict cannot be ended, but it must be moderated. Otherwise, we are we doomed to witness an eternity of doomed revolutions.

An Insoluble Problem?

Discussions about how to persuade intellectuals to give up or moderate their hostility to capitalism usually fail to take their social and psychological identity into account. For example, some have suggested that improving the material situation of the average intellectual might change her attitude. As one observer noted, "Nature has no cure for this sort of madness, though I have known a legacy from a rich relative to work wonders." Others think intellectuals are dissatisfied because ever-increasing numbers of them are unable to find jobs, or are unsatisfied with the jobs they do find. But the most professionally successful and well-paid intellectuals are often the most critical of capitalism. If you want to find intellectuals who don't like capitalism, the best places to look for them are the liberal arts faculty at Harvard or Oxford or the College de France. Doubling or tripling the salaries of college professors, even cutting their teaching responsibilities in half, is not likely to change their attitude towards capitalism. As the writer Arthur Koestler noted, "in 1931, when at last I had achieved a comfortable income, I found that it was time to join the ranks of the proletariat," and he joined the Communist Party. An infusion of cash does nothing to change an intellectual's identity or social position, since money is not the source of either.[26]

It has also sometimes been suggested that the reason intellectuals don't like capitalism is that they don't really know anything about it. From this point of view, the hostility of intellectuals for capitalism over the past 150 years is the history of an intellectual error, another chapter in the long story of human ignorance and its terrible consequences. Indeed, the average professor in the liberal arts, not to mention the average artist or writer, is woefully ignorant of the rudiments of economics. But ignorance is not a good explanation for intellectuals' hostility to capitalism. Intellectuals are not unusual in their ignorance of the basic principles of free-market economics. Many people who do not object to capitalism are equally ignorant. Requiring college students—apprentice intellectuals—to take basic economics courses is unlikely to have any considerable effect on most intellectuals' attitudes. The problem is that their morality and the economic system don't mesh. As George J. Stigler, himself a Nobel prize-winning conservative economist, noted, no amount of economic training "would wholly eliminate the instinctive dislike for a system of organizing economic life through the search for profits. It will still appear to many intellectuals that a system in which men were driven by a reasonably selfless devotion to the welfare of other men would be superior to one in which they sought their own preferment. This ethic is deeply embedded in the major religions...," as well as, we might add, in all the secular religions, e. g. socialism, ecologism, etc., preached by intellectuals since the nineteenth century.[27]

To say that capitalism stinks to high heaven but that manure improves productivity is not a satisfactory solution. It begs the moral question. Socialism retains intellectuals' sympathies despite a dismal economic performance. Capitalism attracts intellectuals' contempt regardless of its economic performance. Its economic successes over the past 150 years have merely changed the *forms* of intellectuals' opposition. Instead of becoming socialists, intellectuals in the twenty-first century usually call themselves something else, ecologists or anti-globalization protestors. But the basic attitude does not change.

Permanently alienated, intellectuals have been the permanent revolutionaries of the modern world. Karl Marx claimed that the bourgeoisie's situation required it to continually revolutionize the world. He wrote that "the bourgeoisie cannot exist without constantly revolutionising the instruments of production, and thereby the relations of production, and with them the whole relations of society." True enough, but he left his own kind out of the equation. The complement of the industrial revolution is the intellectual revolution, and the two have accompanied one another throughout modern history. It would be difficult, and pointless, to decide whether the bourgeoisie or the intelligentsia has proven to be the more revolutionary class. Sometimes they have shared an enemy (see chapter 3), but far more often they have been antagonists. Indeed, conflict between intellectuals and capitalism is a constant of modern history.[28]

Hegel thought of human history as progressing through a series of such conflicts. In each one, two great principles would fight with one another. He called these two principles the "thesis" and the "antithesis." In Hegelian terms, the contest between intellectuals and capitalism is the great struggle in Western history since 1850, and in this battle mind and money are the thesis and antithesis. Hegel also argued that such conflicts come to an end when a "synthesis" between the two opponents is found, one that combines the best elements of both of them. But here one must depart from Hegel. The nature of this conflict shows that no synthesis between mind and money is possible. None of the solutions previously proposed for intellectuals' hostility to capitalism will work because they all assume that this hostility can be eliminated. It cannot be. Intellectuals cannot be weaned away from anti-capitalist attitudes, because intellectuals are a permanently alienated elite within capitalism. It is only once we recognize that their hostility to capitalism will not go away that there is any chance of finding a solution that might bring about a truce in the war between mind and money.

The solution lies in changing the terms of the problem. The conflict between mind and money is intimately related to the *positive* social role intellectuals play in a capitalist society. It's their *function* in capitalism to be alienated, their job to provide careful critical discourse to the society around them, to form an adversary culture. They shouldn't be fired for performing their job with enthusiasm. Besides, many of them have tenure—they can't be fired at all. And abolishing tenure at the cost of diminishing the production of careful critical discourse would be a losing proposition. Capitalists and intellectuals are both more productive when there is competition, a competition that limits the power of any one firm or class. The conflict between mind and money is a valuable way of preventing either side from ignoring the truths that the other possesses. It is a necessary stimulant, a crucial element in human progress. But stimulants are dangerous. Badly administered, they can produce sudden death, or addiction. In this case, they have done both. Western intellectuals have been addicted to the opium of revolution, with deadly results.

Intellectuals do a valuable job for capitalism, but this job could be done at a lower cost. The tens of millions of dead in the revolutions and counter-revolutions of the twentieth century were a very high price to pay. Today the culture wars between mind and money prevent America and Europe from seriously addressing many of their vital problems. To find a solution that costs less in blood and tears, we must understand who intellectuals are, and how they relate to democratic society. We must also tell the long story of the wars between mind and money. Only if we understand the conflict and its recurrent patterns can we master it. Understanding battles past is necessary if war is to be avoided in future.

However, the purpose behind this story is not historical, even if much of the book is. This is a polemic, not against intellectuals, but against the role they have too often played. What is needed is a truce between mind and money, not a victory by either side. But "truce" does not really explain the goal. A better word was briefly popularized by Henry Kissinger in the latter years of the Cold War between the United States and the Soviet Union: détente.

Détente does not mean alliance, or even peace—mind and money can never be at peace. But destructive class war can and must be limited. It must be transformed into a productive class struggle. Détente means a relaxation of tensions. A period of lesser tension would be far preferable to the alternating periods of cold and hot war between intellectuals and capitalism the West has experienced. It is not unreasonable to think that a better understanding of the conflict between intellectuals and capitalism could result in détente. In psychotherapy, "the talking cure," as Freud called it, détente is, in a manner of speaking, the result of an individual bringing to consciousness drives and urges that have hitherto unconsciously influenced his behavior. The idea is that "where id was, there ego shall be." In other words, unconscious urges shall be brought to consciousness where they can be rationally examined, and behavior changed in consequence. Irresponsible actions are common among people who are not fully aware of their own motivations. By bringing to light the roots of intellectuals' animosity towards capitalism, we can hope not to eliminate the conflict, but to lessen its potential to become an irrational destructive force. We can end the mutual incomprehension of business-men and intellectuals, and replace it with a more mutually profitable and fulfilling relationship. At least, we can try to persuade one partner that throwing the dishes at the other is counterproductive.

The question is how to go about it. The way to détente is not simply a matter of bringing repressed urges to light, or telling old war stories of the struggles between mind and money. A productive outlet must be found for intellectuals' attitude, a productive function for them as a pseudo-clergy and a pseudo-aristocracy. Intellectuals must have better ways to fulfill themselves within a capitalist society. Capitalism needs the moral criticism of intellectuals acting as a clergy, but it needs it in moderation.

The current struggle of the West with Islamic fundamentalism provides valuable lessons in this regard. It reminds us that Western capitalism needs an intellectual class that is capable of filling the spiritual void that many people feel today. Fanaticisms of one sort or another will fill that void if it is left open. Capitalism needs intellectuals for the moral voice that they bring to the table. Intellectuals must sacrifice their role as revolutionaries. But in return they can be offered a new role, the role of providing moral culture to capitalist society.

As providers of moral culture, intellectuals will not be charged with enforcing any particular morality—that is a job for revolutionaries. Their role will be to offer people what the market doesn't, not to replace the market. "A cynic," said Oscar Wilde, "is someone who knows the price of everything and the value of nothing." But how do we figure out something's value? That is much harder than figuring out the price. The market does not and cannot help us answer that question. Market research tells us the price someone is willing to pay for something, not whether he ought to want it. Intellectuals can help us decide about value. Of course they will disagree about the answer, which leaves us room for choice. But what is important is that intellectuals provide capitalist society with the means to answer questions about value that the market cannot answer.

Intellectuals can provide ideas about how people might live their lives one way and not another. Through careful critical discourse, they can help us analyze what is at stake in our choices, personal and political. Their education, the intellectual traditions which have influenced the struggle of mind against money, teach intellectuals to look at life from a different perspective than that of market capitalism. Through their compulsion to preach, whether in classroom, pulpit, novel or movie, their debates influence society at large. Even intellectuals who don't intend to preach participate in spreading moral culture because they inevitably raise questions about values. Even if there is no clear hero or clear answers, what matters is that the questions are raised. By raising such questions and discussing them, intellectuals can teach people better ways of thinking about what they value, what they might want, rather than simply the most efficient way of getting it. Should I want that car, that house, that spouse, that job, that policy? What direction ought my life and my community to take? Intellectuals should not be in charge of answering such questions, but they can do a great deal to facilitate their discussion. The market is not interested in talking about the meaning of life. Someone must. If Western intellectuals won't, revolutionaries and fanatics will do it instead.

Up to now, intellectual's contribution to capitalism's moral culture has often consisted in giving reasons why it ought to be destroyed. The cost has been terrible. Rather than trying to replace capitalism with something else, intellectuals should be trying to improve it. As outsiders, a permanently alienated elite, they are in a better position to do this than any other group. Aristocracies create the values of their society. If intellectuals were a true aristocracy, perhaps they could overthrow capitalism. But they are merely a pseudo-aristocracy. Instead of creating values, they can only influence them. This is not nearly as exciting or exalting as leading a revolution. But it provides intellectuals with the autonomy that they crave, and capitalism with the criticism it needs.

It is time for the intelligentsia to grow up and assume its responsibilities as a class, instead of pretending that it isn't one. We cannot, surrounded by nuclear weapons and still more frightful inventions, afford to let intellectuals remain in a world of childish absolutes. Intellectuals must turn from what Weber called an ethic of ultimate ends, all or nothing, complete slavery or total freedom, to an ethic of responsibility. Not the abandonment of moral principles—which would mean the end of the intelligentsia—but their reinterpretation. Marx must be turned upside down. He got it backwards when he said that "up to now philosophers have only interpreted the world; the point is to change it."[29] The proper role of intellectuals in a democratic society is not to revolutionize the world, but to interpret it. Their political role is to provide capitalism with a better moral culture. This is a spiritual and social vocation not to be despised. It is one that has the potential to change the meaning of everything, even the means of production. It is time for intellectuals to leave behind their self-imposed immaturity, and assume their proper roles in a capitalist society that needs them. We need to make the world safe for intellectuals at the same time as we make it safe from intellectuals. We need détente between mind and money before their cold war turns hot. Again.

Notes

1.   Christophe Charle, *Les intellectuels en Europe au XIXe siècle: Essai d'histoire comparée* (Paris: Seuil, 1996), 155; U.S. Department of Labor, Bureau of Labor Statistics, Occupational Outlook Handbook, www.bls.gov; Paul Hollander, "American Intellectuals: Producers and Consumers of Social Criticism," in *Intellectuals in Liberal Democracies: Political Influence and Social Involvement*, ed. Alain G. Gagnon (New York: Praeger, 1987), 69; Seymour Martin Lipset, "The New Class and the Professoriate," in *The New Class?* ed. B. Bruce-Briggs (New Brunswick, NJ: Transaction, 1979), 82-3. Some claim that the intellectual, as distinguished from the academic, is a dying breed. The extent to which this argument is both true and false can be seen in chapters 7 and 8. Cf. Russell Jacoby, *The Last Intellectuals: American Culture in the Age of Academe* (New York: Basic Books, 1987).
2.   The term "cultural capital" is borrowed from French sociologist Pierre Bourdieu. Bourdieu fit intellectuals into a Marxist economic category by using the word "capital" to suggest that they act like an economic group. However, their class identity is based not on their money or their relationship to the means of production, but on their status. This appeal from economics to status is derived from Max Weber, but Weber distinguishes between "class," an economic category, and "status," a non-economic category, whereas I consider economics and status alternative means of identifying classes.
3.   Because Socrates held this view, he counts as the first known Western intellectual.
4.   On CCD, see Alvin Gouldner, *The Future of Intellectuals and the Rise of the New Class* (New York: Oxford University Press, 1982), 28, 84. On the theme of the "highbrow," see Stefan Collini, *Absent Minds: Intellectuals in Britain* (New York: Oxford University Press, 2006), 110-37.
5.   Leszek Kolakowski, "The Intellectuals," in *Modernity on Endless Trial* (Chicago: University of Chicago Press, 1990), 36.
6.   Thomas S. Kuhn, *The Structure of Scientific Revolutions*, 2nd ed. (Chicago: University of Chicago Press, 1970), 23-43; Gouldner, *The Future of Intellectuals*, 30.
7.   William James, in David E. Shi, *The Simple Life: Plain Living and High Thinking in American Culture* (New York: Oxford University Press, 1985), 168.
8.   Gouldner, *The Future of Intellectuals*, 33.
9.   Jerrold Siegel, *Bohemian Paris, Culture, Politics, and the Boundaries of Bourgeois Life, 1830-1930* (Baltimore: John Hopkins, 1999), 6, 11. Intellectuals, with their rather vague social identity and stress on personal autonomy, embody leading features of modernity itself. This is neither a surprise nor a coincidence.
10.   Karl Mannheim, *Ideology and Utopia*, trans. Louis Wirth and Edward Shils (New York: Harvest, 1936), 154-55.
11.   The parallel is inexact, since not all secular clergy belonged to wandering orders. Parish priests were also secular clergy, since they did not follow a monastic rule.

12.   Julien Benda, *La jeunesse d'un clerc* (Paris: Gallimard, 1938), 272-74.
13.   See the American sociologist and radical C. Wright Mills, cited in Jacoby, *The Last Intellectuals*, 79.
14.   The term "public moralist" derives from Stefan Collini's excellent book *Public Moralists: Political Thought and Intellectual Life in Britain, 1850-1930* (Oxford: Oxford University Press, 1991). See also Hollander, "American Intellectuals," 69, and Gouldner, *The Future of Intellectuals*, 39.
15.   Alas, the most recent research shows the word to have been in use in French periodicals and newspapers several years in advance of the Affair. In English, it appears that Byron used it as early as 1813, although the word only fully took on its modern connotations at the end of the nineteenth century. See chapter 4 for why, and see Collini, *Absent Minds*, part one, for the history of the word.
16.   On the definition of an aristocracy, See Alexis de Tocqueville, *Democracy in America*, trans. by Arthur Goldhammer (New York: Library of America, 2004), 461.
17.   As Tocqueville notes, "in aristocracies what is held in contempt is not precisely work, but work for profit. Work is glorious when inspired by ambition or pure virtue...." Tocqueville, *Democracy*, 642. See also *Democracy*, 722.
18.   Tocqueville, *Democracy*, 643. Max Weber also makes this point. See "Class, Status, Party" in *From Max Weber: Essays in Sociology*, ed. and trans H. H. Gerth and C. Wright Mills (New York: Oxford University Press, 1946), 191.
19.   Gustave Flaubert, April 1852, *Correspondance*, Bernard Masson, ed. (Paris: Gallimard, 1998), 172. See also his letter of 14 August, 1853, 247.
20.   Julien Gracq, *Lettrines* (Paris: Jose Corti,1967), 78.
21.   E. Shils, "The Traditions of Intellectuals," in *The Intellectuals: A Controversial Portrait*, ed. George B. Huszar (Glencoe, IL: Free Press, 1960), 57; Milan Kundera, interview, in A. Liehm, *Trois Générations: essai sur le phénomène culturel Tchecoslovaque* (Paris: Gallimard, 1970), 96-97; Victor Brombert, *The Intellectual Hero: Studies in the French Novel, 1880-1955*, (Philadelphia: J. B. Lippincott, 1961), 154, 160-61, 230.
22.   Gouldner, *The Future of Intellectuals*, 6-7, 19-20, 31, 86; J. K. Galbraith, *The Affluent Society*, cited in Bruce-Briggs, "Introduction," *The New Class?*, 8. Michael Walzer, *The Company of Critics: Social Criticism and Political Commitment in the Twentieth Century* (New York: Basic Books, 1980), congratulates intellectuals on being the new prophets.
23.   "The first thing we do, let's kill all the lawyers," Shakespeare, *Henry VI* (Act IV, Scene II).
24.   Max Weber, "The 'Rationalization' of Education and Training," *From Max Weber,* 243.
25.   Joseph A. Schumpeter, *Capitalism, Socialism, and Democracy* (New York: Harper, 1962), 146.
26.   F. E. Smith, *Law, Life and Letters* (London: 1927), vol. 2, ch. 19; Lipset "The New Class and the Professoriate," in *The New Class,* ed. Bruce-Briggs, 74-5; Arthur Koestler, in Richard Crossman, ed., *The God that Failed* (New York: Harper, 1950), 15.
27.   George J. Stigler, *The Intellectual and the Market Place* (Cambridge, MA: Harvard University Press, 1984), 154.
28.   Marx, *The Communist Manifesto*, in *The Marx-Engels Reader*, Robert C. Tucker, ed. (New York: W. W. Norton, 1972), 338-340.
29.   Marx, "Theses on Feuerbach," in *Marx-Engels Reader*, ed. Tucker, 145.

2

The Three Don'ts

A Very Brief History of Western Intellectuals

A history of the Western intelligentsia cannot ignore the sophists of ancient Greece, whose activities are known to us from as early as the sixth century B.C. They made their living by teaching and talking about philosophy and rhetoric. Having ideas and communicating them was their chief trade, and they were in many respects the first known intellectuals, even if nothing like the modern intellectual class came into being for many centuries afterwards. People had had ideas and communicated them long before the sophists, of course. But unlike priests, farmers, merchants or warriors, sophists specialized in language. In the fifth century B.C., Socrates, a sophist who didn't like the way other sophists talked, rejected the name "sophist," and afterwards sophists were often known as philosophers, which literally means "lovers of wisdom." There were never very many of them, but they wrote a lot and were well known to the other elite groups of the ancient world. Some, like Socrates, had critical things to say about contemporary politics and culture, but, again like Socrates, they almost always counseled respect for existing institutions.

Unlike modern intellectuals, most ancient philosophers were religious conservatives who were not fond of an upstart new religion. They mostly rejected Christianity, and Christianity's rise led to their decline. There were few left by the fifth century A.D., and in the early sixth century the Byzantine Emperor Justinian closed the philosophers' last stronghold, the so-called University of Athens, on the grounds that it taught paganism and atheism. As an independent social group, the sophists/philosophers disappeared.

But their ideas did not disappear. They found a new home within Christian theology.

For a long time all, or nearly all, those concerned with intellectual matters in Europe were clergy of some sort. From the late first century A.D. onwards, Christian theology adopted and adapted classical philosophy to its needs. By the thirteenth century, Christian theologians regarded the pagan Greek Aristotle with reverence as "the Philosopher." Like the pagans, medieval intellectuals taught, wrote, and on occasion advised politicians. What set medieval Western intellectuals apart was that they were almost all people who had sworn allegiance to Church dogma and taken vows of chastity and poverty. The chief exceptions were also clergy—the relatively small number of Jewish rabbis, whose descendants contributed greatly to the formation of the modern Western intelligentsia.

Although the Church owned a great deal of property, as individuals the medieval clergy, whether wandering friars or bishops, owned nothing. Furthermore, while the Church owned property, it did not engage in commerce, beyond selling the products of its lands and workshops. This divorce between Western intellectuals and property-ownership and trade would cast a long shadow. In medieval times it was most visible among the wandering friars, some of whom were intellectuals who the bohemians of the nineteenth century and the beatniks of the twentieth would have recognized as comrades.

However, from the Italian Renaissance, and still more after the Reformation, increasing numbers of artists and thinkers began to find a base outside the church, although language and popular perception continued to associate them with the clergy. In French, for example, the word *"clerc"* can still mean both clergyman and intellectual. As we have seen, there are many ways in which modern Western intellectuals have retained the clergy's role and language, while no longer affiliating themselves with religion. By the seventeenth century, and still more in the eighteenth, there were a fairly large number of secular intellectuals. Secular intellectuals and clergy then often became competitors. Many eighteenth-century intellectuals, although by no means all, became famous for attacking established religion. The seventeenth and eighteenth centuries saw numbers of secular intellectuals attempting to give lessons in politics, economics, and morals to the world, as the clergy had traditionally done. Claiming to be the "unacknowledged legislators of the world," poets attempted to supplant the Divine Legislator's spokesmen. Intellectuals have continued to preach socio-economic and political sermons in the nineteenth and twentieth centuries, with some success—the gospel according to Marx is but one example.

In the past two centuries the number of intellectuals has vastly increased. There are certainly more intellectuals now than at any previous moment in history. Intellectuals' increased numbers have made it easier for them to influence people and events. By the late nineteenth century, intellectuals' numbers and independent social position had transformed them from a relative handful of individuals into a social class that displayed the traits described in chapter one.

The Three Don'ts

Western intellectuals' hostility for capitalism has deep historical roots, roots that go back as far as the very beginning of their history. These traditions have influenced the war between mind and money, and shaped intellectuals' attitudes, in ways that have only been alluded to up to now. They are the historical point of departure for intellectuals' war against capitalism.

The chief ways in which historical traditions have contributed to modern intellectuals' criticism of commercial society can be summarized in Three Don'ts.

1) DON'T MAKE MONEY (JUST HAVE IT).
2) DON'T HAVE MONEY (GIVE IT TO THE POOR).
3) DON'T HAVE OR MAKE MORE MONEY THAN OTHERS DO (IT'S NOT FAIR).

These Three Don'ts have motivated much of Western intellectuals' criticism of capitalism. They continue to underlay contemporary thinking. Each Don't draws on a multitude of historical sources, but in each case one more than others: Greco-Roman thought inspires the First Don't, Christianity the Second, and the democratic ideas of the eighteenth and nineteenth centuries the Third.

The First Don't—The Classical Background

It begins with the Greeks, like so much else.

The First Don't, "Don't Make Money (Just Have It)" comes oddly from one of the greatest trading peoples of antiquity. The Greek colonies that dotted the Mediterranean and Black Seas were testimony to their far-flung commercial ventures. Nevertheless, in Greek society even the most commercial city-states, such as Athens, harbored ideas and feelings strongly opposed to trade and industry. Among the Greeks, leading intellectuals like Plato and Aristotle made no secret of their dislike for commerce. In both these respects the conflict between mind and money in ancient

Greece resembles the modern West. Where ancient Greece differs is that it was a slave-owning society, with an aristocratic sense of rank.

There were strong cultural differences among Greek states, most famously between Athens and Sparta, but all Greek cultures were more or less biased against commerce. The continuum ran from a mixture of acceptance and hostility in Athens to absolute rejection in Sparta. Sparta went so far as to ban possession of gold and silver by its citizens, and to declare iron the national currency. It is difficult to accumulate a great fortune in iron bars, or to engage in commerce with iron currency. Agriculture, carried on by serfs (*helots*), was the only means by which a Spartan citizen could earn his living.

Trade as a profession was effectively banned at Sparta by the lack of a useful currency, but the Athenians and many other Greeks were enthusiastic and talented traders. The Athenian attitude towards trade and industry was complicated. The Athenian experience of the Persian invasion of 480 B.C. showed that Athens' real vocation was the sea. When the Persian army drew near, the Athenians sent an envoy to Delphi to ask the god Apollo for an oracle about their fate. Apollo responded that they should "trust in their wooden walls." Some took this to mean the wooden wall that surrounded the Acropolis at Athens. They were incinerated by the Persians. The majority understood the oracle to refer to the wooden walls of their ships. The ships won the great naval battle of Salamis, and Athens and Greece were saved from Persian rule. Those ships and the sailors who manned them would not have existed but for Athens' commercial prowess.

It is thus no surprise that trade and to a lesser degree industry were more esteemed at Athens than elsewhere. Solon of Athens (638-558 B.C.), one of the "Seven Wise Men" of Greek tradition, was the author of an early Athenian law-code that forbade insulting people's occupation. He himself sailed on trading voyages. In Thucydides' (c. 460-c. 400 B.C.) *History of the Peloponnesian War*, Pericles, acknowledged as one of the greatest Athenian leaders, an aristocrat of great inherited wealth, gives a speech in which he contrasts Athens and Sparta. One of the characteristics of Athens, he says, is that at Athens, "poverty is no disgrace. The only disgrace is not working hard to cease being poor."[1] But even at Athens trade and especially industry encountered a great deal of hostility. The comedies of the Athenian playwright Aristophanes (448-385 B.C.) constantly contrast the virtues of agriculture and country living with the vices of traders and city life. Many writers thought of the artisan as a free man doing work that should properly be done by a slave. This contempt sometimes spread to all forms of physical labor, even agriculture. Physical labor for money was not worthy of a free man, whose life should be devoted to community service and worthwhile leisure activities, such as physical/military training at the gym. Athenian politicians who earned their money, rather than inherited it, were considered to bear a black mark. Athenian intellectuals, the intellectual leaders of the Greek world, notably displayed none of the ambivalence towards commerce and industry recorded by Thucydides—they were overwhelmingly hostile. Plato and Aristotle are good representatives of Greek thought in this regard. Significantly, they have served as archetypes of what a Western intellectual is supposed to be. Their biographies illustrate this.

Plato (428-348 B.C.) was an Athenian of aristocratic birth who became a student and follower of Socrates. He acquired a lifelong distrust of Athenian democracy when his beloved teacher was condemned to death on charges of atheism and leading the nation's youth astray (some things never change). Plato founded the first formal school for instruction in philosophy and rhetoric at Athens, known as the Academy. Besides doing a massive amount of teaching and writing, he left Athens for several years to act as advisor and teacher to Dionysus the Younger, ruler of the powerful Greek city of Syracuse, on the island of Sicily. The experiment turned out badly, and Plato had to flee for his life.

Aristotle (384-322 B.C.) was Plato's student. Native of a small independent town in northern Greece, his father was court doctor to a king of Macedon. At the age of 17 Aristotle arrived in Athens, where he spent the next 20 years studying under Plato and teaching philosophy. Aristotle rejected much of Plato's teaching, and after Plato's death founded his own school in rivalry with Plato's Academy, which was carried on by Plato's other students. Aristotle was invited to become tutor to the Macedonian crown prince, who eventually became known to history as Alexander the Great. When Alexander left to conquer Persia, Aristotle returned to Athens. He had to flee Athens after Alexander's death, when anti-Macedonian feeling made him fear for his life. He is reported to have quipped that he wanted to save the Athenians from committing a second crime against philosophy (the first being the execution of Socrates). He died a year later.

Plato's and Aristotle's careers illustrate many enduring features of the Western intelligentsia; ties to the aristocracy; a career in teaching and writing; conflicts with political authorities; strong disagreements, especially among those of different generations; and finally and perhaps most importantly, intellectuals' claims to serve as advisor to the ruler, a role which intellectuals have often felt called upon to play. Their writings are representative of Greek thought about trade and commerce and they embody modern intellectuals' claim to be the moral judges of society. Their attitudes towards money are especially important because of the enormous influence their writings have exerted on the Western intellectual tradition.

Plato, who aside from a few fragments is the first Western intellectual whose writing has come down to us, is especially emphatic in his distaste for money:

> We maintain, then, that a State which would be safe and happy, as far as the nature of man allows, must and ought to distribute honour and dishonour in the right way. And the right way is to place the goods of the soul first and highest in the scale;... and to assign second place to the goods of the body; and third place to money and property. And if any legislator or state departs from this rule by giving money the place of honour, or in any way preferring that which is really last, may we not say, that he or the State is doing an unholy and unpatriotic thing?[2]

This passage embodies an idea that would pass into the Christian moral tradition and figure among the moral assumptions by which so many Western intellectuals have been guided: The soul ranks above the body, and money beneath both. Ominously, Plato calls on the state to enforce this view.

Plato made his views about money even more explicit, and more radical, in the *Republic*. The ideas expressed in this book are especially important because the *Republic* may well be the most influential work in the history of Western philosophy. In it Plato told the "Noble Lie," a story designed to make people content with the Utopian regime outlined in that work. According to the noble lie, when human beings were created by the Gods they were fashioned of different metals. Those destined to be the most virtuous were made with gold and silver, while lesser souls were made of iron and brass. When people came together in society, "the iron and brass [people] fell to acquiring money and land and houses and gold and silver, but the gold and silver races, not wanting money but having the true riches in their own nature, inclined towards virtue...."[3] Plato adds that it is not possible to mix the desire for wealth with the desire for virtue:

> [T]he more they think of making a fortune the less they think of virtue; for when riches and virtue are placed together in the scales of the balance, the one always rises as the other falls.
> True.
> And in proportion as riches and rich men are honoured in the State, virtue and the virtuous are dishonoured.

Clearly.
And what is honoured is cultivated, and that which has no honour is neglected.
That is obvious.
And so at last, instead of loving contention and glory, men become lovers of trade and money; they honour and look up to the rich man, and make a ruler of him, and dishonour the poor man.[4]

Plato goes on to argue that this has disastrous political consequences, for then the poor are excluded from political participation, regardless of their merits, and a permanent class struggle takes the place of social harmony: "such a State is not one but two States, one of the poor, the other of the rich; and they... are always conspiring against one another."[5] Plato's preference for harmony, which he associated with economic equality, over strife, associated with competition for wealth, became a commonplace of the Western tradition of criticizing capitalism.

To cap his argument about wealth, Plato ends up suggesting that the class of philosopher-rulers should own nothing individually. They should hold all their wealth in common. Private property is reserved for the lesser breeds, as a means of reconciling them to the rule of their more virtuous betters. This was extreme, even by the standards of Greek intellectuals. Of course, Plato was something of an intellectual extremist by nature. He even claimed that women could be men's intellectual equals, an unheard-of notion in his time.

Plato's rejection of private property in the *Republic* was not followed by other Greek thinkers. In other works Plato himself was more moderate. What is important for Plato is that a man should have inherited enough money to live a leisured life of study and public service. Freedom from the need to earn a living is a basic necessity for the good life. We need to have money to make sure that "the care of riches should have last place in our thoughts."[6] For all their assaults on commerce and the pursuit of Mammon, neither Plato nor most other intellectuals of the classical world thought highly of poverty, at least not of poverty without leisure. Even the philosophical school of the Cynics, who praised poverty (their founder, Diogenes, was famous for living in a barrel), thought poverty worthwhile only when it was accompanied by leisure, not work. Reverence for poverty as such, and for that matter for work, was a Christian innovation, as we will see in the next section. The First Don't, after all, "Don't Make Money (Just Have It)" suggests that having money is a good thing. What Greek intellectuals condemned was earning it.[7]

Aristotle's ideas about money, less radical than Plato's, are perhaps more representative of Greek thought. Indeed, Aristotle, whom the

Middle Ages would refer to as "The Philosopher," may also have had even more influence. His influence extends well beyond the Middle Ages—Rousseau's and Hegel's discussions of money owe much to Aristotle, and Marx quotes him extensively.[8]

Aristotle analyzes commerce in relation to human nature. Human nature makes people into social creatures. The need to form a society, a political community, is built into the human species. Only a beast or a god can live independently. While no individual can be fully independent, the community ought to be: it should capable of supplying all its own needs, either from its own production or, if necessary, by trade with other communities. Within the context of the self-contained community, money and commerce are necessary and good. Since no individual can be completely independent, everyone needs to trade with their fellow-citizens to satisfy their needs. Money is a device to simplify these transactions, and thus a good thing.[9]

Aristotle's conclusion that the invention of money was a good thing was a relatively liberal one. The fifth-century B.C. Athenian playwright Sophocles had not been so kind: "No thing in use by man, for power of ill,/ Can equal money. This lays cities low,/ This drives men forth from quiet dwelling place,/ This warps and changes minds of worthiest stamp,/ To turn to deeds of baseness, teaching men/ All shifts of cunning, and to know the guilt/ Of every impious deed." For Aristotle, the problem is that with the invention of money, a new form of economic exchange becomes possible, one based not on satisfying the real needs of oneself and one's fellow citizens, but on accumulating wealth indefinitely. Aristotle's distinction between satisfying real needs—good—and merely making a lot of money—bad—was another Greek attitude destined for a long future.[10]

The desire to accumulate great wealth separates the individual from the community. He is accumulating wealth that is unnecessary to fulfill real needs. The individual is then no longer pursuing the common good, but a mistaken idea of his own selfish benefit. In a sense, the problem with money from an Aristotelian viewpoint is that it tempts people to try to become gods, that is, to become completely independent of the community. But people are not gods, and when they try to become gods they act contrary to human nature and in so doing lower themselves to the level of beasts.

Aristotle gave a special name to economic activity devoted to accumulating excessive monetary wealth: he called it "chrematistic." Chrematistic means both the desire for unlimited wealth and the art of acquiring unlimited wealth. Chrematistic is an unnatural desire, since it is not a response to real human needs. It is also an unnatural art or technique, since technology is supposed to serve the community, and chrematistic harms it. Today's ecological and anti-globalization protestors accuse corporations and governments of chrematistic practices, although they call it capitalism. Chrematistic desire is by definition limitless, since there is no limit to the amount of money one can have. When people engage in commerce from chrematistic motives, commerce loses its virtue. By extension, when a whole society devotes itself to chrematistic pursuits, it loses its ability to be virtuous. In short, capitalism is evil.[11]

The Aristotelian distinction between real economic needs and false ones has been very influential. It is at the root of many modern assaults on "alienation" and attacks on consumer culture. It also leads to another distinction, between economic behavior that satisfies needs and supports the community, and economic behavior that is independent of the community and destructive of it. It has been suggested that Aristotle was the first to develop what the nineteenth and twentieth centuries would call the opposition between *Gemeinschaft* (community) and *Gesellschaft* (society), as Ferdinand Toennies formulated it (see the discussion of Toennies in chapter 5).[12]

Aristotle, however, makes a distinction between wealth, a good thing, and chrematistic. Wealth, according to Aristotle, consists of possessions that contribute to happiness. It means an abundance of money, land, slaves, herds. Wealth is useful because it contributes to the owner's enjoyment. Aristotle says of the desire for wealth and material goods: "one blames men not for desiring them, for wanting them and loving them, but to love them in a certain way and to show excess in efforts for them." When wealth gives way to chrematistic, money is no longer a means to satisfy anyone's needs, even the owner's. It becomes an end in itself. Chrematistic is an exaggeration of a feeling that is itself perfectly natural. Those who engage in chrematistic "think enjoyment is linked to excessive wealth, and so pervert all their faculties trying to get it."[13]

There are, however, certain means of acquiring even moderate wealth that Aristotle rejects and considers inherently "vile." Acquiring wealth from "commerce… is justly criticized for it is not natural but comes at others' expense; and it is completely natural to hate the profession of moneylender, because his fortune comes from money itself." Money was made for exchange, not for earning interest. Lending money is an unnatural form of acquiring property and inherently despicable.[14]

It is not just banking that Aristotle rejects. In the ideal city, "the citizens should not lead the life of either an artisan or a merchant, for such a life is vile...." Why? "It is because their way of life is bad, because of the fact that the activity to which the mass of artisans, of merchants and of laborers devote themselves is not in accord with any virtue." In keeping with the aristocratic Greek preference for agriculture, Aristotle concedes that the peasant is not inherently vile. But his need to earn his living by the sweat of his brow bars him from the leisure necessary for virtue and political participation. If he only had enough income from his land to be able buy slaves to till it, the peasant would make a good citizen. One needs money, but earning it is either vile or too time-consuming.[15]

Wanting money too much, wanting too much money, earning money by labor, are all things that harm the community as well as the individual in the view of most Greek intellectuals. Certain ways of earning money are inherently objectionable, others merely because they take too much time and deprive one of leisure necessary for education and politics. Agriculture is morally better than trade and industry.

The Romans, avid consumers of Greek culture, took over these attitudes as well, although they probably didn't need much persuading, being an aristocratic, slave-owning society with a strong military streak. Roman authors did not simply parrot Greek writers, however, they added their own nuances to the basic theme of "Don't Make Money (Just Have It)." They had high regard for frugality and thrift, and even for poverty and hard work, provided they were in the right context—preferably the pursuit of political glory or national service. In the heyday of the Roman Republic, the epitome of virtue in the Roman mind (and that of many of the American and French revolutionaries), it was respectable for a Roman aristocrat to do agricultural work with his own hands. The semi-mythical heroes of early Rome did. There was old general Cincinnatus, called away from the plow he was guiding to lead the army in a time of danger, and the revered figure of Cato the Elder, scourge of luxury and Carthage, fond of wearing home-spun clothing. They were Roman archetypes of frugal men devoting themselves to public service.

Cicero and Seneca were the most influential Roman writers on moral subjects, and their attitudes towards money may serve as a summary of Roman attitudes in general. Marcus Tullius Cicero (106-43 BC), was a participant in the bloody struggles for political power in Rome at the end of the first century BC. He served as a consul, one of the heads of the executive branch of government at Rome, and was a partisan of maintaining the Republic against attempts to create an Empire. He eventually lost his life for backing the wrong horse in the conflicts that followed Julius Caesar's assassination. Although he preferred action to contemplation, posterity has found him a better writer than politician.

Cicero was eclectic in his tastes, borrowing arguments from various philosophical schools without overmuch care about their consistency—a failing he himself recognized. But lack of philosophical consistency did not prevent Cicero from becoming one of the best-read authors of the Middle Ages and the Renaissance. If Aristotle marked medieval philosophy more deeply, Cicero penetrated more widely into the culture and the elite educational system of both the medieval and early modern periods. He was a staple of the medieval classroom, and medieval philosophy borrowed many of its terms from him. The Renaissance echoed medieval admiration for Cicero. The great Italian Renaissance poet Petrarch made him his literary model, as did many others. The Protestant Reformation was made by his disciples. Martin Luther preferred him to Aristotle. Praise of Cicero continued to flow from the pens of Locke, Montesquieu, and Hume in the eighteenth century. Since the nineteenth-century, however, Cicero's reputation has been on the decline, and his eclecticism and lack of originality have been held against him. But he long continued to be part of the elite school curriculum and, whether directly or indirectly, remained in a position of influence through World War II.[16]

Cicero's position on wealth was sometimes almost as radical as Plato's: "We can disregard wealth, which I do not include in the category of good things because anyone, however unworthy, can get hold of it—and that could never be true of things that are really good." But while Cicero refused to call wealth good, he recognized its utility. However, it was only useful in proportion as it was despised: "nothing is as good an index of a narrow and trivial spirit as the love of wealth; nothing is more upstanding and glorious than the contempt for wealth if you are not wealthy, or if you have wealth, to apply it to benefits and generosity." Cicero's sympathies were on the side of a modest fortune derived from inheritance and agriculture, and in favor of a frugal limitation of one's needs. He told a story about the Greek philosopher Xenocrates: "envoys from Alexander once brought him 50 talents [more than a million dollars]... Xenocrates took the envoys to dine with him at the Academy and set before them a sufficient quantity of food, but without any luxury trimmings. Next day they asked him the name of the representative to whom he wanted the money given. 'What!' he replied, 'didn't yesterday's frugal dinner show you I don't need any money?'" The story in fact shows two things: that Xenocrates already had enough money to take people out to dinner, and that he didn't want any more. Neither Greeks nor Romans idealized poverty.[17]

Cicero's notion of generosity is a good example of classical thinking about the proper use of wealth. His is not the idea found in the Gospel of "sell your possessions, and give to the poor, and then you will have riches in heaven…." Generosity should not be the cause of poverty. "A man must keep an account, however, of his private means; to let them go to waste would be shameful. But the accounting should be such that no suspicion of harshness and greed arises. Unquestionably, the greatest advantage of wealth is the ability to be generous while not depriving oneself of one's inheritance." Generosity is good, but only within reasonable limits. Cicero thinks it wrong to give away too much of one's wealth.[18]

Thus far we have discussed Cicero's attitude towards the possession of wealth. In his discussion of what constitutes acceptable means of acquiring it, he follows closely the Greek position. It is a summary of classical attitudes worth quoting at length:

> Now the following is the gist of my understanding about professions and trades, those that free men can think of entering and those that are contemptible. First, no one can approve professions that arouse people's dislike, for example, collectors of harbor dues or usurers. Similarly, the work of all hired men who sell their labor and not their talents is servile and contemptible. The reason is that their wages actually constitute a payment for slavery. Another disreputable class includes those who buy whole lots from wholesalers to retail immediately…. All mechanics work in contemptible professions because no one born of free parents would have anything to do with a workshop. The employments least worthy of approval are those that pander to pleasure: "fishmongers, butchers, cooks, sausagemakers, fishermen," as Terence says. Add to this list, if you like, perfume makers, stage dancers, and the whole musical stage. However, those professions that require greater knowledge or that result in more than ordinary usefulness, for example, medicine, architecture, teaching in respectable subjects: these are reputable callings for those whose rank they suit. Commerce should be considered vulgar if it is a rather small affair. If it is extensive and well-financed, importing many products from all over the world and distributing them to many customers honestly, one should not criticize it severely. In fact, there seems to be every justification for praising it if a merchant who has had his fill of trade, or I should say is satisfied with his profit, retires from the quayside to his farmhouse and estates…. Of all the pursuits whereby men gain their livelihood none surpasses the cultivation of the earth. Farming is the most pleasant livelihood, the most fruitful, and the one most worthy of a free man.[19]

These ideas were commonplaces in Cicero's time. How many find an echo in our own? Bankers are still especially unpopular. Cicero cited that archetype of Roman virtue, Cato the Elder, who, when asked whether money-lending wasn't more profitable than agriculture, replied, "And what about murder?"[20]

Cicero was actually relatively liberal in his attitude towards commerce. His contemporary, the historian Livy, wrote that "every form of profit seeking was thought unsuitable for Senators," who nevertheless were required to possess large fortunes, on pain of losing their seat in the Roman Senate. It was illegal for senators to own a seagoing ship (owning vessels to take the produce from one's estates downriver to market was legal). When the Roman historian Sallust (86-35 B.C.) blamed the decline of the Republic on the effects of wealth and avarice in the upper classes, he was citing commonplaces.[21]

Alongside Cicero, the Stoic philosopher and politician Lucius Annaeus Seneca (4 B.C.–65 A.D.) was one of the most read Roman authors in the Middle Ages, and contributed much to the "First Don't" in the Western intellectual tradition. Like Cicero an accomplished lawyer, writer and politician, he rose to prominence during the early Roman Empire, and was forced to commit suicide for suspected involvement in a plot against the Emperor Nero, whose tutor and minister he had once been. He was also celebrated for his love affairs with highly placed women, and for his enormous wealth, much of which was reputed to come from money lending. He did not live up to his philosophical precepts, but that did not prevent his writings on moral and ethical subjects from becoming instant classics.

Seneca's work was particularly prized by early Christian authors. There exists an apocryphal correspondence between Seneca and St. Paul, and he is cited with approval by St. Jerome, Lactantius, St. Augustine, and Tertullian, all prominent theologians and fathers of the Church. In the Middle Ages, Dante placed him, together with Cicero, as second only to Virgil in the *Inferno*, and Chaucer classed him with Solomon and St. Paul in the *Parson's Tale*. Erasmus, Montaigne and Queen Elizabeth I of England all thought highly of him.[22]

Seneca differs from the authors we have previously discussed in his attitude to poverty. To be content with bread and water, the diet of slaves and prisoners, is for Seneca a triumph of self-control and a sign of emancipation from the slings and arrows of outrageous fortune. But Seneca praises poverty as a way of achieving autonomy and independence, not of mortifying the flesh. Nor is poverty a necessity for virtue. Just after a passage praising the virtues of poverty, Seneca goes on to say that "no one is worthy of a god unless he has paid no heed to riches. I am not, mind you, against your possessing them, but I want to ensure that you possess them without tremors; and this you will only achieve in one way, by convincing yourself that you can live a happy life even without them…." Seneca does not suggest actually getting rid of one's wealth, but rather living as if it didn't matter. He defends his own possession of wealth: "Cease therefore to forbid philosophers to have money: no one has condemned wisdom to poverty. The philosopher can possess a considerable fortune…," but it must not be gained by unjust means, and, above all, it must have no hold over the wise man. Seneca does, however, suggest getting rid of luxuries: "we need to look down on wealth, which is the wage of slavery [i.e., work]. Gold and silver and everything else that clutters our prosperous homes should be discarded."[23]

Thus we should *have* wealth, but not show it or need it (the resemblance between Seneca and Calvinist ideas is striking). Which is not to say that we should work for it (unlike Calvinism). Like other classical authors, Seneca looks down on education intended to help people make money: "… I have no respect for any study whatsoever if its end is the making of money. Such studies are to me unworthy ones." Seneca's attitude, consistent with the classical tradition that inspired the "First Don't," has much in common with that of many twenty-first-century academics.[24]

The attitudes of Greek and Roman intellectuals contributed much to the hostility towards capitalism shown by modern Western intellectuals. Even though modern intellectuals reject many of the assumptions of the ancients, for example, slavery, the inferiority of women, and the inferiority of manual labor, they nevertheless condemn with equal fervor a life devoted to acquiring wealth. The forms of acquiring money despised by the Greeks and Romans have been the forms most condemned by the moderns. One has only to think of the typical portrayal of the banker or stock-market speculator to see the resemblance. Unlike the Greeks and Romans, however, modern intellectuals often have little tolerance for the possession of wealth, regardless of the means by which it was acquired. To look for the historical sources of this attitude, we must turn to the Second Don't, and to Christianity.

The Second Don't—The Christian Background

The classical tradition embodied in the First Don't encouraged limits on wealth, and urged generosity to friends and fellow-citizens. The Second, Christian, Don't, Don't Have Money (Give It to the Poor) went well beyond these injunctions.

Christian charity was different in kind from the generosity praised in the classical tradition. In the New Testament, possessions ought to be sold and the money given to the poor—regardless of their citizenship. Wealth is to be given away. St. Paul does suggest a limit to this process, but he goes well beyond Cicero's suggestion that one should not give so much today that one cannot keep on giving tomorrow: "There is no question of relieving others at the cost of hardship to yourselves; it is a question of equality. At the moment your surplus meets their need, but one day your need may be met from their surplus. The aim is equality; as Scripture has it, 'the man who got much had no more than enough, and the man who got little did not go short.'" The charity the Christian apostle had in mind was very different from the liberality of the Roman aristocrat.[25]

If the Christian attitude to charity was different, so was the Christian attitude to the rich and the poor. The well-known saying from the Gospel according to Matthew, that it is easier for a camel to pass through the eye of a needle than for a rich man to enter the kingdom of heaven, neatly summarizes this attitude. It is emblematic of a strand of Christian thinking that sees the wealthy man as exceptionally sinful, and promises that on the day of judgment, "many who are first will be last and the last first," in other words that the social order will be turned upside down and that the poor will turn out to be the ones truly blessed. "How blessed are you who are in need; the kingdom of God is yours. How blessed are you who are now hungry; your hunger shall be satisfied." Aristotle and Cicero would hardly have imagined that "vile" laborers might turn out to be better off than they. The New Testament is full of special warnings to the wealthy: "Next a word to you who have great possessions. Weep and wail over the miserable fate descending on you. Your riches have rotted; your fine clothes are moth-eaten; your silver and gold have rotted away, and their very rust will be evidence against you and consume your flesh like fire." Thus, unlike in Greek and Roman thought, those who possess wealth, not just those who acquire it, are bad. Trying to acquire it is just as bad: "No servant can be the slave of two masters... You cannot serve God and Mammon [i.e., Money]." "The love of money is the root of all evil...."[26]

The phrase, "the love of money is the root of all evil," was destined for a long history. Chaucer would cite it frequently, and it has formed the basis for many a modern Christian Socialist sermon. The consequence drawn from this attitude was, logically enough, that the good life did not involve wealth. The good life was a life of poverty and charity, storing up treasures in heaven instead of on earth. On earth, indeed, one was called upon to distribute one's treasure to the poor. Thus Jesus advises the young man who asks him how to live to follow the ten commandments, and when asked if this is all that is necessary, replies, "if you wish to go the whole way, go, sell your possessions, and give to the poor, and then you will have riches in heaven, and come, follow me." The fact that Jesus himself was a poor man, and that imitating him, the Christian's duty, meant becoming poor, signaled a revolution in the way in which poverty and wealth were viewed. Never before had any god been conceived of as *poor*.[27]

The culmination of this point of view about wealth, poverty and charity were those passages in the Book of Acts which socialists took delight in:

> All those faith had drawn together held everything in common: they would sell their property and possessions and make a general distribution as the need of each required.... The whole body of believers were united in heart and soul. Not a man of them claimed any of his possessions as his own, but everything was held in common,... they had never a needy person among them, because all who had property in land or houses sold it, brought the proceeds of the sale, and laid the money at the feet of the apostles; it was then distributed to any who stood in need.[28]

Ananias sold his estate and gave only part of the money to the apostles. St. Peter criticized him for holding money back for himself and he died. Thus the model Christian community was one in which private property was abolished.[29]

After the writing of the Gospels, Christian thinkers continued to concern themselves with issues that had not seriously troubled most Greco-Roman thinkers, for example the justification of private property. Taking the New Testament as their point of departure, Saints Clement and Augustine argued that private property did not exist before the Fall of Adam and Eve in the Garden of Eden, and was thus the result of sin. This did not mean that they urged its abolition—in humanity's fallen state, there was no alternative. Private property was considered from a religious or moral perspective that emphasized charity, and led many early Church fathers to urge people to give away everything beyond what was strictly necessary. Augustine emphasized that acquiring wealth was not something with which a good Christian should be concerned. For some theologians it was a question of the inward attitude to take towards one's money, as it had been for Seneca. But others maintained an absolute condemnation of wealth. Saints Basil and John Chrysostom likened the rich man to a thief and a robber, and Saint Jerome claimed that wealth is always the product of theft. This went well beyond Aristotle's desire to repress chrematistic.[30]

However, Christian theology absorbed those Greco-Roman attitudes towards money that complemented its own. While it rejected classical disdain for those who worked with their hands, it maintained the special respect accorded agriculture, and the special distaste for trade. Food, after all, was a necessity even for the poor man. Commerce, seemingly, was not. St. Ambrose, archbishop of Milan, had no tolerance for commerce. He condemned merchants' greed and told them to use the sea for catching fish to eat, not for trade: "God did not make the sea to be sailed over." Pope Leo the Great claimed that "a merchant is rarely or never pleasing to God."[31]

In some respects Christian clergy/intellectuals exercised more influence over their communities than their pagan predecessors. No philosopher possessed the power of excommunication. But when Christianity became the state religion of the Roman Empire, it did not use its power to put into practice its draconian attitudes towards wealth and trade. There were no forced expropriations of property for division among the poor, nor was commerce banned. Christianity looked forward to a paradise beyond this world, not in it. Since sin could not be abolished, neither could private property. Monasticism served as an outlet for those anxious to come as close to perfection as possible, but the Church did not try and turn the world into a gigantic monastery, unlike some later secular intellectuals (e.g., Fourier, Lenin, Mao, Pol Pot).

But if primitive Christianity was not a movement for social revolution, the third to fifth centuries A.D. were the beginning of an often-unremarked but extremely remarkable phenomenon, produced by free choice rather than fear: the Great Renunciation. Over the course of the next 1500 years, millions of people would renounce sex and money in God's name. Catholic priests, monks, nuns and many lay people swore oaths to give them up. Whereas it was difficult to tell if the renunciation of sex was real, the renunciation of property-ownership by the clergy was much easier to enforce—since personal ownership of property by a cleric who had taken a vow of poverty was not legally valid (although many clerics enjoyed the practical benefits of the church's institutional wealth). The effects of the clergy's renunciation of sex are beyond the scope of this book. However, the renunciation of private property by so many people, including nearly all the intellectuals of medieval Europe, exercised immense influence on the relationship between intellectuals and capitalism. It gave tremendous moral and institutional force to the Second Don't, and embedded it firmly in the Western intellectual tradition. To get a little ahead of our story, the attitude of even the twenty-first century Catholic Church towards capitalism is far from a whole-hearted embrace, and this continued ambivalence has had an impact extending well beyond the shrinking numbers of the faithful. Sometimes, as in "Liberation Theology," it has culminated in support for the social revolution rejected by the fourth-century Church.

The Christian attitude to wealth and trade continued to develop in the centuries after the end of the Roman Empire in the West. The medieval economic and political system served, if anything, to reinforce both the First and Second Don'ts. The knight of chivalry was no friend of the merchant or the moneylender. Commerce and industry continued to be low-prestige occupations compared to agricultural pursuits. At the same time medieval Christianity encouraged charity and an un-classical reverence for the poor, as epitomized by the favorite medieval theme of the beggar at the door who turns out to be Jesus in disguise.

Nevertheless, the medieval period saw a number of interesting developments in Christian attitudes towards wealth and commerce. For a while, in the world of chivalry, the sin of avarice was subsumed under the sin of pride, considered the worst of the seven deadly sins. Around the end of the tenth century, however, the prominent theologian Peter Damian emphasized once again that money was the root of all evil. He told a monk who asked for advice on how to achieve salvation, "First of all, get rid of money, for Christ and money do not go well together in the same place... the more abundant your supply of the worthless lucre of this world, the more miserably lacking you are in true riches." Greed came to be as much of a sin as pride, or worse.[32]

The intellectuals of the twelfth and thirteenth centuries generally mistrusted the economic sphere, and merchants were not well regarded. Theologians regularly condemned them. Honorius of Autun (early twelfth century) wrote that merchants had only a slight chance of going to heaven, while farmers were likely to be saved. Peter Lombard (1100-1160) wrote that merchants could not perform their jobs without sinning. Leo the Great's judgment that merchants cannot please God was included in Gratian's *Decretum*, a widely read medieval compilation, and became a common aphorism. Gratian went on to say that "the man who buys something in order that he may gain from selling it again unchanged and as he bought it, that man is of the buyers and sellers who are cast forth from God's temple." Buying and selling was regarded as spiritually dangerous.[33]

In the thirteenth century there was a change in this overwhelmingly negative attitude. In 1199 St. Omobono of Cremona (d. 1197) was canonized as the first merchant saint. In a life devoted to charity and good works, he never ceased to trade and make a profit. He became merchants' patron saint. Yet in the same period, St. Francis of Assisi (1182-1226) preached a return to the radicalism of the Book of Acts. The biography of St. Francis is instructive, as it is in some respects the exact opposite of that of St. Omobono. The son of a wealthy merchant, Francis gave up trade, sold all his goods and, following the example counseled by Jesus, gave all his money to the poor. He rapidly found followers and imitators, and soon formed a monastic order of wandering friars. One of St. Francis' own rules for his friars, dating from 1221, was that "in general, they should have neither use nor regard for money, considering it as dust." In his "Admonitions," he described money as something unnatural (following Aristotle's notion of chrematistic but extending it to all uses of money), and regarded it as inextricably bound up with the sin of avarice.[34]

But St. Francis' position ran counter to the tendency of the time. St. Albertus Magnus (1206-1280) and above all St. Thomas Aquinas (1225-1274) saw wealth positively when it was used as an instrument for attaining the right goals. The opinion of Aquinas carried enormous weight. He was the author of the *Summa Theologica*, the most important work of philosophy and theology written in the Middle Ages, and still largely authoritative in matters of Catholic theology and morals. His followers, known as scholastics or schoolmen, dominated medieval universities thereafter.[35]

Aquinas was certainly no proponent of a life devoted to commerce. Indeed, he sometimes quotes "the Philosopher" (Aristotle) at length on the perversity of unlimited moneymaking. Nevertheless Aquinas emphasized the *utility* of trade and traders, the ways in which they contribute to the common good and thus are necessary. The admission can be grudging, but it indicates a new departure. Aquinas rejected the idea that selling a thing at a higher price than what was paid for it is necessarily sinful, a form of cheating. He argued that trade, while not good in itself, might not be evil either, thus promoting it from an immoral to a morally neutral activity. According to Aquinas, profit cannot legitimately be the sole or final purpose of an activity, but it may be aimed at as a means to something else:

> [T]rading, considered in itself, has a certain debasement attaching thereto, in so far as by its very nature, it does not imply a virtuous or a necessary end. Nevertheless, gain which is the end of trading, though not implying, by its nature, anything virtuous or necessary, does not, in itself, connote anything sinful or contrary to virtue: wherefore nothing prevents gain from being directed to some necessary or even virtuous end, and thus trading becomes lawful.[36]

The merchant who imports grain into his country in time of famine is not a blood-sucking vampire, but a benefactor who deserves to make a profit, albeit a profit tempered by the notion of a "just price." By 1320 followers of Aquinas were publishing moral handbooks for merchants that assumed that a merchant was indeed capable of living a moral and indeed a religiously laudable life, something once considered impossible.[37]

Aquinas' attitude to wealth also represents a change in Christian attitudes. In discussing the sin of avarice, Aquinas defines avarice not as the desire for wealth, but as an immoderate desire for wealth—thus returning to Aristotle's formulation. Furthermore, it is acceptable "that man seeks, according to a certain measure, to have external riches, in so far as they are necessary for him to live *in keeping with his condition of life*" (emphasis added). It is thus appropriate for an aristocrat to seek to have more money than a peasant, etc. What continues to be unacceptable, however, is desire for more than what is appropriate to one's station, or indeed the desire to change station, to improve one's social condition. As one fourteenth-century scholastic put it: "He who has enough to satisfy his wants, and nevertheless ceaselessly labors to acquire riches, either in order to obtain a higher social position, or that subsequently he may have enough to live without labor, or that his sons may become men of wealth and importance—all such are incited by a damnable avarice, sensuality, or pride."[38]

One area in which Aquinas re-emphasized earlier Christian economic tradition, however, is the famous question of usury, that is, charging interest on money. Usury had always been illegal in the Church's view, and Gratian's *Decretum* cited 29 authorities against it. As commerce developed, lending money at interest became more and more widespread. However, since Aristotle had found the practice of charging interest "unnatural," Aquinas had no incentive from that quarter to alter his views. He cited Aristotle in rendering his opinion that "it is by its very nature unlawful to take payment for the use of money lent...."[39]

Even though it seems an economic curiosity from a modern point of view, the Church's ban on usury was maintained for centuries. In 1745 Pope Benedict XIV, in a pastoral letter to the bishops of Italy, reminded them that lending money at interest is absolutely forbidden: "One cannot condone the sin of usury by arguing that the gain is not great or excessive, but rather moderate or small; neither can it be condoned by arguing that the borrower is rich; nor even by arguing that the money borrowed is not left idle, but is spent usefully...." In the case of usury, utility was irrelevant—the utilitarian justifications Aquinas had applied to commerce and to the possession of wealth could not be applied to banking. It is no coincidence that the banker has remained one of the most reviled figures in anti-capitalist literature.[40]

Medieval thought about money and commerce always maintained a moral perspective on economics, in which spiritual considerations were more important than utility. Don't Have Money (Give It to the Poor) was the basic attitude. The economic world was a place of potential sin, not salvation. The Protestant Reformation changed that by making production and economic success into religious duties and a sign of divine favor, or in another interpretation, by taking economics entirely out of the sphere of religion, henceforward confined to internal faith.

This is not the place for a lengthy discussion of Max Weber's and R. H. Tawney's controversial theories about the connection between Protestantism and the rise of capitalism, summarized in the preceding sentences. For both, Calvinism especially was a significant factor in the development of capitalism. The thesis has been controversial. What is important here is what Weber and Tawney left unsaid, the development of a specifically Protestant critique of capitalism that grew up alongside Protestantism's encouragement of capitalism. The Protestant critique of capitalism has had enormous influence on modern intellectuals.

The Protestant critique of capitalism is not a criticism of producing wealth, whether by agriculture, trade, or industry. Protestants embraced hard work and new technology. Calvin himself had no special preference for agriculture, and no special contempt for the merchant: "What reason is there why the income from business should not be larger than that from land-owning? Whence do the merchant's profits come, except from his own diligence and industry?" It is easy enough to see why Weber thought there was a special affinity between Protestantism and capitalism, and why Tawney thought that Calvinism made the bourgeoisie feel like the new chosen people, preferred by God because of their good character.[41]

However, while Protestant attitudes contributed to capitalism, among some intellectuals they led to criticism of it, on two grounds. First, because capitalist society does not devote enough of its profits to charity. In the Calvinist view the successful businessman is a "steward of the gifts of God, whose duty it is to increase his capital and utilize it for the good of society as a whole, retaining for himself only that amount which is necessary to provide for his own needs...." One is obliged to make the most efficient possible use of one's property—and then give away most of one's profits (John D. Rockefeller is a good example).

And one is obliged to work—unemployment is a sin, in the Protestant view, a misuse of the gifts of God. That unemployment is a sin cuts two ways vis-à-vis capitalism. The poor man must do his best to find work. Conversely, society must make sure there is work for him to do. If necessary, the community/state must intervene to make sure that wealth is used correctly and there is work for the poor man.[42]

These are roots for a Protestant justification of socialism and a planned economy. Marx's critique of capitalist under-production is partly derived from this attitude. An extreme example is found in the work of Thorstein Veblen, son of Norwegian immigrants to America, and scourge of the leisure class (see chapter 5). He excoriates capitalism because it allows profits to get in the way of production. The Protestant emphasis on productivity (as a sign of divine grace), and some Calvinists' tendency to give the community the power to enforce this productivity could lead to a rejection of the free market. There was a Protestant "Christian Socialism" in Europe and America in the late nineteenth and early twentieth centuries. The Protestant critique of capitalism often acted as a halfway house between the Christian Second Don't and the Third, secular and democratic Don't: Don't Have or Make More Money Than Others Do (It's Not Fair).

Further, and perhaps more importantly, the Protestant critique of capitalism rejects capitalism because it is not based on good intentions. In order to understand the reasons for this, it is necessary to understand something about Protestant theology generally and more particularly about Calvinism. Before Martin Luther began the Protestant Reformation, there existed a certain amount of confusion within Catholic Christianity about whether salvation was attained by faith, by doing good deeds ("works") like giving charity and going on pilgrimages, or by some combination of both. Luther ended the confusion, at least on the Protestant side, by saying that salvation could only be attained by faith. Good works had nothing to do with going to heaven, only one's inner faith mattered (although a person of faith would naturally also do good deeds). Being in a "state of grace," that is, being someone with the proper faith whose sins had been divinely forgiven, was an internal, not an external matter.

Some Protestants arrived at a critical attitude towards capitalism through another side of this belief. Because Protestants believed that salvation came only from faith, from within the individual's conscience, they rejected the idea that external things could bring about an individual's salvation. External things had no value in themselves. Therefore, capitalism could not be justified ("justified" was also the word used to speak of salvation) by its greater productivity. It needed a good conscience, good intentions. It didn't have them.

Many modern intellectuals far removed, or so they think, from Calvinism, take this point of view. It is easier for modern intellectuals to adopt this attitude because Immanuel Kant secularized the Protestant idea of salvation by faith alone. Faith is an internal matter, a question of attitude, known in the end to God alone. At the end of the eighteenth century Kant replaced "faith" with "good intentions." Kant argued that the only thing that is absolutely morally good is a good intention, and that the morality of acts is dependent upon the intention with which they are performed. For example, when a baker gives the correct change to a four-year-old, it is impossible to tell whether he has committed a moral action, according to Kant, unless you know his motivation. If he gave the correct change because he thought it was the right thing to do, he acted out of a sense of moral duty and the action is morally good. If he did it because he was afraid that the customer next in line would see him cheat, would make a scene about it, and he would end up losing the other customers' business, then his action was based on selfish motives and, according to Kant it is at best amoral and possibly immoral.

This vision of morality has far-reaching implications for how one evaluates capitalism. While from a Protestant/Kantian point of view there is no moral benefit to be derived from self-interest, for Adam Smith, on the other hand, the baker's correct action from self-interested motives is a proof of the moral benefits of commercial society. Intentions are irrelevant to the benefits of the marketplace as Smith conceived them. For Smith, the merchant "intends only his own gain, and he is in this, as in many other cases, led by an invisible hand to promote an end which was no part of his intention. Nor is it always the worse for the society that it was no part of it. By pursuing his own interest he frequently promotes that of the society more effectually than when he really intends to promote it." Selfishness and competition result in social good, for Smith, because of their fruits: intention is irrelevant, and good intentions may even result in harm. A Kantian morality based on intentions, however, on faith rather than deeds, will find little to praise in a capitalist society with selfish motives. If businessmen don't have good intentions, they are not morally good, regardless of how much they produce. This is true even if commercial practice leads to apparently good behavior, e.g., honesty and fair dealing. Smith's shopkeeper giving honest change out of prudence is, for Kant and Calvin, an immoral or at best amoral man.

His intentions are not good, merely selfish. The good fruits of one's bad intentions are irrelevant, good works will not get you to heaven—only a good conscience. Smith's commercial paradise is Calvin's gateway to Hell.[43]

From the Protestant/Kantian point of view capitalism is at best amoral, and more often immoral, because it relies on selfishness and vice rather than good intentions and virtue. Intellectuals, a secular pseudo-clergy, have been particularly inclined to this Protestant critique of capitalism. Already alienated from capitalism because of their identity and their social situation, intellectuals are further alienated from it by their cultural heritage and their moral judgment. The Protestant emphasis on intentions combines with the intellectual's preoccupation with autonomy to make the effects of capitalism on individual character into a widespread subject of condemnation by intellectuals. The capitalist's character and the character traits fostered by capitalist society have been central to intellectuals' attacks on capitalism.

The Christian Second Don't, "Don't Have Money (Give It to the Poor)", thus joins the First, classical Don't, "Don't Make Money (Just Have It)", in the anti-capitalist historical tradition. Together they have sustained and influenced many intellectuals' attacks on capitalism.

However, there is an important caveat to bear in mind. If Christianity is the historical source of the Second Don't, this does not mean that Christianity, at any period in its history, was wholly opposed to either private property or commerce. There were many elements in the Christian tradition that favored the development of capitalism, not just the Protestant Ethic. The argument is thus not that Christianity and capitalism cannot co-exist. Any such suggestion would be patently absurd. But the ways in which Christian attitudes *encouraged* the development of capitalism are beyond the scope of this book. The point is that the Christian tradition harbored attitudes toward commerce and wealth that became an important element in the anti-capitalist attitudes taken up by Western intellectuals in the nineteenth and twentieth centuries. Christian attitudes lay behind many an atheist's attack on capitalism.

These two Don'ts, and the democratic Don't discussed below, hardly exhaust the historical sources of modern anti-commercial attitudes. If only to illustrate the selective nature of this account, it is useful to very briefly mention another source, which appeared chronologically in between the Second and Third Don't, and which plays a lesser role in forming the attitudes of modern intellectuals: the Duke's Don't.

The "Duke's Don't" played a relatively small part in forming modern intellectuals' attitudes, but it is by no means negligible. It can be summed up as: "Don't Make Money, Take It and Spend It." The noble was not supposed to be concerned with money. Indeed, he despised it (and those who concerned themselves with it) as much as any monk. But he needed money in order to live up to his status and his ideals, so he took it from peasants and merchants as his due, whether by outright robbery or through legal privileges. Once the noble had money, he spent it. "To spend, to give without counting the cost, without thought for the future, are aspects of the... chivalric ideal, that of honor and glory." Partly the nobleman spent it more or less in the Christian manner, on charity—although that charity often took the form of a display of wealth and power. But the noble also spent lavishly on personal display, on clothing, ceremony, tournaments, feasts, and so on. "To be noble means an obligation to display, it means to be condemned, under pain of loss of status, to luxury and expense." Once, a duke wanted to teach his son the proper attitude towards money. He gave him a purse full of coins, so that he would learn to spend money in a manner befitting a great lord. When after a period of time the young man brought the purse back still full of cash, his father took it and, in his son's sight, threw it out the window.[44]

In practice, modern intellectuals rarely take pride in throwing money out the window (although there have been exceptions). But more than one, whether bohemian spendthrift or tenured professor, takes pride in being careless and ignorant about money. It is striking to find an intellectual taking pride in ignorance. Many reasons, some derived from the First and Second Don'ts, play a role in the adoption of this attitude towards money. But a large part of the explanation lies in the Duke's Don't, an attitude that intellectuals are liable to adopt just as they retain other aristocratic traits. It is also worth noting that the sense of entitlement many intellectuals feel, the idea that society owes them a living, is similar to the medieval noble's sense of entitlement.

The first two Don'ts and the Duke's Don't were part of the historical background for the development of the Third. However, the most important historical source of modern intellectuals' rejection of capitalist society did not spring from feudal society, nor even from ancient Rome or medieval Christendom, sources of the first Two Don'ts. The most important source of modern anti-capitalism as found in the democratic Don't—Don't Have or Make More Money Than Others Do (It's Not Fair)—is capitalism itself.

Unlike any preceding critique of commerce, the Third Don't was formulated in a capitalist society. Europe in the late eighteenth and early nineteenth centuries was a capitalist society, or at least far along in becoming one. An increasingly market-based economy, rapidly developing technologies, growing middle classes and spreading bourgeois values, and not least a new class of intellectuals were coming together to create "capitalism," a term that was eventually coined to describe it around 1850.[45]

The capitalist context gave new importance to criticisms of commerce. Before capitalism, such criticism by Socrates or St. Augustine did not imply the destruction of the prevailing socio-economic system, because capitalism was not the basis of the prevailing system. But when the attitudes embodied in the first Two Don'ts were transferred to a capitalist society, they potentially entailed the overthrow of that society. In the new context of capitalism, the philosopher and the preacher became what they had not been before—reformers and revolutionaries.

The Third Don't—The Democratic Background

The First Don't endorsed economic inequality, provided it was achieved in the right way. The Second Don't rejected economic inequality in the abstract, but did not challenge it in practice. The Christian Revolution, when the last would be first, was delayed until the Last Judgment. The Third Don't—Don't Have or Make More Money Than Others Do (It's Not Fair)—provided no excuse for economic inequality, and no reason to wait for the Apocalypse. Revolution is a logical conclusion from the Third Don't, although not the only one possible. The Third Don't set the stage for the confrontation between intellectuals and capitalism that has influenced so much of modern history.

One reason the Third Don't is more revolutionary than either the classical or Christian traditions of anti-commercial criticism is because it is democratic. It emphasizes equality above all else. At the same time, in contrast to the first two Don'ts, the Third Don't legitimizes making money and creating wealth, provided it is distributed equally. This legitimation of moneymaking is also a characteristically democratic attitude (see chapter 1). Like democratic society itself, it is relatively recent. Nevertheless it was not formed in a day. The Third Don't too has a history. Its development can be glimpsed ever-more clearly in three historical contexts: the work of Rousseau in the eighteenth century; the Jacobins and sans-culottes of the French Revolution; and finally in early socialist thought at the beginning of the nineteenth century.

It is hard to imagine today, but many Western intellectuals greeted the rise of capitalism with joy. They mustered a principled defense of commerce, industry, and moneymaking, even when such things were pursued from mere hope of profit. The late seventeenth and eighteenth centuries (albeit not without challenges) saw a rare honeymoon period between the majority of Western intellectuals and commercial society, an appreciative relationship that was dominant until the mid-nineteenth-century in Europe, and still later in the United States. This halcyon period will be discussed in chapter 3, as will the reasons for its end.

However, a reaction against capitalism began even before it had won the day. The reaction was new, too, based on secular, egalitarian grounds, although the new arguments never altogether replaced the old ones. Capitalism continued to be criticized in the eighteenth century on the basis of the first two Don'ts. However, by the late eighteenth century condemnation of capitalism was increasingly based on the idea that it led to greater inequality. For all his harking back to classical tradition, this new affirmation of equality can be clearly seen in the work of the greatest eighteenth-century critic of luxury and commercial society, Jean-Jacques Rousseau (1712-1778) Rousseau was probably the most influential critic of commercial society writing in the eighteenth century, and one of the most influential ever.[46]

Rousseau lived partly in the traditional way of intellectuals, that is, from the patronage of the wealthy, and partly in a new way, from the income his writing produced. He was a good representative of the intellectual class in the making in eighteenth-century Europe, as will be discussed in the next chapter. He was also typical in the way he mixed attitudes drawn from the first two Don'ts with newer arguments related to the emerging Third. Like St. Augustine and many early Christian theologians, Rousseau associated the invention of private property with sin. Private property is, for Rousseau, the origin of all social evils:

> The first person who, having marked off some ground, said 'this is mine', and found people stupid enough to believe him, was the real founder of civil society. How many crimes, wars, murders, hardships and horrors the human race would have been spared by someone who, tearing out the markers or filling in the ditch, had shouted to his fellows: 'Don't listen to this imposter; you are lost if you forget that the harvest is for all, and the land belongs to no one'.[47]

This is a secularized version of the Christian account of the Fall of Man, in which Adam's sin is visited upon the heads of all his descendants.

Rousseau followed Christian and Greco-Roman traditions in showing particular distaste for money transactions (shades of Aristotle!) and those who specialized in them, the merchants. He argued that the use of money discourages people from farming, which is morally and politically preferable to any other occupation. There are no exceptions to this rule: "I regard any system of commerce as destructive of agriculture. I do not even except commerce in agricultural products." When farmers are forced to sell their goods for cash, they become "petty merchants, petty scoundrels, petty thieves." For Rousseau there is no difference between a merchant and a thief. Rousseau consistently rejects making money by commercial or industrial means, and he remains wedded to the views summarized by our first two Don'ts.[48]

But from the perspective of the development of the Third Don't, what is important is Rousseau's overriding concern for *equality*. For example, for tax purposes he distinguished between "necessary" property, and "superfluous" property. Rousseau rejected the idea that some people needed more worldly possessions than others. Everyone's needs were equal. Many commentators have suggested that what Rousseau cares most about is not economic equality, but political equality, which he thinks will be destroyed by economic inequality. Actually, Rousseau is concerned with *all* aspects of equality, and this is characteristic of modern intellectuals' criticism of commercial society. Rousseau states his perspective very simply: "What is necessary is that everyone should be able to live and that no one should be able to get rich. This is the fundamental principal of national prosperity." Rousseau also believed that everyone should equally have to work. Perhaps Rousseau's upbringing in Calvinist Geneva shows in his view that "He who eats at leisure what he has not earned himself, steals." No latter-day socialist could have stated it better—although some might amend Rousseau to suggest that everyone ought to become rich and leisured, through the spread and development of the luxuries and technologies that Rousseau rejected.[49]

Rousseau's ideas were considered amusing intellectual fantasies by many, perhaps most of his readers. But intellectuals' egalitarian dreams have a way of taking on reality. The French Revolution did much toward making the Third Don't the leading influence on the criticism of capitalism. Egalitarian criticism of commercial society was represented during the Revolution by the Jacobins of the Committee of Public Safety, such as Robespierre, and by the Paris sans-culottes who supported them, many of whom could and did quote long passages of Rousseau from memory during political debates. It is worth noting that just as the development of the Christian Second Don't owed much to non-intellectuals, the same is true of the Third.

It was once common to see the Jacobins and sans-culottes as early socialists, but that error has long been corrected. Despite their liking for Rousseau, even the most radical sans-culottes were firm supporters of private property. They were themselves often shopkeepers. Their superficial resemblance to socialists comes from their ferocious attacks on the wealthy and large-scale commercial middlemen. They wanted to limit property rights, not abolish them. Their ideal was a community of independent small producers, not exactly equal with one another, but not too different, materially, either. As Robespierre put it, "the extreme disproportion of fortunes is the source of many evils and many crimes; but we are no less convinced that equality of property is a chimera."[50]

Thus property is fine (society needs to produce as much as possible), as long as it is earned by work (so much for the aristocratic First Don't), but too much property in individual hands is bad (hence the Third). One sans-culotte body declared that "Anyone who has more than he needs cannot use it, he can only abuse it; thus while leaving the individual what is strictly necessary, all the rest belongs to the Republic and to its unfortunate citizens." This idea came straight from Rousseau, who had proclaimed that what was necessary should not be taxed at all, while what was superfluous could be taken away entirely in case of need. Possession of "superfluous" property is a "violation of the people's rights." Billaud-Varenne, a leading member of Robespierre's Committee of Public Safety, wrote that the political system should establish "as much as possible a division of wealth if not absolutely equal, at least proportional among the citizens." Everyone should have something, but no one should have too much.[51]

There were a handful of revolutionaries who went beyond this. The most well known was Babeuf, whose "conspiracy of equals" was a failure, but whose revolutionary ideas were passed on to future generations of conspirators and revolutionaries by his companion Buonarroti (Babeuf was guillotined). Buonarroti reports that the plotters concluded that "the permanent cause of the enslavement of nations lay entirely in inequality... to destroy that inequality was therefore the task of a virtuous legislator...." Since every citizen worked, or ought to work, for society, "it follows that the burdens, productions and advantages ought to be shared equally. Furthermore the real purpose of society is to avoid the effects of natural inequalities...." Anticipating later anti-capitalist criticism of new technology, they argued that until private property was abolished, the invention of new machines would be a misfortune, because they caused unemployment for the poor while giving profits only to the wealthy. Once their product was equally distributed, new machines would be good.[52]

For the first time in history, the French Revolution saw significant numbers of people adopting the view that it was wrong to have or make more money than other people did. This view was no longer associated with any Christian notion of the renunciation of worldly goods in order to attain salvation. It was asserted as the correct way to organize economic life in this world, with no thought of any other. If the Jacobins and sans-culottes still spoke a language full of "virtue" and other moral terms, these terms were no longer endowed with religious significance. The secular moral critique of capitalism had been born.

And, perhaps, the intellectuals had begun their career as a revolutionary class. This is not the place to discuss the many arguments over whether the Enlightenment caused the French Revolution, whether it was "Rousseau's and Voltaire's fault" as many conservatives have alleged. In any case, both the Revolution and the Enlightenment contained much that was pro-commercial as well as anti-commercial. If the Third Don't was born of the Enlightenment and the French Revolution, its outlines still remained hazy at the Revolution's end in 1815, partly because the French Republic and the Jacobins and sans-culottes rapidly disappeared from the scene. The Third Don't was perfected in other contexts. The most obvious was that of early socialism, a good example of which is the writings of Pierre-Joseph Proudhon (1809-1865).

Proudhon was the first person to call himself an "anarchist." He was a political activist and journalist, served briefly in the French National Assembly in 1848, and was one of Karl Marx's many rivals in the nascent socialist movement. In short, he had a classic intellectual's career, of a kind that only began to be possible in the modern era. He wrote several books and a vast number of articles and letters.

Like many modern intellectuals, Proudhon was influenced by the first two Don'ts. As a high school student, he learned Latin and Greek and became familiar with many of the authors cited in the discussion of the First Don't. His works are also liberally sprinkled with references to early Christian theologians' condemnation of wealth and commerce, as well as to Biblical sources (he learned theology working as a printer of theological works). Although he didn't like Rousseau, he read him. Indeed, he echoed Rousseau about the consequences of the invention of private property: "The right to private property was the beginning of evil on earth, the first link in that long chain of crimes and hardships that the human race has dragged behind it since birth." Thus, as would so often be the case, Proudhon's intellectual background included anti-commercial authors from many times and places.[53]

In his criticism of capitalism, Proudhon emphasized equality to an extent rarely equaled before. He made it not merely the foundation of his own views, but found it at the bottom of every human being's heart: "Yes, all men believe and repeat that equality of conditions [i.e., wealth and status] is identical to equality of rights; that *property* and *theft* are synonymous terms; that all social pre-eminence, given or better-said usurped under the pretext of superiority of talent or service is iniquity and robbery: all men, I say, attest to these truths in their soul...." Proudhon's rejection of private property, summed up in his famous slogan, "property is theft," is actually more nuanced than it appears. He distinguished between "individual ownership" (bad) and "individual possession" (good). He considered the communal property of the early Christians in the Book of Acts unworkable. Individuals ought to have exclusive use of their tools, land, etc. But he insisted that an individual's private use of their land, their tools, or their abilities must not lead to inequalities of income. Proudhon titled a chapter of his most famous work, *What is Property?*, "That in society all salaries are equal," or ought to be. If I do my work more quickly than you do, I have a right to more leisure, according to Proudhon, but not to more money.[54]

If I am smarter than you are, that too should not have any effect on our material positions: "it is impossible to evaluate any kind of talent in money terms, *since talent and money are incommensurable qualities*" (emphasis added). Proudhon took pains to reject the idea that intellectuals or other people with above-average talents ought to be better-paid than others (a hint of the democratic self-abasement common among this pseudo-aristocracy). Insofar as ability and education are translatable into money, they are, according to Proudhon, the property of the community. "Talent is a creation of society much more than a gift of nature; it is an accumulated capital, of which he who receives it is only the depositary." Talent thus gives no moral right to any greater reward than that received by any one else.[55]

This attitude of Proudhon's is obviously against an intellectual's self-interest. Its early appearance among anti-capitalist intellectuals, almost simultaneous with the formation of an intellectual class, is significant. It shows that intellectuals' tendency to self-abasement, their adoption of pseudo-clerical attitudes (e.g., voluntary poverty, or at least equality), and their refusal to be subject to the laws of the market, are all closely associated with their embrace of equality and the Third Don't. Pseudo-aristocrats they may be, but their devotion to equality is no less for all that.

The basis on which Proudhon rejected any deviation from equality is particularly significant, because it is the basis on which many intellectuals would reject commercial society for the next 150 years. It is morality. Like many a later intellectual, Proudhon denounced the morality of the middle classes. He tells a story of how a clever man persuaded other men to work for him, and soon became the owner of their land, while they were reduced to wage-earners. "In this century of bourgeois morality in which I had the good luck to be born, the moral sense is so weakened, that I would not be at all surprised to find myself asked by many an honest landowner what it is that I find unjust and illegitimate in all this."

For Proudhon, any contract that has a loser is morally invalid: "Thus, in every exchange, there is a moral obligation that none of the contractants gain anything at the expense of the other; that is, in order to be true and legitimate, commerce must be exempt from all inequality." In his view of commerce Proudhon is, perhaps knowingly, following Aquinas and reviving the Second Don't, but in the secular moral form typical of modern intellectuals. Proudhon's moral criticism of capitalism was typical of much later intellectual criticism of commercial society, more so than Marx's emphasis on capitalism's flaws as a system of economic production.[56]

With Proudhon and other early socialists the Third Don't comes into its own as a tradition of criticizing capitalism. The attitude of Don't Have or Make More Money Than Others Do (It's Not Fair) became central to mind's war on money. In the hands of Proudhon and his fellow socialists it is a revolutionary attitude. This has been one of the most striking forms taken by the Third Don't, but not the only one. Socialist revolution is only one of the remedies intellectuals propose for capitalism. Many intellectuals reject capitalist society without any particular replacement in mind, except general moral improvement. A characteristic of moral criticism is that it is often open-ended. One can criticize human faults without any intention of replacing human beings with something else. In the same way intellectuals can criticize capitalist society on the basis of the Third Don't without any intention of doing away with it. Sometimes they want to reform it, and this can be very useful to a capitalist society. Other times the intent is purely negative, a kind of attack on original sin without any recipe for salvation, whether socialism or something else. Intellectuals condemn capitalism's immorality not in heaven's name, but in the name of holy equality. But like many a preacher, the images they paint of sin are much more concrete than their pictures of heaven. After all, it is so much easier to find examples of sin as models.

Particularly since the end of communism, many intellectuals have attacked capitalism without any alternative in mind, whether a revolution or a reform. One reason for this is the nature of the Third Don't, compared to the others. The classical tradition of criticizing commerce had a specific alternative lifestyle in mind, that of the leisured landed gentleman engaged in either philosophical contemplation or political service. The medieval Christian tradition also proposed an alternative lifestyle, that of the Christian vowed to poverty and prayer. The Duke's Don't proposed the chivalric ideal. The Third Don't, Don't Have or Make More Money Than Others Do (It's Not Fair), does not prescribe any particular alternative to capitalism. It can even be seen as an incentive to make as much money as possible so that all may share in the benefits of greater collective wealth. In some ways the modern intellectual has a special affinity for the Third Don't because of its open-ended nature. It allows intellectuals to use any stick with which to beat capitalism. Thus it permits the intelligentsia to ally itself with any group opposed to it—artisans, peasants, industrial workers, the Third World, racial and ethnic groups, etc. For a pseudo-aristocracy looking for a way to form a connection with some other part of society, the attitude summarized in the Third Don't provides an excellent bridge. The bridges thus formed have led to many different places, and sometimes the abyss.

Taken together, the Three Don'ts are a handy device for grasping the historical point of departure for modern intellectuals' discontent with commercial society. All three provide resources with which to attack representatives of commercial society, the capitalist or the bourgeois, as individuals who have gone astray. They also provide means for criticizing capitalist society as a whole. The forms taken by the struggle between mind and money since 1850 have been influenced by the nature of modern intellectuals as a group, the subject of chapter one, and by the traditions discussed here. But this is merely the point of departure from which intellectuals set forth on their great campaign. It brings the intellectuals onto the battlefield, into position for the struggle between mind and money yet to come. An account of the origins of a conflict is not the same thing as an account of the war itself, and the course of a war is often hard to predict from its origins. Nevertheless, the sources discussed in this chapter have influenced the struggle, in ways not always immediately visible, but often vital. The following chapters describe the evolution of that struggle.

Notes

1.   Thucydides, "Pericles' Funeral Oration," *The Peloponnesian War*, Book 2, chapter 6. Since so many translations of the Greco-Roman classics are in wide circulation,

references to them will be to books and chapter divisions, and where possible line numbers.

2.   Plato, *The Laws*, Book 4.
3.   Plato, *The Republic*, Book 8.
4.   Plato, *Republic*, Book 8.
5.   Plato, *Republic*, Book 8.
6.   Plato, *Laws*, Book 5.
7.   Plato, *Republic*, Book 1; *Laws*, Book 5.
8.   See Arnaud Berthoud, *Aristote et l'argent* (Paris: Maspero, 1981), 100.
9.   Aristotle, *Politics*, Book I, 2:1252b.
10.   Sophocles, *Antigone*; Aristotle, *Politics*, Book I, 9:1257a; 1258a.
11.   Aristotle, *Politics*, Book I, 9:1256b; 1257b; Berthoud, *Aristote et l'argent*, 100, 165.
12.   For the parallel with Toennies see Pierre Pellegrin, introduction, in Aristotle, *Les politiques* (Paris: Flammarion, 1993), 60-61.
13.   Berthoud, *Aristote et l'argent*, 108, 165; Aristotle, *Politics*, Book I, 9:1257b.
14.   Aristotle, *Politics*, Book I, 10:1258a.
15.   Aristotle, *Politics*, Book VII, 9:1328b; Book VI, 4:1310a; Book III, 5:1278a.
16.   Michael Grant, introduction, *Cicero on the Good Life* (London: Penguin, 1971), 35-43.
17.   Cicero, "Discussions at Tusculum," Book V, 15:45, 31:88-32:90; *On Duties*, Book 1:19-25, 68, 106.
18.   Matthew 19:21-23; Cicero, *On Duties*, Book 2:54-55, 64.
19.   Cicero, *On Duties,* Book 1:150-51.
20.   Cicero, *On Duties*, Book 2:89.
21.   See John H. D'Arms, *Commerce and Social Standing in Ancient Rome* (Cambridge, MA: Harvard University Press, 1981), 4-6; Sallust, *The Conspiracy of Catiline*.
22.   Robin Campbell, introduction, Seneca, *Letters from a Stoic* (London: Penguin 1969), 24-26.
23.   Seneca, *Letters from a Stoic*, Letters 18, 104; *La vie heureuse* (Paris: Arlea, 1995), 66-67; *De Vita Beata*, 21:6, cited in Christopher J. Berry, *The Idea of Luxury: A Conceptual and Historical Investigation* (Cambridge: Cambridge University Press, 1994), 65.
24.   Seneca, *Letters*, Letter 88; D'Arms, *Commerce and Social Standing*, 153.
25.   2 Corinthians 13-15.
26.   Matthew 19:21-25; Mark 10:23-31; James, 1:9-11, 2:5-6; Matthew, 6:24; 1 Timothy 6:9-10. See also Luke 6:20, 16:19-31.
27.   Matthew 19:21-23; See 2 Corinthians 8-9.
28.   Acts 2:43-45; 4:22-26.
29.   Acts 5:3-5.
30.   Augustine, in Janet Coleman, "Property and Poverty" in *Cambridge History of Medieval Political Thought c. 350–c. 1450*, ed. J. H. Burns (Cambridge: Cambridge University Press, 1991), 617; Augustine, *City of God*, Book 19, ch. 17; Ernst Troeltsch, *The Social Teaching of the Christian Churches*, trans. by Olive Wyon (Louisville, KY: Westminster/John Knox Press, 1992), 1:115-16, 118.
31.   Ambrose, cited in Coleman, "Property and Poverty," 619, 628; D'Arms, *Commerce and Social* Standing, 3; Leo, cited in Lester K. Little, *Religious Poverty and the Profit Economy in Medieval Europe* (London: Paul Elek, 1978), 38.
32.   Damian, cited in Little, *Religious Poverty*, 36.
33.   Jacques Le Goff, *Your Money or Your Life: Economy and Religion in the Middle Ages*, trans. by Patricia Ranum (New York: 1990), 57; Little, *Religious Poverty*, 36, 38, 75; D'Arms, *Commerce and Social Standing*, 3n.5; R. H. Tawney, *Religion*

and the Rise of Capitalism, intro. by Adam B. Seligman (New Brunswick, NJ: Transaction, 1998), 34-35.

34. Coleman, "Property and Poverty," 632.

35. Coleman, "Property and Poverty," 624, 626, 628-29; Little, *Religious Poverty*, 176, 215; St. Thomas Aquinas, *Summa Theologica*, II, II, q. 117

36. Aquinas, *S. T.*, II, II, q. 77.

37. Little, *Religious Poverty*, 195.

38. Aquinas, *S. T.*, II, II, q. 117; H. von Langenstein, quoted in Tawney, *Religion and the Rise of Capitalism* (New York: Mentor, 1960), 36.

39. Le Goff, *Your Money or Your Life*, 22, 24, 28; Aquinas, *S. T.*, II, II, q. 78.

40. Benedict XIV, *Vix Pervenit*, 1 November, 1745, www.papalencyclicals.net/ Ben14/ b14vixpe.htm.

41. Calvin, cited in Tawney, *Religion and the Rise of Capitalism*, 105. Luther himself usually rejected usury, and was on the whole much less friendly to capitalism. See Tawney, 94-96; Troeltsch, *Social Teaching*, 2:554-57, 560, 642, 870.

42. Troeltsch, *Social Teaching*, 2:648.

43. Adam Smith, *The Wealth of Nations*, in *The Essential Adam Smith*, ed. Robert L. Heilbroner (New York: W. W. Norton, 1986), 265. Smith is, however, nuanced about commercial society's benefits.

44. Philippe Perrot, *Le Luxe: Une richesse entre faste et confort XVIIIe-XIXe siècle* (Paris: Seuil, 1995), 43, 46.

45. The word is used in a novel by Thackeray published in 1854.

46. See Berry, *The Idea of Luxury*, 227.

47. J. J. Rousseau, "Second Discourse," in *Œuvres Complètes*, ed. Bernard Gagnebin and Marcel Raymond, with, for this volume François Bouchardy, Jean-Daniel Candaux, Robert Derathé, Jean Fabre, Jean Starobinski and Sven Stelling-Michau (Paris: Gallimard, 1964), 3:231.

48. Rousseau, "Constitution for Corsica," in *OC*, 3:920.

49. Rousseau, "Constitution for Corsica," *OC*, 3:920, 924.

50. Albert Soboul, "Utopie et Révolution Française," in J. Droz, *Histoire générale du socialisme* (Paris: PUF, 1997), 1:202-03, 205; Robespierre, *Discours* (Paris: Union Générale des Editions, 1965), 117.

51. Cited in Soboul, "Utopie," Droz, *Histoire générale*, 202, 204, 214-15, 220.

52. Buonarroti, *La conspiration pour l'égalité, dite de Babeuf* (Paris: Editions Sociales, 1957), 80-81, 157, 159.

53. Droz, "le socialisme français," in *Histoire générale du socialisme*, 1:387; Proudhon, *Qu'est-ce que la propriété?* (Antony: Editions Tops, 1997), 99.

54. Proudhon, *Qu'est-ce que la propriété?*, 35.

55. Hervé Trinquier, introduction, in Proudhon, *Qu'est-ce que la propriété?*, 16; Droz, "le socialisme français," *Histoire générale du socialisme*, 1:387; Proudhon, *Qu'est-ce que la propriété?*, 120, 123, 136, 232, 251-52.

56. However Marx too used moral weapons. The secular prophecy of Marxism had roots in Marx's own thought, despite Marx's well-known denial that he was a "Marxist" (see chapter 5). Proudhon, *Qu'est-ce que la propriété?*, 115, 129, 238; Droz, "le socialisme français," *Histoire générale du socialisme*, 1:388.

3

The Unexpected Honeymoon of Mind and Money, 1730-1830

The previous two chapters prepare us for war between mind and money. They do not prepare us to understand the intense yet troubled romance between them that preceded their struggle. There is little in the background of the Western intelligentsia to explain their embrace of capitalism in the early modern period. Every divorce begins with a honeymoon. In this case, however, the surprise is not the divorce, but the fact that there was a honeymoon in the first place. Western intellectuals had a long history of contempt for trade, commerce and industry. Why, from the late seventeenth to the early nineteenth century, did many leading Western intellectuals decide that capitalism was good? Without understanding the unprecedented attraction commercial society once held for intellectuals, and why it came to an end, we will not understand the war that followed. The honeymoon tells us a great deal about the conflict between mind and money. The divorce tells us even more—it tells us why there is unlikely ever to be a second honeymoon.

The Point of Departure

There are several important differences between the eighteenth-century intellectuals who praised capitalism and the intellectuals of earlier and later periods. These differences made it easier for intellectuals to change their attitude towards commerce then, and much more difficult afterwards. One very important difference is that, of the "Three Don'ts," the Third, Democratic Don't ("Don't Have or Make More Money than Others—it's not fair") was still being formed. It was still unclear what its relationship to capitalism would be. In this crucial respect eighteenth-century[1] intellectuals who fell in love with capitalism differed from both their earlier and later counterparts. Unlike their predecessors, they were

65

partisans of equality. Unlike their successors, they did not associate capitalism with inequality.

However, they were well aware of the other two Don'ts, and of the anti-commercial attitudes of their predecessors. To restore the reputation of commerce, writers had to turn traditional moral judgments upside down. One way of doing so was to rewrite history. So they praised commercial Athens over agricultural Sparta, and came up with new explanations for the fall of Rome: "The luxury of Athens produced great men of every kind. Sparta had a few generals, and even those in smaller number than other cities," wrote Voltaire. Hume noted that "What has chiefly induced severe moralists to declaim against refinement in the arts, is the example of ancient ROME...." But Hume refused to blame the fall of the Roman Empire on luxury, and attributed the loss of Roman virtue to too much conquest, rather than too much money. His arguments about Roman history (like those of Montesquieu before him) were meant to open readers' minds to the possibility that commercial society could have unsuspected merits.[2]

The Enlightenment, as the reforming intellectual movement of the eighteenth century is called, had something to do with this change in attitudes. Declaring that old authorities were no longer to be trusted was part of the Enlightenment's stock in trade. From the new, Enlightened perspective, the ignorant medieval world had been "misled by Aristotle." The partisans of commercial society made a point of ridiculing the economic ideas held by Aristotle, Aquinas, and their followers, in particular the medieval ban on charging interest on loans. Eighteenth-century intellectuals were prepared to free themselves from Aristotle's ghost and embrace capitalism in the name of modernity.[3]

How long this honeymoon period lasted is hazy. It happened roughly from the late seventeenth century until around 1820 or 1830, with allowance for a violent return to anti-commercial attitudes during the radical phase of the French Revolution. By the mid-nineteenth century, however, anti-commercial attitudes prevailed once again, and many intellectuals no longer loved capitalism. Although the honeymoon endured longer in isolated pockets and disciplines like "political economy" and eventually modern economics, it was not even a memory among the intelligentsia generally by the end of the nineteenth century. Even the honeymoon period had been troubled. While some of the most famous Enlightenment intellectuals performed unheard-of defenses of capitalism, they were not the majority. Eighteenth-century debate about commercial society was intense.[4]

Three prominent authors will act as our chief exemplars of intellectuals' pro-commercial attitudes during the honeymoon between mind and money: Adam Smith (1723-90), the famed Scottish author of *The Wealth of Nations*, founder of modern economics; David Hume (1711-76), another Scot, better known as philosopher, historian, and religious scandal (he died a public agnostic) than as a commentator on economics, but a prominent voice nonetheless; and Baron Montesquieu (1689-1755), French author of *The Persian Letters* and *The Spirit of the Laws*, perhaps the greatest political theorist of the French Enlightenment. If all three are exceptional individuals rather than representative of the majority of their contemporaries, all were among the most influential intellectuals of their time. They justified commercial society in many ways.

Justifications of Commerce

The term "justification" has meanings that are now largely forgotten. According to the dictionary, the word "justify" means "to show to be just, right, or reasonable." This definition itself mixes moral ("just") and amoral ("reasonable") meanings. Closer to the old meaning is the 2nd definition given: "To declare or prove guiltless or blameless: absolve; excuse"—here the moral emphasis is stronger. Only the 6th definition, described as "theological," gets to an important part of what is at issue here: "To cause to be free of grievous sin, and reconciled with God." As the Puritans used the word, to be "justified" meant to have received God's grace and be free of sin. When we talk about intellectual defenses of capitalism, particularly with reference to the Christian, Second Don't, this is the meaning we need to bear in mind, as much as its secular counterparts. Moral references, secular and not so secular, abound in eighteenth-century intellectuals' justifications of commerce. To us, increased economic productivity seems the most obvious place to begin a defense of capitalism. Yet even when defending capitalism because of its productivity, eighteenth-century intellectuals often brought in moral considerations, sometimes as paradoxes, sometimes to provide unexpected new moral support for the market.[5]

In looking at how intellectuals justified capitalism, we can isolate several distinct approaches. First, commerce was sometimes justified on amoral, pragmatic grounds that ignored or even embraced its immorality. This was the most radical, and least common, means of justifying commerce. Second, much more often commerce was found, despite appearances, to promote morality. Thirdly, the political and social benefits of capitalism were emphasized. In this case, one particular good result was often appealed to: equality, a term that had increasing moral and political weight. Strikingly, from a twenty-first century perspective, many Enlightenment thinkers defended capitalism as a force for greater equality. This is perhaps the least well recognized of the eighteenth-century justifications of capitalism. In practice, thinkers often combined one or more of these approaches, just as anti-capitalist thinkers usually lean on more than one of the Three Don'ts.

The most radical argument for commerce was based on "de-moralizing" issues like luxury, taking them out of the realm of moral debate so that they could be evaluated on purely utilitarian grounds.[6] This strategy, and the language in which it was deployed, was perhaps the most "modern" one, and certainly the least common. An example is Adam Smith's suggestion that the benefits of commerce, regardless of the motives that produced them, justified it. The merchant:

> ...intends only his own gain, and he is in this, as in many other cases, led by an invisible hand to promote an end which was no part of his intention. Nor is it always the worse for the society that it was no part of it. By pursuing his own interest he frequently promotes that of the society more effectually than when he really intends to promote it.[7]

Defenders of capitalism were not content to merely ignore intentions. They sometimes appealed directly to vice to achieve their ends. Since, wrote Hume, "these principles [virtues] are too disinterested and too difficult to support, it is requisite to govern men by other passions, and animate them with a spirit of avarice and industry, art and luxury." Appealing to avarice, a mortal sin, as a motor for the economy was novel (even if Mandeville had done so earlier). Montesquieu was equally blunt in praise of vanity: "Vanity is as good a spring for a government as arrogance is a dangerous one. To show this, one has only to imagine to oneself, on the one hand, the innumerable goods resulting from vanity: luxury, industry, the arts, fashions, politeness, and taste...." Smith too had no doubt that civilization was partly the result of vanity. In his view, one reason people wanted to become wealthy was vanity. More money did not really make people happier, although they thought it would. But "it is well that nature imposes upon us in this manner. It is this deception which rouses and keeps in continual motion the industry of mankind. It is this which first prompted them to cultivate the ground, to build houses, to found cities and commonwealths, and to invent and improve all the sciences and the arts...." Vanity and luxury, hitherto regarded as a character flaw and its evidence, were transformed into instruments of Providence.[8]

These novel arguments allowed defenders of capitalism to attack its opponents as enemies of humanity, regardless of their good intentions. Old-fashioned clergy who preached against luxury and commerce, whether traditional Christians or admirers of Sparta, were doing humanity a disservice: "The reformer, who by the severity of his way, would also render life more severe, may perhaps be revered by the populace, but he will be slighted by wise men, who make it their rule, to procure ease and comfort to society." Without trade, industry and luxuries, wrote Hume, there was no incentive to work hard or to improve technology.[9]

Amoral justifications of commerce represented a radical break with Western intellectual traditions. They were problematic even for radical intellectuals. As secular clergy, intellectuals' inclination was to moralize rather than de-moralize topics of discussion, and they found ways to discover hitherto unsuspected virtues in commerce and trade. Alongside the de-moralizing of commerce went arguments that found in capitalism a new, and better, morality. Even intellectuals who used "de-moralizing" arguments (e.g., Smith) often, and usually more often, provided parallel justifications of commerce on moral grounds.

For example, all human beings, according to Smith, naturally sympathize with one another and naturally desire praise from others. Human action springs in large part from this desire for praise and approbation. In the marketplace we find sources of approbation and praise, not through exemplary obedience to a religious or moral order, or by successful hand-to-hand combat, but in buying and selling and making and keeping contracts. Our desire for love and praise is fulfilled by making money. Every transaction is an example of the confidence other people have in us, every sale a recognition of our self-worth. Smith's vision of the market foreshadows Simmel's declaration that market relationships are analogous to love relationships. In both love and the market participants try to anticipate and satisfy the desires of the loved one, the customer. In Smith's analysis, in a capitalist society the persuasion once devoted to political rhetoric (or, we might add, to sexual seduction) is devoted instead to commerce—with beneficial results. "In this way, the market transforms potentially disruptive forms of conflict for recognition into regularized, ordered, competition," as one commentary puts it. Instead of the boundless conquests sought by the noble warrior, or the ultimate salvation sought by priests, the merchant sought wealth as his path to praise and approval. It was better that the merchant focused on salesmanship, rather than religion or revolution. Society was better off for the change. Society and economic productivity gained. So did the individuals concerned, both morally and materially. They were preserved from fanaticism and berserker rage.[10]

Commerce itself, as well as the merchant, was given a positive moral role to play in this account:

> Commerce cures destructive prejudices, and it is an almost general rule that everywhere there are gentle mores, there is commerce and that everywhere there is commerce, there are gentle mores.
>   …. Commerce has spread knowledge of the mores of all nations everywhere; they have been compared to each other, and good things have resulted from this. [11]

Montesquieu goes on to give an impressive list of the virtues fostered by capitalism: "the spirit of commerce brings with it the spirit of frugality, economy, moderation, work, wisdom, tranquility, order, and rule. Thus as long as this spirit continues to exist, the wealth it produces has no bad effect." Indeed, noted Hume, "the more men refine upon pleasure, the less they will indulge in excesses of any kind," and if luxury encouraged marital infidelity, it nevertheless diminished drunkenness, which was worse. Capitalism made most people more virtuous. Thus, in the same way amoral justifications of capitalism argued that it materially benefited everyone, so moral justifications of capitalism suggested that it improved, if not everyone's morals, at least those of the "greater part of mankind."[12]

Intellectuals like Smith and Montesquieu and Hume weighed capitalism in modern scales, and found the balance more favorable than a traditional moral perspective would have. We have become accustomed to intellectuals of all kinds, and particularly artists and writers, condemning the businessman's character and lifestyle. But to Smith and many other intellectuals of the eighteenth century, the business personality was a promise of peace and prosperity. The conclusion was that, in Dr. Johnson's words, "There are few ways in which a man can be more innocently employed than in getting money."

The moral consequences of capitalism were central to another set of arguments intellectuals used to defend it, arguments which stressed its political benefits. If the ways in which commerce strengthens the state are viewed as a triumph of *raison d'état*, this tactic seems like an example of de-moralizing commerce. However, intellectuals who defended capitalism because of its political benefits usually appealed to moral considerations. In itself, doing something that was good for the commonwealth had positive moral connotations, particularly from an Aristotelian perspective in which human beings were seen as political animals, and political and moral benefits were largely identical. Here defenders of capitalism retained a traditional moral perspective while turning the old conclusions about commerce upside down. Arguments for the virtues of commerce upended Greco-Roman and feudal ideas that only land-ownership gave people the necessary financial and intellectual independence for freedom. From the perspective of those who defended capitalism, commerce destroyed the economic basis of subjection, by creating new sources of wealth that could not, unlike land, be monopolized.

There is a limited amount of land. All of it is already owned, and most of it is in the hands of a very few people. Trade and industry, however, are potentially unlimited resources. "An estate's a pond, but trade's a spring: the first, if it keeps full, and the water wholesome... is all that is expected; but the other is an inexhausted current, which not only fills the pond,... but is continually running over, and fills all the lower ponds and places about it." Commerce frees people from dependence on land-owners. The springs of wealth are the springs of freedom, and they are fed by trade. Commerce not only creates new wealth, but "calls forth sentiments that had never been felt, and virtues that had no objects." It leads to "that last and greatest of mental improvements, a true political knowledge and sense of Liberty." By producing a "monied interest," it creates rivals to the previously unchallenged superiority of aristocratic landowners, and by refining manners and ideas, produces a demand for political freedom.[13]

Benjamin Constant shows how the economic independence created by capitalist society created a demand for political freedom, even in men otherwise without virtue. During Napoleon's despotic reign, Constant has dinner with a Monsieur Amyot, whom he describes as lacking both intelligence and character: "However, by the sole fact that he is a proprietor he has a tendency to resist oppression, a tendency susceptible of producing, given the opportunity, effects worth far more than their motives." Here is Smith's invisible hand working to create political benefits. The political defenders of commerce produced a crucial justification for commerce when they established its political utility. "Commerce and manufactures gradually introduce order and good government, and with them, the liberty and security of individuals.... This,... is by far the most important of their effects."[14]

Not that eighteenth-century intellectuals, unlike some later defenders of commerce and "civil society," were ever foolish enough to say that commerce *necessarily* led to political freedom. Hume says that although "it has become an established opinion, that commerce can never flourish but in a free government the example of France seems to prove that the connection is not infallible." Nevertheless, "I would assert, that, notwithstanding the efforts of the French, there is something hurtful to commerce inherent in the very nature of absolute government, and inseparable from it." A whole complex of reasons is given for how and why commerce is linked, if not infallibly, to freedom. The links are not just direct, as when commerce requires secure title to property, a way of enforcing contracts with the government, etc. They are also indirect. For example, commerce and luxury lead to progress in technology, and "progress in the arts is rather favourable to liberty, and has a natural tendency to preserve, if not produce a free government." Commerce also enriches the peasants, as well as traders and merchants, which creates a larger middle class, and "draws attention to that middling rank of men, who are the best and firmest basis of public liberty.... They covet equal laws, which may secure their property, and preserve them from monarchical, as well as aristocratical tyranny."[15]

Capitalism makes wealthy people, too, of course. The more wealthy people there are, the less absolute power can be exercised: "Wealth in the subject then, is the natural poise against arbitrary power in the state." But it is also the manner in which it enriches people which makes capitalism favorable to freedom: "How much better calculated for the interests of freedom this commercial arithmetic of multiplication is, that regulates the national property, by increasing every particular person's share, than that of agrarian division [re-distributing landownership equally to all], projected by the ancients to serve the same purpose." Commerce creates "a new species of property, entirely its own creation, that lifts the humble vassal within sight of his haughty lord."[16]

These are the political effects of commerce from the bottom up. Commerce also works from the top down to encourage freedom. After suggesting that trade and industry are initially established only with the support of rulers, Dugald Stewart continues "When once a state begins to subsist by the consequences of industry, there is less danger to be apprehended from the power of the sovereign.... he finds himself so bound up by the laws of his political economy, that every transgression of them runs him into new difficulties.... modern economy, therefore, is the most effectual bridle ever invented against the folly of despotism." Montesquieu gives an example of this, describing how Roman emperors, ruling a non-commercial society, could profitably manipulate the value of their currency, whereas "these violent operations could not occur in our time; a prince would deceive himself and would deceive no one else.... The exchange... has curtailed the great acts of authority, or at least [their] success." Another example used is how "commerce makes... [property] virtually impossible to seize." Land is easy to confiscate. Money in accounts and bills of exchange can rapidly be transferred beyond the despot's reach. The converse was also true, in Montesquieu's view: "Muscovy [Russia] has tried to leave its despotism; it cannot. The establishment of commerce requires the establishment of the exchange, and the operations of the exchange contradict all Muscovy's laws." Without guarantees for commerce, there can be no political freedom in Russia—a lesson demonstrated at the end of the twentieth century.[17]

Along with freedom, another moral and political benefit intellectuals expected from capitalism was peace. Capitalism led to peace because peace was more profitable than war, and trade had taught men to control their other passions in the name of gain. "War is all impulse, commerce, calculation. Hence it follows that an age must come in which commerce replaces war. We have reached this age," wrote Constant. Commerce created new interests that encouraged peace. Montesquieu demonstrated that "the natural effect of commerce is to lead to peace. Two nations that trade with each other become reciprocally dependent; if one has an interest in buying, the other has an interest in selling, and all unions are founded on mutual needs."[18]

Many eighteenth-century intellectuals thus defended capitalism as a source of moral and political benefits to the individual and society. Capitalism produced a new, private, secular morality accessible to ordinary people who were neither heroes nor saints, but businessmen. The benefits capitalism brought society as a whole came about through the good capitalism did for individuals. "'Private virtues, public benefits' would be a fair description."[19] By adopting this view of capitalism, intellectuals could use their traditional moral voice while taking an untraditional position in defense of commerce.

For all these reasons, amoral, moral, and political, commercial society was superior to its predecessors, and particular intellectuals were happy to use some or all of these justifications in its defense. But there was yet another effect of commerce that was of great importance to eighteenth-century intellectuals, an effect with economic, moral, and political connotations—greater equality. It has long been recognized that inequality was an issue in eighteenth-century debates over commercial society. What has not been recognized is the extent to which a desire for equality motivated its supporters, as well as its opponents. In the eyes of capitalism's supporters, capitalism was not opposed to the Third Don't, to a more equal distribution of wealth. In fact, it was a manifestation of it. No one defended commerce on the grounds that it contributed to inequality. Many defended it because it lessened inequality, either absolutely or relatively.

Eighteenth-century *opponents* of capitalism sometimes defended inequality. In particular they declaimed against the "luxury" of the poor. Food riots in the summer of 1757 prompted one English periodical to declaim against the luxury of "the lower sorts of people," arguing that unless it was suppressed, Britons would lose their property.[20] The novelist Fielding blamed the troubles on commerce: "Nothing has wrought such an alteration in the [lower] Order of People, as the Introduction of Trade.... The narrowness of their Fortune is changed into Wealth; the Simplicity of their Manners changed into Craft, their Frugality into Luxury, their Humility into Pride, and their Subjection into Equality."[21]

This was precisely why supporters of commercial society favored it. Justifications of capitalism often combined a utilitarian appeal to material improvement with a moral/political appeal to egalitarianism. Greater productivity was in everyone's interests: "Among civilised and thriving nations... a workman, even of the lowest and poorest order, if he is frugal and industrious, may enjoy a greater share of the necessaries and conveniences of life than it is possible for any savage to acquire.... in a well-governed society, universal opulence... extends itself to the lowest ranks of the people." Smith anticipated and rejected Fielding's complaint. He knew that one of capitalism's great advantages was that *everyone*[22] was better off in it than they had been in previous stages of human civilization, and that this was a good thing: "Is this improvement in the circumstances of the lower ranks of the people to be regarded as an advantage or as an inconvenience to society? The answer at first sight seems abundantly plain... what improves the circumstances of the greater part can never be regarded as an inconvenience to the whole." For Smith "the common complaint that luxury extends itself even to the lowest ranks of the people" has no merit. "We do not think civilization commits a crime by procuring many material enjoyments and making their acquisition easier." Hume stressed the improved productivity that would result if the poor were better off. Rather than becoming lazy, the laborer would work harder if he had more opportunity to make money and more things to buy with it. Montesquieu supports the ban on nobles engaging in trade on egalitarian grounds: "The law must prohibit nobles from engaging in commerce; merchants with such rank would set up all sorts of monopolies. Commerce is the profession of equal people...."[23]

This is the heart of the matter. *Commerce is the profession of equal people*. It lessens not only material inequalities, but social and political ones. It tends to destroy inherited differences of status, lower the great and raise up the middle class and even the poor. "For a continual addition of wealth, communicated alike thro' all the various stations of civil life, must hasten the several heaps to a level; must bring the fortunes of fellow citizens towards that unattainable limit of equality near which all the safeguards of freedom lie." Commerce will bring us greater equality, the foundation of political freedom (the defense of commerce as a source of freedom had links with the "republican" tradition of antiquity and the Renaissance, which for reasons of space must be left out of this account).[24] Capitalism was justified because its ever-increasing productivity led to greater equality.[25]

On behalf of capitalist equality, Smith and other intellectuals fiercely attacked monopolies, entails, primogeniture, etc. It is the offense to equality, more than economic arguments, that motivates the attack. Monopoly is a way in which trade and industry can be limited like feudal land-ownership, and more or less permanently concentrated in a few hands. Smith himself compares land-ownership to a monopoly: "The rent of land,... is naturally a monopoly price." Monopolies re-establish within capitalism those permanent dependencies and differences in status which commercial society was supposed to break down. By contrast competition is like the equal division of wealth among children, because competition, "by cutting into many different channels the overflowing stream of wealth, the torrent soon subsides within its proper bounds." Commerce thus promotes equality, while monopoly promotes inequality.[26]

Eighteenth-century intellectuals' honeymoon with capitalism comes at the beginning of their long-term espousal of equality. But before we equate eighteenth-century support for commerce with support for equality, we must add a caveat. While the supporters of capitalism supported more equality, they also recognized an "unattainable limit to equality." They wanted greater equality, not absolute equality. For the Scottish Enlightenment generally, with its "four stages" theory of human development (primitive, pastoral, agricultural, commercial), material equality is left behind in the primeval forest. Commerce is deadly to inherited, aristocratic hierarchies of wealth and status, it tends towards equality in some respects, but not all. Hume says that without some inequality, government would be impossible, and Morellet argues that without inequality people would have no need for one another and society would become impossible (a neat inversion of Rousseau, who thinks primitive humans don't need each other, and hence are solitary). What supporters of capitalism and equality support is the growth of the "middling ranks." They maintain that capitalism, like the tide, raises all boats, but unlike the tide not by an equal amount. And this is good enough. Indeed, it is a revolutionary change. Like all revolutions, it produced some unlikely bedfellows: mind and money experienced a honeymoon.[27]

Intellectuals' concern for showing that the benefits of capitalism extended to all showed that the egalitarian imperative summarized in the Third, democratic Don't (Don't Have or Make More Money Than Others) was already at work, and that it was not necessarily hostile to capitalism. The love-talk of mind and money was often couched in egalitarian language, appealing to a more equal distribution of wealth and opportunity. Although the argument that capitalism made everyone better off was not quite the same as saying that capitalism made everyone equal, or even equally better-off, the themes were related. Many eighteenth-century intellectuals saw capitalism as the road to greater social equality. While nineteenth to twenty-first century thinkers usually assume that capitalism leads to greater economic and social inequalities, eighteenth-century defenders of commerce made the opposite assumption. This difference is an important reason why many eighteenth-century intellectuals favored capitalism, and those afterwards mostly criticize it. Praising capitalism for not merely producing more things, but for distributing some of them to everyone is a moral judgment as well as an economic one. It is only because of their positive moral evaluation of capitalism that many intellectuals could praise it. For many eighteenth-century intellectuals, the foundation of morality was already found in equality. In that judgment lay one of the roots of divorce.

But even pro-capitalist eighteenth-century intellectuals harbored some mixed feelings. Smith wondered whether specializing the tasks involved in pin making, which increased productivity a thousand-fold and cut the price of pins by 99 percent, was on balance a good thing. Was the boredom and stunted development of the pin makers performing their specialized tasks too high a price to pay? All the major authors who defended capitalism were aware that not all its consequences were desirable. Montesquieu noted that "in countries where one is affected only by the spirit of commerce, there is traffic in all human activities and all moral virtues; the smallest things, those required by humanity, are done or given for money."[28]

The ambivalence capitalism's defenders displayed about the relationship between capitalism and virtue is most pronounced when it comes to military questions. Though Smith and Montesquieu were supporters of commercial society, they accepted the idea that it weakens the military virtues and regarded this as a flaw. Other defenders of capitalism felt compelled to make a case that it promoted the martial virtues too. Hume claimed that ages of great generals, as well as great philosophers and poets, were usually ages which abounded in skillful weavers and ship-carpenters, ages of "industry and of refinements in the mechanical arts." Daniel Defoe defended merchants against the charge (admitted by Montesquieu and Smith, however,) that the pursuit of material well-being made one unfit for war, describing an English army that was "full of excellent officers, who went from the shop, and behind the counter, into the camp, and who distinguished themselves there by their merits and gallant behaviour!" François Melon went so far as to attribute warrior virtues to avarice, citing the glorious exploits of French privateers (legalized pirates), and suggesting that "Glory alone, without those advantages, which are inseparable from a happy existence, is not a sufficient spur for the multitude." If the privateers had returned with only honour instead of prize money, they would not have gone back to sea.[29]

These qualms afflicting capitalism's staunchest defenders show how even during the honeymoon between mind and money, older affections, Greco-Roman, aristocratic, and "republican" lingered. It was hard for many intellectuals to wholeheartedly embrace capitalism without casting a wistful eye back towards the ancient virtues and traditional moral attitudes. The best example of this is perhaps Constant, who admired the Greeks and Romans while regarding their political virtues as impossible to duplicate in the modern world. Attempts to revive the glorious old virtues would only lead to Jacobin despotism, he wrote. But unlike Montesquieu and Smith, in the end Constant decided that commercial society was capable of overcoming its flaws in this regard: "Civilization is like Achilles' spear, it cures the ills it causes. The ills are only passing, and the cure is eternal."[30]

Why the Honeymoon Began

Eighteenth-century intellectuals defended capitalism because of its direct and indirect benefits. These benefits were material and moral, political and social, and above all egalitarian. This defense flew in the face of much of the Western intellectual tradition. Why did this happen? There were changes in eighteenth-century society that distinguished it from past eras, but they were less radical than the new ideas intellectuals had about them. What we have here is a case of people faced with circumstances fairly similar to those of the past, but having revolutionary new ideas about them. What caused this?

This is the kind of direct question about causes that typically gives historians difficulties. In response, they usually produce volumes that provide greater understanding, and not much explanation. Attaining at least a partial explanation, however, is necessary for understanding the conflict between mind and money that has endured ever since the honeymoon came to an end. In fact, what is needed are two explanations, one of why the honeymoon began, and the other of why it ended. Both can be derived from the summary of the honeymoon we have just finished.

The first explanation, for why the honeymoon began, can be approached in several ways. There were intellectual reasons why capitalism suddenly seemed attractive, there were sociological reasons which contributed to intellectuals finding these new arguments convincing, and there were particular historical events and circumstances which added force to both the intellectual and sociological reasons. These headings, intellectual, sociological, and historical, are somewhat arbitrary, since things considered under one could often be considered under another. What is important is to recognize the constellation of causes that contributed to the honeymoon.

To begin with the intellectual reasons, the broadest is the effect of the Enlightenment. Without attempting to define that highly elastic term, it is safe enough to attribute to the Enlightenment widespread rejection of many traditional ways of thinking. In this respect the honeymoon between mind and money was just another aspect of a far wider intellectual movement.

A fashion for trashing tradition, however, does not explain why intellectuals were suddenly fond of commerce. Some specific reasons have been given above. A more general answer is given by Albert Hirschman, in *The Passions and the Interests: Political Arguments for Capitalism before its Triumph*. He suggests that intellectuals' support for capitalism in the eighteenth century derived from a "desperate search for a way of *avoiding society's ruin*, permanently threatening at the time because of precarious arrangements for internal and external order." What threatened to ruin society? Fanaticism and despotism, both of which were founded on violence, the violence that "*doux commerce*," "gentle trade," was intended to prevent.[31]

Late seventeenth-century Europe had just emerged from a long series of wars and revolutions unleashed by the Protestant Reformation and Catholic attempts to overcome it. From the Thirty Years War in Germany, to the Wars of Religion in France, to the English Civil Wars, Europe had been devastated by over a century of religious violence. One result was to send many intellectuals scurrying to find some basis outside religion, or at least outside traditional Christianity, on which to found human relations. Intellectuals were moralists, and they were firmly convinced of the need to find a moral basis for society. But their historical experience caused these moralists to consider rejecting morality as a foundation for social relations, because morality was so strongly associated with religion, and religion with war (in 2009, this seems very familiar!). Thus amoral justifications for social relations like those created by commerce suddenly seemed a safer ground on which to rest. Better people buy luxuries and go to the theater than fall prey to religious fanaticism: "Public diversions have always been the objects of dread and hatred to all the fanatical promoters of those popular frenzies [of religious zeal]. The gaiety and good humor which those diversions inspire were altogether inconsistent with that temper of mind, which was fittest for their purpose, or which they could best work upon." Salvation could go by the wayside, if it had to be purchased at the cost of vast quantities of blood, sweat, and tears.[32]

Insofar as intellectuals continued to be moralists, they thought it better to rest their moral judgments on secular rather than religious foundations. One well-known example of this is the "social contract," from which some intellectuals derived individuals' rights and duties. Another was commerce. Capitalism would produce the moral fruits that Christianity had promised in vain. Consumerism was the antidote to fanaticism. Preachers produced violence. Merchants produced peace. Of the two unintended by-products, war and peace, intellectuals knew which they preferred. The passions, at least the violent ones, including religion, were to be moderated by the interest in making money and the material diversions (shopping!) of a nascent consumer culture. Making money was a more innocent occupation than religious warfare, robbery, or rape. Religion might be a useful or even necessary element for encouraging morality, but only if it was prevented by commerce from turning into fanaticism. God and Mammon would make good bedfellows, whose union would lead to peace and prosperity. Under these auspices, mind was ready to embark on its honeymoon cruise with money.

A final intellectual motive for supporting capitalism was the alternative it provided to aristocracy. Any eighteenth-century intellectual lived in a world we can only imagine today, a world dominated by inherited status and privilege. We have to take classes to learn what an aristocracy was, a "society of orders," in which inequality was the accepted norm and rank and status were inherited. The intellectuals of the eighteenth century knew what such a society was by personal experience, often bitter. While they rarely came from the bottom, they were usually far from the top in rank, and they resented it. There is much satisfaction behind Smith's description of how the landed aristocracy was in the process of losing its power. After describing how the great landowners, rather than paying armed men, had begun to spend their money on luxury goods, he continues:

> The tenants having in this manner become independent, and the retainers being dismissed, the great proprietors were no longer capable of interrupting the regular execution of justice, or of disturbing the peace of the country. Having sold their birthright... for trinkets and baubles, fitter to be the playthings of children than the serious pursuits of men, they became as insignificant as any substantial burgher or tradesman in a city.[33]

The picture drawn by Smith here is all the more significant because it is inaccurate. The claim that the lords were now insignificant, no longer the superiors of the bourgeois, was false politically, socially, and even economically when Smith wrote. But it was the dream Smith *wanted* to see come true. However unrealistic it was as a representation of eighteenth-century Europe, it had a strong emotional and intellectual appeal to many intellectuals, as for other commoners.

It was capitalism that would make the dream come true. The equality produced by capitalism was less an equality of wealth (Enlightenment intellectuals were rarely foolish enough to believe that) than an equality of status. At the time, this seemed like plenty. An artistic representation of intellectuals' appeal to commerce to make us equal can be found in Mozart's opera *The Magic Flute*. Its libretto exalts the value of work, and the "Masonic Lodge" that represents the heroes embodies the equal status of its members, along with all the other bourgeois virtues.

Intellectuals had sociological as well as intellectual reasons for favoring capitalism in this period. Intellectuals had historically been close to whoever ruled society. Although they had always been hostile to commerce, they had generally been favorable to property, and the owners of property. Greek sophists and Roman philosophers had supported the aristocratic landowners of their day. Christian theologians had, once Christianity became the state religion, been equally friendly to feudal magnates. There was a long history of alliance between those with property and those with education in the West. It had been a necessity for intellectuals dependent on clerical positions or lay patrons for their subsistence.

In the eighteenth century, there was an incipient change in intellectuals' social position, and a related change in the nature of the society that surrounded them. An independent intellectual class began to take shape, and commerce and industry were beginning to play a leading economic role. During the honeymoon, it seemed that these changes would lead to an even closer alliance between the propertied and the educated, with the former now being traders and industrialists rather than landowners. Let us begin with the intellectuals themselves, and go on to the growth of what Tocqueville called "democratic society."

There were more intellectuals in eighteenth-century Europe than there had ever been before, and they held different kinds of jobs. The medieval and renaissance intelligentsia was bigger than the classical intelligentsia. In the eighteenth century this growth continued, amid the growing demand for higher education in the age of Descartes and Newton and expanding royal bureaucracies. Not only were there more intellectuals, but they were more frequently outside the employ of Church and State. They had new means of earning a living and new lifestyles to lead. They could more or less publish what they pleased, at least anonymously, and find readers and perhaps more importantly, publishers willing to pay them. They could earn a precarious living, and sometimes more, in this way. Capitalism vastly expanded the private space free of religious and political intervention (the market), and encouraged a new kind of people to fill it—the commercial and industrial middle classes, as well as intellectuals. All kinds of new markets were opening up for intellectuals, markets that valued the intellectual more for his independence than for his orthodoxy. If capitalism and the markets it created for intellectuals were still dwarfed by more traditional sources of patronage in the eighteenth century, they had begun to make their presence felt.

This contributed to the creation of a more autonomous social position for intellectuals. Intellectuals had always been an identifiable group. In the eighteenth century, however, the "man of letters" was becoming part of a new class, with a new social position that was recognized by the widespread use of the term "man of letters" (and sometimes even "woman of letters"). Socrates and Aquinas had been intellectuals in their time. But describing them and their fellows as intellectuals also results in a certain confusion. Individually, they *were* intellectuals because they *did* manifest very strongly as individuals the characteristic markers of the intellectual. They possessed the best educations available in their day, they exercised certain occupations, they played a moral role, and they used careful, critical discourse, CCD. But intellectuals as a class are defined not just by their personal identity, but by their social position. As a group, they stand in a certain relationship to society. Socrates and Aquinas stood in a very different relationship to their society than eighteenth-century men of letters stood to theirs, not least because the world of Ancient Greece or medieval Europe was neither democratic nor commercial. Although there are similarities between Plato, Aquinas, and Montesquieu (partly because Montesquieu read Plato and Aquinas), socially it is the differences that matter. The role Montesquieu played in society was vastly different.

One reason an increasingly autonomous intellectual class sought to emancipate morality from religion, and used commerce as a tool to do so, was that as a class it needed both freedom and morality. It needed freedom to be able to engage in careful critical discourse, independent of Church and state. It needed a moral role to provide its social function and justification. Threats to their freedom and their moral role came from the churches. They also came from rulers, who throughout much of eighteenth-century Europe were seeking to expand their powers. Intellectuals saw that capitalism could help them in both respects. It was not only religious fanaticism that would be diminished by commerce, it was also government despotism. Capitalism promised to limit the power of the ruler. These developments laid the foundation for a new kind of politics, a new kind of political freedom, and, for intellectuals, much greater freedom for criticism.

The formation of the intellectual class was linked to the development of democracy. Intellectuals need a democratic, that is, egalitarian and technological, society in which to be fully independent. They need to be independent of crown and altar, king and pope. The social changes that took place in Europe in the eighteenth century, i.e., the development of democracy, made possible their emergence as a class and made it logical for them to embrace capitalism in ways the mass of intellectuals had never done before. The eighteenth century saw the beginnings, not just of the class of intellectuals, or of capitalism, but of democratic society, the society that assumed that equality was the natural and only justifiable condition of humanity. Although eighteenth-century society was far from embodying this ideal, nevertheless the foundations of aristocratic hierarchy were crumbling. If the process was too slow for some, it was fast enough to be striking to others. The development of democratic society was epitomized by the Third Don't. It added yet another reason for intellectuals to support capitalism—as long as capitalism was seen as promoting, rather than retarding, equality.

Archimedes said that if he had a lever long enough, and a place on which to rest it, he could move the Earth. In democratic capitalism, eighteenth-century intellectuals found a place to stand far enough removed from the state and religion from which to exercise their independent moral judgment. If the Earth was not necessarily moved by the levers intellectuals had at their disposal, it was not for lack of trying. Sometimes they even thought they moved it. Shelley claimed in 1822 that poets were the unacknowledged legislators of the world. For the most part, however, eighteenth-century intellectuals were still relatively modest, at least before the French Revolution. As a nascent class still in the early stages of formation, they were not yet the pseudo-aristocracy they would become—their pretensions were not yet that great. They were already hostile to the traditional aristocracy of birth (if still often dependent on it for patronage, another source of resentment), but not yet hostile to what some of them would call a new aristocracy of capital.

Alongside intellectuals' new ideas and social situation, there were particular historical events and circumstances encouraging intellectuals to take a more positive attitude towards capitalism. The most important of these was perhaps the sheer novelty of the situation. While from the perspective of the frenetically changing twenty-first century change in eighteenth-century Europe seems slow and marginal, at the time it seemed rapid and revolutionary. If one looks at the available econometric statistics, the changes between 1750 and 1830 seem small, but if one looks at the literary evidence, they seem enormous. Since it is intellectuals with whom we are concerned, it is the literary evidence that is relevant. Smith, Hume, Montesquieu and their fellows perceived the world to be turning under their feet, moved by the rapid development of capitalism. The growing wealth and productivity struck them forcefully, and the impression they took away was in most cases favorable. Unlike in the 1840s, when the factories and slums of Manchester appeared to Engels as proof of capitalism's depravity, in 1727 it was how much better-off the English poor were than those of other countries that struck Defoe: "the working manufacturing people of England, eat the fat, drink the sweet, live better, and fare better, than the working poor of any other nation in Europe." The new economic situation impelled intellectuals to rethink old ideas about trade and industry. Gains in the standard of living, the past two centuries have shown, are not necessarily enough to justify capitalism in intellectuals' eyes. We have become accustomed to the idea of a rising standard of living for everyone, even the poor. But in the eighteenth century, the novelty of the change did much to encourage intellectuals to support capitalism. It even seems surprising that a substantial minority of intellectuals continued to reject capitalism—testimony of the residual strength of the first Two Don'ts.[34]

Yet the honeymoon ended, and was immediately followed by a bitter quarrel. In England, as early as 1790 people worried that attacks on businessmen were contributing to "disdain for trade and industry," while in France the Revolution led to a return to praise for the anti-commercial values and attitudes of Greece and Rome. In the early nineteenth century Romanticism adopted anti-commercial attitudes as well, in part in reaction against new technology. But pro-commercial thinkers, such as Constant (d. 1830), or Smith for that matter, continued to be highly influential. It is impossible to give a precise date for when the balance of intellectual opinion swung against capitalism. However, by 1848, if one likes revolutions, or 1850, if one prefers round numbers, the turning point had been passed. Hostility grew over time, gathering momentum until 1880 or so, when it was firmly established. By 1902 Friedrich Paulson could write that "to a large extent, the academically educated classes have the sense of being an aristocracy of the mind, which is called upon to be a counterweight against the aristocracies of birth and wealth."[35]

When the honeymoon ends in divorce, the former partners rarely go back to the relationship they had before they married. Too many things have changed. The same was true of mind and money. What led to an unprecedented state of war between them was not the fact that intellectuals returned to their old hostility to commerce. That was ancient, and had only been briefly interrupted by their honeymoon. What was new were the new social, intellectual and historical contexts of the nineteenth century. In the nineteenth century the hostility between mind and money existed within a much more democratic and overwhelmingly capitalist society. The conflict's point of departure was the breakdown of the old, pre-capitalist, pre-honeymoon alliance between those with property and those with education.

Between 1850 and World War I there was a complete breakdown of this alliance, which had previously been a constant factor in Western history. In the Greco-Roman world, the First Don't deplored commerce, but supported property. In medieval Europe, throne, altar, aristocracy and clerical intellectuals bonded together, despite occasional attempts to revive the Second Don't in its fundamentalist rigor. Hostility to commerce had not implied hostility to property when most property was land and Europe was a predominantly agricultural society. In any case, what did it matter if intellectuals hated commerce, when intellectuals were a dependent group tightly bound to non-commercial institutions? Even in the dawn of capitalism in the late eighteenth century, the old alliance between property and education was confirmed by the honeymoon period between intellectuals and rising merchants, however revolutionary that period was in other respects. But when the honeymoon was over, large numbers of Western intellectuals were again hostile to commerce when, for the first time in history, capitalism had become the dominant factor in Western life, and Western society had become largely democratic. The combination was enough to transform intellectuals from pillars of the establishment into wild-eyed Samsons, often with long hair to match.

The beginning of this war will be described in chapter 4. What requires explanation here is why the honeymoon between mind and money came to such a bitter end. Why was the combination of a democratic society, capitalism, and an intellectual class so explosive? At the beginning of the honeymoon there had been intellectual reasons why capitalism suddenly seemed attractive, sociological reasons that contributed to intellectuals finding these new arguments convincing, and particular historical events and circumstances that gave them added force. At the end, all these causes conspired to destroy the tenuous harmony between intellectuals and capitalism.

Why the Honeymoon Ended

The most important reason for the outbreak of war between mind and money was the full emergence of the intellectual class described in chapter 1. Without it, the conflict could never have begun. Intellectuals' status as a group had begun to change in the eighteenth century, when "men of letters" and some women, made their weight felt in the salons. However, the intelligentsia was not fully formed until well into the nineteenth century. This is one reason why the alliance between property and education was one of the few things that spanned the abyss of the French Revolution. As long as intellectuals were not a fully defined group, and as long as capitalism was not fully developed and the old aristocratic regime persisted, the alliance of property and education could endure, and the ideas of the honeymoon period could find a receptive audience here and there. This is why the alliance, and even some shreds of the honeymoon, lasted well into the nineteenth century, into the 1830s, 1850s, or even 1870s, depending on circumstances.

The emergence of an intellectual class was not rapid. Intellectuals were slow to develop an independent social identity, partly because many of the social and professional niches they occupy today were still very sparse.

There was, compared to a century later, little employment to be had in academia or the press, and painters and poets still depended largely on aristocratic patronage. But throughout the nineteenth century the number of intellectuals grew rapidly. In academia, the number of university faculty in Britain, France and Germany almost tripled during the second half of the century, growing from fewer than 3,000 in 1864 to about 8,500 in 1909.[36] Even more impressive was the increase in university students. Whereas in 1860 only about 23,000 students attended universities in the three countries, by 1910 it was 133,000, a five-fold increase. The number of books published in these same countries, which gives some indication of the number of authors, rose from 22,000 in1850 to 50,000 in 1891. The number of people employed in independent intellectual professions, such as writers and journalists, rose in France alone from about 4,100 in 1876 to over 9,000 in 1906. In Germany in 1882 there were 5,000, and in England and Wales, 6,800 in 1881. One historian has put the number of "intellectuals" of all sorts in France alone in 1901 at about 30,000. The numbers in America were initially smaller, but with the creation of land-grant universities beginning after the Civil War ended in 1865, they too rapidly increased.[37]

These are tiny numbers in comparison to the population at large, of course. The number of people who received the minimum education necessary to become an intellectual remained very small. Even in 1914, only 1.1 percent of French and German eighteen-year-olds were enrolled in the final year of an academic high school. In absolute terms, however, these figures mark an enormous increase over the past. It does not take a large *percentage* of a population to form a class, even a dominant class—the French nobility in 1789 was only 1-2 percent of the total population, including their children. But it does take a certain absolute number, and this is the period in which intellectuals attained those numbers. This process of class formation continued throughout the nineteenth century.[38]

The formation of an independent intellectual class in the late nineteenth century was confirmed by the invention of the word "intellectual" to describe them. The word was first widely used in France. It is characteristic of France, and perhaps of intellectuals, that "intellectual" first entered common use in the course of a violent political struggle, the Dreyfus Affair. Captain Alfred Dreyfus was falsely accused of being a German spy and convicted based on forged evidence. On 13 January, 1898, a French newspaper published an open letter to the president of France, written by the great novelist Emile Zola, protesting against this injustice.

Over the course of the next several weeks, the newspaper published the names of several hundred people who supported Zola's protest. The list was made up almost exclusively of professors, writers, and artists, often identified by their diplomas—'M. Péguy, Ph.D in literature', for example. However the word "intellectual" was never used. On 1 February, 1898, another great writer, Maurice Barrès, who opposed Dreyfus, referred to Zola's letter and its backers as "the protest of the intellectuals." From that moment the word entered into common usage.

Contrary to legend, however, this was not the first printed use of the term. It had been in use in France since the beginning of the decade. Barrès himself had used it in print as early as 1892.[39] But the class of intellectuals was not suddenly created in 1892 or 1898. The English poet Lord Byron had used the word in a letter as early as 1810. People often used other words to talk about intellectuals before the 1890s, and the class of intellectuals was present long before the word was invented, even if its presence was expressed more vaguely. The creation of the word is not the creation of the thing.[40] Still, the coining of the word "intellectual" was the culmination of a long process of class formation. It recognized intellectuals' new status. "Intellectual" increasingly replaced the older "man of letters," and the intellectual became an easily recognizable and recognized type. Emancipated from Church, aristocratic, and to a lesser extent from government patronage, the intellectual could imagine herself as the "free-floating," unattached and unattachable being that Karl Mannheim would conceive her to be (this was especially true of women intellectuals, who were detached even from their conventional gender role).

Even more revelatory of intellectuals' new social status than the creation of the word "intellectual" was the fact that intellectuals were now playing a political role *as* intellectuals. The Dreyfus Affair is but one example of a wider phenomenon of the later nineteenth century. In England, indignation over the "Bulgarian Atrocities" in 1876, largely whipped up by intellectuals, helped put Gladstone back in power in the elections of that year. As early as 1871, the new political role intellectuals were playing had struck observers. Commenting on the uprising of the Paris Commune in that year, *The Nation* wrote that the strangest thing about the rebellion was "the appearance in it of a swarm of adventurers from the *Quartier Latin*, with pretensions more or less well-founded to education, and who had nothing in common with the working-classes…." The *Nation* went on to complain about a "bohemian element" (the word "intellectual" was not yet in common use in English) who had done so much "to make the

Commune possible, and who played so large a part in carrying it on...."
The *Nation* was not alone. The *Revue des Deux Mondes*, the authoritative
journal of French liberalism, also thought the Commune differed from
previous uprisings because of the role intellectuals played.[41]

Fear of intellectuals had made its appearance here and there before
the Commune. Afterwards the alliance between those with property
and those with education seemed increasingly dubious to those on both
sides of the barricades. After the honeymoon, intellectuals no longer
allied themselves with capitalism and the middle classes in the name of
equality and freedom. Instead they opposed them in the name of equality
(the Third Don't) and freedom—and the first two Don'ts as well. By the
late nineteenth century hostile attitudes towards commercial society by
intellectuals of both left and right had become widespread. Both Barrès
and Zola, on opposite sides in the Dreyfus Affair, wrote novels in which
capitalism was held up for contempt.

Intellectuals were not always the aggressors in this conflict. Philistine
hostility towards effete intellectual snobs is as characteristic of the war
between mind and money as intellectuals' contempt for philistines. Intellectuals' distaste for capitalism was balanced by a growing resentment
of their pretentions. As Friedrich Meinecke, a leading German historian,
wrote: "The academically educated, who had once been on the offensive
against the old ruling classes, and then united with them in a certain part-
nership and in part incorporated in them, from now on felt themselves on
the defensive against [them]." It was only natural that as the intelligentsia
became a separate class, it became a target of middle-class hostility. In
America too an early nineteenth-century alliance between property and
education gave way to persistent mutual hostility.[42]

During the same period when the intelligentsia emerged (1830-
1880), another social development was taking place: the decline of the
aristocracy and the rise of the middle classes. This too helped ignite the
war between mind and money. Intellectuals' pro-capitalism had been
fueled to some extent by their resentment of the rank, privileges, and
status of the aristocracy. To put it baldly, since capitalism undermined
aristocracy, it was a good thing from an intellectual's point of view. To
the extent that the intellectual class became a pseudo-aristocracy itself,
this was even more true, as the traditional aristocracy were their rivals.
Once the traditional aristocracy had been put into the shade by rising
middle classes, the situation was different. Now, rather than diminishing
the status of their rivals, the old aristocracy, capitalism was the support
of a new rival, the businessman.

Whether the bourgeoisie was the ruling class in nineteenth-century Europe (probably not) is not the issue, what matters is that they were perceived to be by people like Karl Marx. Many nineteenth-century intellectuals, not just Marx, saw the bourgeois as the new, and newly dominant, enemy. The bourgeois and the bourgeoisie were more inviting targets than the aristocracy, or even the Church, had ever been, because the new intellectual class no longer needed to identify with its social superiors. The hostility of intellectuals to capitalism was correspondingly unprecedented in scope and fervor.

Another social development that helped end the honeymoon between mind and money was the emergence of the proletariat. Hard as they might try, it was difficult for many European intellectuals to sympathize much with peasants, as Marx's well-known remarks about "the idiocy of rural life" and peasants as so many "sacks of potatoes" indicate. But the newly-industrialized factory worker was another thing. In England the Chartist movement, on the continent the revolutions of 1848, showed that a new set of actors was appearing on the scene, potential allies for intellectuals in any assault on capitalism. The proletariat provided intellectuals with opportunities for pseudo-aristocratic social bonding that peasants did not. They offered not just potential allies, but examples of the perfidy of commercial society as well. They provided a moral focus for intellectuals' jeremiads against capitalism, people on whose behalf intellectuals could write and talk. While it was useful to complain that capitalism deformed the middle-class character, it left one with the unsatisfactory image of someone whose chief victim was himself. The proletariat provided a class of victims on whose behalf intellectuals' could fight.

At the same time as the proletariat provided intellectuals with a cause, in the late nineteenth century intellectuals often developed some sympathy for the old aristocracy of birth. Partly this was due to its cultural pretensions. But there was a deeper reason at work. For intellectuals, the fact that commerce, what people *have*, displaces *being*, what people *are*, is a threat. Their class position is based on being, not having, on status, not money. Although during the honeymoon period they saw the rejection of being, i.e., being a hereditary aristocrat, or an anointed bishop, as opening the door to their independence as individuals and as a class, this view did not survive the honeymoon period. It was replaced by the idea that a capitalist society that prefers having to being is rejecting *them*, along with the old nobility. This made intellectuals more inclined to pity the old nobility in a kind of displaced self-pity. After all, capitalism was trying to displace them, too.

All this sociology is easy to make into a family drama. The bourgeoisie and the intellectuals were siblings who became rivals. They were united in their struggle against their parents, the aristocracy and the Church. Once victory was in sight, their alliance turned into a rivalry made all the more bitter by their common origin.

Here there is a difference in the family history of the American and European intelligentsia that influenced the slightly later development of anti-capitalist attitudes among American intellectuals. There was no aristocracy to fight in the United States. Superficially, this would seem to suggest that American intellectuals should have become anti-capitalist even more quickly than their European counterparts, since there was nothing to distract their attention from the middle classes. But because American intellectuals, along with the rest of the world, perceived American society as strongly egalitarian, they were late in perceiving the American businessman as a threat to equality.

Another reason for the relatively late development of anti-capitalist sentiment in the United States was America's "peculiar institution," slavery. Slavery was the great exception to the egalitarian pattern of American life. Slavery was perceived by intellectuals as a non or anti-capitalist institution, while capitalism was seen as slavery's opponent and (by Northern intellectuals) the slaves' liberator. What early anti-capitalist sentiment there was in America was largely the work of Southern writers, most notably John Calhoun, who proclaimed the factory-owner morally worse than the slave-owner. But Northern intellectual dominance, and Northern victory in the Civil War, retarded the development of anti-capitalist attitudes among mainstream American intellectuals. They did not become prevalent until well after the Civil War, or even World War I. With respect to the war between mind and money, America therefore lagged behind Europe.[43]

The conflict between mind and money depended not only on social changes, but on intellectual changes in nineteenth-century society. Just as many social developments must be taken into account, intellectual causes also contributed to the end of the honeymoon between mind and money. One was the continued intellectual pressure exercised by the First and Second Don'ts. It had been partly overcome during the honeymoon period, but it exerted renewed influence afterwards, in the new social circumstances in which intellectuals found themselves. Alongside the return of old attitudes, the new democratic Don't (Don't Have or Make More Money Than Others—It's Not Fair), took on a strongly anti-capitalist meaning. The new understanding of capitalism as antagonistic to equality was so strong that it soon became unimaginable that it had once meant greater equality. Based on all three Don'ts, there came about a new moral evaluation of both the individual capitalist and of capitalism as a whole.

Capitalism's mores, values, and new technology were all subject to condemnation. The merits of technology in particular were reconsidered by many intellectuals. Although intellectuals with reservations about capitalism did not necessarily have reservations about technology as such, and some continued to praise it, new and unprecedented attacks on technology were made. The Romantics were to a certain extent continuing an older tradition of preferring the countryside over the town, but there was a new edge to their criticism of the ugly mill. As the century progressed, new kinds of criticism arose of technology and its economic consequences. This was sharply different from the eighteenth-century attitude. Consider the following extract from the article "Industry" in the *Encyclopédie* (1751-1772):

> Let no one object any more against the utility of industrial inventions, that any machine which diminishes the need for labor by half, at that very moment takes their livings away from half the workers in the industry; that the unemployed workers will become beggars at the expense of the government, rather than learning another job, that consumption has limits.... It is characteristic of such objections to be devoid of good sense and education.[44]

A century later, "such objections" would be far more common than they had been in the eighteenth century, and they would be made by intellectuals.

Finally, together with the social and intellectual reasons for the honeymoon period's end, the reaction to one particular historical event must be singled out as a unique circumstance that helped determine *when* many intellectuals turned against commercial society: the French Revolution. The revolutionary Terror of 1793-94 revolted most intellectuals. The Terrorists had used a highly moralistic, anti-commercial language. By doing so, they discredited that language in the eyes of all but a few extremists. Quite possibly the anti-commercial rhetoric of the Jacobins prolonged the honeymoon period between mind and money by several decades. As time passed, however, the evaluation of 1793 (the year the Terror began) changed. Instead of appearing as an attempt, doomed to bloody failure, to turn back the clock and restore ancient liberty on the ruins of modern freedom, 1793 became the bold forerunner of a distinctly modern kind of freedom: equality defined in economic terms. Instead of being the last Roman, Babeuf, the leader of a radical sect guillotined in 1797, became the first socialist, an early martyr and saint in Marxist hagiography.

This re-evaluation of 1793 was promoted by the recognition that the era of revolutions had not come to a close in 1815, and that capitalism, far from inaugurating an era of peaceful stability, had brought with it ever more rapid and, at least potentially, ever more violent change. Nineteenth-century intellectuals, left and right, anti-capitalist and even pro-capitalist, recognized that they were living in an "era of transition" as John Stuart Mill, among many others, put it. The Revolution had taught intellectuals, and everyone else, that everything could be changed, that even the most ancient and apparently stable institution could be overthrown. If you could get rid of the king, why not private property? The possibilities of social engineering seemed vastly greater. Intellectuals' confidence in their ability to guide social reconstruction rationally suffered a blow during the French Revolution, but intellectuals gradually recovered from the Terror, even to the point of defending it. Eventually they would feel capable of the Russian Revolution.

The feeling of living in an era of transition has never left intellectuals, and it works in their favor. As practitioners of critical discourse, it is the environment in which their discourse can have the most impact, an environment in which everything is open to question, and no authority is safe. The circumstance of living in a revolutionary period, in an era of transition, contributed much to cutting the bonds that had linked mind and money.

There were thus many factors, social, intellectual, and historical, which contributed to the end of the honeymoon between mind and money. Some of them, like the first two Don'ts or the rise of the middle classes, were extremely long-term influences. They are examples of what the great French historian Fernand Braudel called the *longue durée,* long-lasting patterns that have a persistent influence on events over long periods of time. Braudel had things like climate and geography in mind when he spoke of the *longue durée*, but the hostility of intellectuals to capitalism is an example of the *longue durée* in intellectual history. The honeymoon between mind and money was a brief interruption in these long-term patterns. Like most disturbances in long-term weather patterns or well-established ecologies, eventually relations between mind and money returned to an equilibrium only modestly altered from its starting-point. In this case, the alteration turned out to be a greater hostility than ever before.

But the story told in this chapter is in some respects a Hegelian, not a Braudelian story. Hegel liked to talk about "the cunning of Reason," the way in which history moves in unexpected ways to reach its goal.

It is a truly Hegelian irony that the intellectual, social and historical circumstances that encouraged the honeymoon, *and* those that ended it, are all, in many respects, products of capitalism itself. As Hegel might have put it, the "thesis" of capitalism called into being the "antithesis" of intellectual hostility to it (the fact that intellectuals *contributed* to the rise of capitalism in the eighteenth century is just another of Reason's cunning little tricks). Just as Hegel's theory of history would have it, the rise and spread of capitalism created the widest possible battlefield for the struggle of thesis and antithesis, mind and money. The war between mind and money has embraced most of the fields of human activity, and it has spread, with the expansion of Western civilization and the continually improving technology capitalism encourages, to every corner of the globe. When it comes to the relationship between mind and money, it turns out in the end that capitalism brings not peace, but a sword.

Neither Braudel nor Hegel could have predicted this on the basis of some perennial conflict between mind and money within Western civilization, some traceable development of Reason. The war between mind and money could only take on its enormous and global dimensions in the new social, intellectual and historical constellation described above. Only Tocqueville's democratic society could set the stage for a theater of war that would extend to every corner of the planet once the alliance of property and education collapsed.

Part II of *Mind vs. Money* is devoted to describing this conflict, beginning with how nineteenth-century intellectuals attacked capitalism. What is common to almost all their assaults is an emphasis on its moral failings. Both capital*ism* and capital*ists* are attacked, and neither the character nor the lifestyle of the businessman escapes intellectuals' censure. Much of nineteenth-century literature can be read as one long sermon against capitalism. Like most sermons, it did not persuade its largely middle-class audience to give up its sins. But it was very effective in spreading the word that they were sinners.

Notes

1.   The period roughly 1680-1830 will be referred to as the "eighteenth century."

2.   Hume, "Of Commerce," in *Essays Moral, Political, and Literary* ed. Eugene F. Miller (Indianapolis: Liberty Fund, 1985), 259; "Of Refinement in the Arts," *Essays*, 275-76. See also Montesquieu, *Considerations on the Causes of the Greatness of the Romans and their Decline*.

3.   Turgot, "Reflections on the Formation and the Distribution of Wealth," in Henry C. Clark, *Commerce, Culture, & Liberty: Readings on Capitalism Before Adam Smith* (Indianapolis: Liberty Fund, 2003), 548-49; Voltaire, "Luxury" in *Philosophical Dictionary*, ed. and trans. Theodore Besterman, (New York: Penguin,

1972), 291; Montesquieu, *Spirit of the Laws*, trans. Anne Cohler, Basia Miller, and Harold Stone (Cambridge: Cambridge University Press, 1989), 387-88; William Robertson, "A View of the Progress of Society in Europe" in Clark, *Commerce, Culture, & Liberty*, 513.

4.   The duration of the honeymoon period is subject to scholarly dispute and varied nationally. See James Raven, *Judging New Wealth: Popular Publishing and Responses to Commerce in England, 1750-1800* (Oxford: Clarendon, 1992), 3-4, 9, 11-12, 244, 261; John Sekora, *Luxury: The Concept in Western Thought, Eden to Smollet* (Baltimore: Johns Hopkins University Press, 1977) 66, 111; M. R. de Labriolle-Rutherford, "L'évolution de la notion du luxe depuis Mandeville jusqu'à la Révolution," in *Studies on Voltaire*, v. 26, 1963; Henry C. Clark, "Commerce, Sociability, and the Public Sphere: Morellet vs. Pluquet on Luxury," *Eighteenth Century Life*, v. 22, 1998, 89.

5.   "Justify," *Funk & Wagnalls Standard Collegiate Dictionary* (New York: Funk & Wagnalls, 1977).

6.   Berry, *The Idea of Luxury*, 138. However, Clark's criticism of Berry's view that the defense of luxury came *chiefly* through "de-moralization" is justified. Clark, "Commerce, Sociability and the Public Sphere," *Eighteenth Century Life*, 98n.3.

7.   Smith, *Wealth of Nations, The Essential Adam Smith*, 265. For this point among eighteenth-century intellectuals in general, see Labriolle-Rutherford, "L'évolution de la notion du luxe," 1032.

8.   Montesquieu, *The Spirit of the Laws*, 312; Smith, *Theory of Moral Sentiments, The Essential Adam Smith*, 122.

9.   Jean-François Melon, "A Political Essay Upon Commerce," in Clark, *Commerce, Culture, & Liberty*, 259; David Hume, "Of Commerce," *Essays*, 261.

10.   Andreas Kalyvas and Ira Katznelson, *Liberal Beginnings: Making a Republic for the Moderns*, (Cambridge: Cambridge University Press, 2008), p. 41n.91, and pp. 24-46. See also Albert O. Hirschman, *The Passions and the Interests: Political Arguments for Capitalism before Its Triumph* (Princeton: Princeton University Press, 1977), 132.

11.   Montesquieu, *The Spirit of the Laws*, 338.

12.   Montesquieu, *The Spirit of the Laws*, 48; Hume, "Of Refinement in the Arts:, *Essays*, 271-72; Melon, "A Political Essay upon Commerce," in Clarke, *Commerce, Culture, & Liberty,* 257; Smith, *Wealth of Nations, The Essential Adam Smith*, 87.

13.   Berry, *The Idea of Luxury*, 154-55; Defoe, "Complete English Tradesman," in Clark, *Commerce, Culture, & Liberty*, 244; William Hazeland "A View of the Manner in Which Trade and Civil Liberty Support Each Other," in Clark, *Commerce, Culture, & Liberty*, 409.

14.   Constant, *Journal*, 17 February, 1805, in Constant, *Ecrits politiques*, ed. Marcel Gauchet (Paris: Gallimard, 1997), 657n.1; Smith, *Wealth of Nations, The Essential Adam Smith*, 253.

15.   Hume, "Of Civil Liberty," in *Essays*, 92-93; "Of Refinement in the Arts," *Essays*, 277.

16.   Hazeland, "Trade and Civil Liberty," *Commerce, Culture, & Liberty*, 406-07.

17.   Dugald Stewart, cited in Hirschman, *Passions*, 83-85; Montesquieu, *The Spirit of the Laws*, 416; Constant, "The Spirit of Conquest and Usurpation," in Constant, *Political Writings*, ed. and trans. Biancamaria Fontana (Cambridge, Cambridge University Press, 1988), 140.

18.   Montesquieu, *The Spirit of the Laws*, 338; Constant, "The Spirit of Conquest," *Political Writings*, 141; "The Liberty of the Ancients Compared with that of the Moderns," 313. See also Hirschman, *The Passions and the Interests*, 79-80. As

Hirschman notes, in the same chapter Montesquieu says that commerce has the opposite effect on individuals, destroying natural solidarity and leading them to sell things they once would have given away. Some writers like commerce for its social benefits, some for its individual benefits, others for both. Some struggle with ambivalence.

19. Clark, "Commerce, Sociability and the Public Sphere," *Eighteenth Century Life*, 93.

20. Sekora, *Luxury,* 65, 78, 97.

21. Fielding, cited in Sekora, *Luxury*, 91.

22. Or almost everyone. Those who were not "frugal and industrious" might not benefit. Intellectuals are inveterate moralists.

23. Smith, *Wealth of Nations, The Essential Adam Smith*, 159, 166, 203; Nicholas Phillipson, "Adam Smith as Civic Moralist," in *Wealth and Virtue: The Shaping of Political Economy in the Scottish Enlightenment*, ed. Hont and Ignatieff (Cambridge: Cambridge University Press, 1986), 189-90; Hume, "Of Commerce," *Essays*, 262; Montesquieu, *The Spirit of the Laws*, 53.

24. The relationship between nascent, pro-capitalist "liberalism" and republicanism has been the subject of enormous debate, most recently in Kalyvas and Katznelson, *Liberal Beginnings: Making a Republic for the Moderns* (New York: Cambridge University Press, 2008).

25. Hazeland, "Trade and Civil Liberty," *Commerce, Culture, & Liberty*, 406; Hume, "Of Commerce," *Essays*, 255, 261-62; Hume, cited in John Robertson, "The Scottish Enlightenment at the Limits of the Civic Tradition," *Wealth and Virtue*, 152.

26. Smith, *Wealth of Nations, The Essential Adam Smith*, 220; Hazeland, "Trade and Civil Liberty," *Commerce, Culture, & Liberty*, 407-08. See Constant, "De la division des propriétés foncières," in *De la liberté chez les modernes*, 599-601.

27. On Hume, see Robertson, "The Scottish Enlightenment" *Wealth and Virtue*, 158; Morellet, cited in Clark, "Commerce, Sociability and the Public Sphere," *Eighteenth Century Life*, 97.

28. Smith, *Wealth of Nations, The Essential Adam* Smith, 302; Montesquieu, *The Spirit of the Laws*, 312, 338-39.

29. Hume, "Of Refinement in the Arts," *Essays*, 270; Daniel Defoe, "The Complete English Tradesman," *Commerce, Culture & Liberty,* 246; Melon, "A Political Essay upon Commerce," *Commerce, Culture & Liberty,* 258.

30. Constant, *Ecrits politiques*, 550.

31. Hirschman, *The Passions and the Interests*, 130. He describes their method as the taming of passion by interest, or the taming of the other passions by the passion for money, what is here called the "amoral" justification of commercial society. But he fails to take into sufficient account what he acknowledges to be the continued use of moral vocabulary by the defenders of commerce, and he is oblivious to their desire for greater equality. See *Passions*, 43-44, 100, 105-06, 110.

32. Smith, *Wealth of Nations, The Essential Adam Smith*, 310.

33. Smith, *Wealth of Nations, The Essential Adam Smith*, 256.

34. Coleman, *Myth, History and the Industrial Revolution*, (London: Hambledon, 1992), 38-39. The question is how big is big, and the econometrics can furnish no guide to this. See Deirdre N. McCloskey, *The Vices of Economists—The Virtues of the Bourgeoisie* (Amsterdam: Amsterdam University Press, 1996). Defoe, "The Complete English Tradesman," *Commerce, Culture, and Luxury*, 249.

35. Raven, *Judging New Wealth*, 259; Paulson, Cited in Ulrich Engelhardt, *Bildungsbürgertum: Begriffs- und Dogmengeschichte eines Etiketts* (Munich: Klett-Cotta, 1986), 174.

36.   These statistics do not include those teaching in engineering schools, or in Germany the *Privatdozenten,* university lecturers who would add 1-3,000 to the numbers.

37.   Charle, *Les intellectuels en Europe,* 146-47, 151, 155. Pascal Ory and Jean-François Sirinelli, *Les intellectuels en France de l'Affaire Dreyfus à nos jours* (Colin: Paris, 1992), 45.

38.   Charle, *Les intellectuels,* 146.

39.   For the history of the word in France, see Ory and Sirinelli, *Les intellectuels en France,* 5-7.

40.   People often make up words and rules as a game goes on, sometimes not until they've finished playing the game a few times. The creation of new language is an important act with important consequences, but often it is the last act of a series begun long before.

41.   See Collini, *Public Moralists* 231; *Absent Minds,* 75; *The Nation,* "Bohemianism in French Politics," in *On Bohemia: The Code of the Self-Exiled* (New Brunswick, NJ: Transaction, 1990), 241-67; E. Caro, *Revue des Deux Mondes,* July 15, 1871, cited in Seigel, *Bohemian Paris,* 182.

42.   Meinecke, Cited in Hans-Ulrich Wehler, *Deutsche Gesellschaftsgeschichte. Dritter Band. Von der "Deutschen Doppelrevolution" bis zum Beginn des Ersten Weltkrieges, 1849-1918* (Munich: Klett-Cotta, 1989), 745; Richard Hofstadter, *Anti-Intellectualism in American Life* (New York: Alfred A Knopf, 1969), 247-60. Hofstadter emphasizes money's dislike for mind.

43.   Hofstadter, *Anti-Intellectualism,* 234, 406; Hofstadter suggests 1890 as the turning point. See also Daniel Aaron, *Writers on the Left: Episodes in American Literary Communism* (New York: Harcourt, Brace and World, 1961), 199, and Arthur A. Ekirch Jr., *Ideologies and Utopias: The Impact of the New Deal on American Thought* (Chicago: Quadrangle Books, 1969), 128.

44.   "Industrie," *Encyclopédie,* ed. Alain Pons (Paris: J'ai Lu, 1963), 373.

Part II

Intellectuals and Their Discontents: The Nineteenth Century (1850-1914)

4

How Capitalism Lost the Struggle
Over Character

A Fairy Tale

Once upon a time, in a far-away land, there lived many merchants. These merchants, purely out of self-interest, devoted their lives to satisfying the needs of their fellow men. They spent untold hours, and almost unimaginable ingenuity and inventiveness, manufacturing and transporting that which best pleased their fellows, and would fetch the highest price. They soon learned that honesty was the best policy, and that peace and virtue were far more profitable than war and vice. Their example helped to spread this good news.

But then, one dark and stormy night, there came a sudden change in the weather. When merchant Smith woke up early, as was his habit, and opened the door to head off to his business, he saw by the gleam of the lamplight that the brass nameplate on his front door no longer read "A. Smith, merchant to the nations and benefactor of humanity." For reasons he could not comprehend, it now proclaimed that this was the dwelling of "Mr. Scrooge." Underneath the nameplate, scrawled in red paint on his door, were the words: "workers of the world unite, you have nothing to lose but your chains!" Mr. Smith shook his head and went off to work. He was not sure exactly what had happened, and he had no idea why, but he knew that somehow things would never be the same again.

He was right. By the time men like Dickens and Marx had gotten through with him, "bourgeois capitalist" would have turned from a compliment into an epithet. Even defenders of capitalism would be forced to apologize for its regrettable immorality before extolling its productivity. This transformation was accomplished by several generations of anti-capitalist intellectuals over the course of the nineteenth century. They

99

were of many kinds, from the novelists, poets and critics discussed in this chapter, to the academic theorists discussed in chapter five. Being intellectuals, they disagreed with each other about many things, but they knew capitalism was bad, and that the people who made it work were bad people. They knew this because they knew that commercial society and its denizens did not have good intentions. Or even if they did, it would not help.

Thus capitalism lost its good name. For many intellectuals it became a dirty word. Even among those who were largely apolitical, or thought they were, it left an unpleasant taste in the mouth. In good company people learned to avoid using it.

Literature played an enormous role in this process. Novelists did even more than professors to make "capitalist" a dirty word. Through novels, essays, and poems, writers turned the paragons of commercial virtue into the pillars of capitalist vice. They were so successful in this enterprise that today the idea that capitalism and commerce ever had a good literary reputation may seem incredible. For many of our contemporaries "virtuous capitalist" is an oxymoron, or at least a dubious and counter-intuitive proposition. How many of the movies, TV shows and novels of the twenty-first century have an entrepreneur for a hero? Or the CEO of a large corporation? This was not always so. The fact that modern-day fictions often register strong anti-capitalist bias is a result of the war mind has waged against money.

Because the evil banker, the hard-hearted factory-owner, and the soulless corporation are so familiar to us, it is worth beginning our account of how capitalism lost the struggle over character by looking first at something once commonplace: a morally positive image of the capitalist, as portrayed by Horatio Alger, Jr. Alongside it we will put its now-commonplace mirror-image—the criticism of this picture by William Dean Howells. Alger and Howells were contemporaries who lived in a state of complete mutual incomprehension. It was a situation that would become increasingly representative of the relations between mind and money. A case in point is their contrasting evaluation of a classic figure of capitalism, the "self-made man."

The Self-Made Man

On the surface, the ideal of the self-made man would seem to be one both intellectuals and businessmen could accept. His achievements embody the independence and autonomy that intellectuals value so strongly. Intellectuals are themselves self-made. No one is born an intellectual, and intellectuals must acquire their own education and write their own books. They succeed or fail in what is sometimes called "the marketplace of ideas." Are intellectuals not also entrepreneurs of a sort, especially those who make their livings outside academic and government institutions? This is how Jules Vallès saw the issue:

> Messieurs! There is a misunderstanding between us! In every man who takes up a pen, a palette, a chisel, a pencil, whatever, the bourgeois sees a useless person; in every bourgeois, the man of letters sees an enemy. Sad prejudice, foolish opinion, unhappy antagonism. Our cause is the same, the valiant cause of the parvenus![1]

Because points of contact between intellectuals and entrepreneurs do exist, a positive image of the self-made man persists in Western literature despite equally persistent attempts to blacken it, and the self-made man has found more literary defenders than capitalism in general.

Nevertheless, the ideal of the self-made man came under attack in the nineteenth century. Indeed, for some anti-capitalist intellectuals, the self-made man was especially nasty, without the redeeming cultural qualities of those born to wealth. He had to overcome the traits that enabled him to make his fortune in order to redeem himself morally. In the negative view of the self-made man, character and commerce contradict, rather than complement, each other.

These opposing views of the self-made man can be found in Alger and Howells. Let us begin with the positive case: "To be born to wealth removes all the incentives to action, and checks the spirit of enterprise. A boy or man who finds himself gradually rising in the world, through his own exertions, experiences a satisfaction unknown to one whose fortune is ready-made." So writes Alger in his novel *Store Boy*, one of the many rags-to-riches, or more accurately rags-to-moderate-wealth stories that made Alger's name synonymous with American optimism.[2]

There is no more fervent defender of the ideal of the self-made man than Horatio Alger. His characters make their way in the world displaying their virtues and teaching them to others: Ambition is a virtue for Alger, and lack of ambition a character flaw. The virtuous hero teaches others to be as ambitious as himself. "A wonderful change came over Mike Flynn. Until he met Rodney he seemed quite destitute of ambition.... as long as he made enough to buy three meals a day,... he was satisfied." Another character notes: "It did me good to leave town. I didn't drink, but I had no ambition."[3]

There are many kinds of ambition. But in Alger the chief ambition is not for love or glory, it is for wealth. In the hands of many a nineteenth-century novelist, putting money above love would be one of capitalism's sins. Not for Alger. One character explains to another why he won't get married and move back East:

> "Yes; I ain't in a hurry to travel in double harness. I'll wait till I am ready to leave Montana, with enough money to live handsomely at home."
>
> "You have got enough now."
>
> "But I may as well get more. I am only thirty years old, and I can afford to work a few years longer."
>
> "I wish I could be sure of being worth fifty thousand dollars when I am your age."
>
> "You have been worth that, you tell me."
>
> "Yes, but I should value more money that I had made myself."[4]

A human being's worth is measured in dollars, by himself and others, provided they are dollars he has earned himself. Love can wait until money has been made. Ambition is good. Money, self-earned, is good. And they lead naturally to virtue:

> "You know how to feather your own nest."
>
> "In a good sense, I hope I do. I don't suppose anyone else will take the trouble to feather it for me. I think honesty and fidelity are good policy, don't you?"[5]

Just as in Adam Smith or Montesquieu, but without their occasional doubts and reservations, commerce and morality are natural friends in Alger's work: "Money is said, by certain moralists, to be the root of all evil. The love of money, if carried too far, may indeed lead to evil, but it is a natural ambition in any boy or man to wish to raise himself above poverty. The wealth of Amos Lawrence and Peter Cooper was a source of blessing to mankind, yet each started as a poor boy, and neither would have become rich if he had not striven hard to become so."[6]

Alger has no reservations about the self-made businessman. By contrast, he is ambivalent about the value of formal education. Nineteenth-century defenders of capitalism occasionally recognize that classical education is the province of their enemies. One of Alger's heroes had learned some Greek and Latin before his family's loss of fortune compelled him to leave school. Of that boy Alger writes that "the discipline which he had received as a student stood him in good stead, and enabled him to make a more rapid advancement than some who had been longer in the employ of the firm." On the other hand, a character in the same story comments, on learning that the hero knows some Greek, "That's what prejudiced me against you. I hired a college boy once as a clerk and he was the worst failure I ever came across. He seemed to have all kinds of sense except common sense."[7]

The growing mutual incomprehension between intellectuals and businessmen is frequently displayed in nineteenth-century literature.

William Dean Howells takes the negative view of the self-made man in *The Rise of Silas Lapham.* Alger's novels begin with a hero in rags, or else about to lose his inherited wealth. Howells begins his story well after Silas Lapham has become a rich man. Once you know this, the title is a giveaway. For in the course of the novel Lapham *loses* his self-made fortune. His financial ruin is accompanied by his moral rise, and indeed his newfound moral sensitivity forces him to refrain from making a shady business deal that would restore his fortunes.

At the beginning of the book Lapham has allowed the desire for making money, whether in the stock market or in his paint business, to become his only desire. "Seems as if the more money he got, the more he wanted to get. It scares me to think what would happen to him if he lost it" says his wife. However, in a manner typical of much anti-commercial writing since Aristotle, Howells distinguishes between the paint business, which is not described as immoral in itself, and the stock market, which is. "Oh, I've made a very good thing in stocks lately," says Lapham. "In stocks? When did you take up gambling for a living?," replies his wife, who plays the Victorian role of guardian of the family's morals. The further one gets from the direct satisfaction of human needs (paint), the closer one gets to the pure manipulation of money (stocks), the more the classical and Christian Don'ts find capitalism objectionable.[8]

A turning point in the novel, which is set in 1882, comes in a discussion at a gentlemen's club. Many of the men there, including Lapham, are veterans of the American Civil War. At the club, to which Lapham has been invited for the first time because his daughter is about to marry into a patrician family, Lapham is forced to remain silent out of fear of making a fool of himself in culturally refined company. He is thus a silent witness to the crucial conversation. After dinner a younger man is asked whether he thought most of his friends would be willing to sacrifice their lives in combat for their country:

> "[W]hat has become of all the heroism? Tom, how many club men do you know who would think it sweet and fitting to die for their country?"
> "I can't think of a great many at the moment, sir."
> "And I couldn't in '61," said his uncle. "Nevertheless they were there."
> "Then you think it is the occasion that is wanting...."[9]

The point is that the modern world of business lacks occasion for heroism. The rest of the novel refutes this claim, by allowing ex-Colonel Lapham to display moral heroism by losing his money. He refuses to profit from the ignorance of some visiting Englishmen who want to buy his business, not knowing that he is about to be ruined by a new competitor.

It would have been possible for Howells to make this into a celebration of commercial morality and the steadfast virtue of the self-made man. The hero displays real heroism in the course of doing business. But Lapham is heroic precisely because he has changed, and is no longer what he was when he was making his fortune. His early business career did not involve lawbreaking, but was conducted on other moral principles—he owed much of his fortune to squeezing out a partner who was short of capital. The businessmen around him are always suggesting shady deals to him—his former partner comes back to urge Lapham to help him cheat the Englishmen. It is only his family and his newfound conscience that encourage him to act otherwise. If he is a businessman-hero, the shining light of his actions only serves to make the businessmen around him seem even blacker.

Silas Lapham is as close as Howells ever got to saying nice things about a businessman. He later wrote a Utopian novel, *A Traveler from Altruria*, in which the clash between mind and money is stated directly. In *Altruria* Howells confirms Alger's suspicion of a contradiction between formal education and business acumen: "'So you admit, then,' said the professor, 'that the higher education elevates a business man's standard of morals?' 'Undoubtedly. That is one of its chief drawbacks,' said the banker, with a laugh." In *Altruria* education is the chief rival of commerce, and the means of overcoming its injustices. After a discussion about how giving businessmen a liberal arts education might change business mores, a character says that "it is education, after all, that is to bridge the chasm between the classes and the masses, though it seems destined to go a long way round about it. There was a time, I believe, when we expected religion to do that." A nice example of the sermon being preached by the new secular clergy.[10]

The contrast between Alger and Howells testifies to the mutual estrangement between capitalism and intellectuals that followed the divorce between mind and money. As is often the case in such circumstances, name-calling soon followed. Writers and artists charged businessmen with every sin under the sun. Greed led the list, of course, and in some form greed was part of every complaint about capitalism, whether by writers or by the academic social theorists discussed in the next chapter. But there were many other complaints. Rather than compiling a complete catalogue of the sins of the bourgeoisie as seen in nineteenth-century literature, we will examine only a few of the most typical, and most telling, charges. Hypocrisy, family-wrecking, and just plain stupidity made middle-class greed all the more loathsome to contemplate.

The Hypocrite

One of the charges the Protestant Critique makes against capitalism and its lack of good intentions is that commerce is based on hypocrisy. The "honest" baker obeys not moral duty but self-interest when he gives the blind man correct change. He calls himself an honest man, but what really motivates him is greed. He is a hypocrite. Hypocrisy is one of the most common charges intellectuals make against commercial society and the middle classes in particular. The description of capitalism as a compound of hypocrisy and greed has become a literary commonplace. Perhaps the greatest critic of hypocrisy was the best-selling French novelist Emile Zola. Though Catholic by birth and atheist by conviction, Zola embodied the Protestant Critique of capitalism.

In Zola's novels the middle classes are hypocritical about money, about sex, and finally about just about everything. In *Pot-Bouille,* the hypocrisy mixes sex and money, and it is no surprise that the result smells like a pig-sty. In one instance the bourgeois inhabitants of an apartment building force a worker to be thrown out of his cheap ground-floor apartment because he is living with a woman he is not married to. This is prostitution, in their eyes, and affronts them. Meanwhile, courtship and marriage among the middle class, as taught by mothers to daughters, is "a whole course in decent and accepted prostitution," "the immodesties of innocents speculating on the sexual appetites of fools." One bourgeois matron counsels her daughter that "only money matters today" when considering a husband. And a cuckolded middle-class husband, trying to understand the cause of his misfortune, says of his adulterous wife, "again, if she had done it for money, I would understand,… but she was not paid, I'm certain of it." Thus Zola describes the bourgeois of *Pot-Bouille* as *"cochon et compagnie,"* (pigs one and all). In only one thing are these bourgeois pigs sincere: "the respect, the furious appetite for money, that whole religion of money…." The religion of money is the one unpardonable idolatry for the new intellectual clergy. One can worship the nation, the people, trees, or pop stars and receive a sympathetic hearing from the intellectual. But not money.[11]

It would be misleading to leave the impression that this is all Zola has to say about capitalism. In some of his other novels he considers another perspective, that these pigs, although pigs, might be doing the world a service. The hypocrite might actually be doing some good after all. This seems like a "honeymoon" vision, something like the baker giving the right change for the wrong reasons, but on closer examination it proves to have very different connotations.

Zola's novel *Money* is a fictionalized account of a real bank crash in late nineteenth-century France. More than that, it is a novel about stock-market speculation, with bank stock playing the role that dot-com stocks did in the U.S. stock market of the 1990s. The "hero," Saccard, is a fraud. Saccard says, "with reason," that work won't earn you a living, it just fattens those you work for. Only gambling, i.e., speculating on the stock market, can give "material well-being, luxury, a wide life, life as a whole" at one stroke. The stock market can be manipulated by whipping up the emotional passions of the crowd, "the eternal crowd to be exploited, the stockholders of tomorrow, who couldn't walk in front of that shop-window of speculation without turning their heads, desiring and fearing what was going on in there." So Saccard hypo-critically sets up a bank that is the epitome of honesty and Christian virtue, unlike the nasty Jewish bankers down the street, the Rothschilds. Their love for stock-market speculation, their faith in Saccard, even occasionally their Catholic solidarity or anti-Semitism, make people invest in his bank stock, while he manipulates the price ever higher. Needless to say it ends up in bankruptcy for one and all, while Saccard skips across the frontier.[12]

But bankruptcy is not the only result. As Saccard points out, speculation is a necessary part of business. Without the hope of great gain, no one would risk their money. Speculation builds all kinds of useful things (in the 1990s, fiber-optic networks). Excess is necessary to investment, Saccard says, on the analogy that one may need to have sex a hundred times to make a single baby. With ordinary profits or work, not much happens, but speculation leads to ten times the energy, etc., and makes things happen that otherwise would never come to pass. The money Saccard's bank gathers is invested in many projects, not all of which build castles in the air. The bank amalgamates several steamship companies, and the new firm builds bigger and faster ships than ever before, and provides more efficient service. The bank creates a silver mine which in the long run turns out to be a failure, but first causes new roads to be built and attracts new populations, so that alongside the silver mine grow fields of wheat and villages where there was nothing before. And they remain, after the crash.[13]

Looking at this, Mme. Caroline, who is called upon to pronounce moral judgment in the novel, veers from one side to another. Seeing Saccard's immoralities, his hypocrisy, his frauds, his cheats, she realizes that Saccard has betrayed everyone and would do it again. Why? For money's sake:

Oh! Money, that rotting, poisoning money, that dried up souls, driving out generosity, tenderness, the love of others! Money alone was the great villain, the middleman of all the cruelties and all the baseness of humanity…. If she had had the power, she would have annihilated all the money in the world at one stroke, as one would crush evil under a heel, in order to preserve the world's health.[14]

This is partly a traditional moralist's rejection of greed. But it is a greed intimately associated with commerce itself. Zola condemns not just Saccard, but the economic system that makes Saccard possible, even necessary.

But then Mme. Caroline takes it all back. She thinks of the new villages, the new wheat fields, the new steamships, and she decides that money is the "dung-hill on which grows the humanity of tomorrow." "Above all the mud stirred up, above all the victims crushed to death, above all the abominable suffering which each forward step costs humanity, is there not an obscure, far-off goal, something superior, good, just and final, whither we are going without knowing it…?" Thus Zola returns to Smith's notion of Divine Providence acting as an Invisible Hand. If money is a curse, it is also a blessing, "all good came from it, from it which did all evil." This seems to be Zola's final judgment. The last words of the novel compare money with love: "Why therefore blame money for all the filth and crimes it causes? Is love, which creates life, any less soiled?"[15]

Zola is ambivalent about money in *Money*. He musters moral indictments only to wonder if money, commerce, and even stock-market speculation do not justify themselves in the end. His picture of capitalism is more balanced than that of most critics. But while money may be justified in the end, throughout most of the book it is damned. Pictures of hell are always far more realistic and convincing than pictures of paradise. The image of far-away wheat fields and villages cannot compete with the image of the great stock market crash and the grieving widows and orphans who have lost their life's savings. This was certainly the effect the book had on André Wurmser, a literary critic who wrote that in *Money* "it is the bourgeois who is dirty…." Zola's justifications of capitalism are less emotionally convincing than his denunciations. The immorality of commerce is portrayed far more strikingly than its benefits, regardless of Zola's intentions.[16]

Is it Zola, the intellectual, who ends up the hypocrite? One bourgeois response to literary criticism is indeed that it is the intellectual, not the bourgeois, who is the real hypocrite. The bourgeois admits he lives to make money and have nice things, while intellectuals hypocritically conceal their own desire for wealth, or at least for the respect that money brings. The charge is old. In 1665 La Rochefoucauld wrote that "the contempt for riches among the philosophers was a hidden desire to revenge themselves on the injustice of Fortune, by contempt of the very advantages of which she deprived them... It was a by-road to arrive at that consideration which they could not obtain by riches." A bad conscience on this subject indeed troubled many intellectuals. Whether the intellectual is guilty of hypocrisy is debatable. What matters is that the charge of hypocrisy has stuck far harder to the businessman.[17]

Family Values

Can a hypocrite love? Who can tell? After accusing the businessman of hypocrisy, it was a short step to attacking his family life. In positive portrayals of capitalism, now mostly forgotten, the businessman was the family man. Unlike the cold and unloving aristocratic castle, too big and drafty for intimacy, the warm and cozy middle-class hearth surrounded the businessman with love. But among the charges brought against capitalism by its opponents was that its greed wrecked the family. In the *Communist Manifesto* Marx charged that "the bourgeoisie has torn away from the family its sentimental veil, and has reduced the family relation to a mere money relation." The charge brought by Marx is typical. Nineteenth-century novelists made it even more effectively. They lavished description on the ways in which hypocrisy and greed destroyed the middle-class family. Once money entered the picture, love fled. The family is the most "natural" of human relationships. Money, and the relationships money spawns, the most artificial. This contrast is as old as Aristotle (see chapter 2). Aristotle's unwitting heirs, the best-selling authors of the nineteenth century, repeatedly called it to their readers' attention. Almost all the novels mentioned in this chapter devote attention to the damage capitalism does to family relations. Ever since the nineteenth century, the moral contrast between the warm family and the cold business world has been a literary staple.[18]

In different ways and under very different circumstance, Charles Dickens and Thomas Mann show the destructive impact of capitalism on family life. Although Dickens' *Hard Times* has a happy ending and Mann's *Buddenbrooks* a sad one, it is hard to tell which has a more negative attitude towards capitalism. Let us begin with Dickens, whose depiction of the destructive effects of capitalism is easiest to trace, and more closely associated with commerce in its modern industrial form.

Hard Times is centered around the Gradgrind family and the city in which they live, Coketown. Coketown seems to be largely based on mid-nineteenth-century Manchester. Its waterways are black and stinking, or purple and stinking, the result of industrial pollution. Its architecture is a uniform "red brick, or of brick that would have been red if the smoke and ashes had allowed it." Its streets are identical except for their size, and their "people equally like one another, who all went in and out at the same hours, with the same sound upon the same pavements, to do the same work...." Everything in Coketown is oriented around work, around facts, around utility and production, at which it succeeds wonderfully well, making "comforts of life which found their way all over the world." But these hardly seem to justify it.[19]

The *Hard Times* of the title are not some exceptional economic depression. They are the ordinary times of modern life in a capitalist society. They are hard, indeed. The poor of Coketown are many, wretched, and often drunk. They do not go to church, to the drab churches reserved in practice for the middle classes, despite much hand wringing. It seems surprising that even the middle classes attend church regularly, for theirs is a life from which, as from that of the poor, all fantasy, imagination, and wonder have been wrung out. Nevertheless the industrialists, the leading characters Mr. Gradgrind and Mr. Bounderby, complain that the lending libraries of the town do more business in stories and novels and fables than in practical primers of mathematics and self-improvement.[20]

It is quite remarkable there is a library that poor people use at all, for the workers of Coketown have been largely dehumanized (at least this is true when Dickens speaks of them in general, his individual characters are as vibrant as any of Dickens' stick figures ever are). The following summarizes Dickens' view of their lot:

> In the hardest working part of Coketown; ... at the heart of the labyrinth of narrow court upon courts, and close streets upon streets, which had come into existence piecemeal, every piece in a violent hurry for some one man's purpose, and the whole an unnatural family, shouldering, and trampling, and pressing one another to death...among the multitude of Coketown, generically called 'the Hands',—a race who would have found more favor with some people, if Providence had seen fit to make them only hands, or, like the lower creatures of the seashore, only hands and stomachs....[21]

Modern urban industrial society is an "*unnatural* family," devoted to deadly competition. A family which would have pleased the factory-owners more if it had been composed of unnatural human beings, just hands and stomachs, a workforce of subhumans. How inhuman those factory-owners must be, to want such workers!

Most of *Hard Times* is not about the poor workers, however. Dickens wanted to avoid his work being seen as an "industrial novel" about factory-workers. He concentrates his attention on the effects of capitalism on those who were supposed to profit from it, the bankers and industrialists. There is Mr. Gradgrind, factory-owner. "A man of realities. A man of fact and calculations.... With a rule and a pair of scales, and the multiplication table always in his pocket, sir, ready to weigh and measure any parcel of human nature, and tell you exactly what it comes to." His home life, just like his factories, "went monotonously round like a piece of machinery which discouraged human interference." His children pay the price. They make their father pay as well. When Gradgrind's son proves a thief, Gradgrind is outraged. His son tells him that it is the law of averages that a certain proportion of people are thieves, and that he should not be surprised by the operation of a well-known statistical fact. His daughter makes a loveless marriage with Mr. Bounderby, a banker, and runs away from it to tell her father that "it has been my task from infancy to strive against every natural prompting that has arisen in my heart." In the capitalist family, she has been trained to calculate, not to feel. Only at the end of the novel does Mr. Gradgrind discover the value of emotion, and the barrenness of utilitarian calculation. When the former charity pupil at the school Gradgrind has sponsored comes to arrest Gradgrind's son, he pleads with him to let the son escape. Bitzer replies, "I am sure you know that the whole social system is a question of self interest. What you must always appeal to, is a person's self interest. It's your only hold. We are so constituted. I was brought up on that catechism when I was very young sir, as you are aware." And with this caricature of Jeremy Bentham, the Gradgrind philosophy is summarized: "Gratitude was to be abolished, and the virtues springing from it were not to be. Every inch of the existence of mankind, from birth to death, was to be a bargain across a counter. And if we didn't get to Heaven that way, it was not a politico-economic place, and we had no business there." Could anything be further from the *doux commerce* theory of the honeymoon period?[22]

The other leading middle-class character in *Hard Times* is Mr. Bounderby. He is "as near being Mr. Gradgrind's bosom friend, as a man perfectly devoid of sentiment can approach that spiritual relationship towards another man perfectly devoid of sentiment." He is rich, coarse, self-made, and proud of it. "This again, was one of the fictions of Coketown. Any capitalist there, who had made sixty thousand pounds out of sixpence, always professed to wonder why the sixty thousand nearest Hands didn't each make sixty thousand pounds out of sixpence, and more or less reproached every one for not accomplishing the little feat."

In Alger's novels, the self-made man is an example of equality in the making. For Dickens and much other nineteenth-century fiction, the self-made man is an example of the triumph of inequality, or immorality, or both. At the end of the novel, it is Mr. Gradgrind, whose fortune is not wholly self-made, who is redeemed by natural emotions and turns to works of faith, hope and charity, while Mr. Bounderby dies unrepentant and unloved.[23]

It is the role of the (secular) clergyman to point the way to salvation. It is possible for the most merciless businessman to be redeemed. Gradgrind is morally redeemed at the end of the novel when he puts his daughter's happiness ahead of her financial security. Although his son must flee overseas and ends up badly, Gradgrind succeeds in re-establishing a natural family relationship with his daughter. On balance Dickens is an optimist. He is a reformer, not a revolutionary—capitalism may yet be saved if it turns its heart away from the factory.

In more extreme criticism of capitalism for its effects on family values, there is no redemption. Thomas Mann is no revolutionary, and he has no blueprint for a new society. But *Buddenbrooks: The Decline of a Family* describes its archetypal capitalist family as rotten to the core. Mann's title must be understood to be at least partly ironic. While the book is a decline and fall story, this is true only with regard to money. Morally it is a Greek tragedy, in which flaws present from the beginning are steadily revealed, flaws inherent in capitalism.

The Buddenbrook family saga displays three generations of a wealthy merchant family in a North German port, beginning in the early nineteenth century. The first significant thing we learn about the family is that there is a rift between the family patriarch and his eldest son. The father has cut off all relations with him because he has "married a shop," married, for love, a woman of lesser social rank and wealth, a mere shop-owner. This son is to be partly disinherited, and the family firm given to the second son, Johann. When the elder son writes a letter to his father demanding his share of the inheritance, his half-brother's comment is, "As regards my personal concerns in the matter, I would have to say: Father, pay up. But I'm joint partner, too, who must represent the firm's interests, and if Papa doesn't think he has any obligation to withdraw moneys from our working capital for a disobedient and rebellious son...." The pattern for the novel is set. The firm's interests will conquer love and natural family relationships. In the end both family and firm will be destroyed.[24]

Money (unnatural) always wins out over family and love (natural) in this story. When Johann's eldest son Thomas begins work in his turn, after the elder Buddenbrook's death, he and his father Johann work hard "to recover the considerable losses that the old man's death had meant for the "firm"—the very word was cloaked in a certain divinity." Commerce as personified in the "firm" has become God, and the Buddenbrooks are its hard-working priests, from generation to generation. Johann is also a very fervent Protestant, but his son Thomas has no particular religious faith, except in money. Money is always at the heart of every judgment made. When his sister Toni complains about some unsavory newcomers to town, Thomas replies, "Yes, but, good lord, Strunck and Hagenstrom have built up a fine business; and that's the main thing.... The main thing is that he's making money." When the Buddenbrooks lament the faster pace of the late nineteenth-century business world, where the telegraph and railroad have replaced the horse-drawn carriage, they are no romantics in love with green trees and history: "Markets are easier and easier to open up, we get our price quotes faster and faster. The risks grow less and less—and so do the profits." It is the last clause that matters. The Buddenbrooks' only standard, socially, culturally, and in the end morally, is profit.[25]

Thus her father and her brother urge Toni to marry a man she does not love. Why? "If she would say yes, she could take her place in the world, set herself up quite nicely, which is what she really wants, and within a matter of days she would love her husband." They crush her budding love affair with a young student of poor family. The "respectable" businessman she is persuaded to marry turns out to be a fraud and eventually a bankrupt. He appeals to Johann to bail him out. Johann, feeling guilty for what he has forced his daughter to do, asks his daughter her wishes. He tells her he will pay, if she wants, but that it is a large sum, one that would seriously impact the "firm." The response from Toni is in the best family tradition: "Enough! Never!" "She looked almost heroic. The word "firm" had hit its mark. It was highly likely that is was a more decisive factor than her dislike of [her husband]." The firm comes first, and duty lies that way. Toni is divorced, and her ex-husband goes bankrupt.[26]

Thomas seems to break the family pattern by marrying for love, but appearances are deceiving: "I adore Gerda Arnoldsen, ardently adore her, but I am not in the least inclined to delve deeper into myself to determine whether and to what extent her large dowry—a sum someone cynically whispered into my ear on that first evening—contributed to my adoration. I love her, but it only makes me that much happier and prouder that at the same time I shall be gaining a significant source of capital for our firm." His love is sincere, but he can no longer tell where love ends and greed begins. He is a man deeply flawed by his devotion to commerce.[27]

The last marriage in the book is Toni's second marriage. Once again it is no love match, but something she feels she owes to the family/firm after the dishonor of her divorce. She marries a Bavarian, a man from south Germany whose speech and manners are very different from those of the North Sea Buddenbrooks. Herr Permaneder, in Toni's eyes, is too comfortable, lacks ambition. "He takes life too easy—which is, however, a fault in its own way, too. Because he'll certainly never be a millionaire...." Shades of Horatio Alger! She thinks that once married, "I'll make sure that he's more ambitious, puts out some effort and gets ahead, and is a credit to me and to all of us—that *is* his duty, after all, if he's going to marry a Buddenbrook." She is devastated when shortly after their marriage, he decides that with her dowry and his own savings, he has enough money to retire from business and live comfortably. Eventually there is a quarrel and she leaves Permaneder and returns home. It turns out that she could not bear Munich, and that what most offended her was the way she was treated as just an ordinary person. "Yes. Tom, we feel that we are aristocrats, and we're aware of that distance, and we should never try to live where people know nothing about us and don't understand our worth...." "I come from here, from this house. And that means something—it means people work hard and have goals."[28]

Toni and the other Buddenbrooks are part of a merchant aristocracy which Mann, representing the intellectual aristocracy/clergy, has judged and found wanting. In the end, even Thomas Buddenbrook begins to find his milieu morally deficient. He suffers some serious business reverses, and discovers to his surprise that his fellow-merchants' attitude is not what he would wish, that business is "cruel and brutal." He even comes to wonder whether a trader like himself is not always in a dubious moral position when compared to the farmer from whom he buys his grain. He is stunned that he can think this way, and tries to shake it off. He cannot, but he cannot change, either. There is no redemption. His musically-inclined son dies young, Thomas dies old in spirit if not in years, his wife goes back to her father's house, the parvenus take over the family house from the once-proud, now vanished house of Buddenbrook, as the Buddenbrooks had once taken it over from another bankrupt old firm. One family and one firm are dead, another has arisen. The drab, futile cycle is ready to repeat itself again.[29]

The Aristocratic Critique of Stupidity

Criticizing the bourgeois for their stupidity is not necessarily a moral criticism. After all, no one is intentionally stupid, stupidity is not a choice that anyone makes. However, becoming a businessman *is* a choice, and in the anti-capitalist intellectual's eyes, the choice is both a stupid one and the guaranty of a stupid life—the life of Mr. Bounderby or Thomas Buddenbrooks. For some intellectuals, in particular those who assert the aristocratic aspect of their situation, it is the choice of a *stupid* lifestyle that is the fundamental sin of the middle classes. What gives intellectuals' criticism of stupidity its aristocratic flavor is that it emphasizes their own elite intelligence and education in comparison with the stupidity of the mass. A natural corollary of such a position is that intelligence becomes a moral virtue. This is not the position taken by Dickens or Mann, and it is not the most common literary criticism of capitalism. But it is significant, and we can find it in a significant novelist: Flaubert.

For Flaubert, the fundamental conflict of modern times was between intelligence and stupidity. Stupidity was embodied in the middle classes, while intellectuals incarnated intelligence. For example, like every other nineteenth-century observer, Flaubert was appalled by the effects of factory work summed up by the name "Manchester." But Flaubert was most struck by its intellectual effects: "have you ever thought about the quantity of stupid professions industry creates and about the mass of stupidity that must come from it in the long run? That would be a frightening statistic to compile! What can one expect from a population like that of Manchester, which spends its life making pins?" Adam Smith had remarked on the same problem. But unlike Smith, Flaubert saw no redeeming features in capitalism.[30]

For Flaubert, the word "bourgeois" was a summary of all capitalism's faults. It was the "bourgeois" against whom Flaubert directed his most vitriolic comments. "Me, the older I get, the more I feel myself full of an inexpressible disdain for the bourgeois...," "one single thing makes me indignant, that is the stupidity, the crass ignorance, the blindness of the bourgeois." Bourgeois = willfully stupid. There could be no greater sin in the eyes of an aristocratic intellectual. This contempt is the backdrop for Flaubert's *Madame Bovary*, a novel in which all the main characters are bourgeois and stupid. What flashes of intelligence there are are directed solely towards satisfying greed. The leading male character (not hero), Charles Bovary, is exceptionally dim-witted in every way. The beautiful heroine, Emma, has a lust for life unmatched by anyone else in her dreary world, and no idea how to go about satisfying it. Her every foolish attempt leads only to greater dissatisfaction and eventually to financial disaster and suicide. None of the other characters are any more appealing, or at least any smarter. They are all caricatures of different bourgeois stereotypes. Suffice it to say that Flaubert wrote that in *Madame Bovary* he had devoted his talent to "writing well about mediocrity." Without attacking the bourgeoisie explicitly, he had portrayed and condemned their stupidity once and for all.[31]

Flaubert's contempt for the bourgeois was not unusual. What was unusual was his frank avowal of allegiance to an aristocratic ideal. According to Flaubert, the masses were condemned to stupidity by the nature of industrialism: "Education for the lower classes and the morality of the poor are, I believe, things of the future. But as for the intelligence of the masses, that is what I deny, whatever may come...." Government, therefore, should be in the hands of an intellectual elite. "The only reasonable thing (and I always come back to this), is a government of mandarins, provided that the mandarins know something, and even that they know many things.... Our salvation now lies in nothing but a *legitimate aristocracy*, by which I mean a majority composed of something other than numbers." An aristocracy composed of the educated was the only kind capable of political competence. But Flaubert carried his intellectual snobbery so far as to look down on even this kind of politics: "A country's government ought to be a section of the Institute [of Sciences], and *the least important of them all*." Plato's philosopher-kings are back with a vengeance.[32]

From which of the Three Don'ts does this aristocratic attack on capitalism stem? Certainly not from the Third—Flaubert was no partisan of equality. From the Second? Flaubert held Christian morality in contempt, because it had too much grace and not enough justice. From the First? Perhaps. Flaubert was extremely well versed in classical literature, but unlike the Greeks and Romans he did not think politics was the highest human occupation. Mostly his attitude was shaped by the particular social and political situation of his time. Western intellectual traditions inform intellectuals' criticism of capitalism, but they are not the whole story. The point of departure does not dictate the whole course of the voyage. The intellectuals' critique of stupidity in the nineteenth century is a new one.[33]

Flaubert's frank assertion of intellectuals' aristocratic superiority to commercial society was typical of the extreme bohemian wing of the intelligentsia, though outwardly Flaubert was the most conventional of men. But it was not unparalleled. In Howells' *Altruria*, the Altrurian says: "We regard all artists, who are in some sort creators, as the human type which is likest the divine, and we try to conform our whole industrial life to the artistic temperament." However, Howells is no Flaubert. The superiority of the intellectual and creative life, while repeated several times in *Altruria*, is always limited by the democratic Don'ts' emphasis on equality, with a little of the classical and Christian preference for agriculture thrown in: "All occupations are equal in Altruria, although agriculture is perhaps especially honored." This slightly shamefaced retraction of aristocratic claims is much more common among intellectuals than Flaubert's frank pride. The pride of the intellectual aristocrat is usually tempered by his longing for a bond with the people and democratic society's egalitarian imperative.[34]

Yet there have always been groups of intellectuals more than willing to cut themselves off from the rest of society. These are the "bohemians." They condemn capitalism and the bourgeoisie not for this or that individual sin, not for greed, or hypocrisy, or lack of family values, or even for stupidity, but as an inherently wrong way of life.

Bohemian vs. Bourgeois: Criticizing a Lifestyle

Damning the capitalist as an individual, however satisfying to the intellectual's clerical streak, was not enough to destroy the reputation of capitalism and commercial society as a system. The existence of vile capitalists did not necessarily demonstrate that capitalism was evil. Moralists, after all, had been condemning individual evildoers since the beginning of time. What was new about intellectuals' rejection of capitalism in the nineteenth century was modern intellectuals' rejection of commercial society as a whole. This meant not merely that there were many morally objectionable bourgeois, but that being a bourgeois was inherently wrong, even if the individual merchant somehow turned out to be a good man with a happy family. The bourgeois' *lifestyle* was enough to condemn him. As César Graña perceived, "literary men in the nineteenth century were often more profoundly repelled by the psychological and cultural features of the bourgeoisie, the inherent valuelessness of their lives and the internal anonymity of their souls, than by their moral sins...." But rejection of the bourgeois lifestyle was not just a rejection of its internal flaws, of the "valueless," anonymous lives lived by the world's salesmen and middle managers. It was also a rejection of the externals of bourgeois life, from its regular hours and regulated pleasures to the technological advances it cherished.[35]

To explore this facet of the struggle between mind and money, we must turn from examining the literary assault on the capitalist as an individual, to exploring the bohemian rejection of the bourgeois lifestyle. Although the novel was again a weapon intellectuals employed in this battle, our bohemian sources will be a more varied group than those discussed above: Henri Murger, George Gissing, Oscar Wilde, William Morris, and John Ruskin.

Since attacking the middle-class lifestyle was an aristocratic form of attack, it makes sense that it most commonly came from a group that was in a sense the elite of the intelligentsia—the elite of an elite. *Not* the academics—they had the wrong kind of social prestige, they were almost bourgeois, like old-regime bishops who were really nobles. Its source was the bohemians, the most autonomous and thus the most aristocratic, of intellectuals. Often the most materially deprived, true bohemians are nevertheless the proudest and most aristocratic of all. Their criticism of the bourgeois lifestyle is the same sort of criticism the medieval noble had once made. In medieval Europe, to enter the aristocracy a bourgeois had to "live nobly." That meant adopt a new lifestyle that included everything from hunting to spending money lavishly to abandoning commerce. Bohemians too vaunted the merits of a "noble" lifestyle. But they insisted even more fiercely than the noble that the bourgeois give up his shop-keeping ways, and start going to bed at daybreak instead of getting up at dawn. Lifestyle criticism has gone in and out of fashion, as have the beatniks and hippies of the late twentieth century, but it remains an enduring aspect of the struggle between mind and money.

"Bohemian" requires some clarification. In chapter 1 it was argued that *all* intellectuals are bohemians, that academia and bohemia are merely far-flung provinces of the same country, and that a "bohemian spirit" of autonomy is central to the self-definition of the intellectual. In this sense many professors and mainstream novelists and a few plumbers, despite their conventional clothing, are bohemians. But there is another, narrower meaning of the word "bohemian," which can be used to describe a particular sub-group among intellectuals who display the common traits of the species "intellectual" in an extreme degree.

Another analogy already used helps us understand the differences between common intellectuals and bohemians—the distinction between the secular clergy, who live in the world, and the regular clergy, the monks, who live outside it, isolated in their cloisters. Mainstream novelists dress respectably and lived in commercial society, although they are not of it. They are the parish priests of the intelligentsia. True bohemians choose to live outside respectable society, even if they possess the educational requirements to join it. They are cloistered in cafes, just as another order of intellectual clergy are cloistered on campuses. They seek spiritual perfection, without any compromise with the secular world, unlike the majority of their academic brethren. They are the ones called "bohemians" in the nineteenth century, and beatniks and hippies in the twentieth. In the late twentieth century the "hippies" liked to organize themselves in "tribes." Bohemians indeed have always practiced a kind of intellectual tribalism.

Bohemia "originated in France,... and the approximate date of its birth was 1830," wrote Malcolm Cowley, a denizen of New York's bohemia in the 1930s. Balzac used the word in 1830s novels, but it still needed to be explained to readers in the late 1840s when Henri Murger's book, *Scenes from Bohemian Life*, source of Puccini's opera *La Bohème* and the Broadway musical *Rent,* was written. The growth of bohemia was symptomatic of the expansion of the intellectual class generally. If bohemia began in Paris, on the left bank of the Seine in the Latin Quarter, it soon conquered neighborhoods as diverse as London's Soho, Munich's Schwabing, and New York's Greenwich Village.[36]

Former bohemians have a habit, when their favorite café goes out of business, of proclaiming bohemia dead. But a new café always opens somewhere. Since 1830 bohemia has been a territory populated by intellectuals, with enclaves scattered throughout the Western world. Throughout the nineteenth century it was expanding its territory. For much of the nineteenth century bohemians were more numerous than professors. Garrets are cheaper to rent than Ivory Towers.

Usually bohemians are young, but not always. Usually they are poor, but not always. They always have "artistic" ambitions, whether writers, poets, or painters, but not necessarily any artistic accomplishments. It is their lives as much as their works that are works of art. The poet Erich Mühsam, writing in the early twentieth century, defined these "artists": "Only those should be considered artists who do not lower their art to a business, and thus those who under all circumstances refuse to produce art without an artistic motive.... On the other hand there belong among the artists, whom I define as the 'outsiders', also those who *without being artistically productive*, [emphasis added] are lead by artistic impulses throughout their lifestyle." It is the lifestyle that matters above all. Bohemians epitomize rejection of the ordered world of the middle classes and capitalism. As Charles Demailly, the bohemian character in the Goncourts' 1860 novel of that name proclaims, "Yes, we are an undisciplinable world. We are rebels, we are jokers.... We are without catechism, without respect, without pity in our games, and we make everything into a game... Yes, but in the final analysis we are a great and noble race, a free, wild race.... which does not recognize the divine right of money."[37]

In short, bohemia was made up of artistic sorts who rejected conventional lifestyles and capitalism. Bohemians' rejection of commercial society was all the stronger because of their relative isolation from it. Their isolation was not complete, of course, and the impossibility of cutting themselves off from capitalism infuriated them. Imagine a St. Anthony, the fourth-century Egyptian hermit, setting out to find a cave in the desert, and finding the road strewn with billboards, a neon sign above the cave where he fasted, flagellated himself, and struggled with the devil, and tourists trooping past to gawk. Of course, there would be a McDonald's built across the gully. St. Anthony would not have been a happy camper. Bohemians were (and are) in something of this position, compounded by the fact that they could not rely solely on charity for their living, unlike St. Anthony, and instead had to sell bits of their souls to the commercial devils, usually at a low price.

How did this oddly-dressed monastic community express its attitude towards capitalism? Naturally bohemians, the most autonomous, most "bohemian" of intellectuals, disagreed with each other, and so their criticism of the bourgeois lifestyle and the alternatives they proposed were as ill-assorted as their clothes. Yet their criticism of the bourgeois lifestyle makes up a recognizable spectrum. Let us begin with Henri Murger, the first chronicler of this world.

Murger, a bohemian himself, vividly described the lifestyle in his autobiographical novel, *Scenes from Bohemian Life*. In it he chronicles the lives and loves of a number of bohemians in the Paris of about 1840, but it could have been set in any of the many bohemias of the nineteenth or twentieth century (Murger's claim that bohemia could only exist in Paris should be understood as a claim that it could not exist in a provincial town). It is a life of alternate poverty and abundance, living off one's wits and not paying the rent, sleeping at friends' houses or sometimes on the street, throwing enormous parties and half-starving for days. "These people know how to borrow money from the world's worst miser, and they would have found truffles in a lifeboat. If necessary they know how to practice abstinence with all the virtue of a hermit; but if they come into a little money, you'll see them immediately shower it on the most ruinous fantasies...." The nearest thing to this conduct is that of the medieval noble referred to in chapter 2, who throws out the window the money his son has neglected to spend, to show him the proper attitude. The bohemians indeed emulated the Duke's Don't, "Don't Make Money, Take it and Spend it." And as they throw away their money, bohemians mock those who save it. When Rodolphe, the main character of Murger's book, and his friends have spent a sudden windfall on a week of partying, they suddenly discover they have the equivalent of $5 left over. The suggestion is made to invest it in government bonds.[38]

Murger identifies bohemian behavior with the ideal of "art for art's sake." Bohemians are "that race of obstinate dreamers for whom art has remained a faith and not a trade." He doesn't call them priests, but he recognizes the religious role they play. The book describes what might be characterized as a bohemian religious order, "The Society of Water-Drinkers." The Water-Drinkers swear an oath that devotes them to art and governs their conduct. Murger tells us that all the members died in obscurity. No matter. The point is that they swore never to prostitute their art to any practical money-earning purpose, so that the poets will not write advertising copy, the painters will not do a tailor's portrait to pay his bill, etc. When a sculptor, who needs to earn money to buy medicine for his dying wife, announces that he must resign from the society, the president responds to him: "My friend, your declaration of love was your resignation as an artist…. Practice your trade; but for me, you are no longer a sculptor, you're a waster of plaster. It is true that now you will be able to drink wine, but we, who will continue to drink water and eat day-old bread, we will remain artists." Bohemians recognized the enormous *temptation* to hypocrisy with which they lived—yet another crime for which capitalism was responsible, in their eyes. Rather than the capitalist's hypocrisy, it was their own which tormented them, a torment they blamed on capitalism. Bohemia, because of its poverty, the purity of its intentions, and the ever-greater temptation to sell out, was where hatred of commercial society, hatred of *sin*, was at its most fierce.[39]

The issue of hypocrisy, of selling out, torments George Gissing. He does not think that money is unimportant to an artist's life. Himself a veteran of many years living in British slums in real poverty, he knows better. As one of his autobiographical characters puts it: "You tell me that money cannot buy the things most precious. Your commonplace proves that you have never known the lack of it. When I think of all the sorrow and the barrenness that has been wrought in my life by want of a few more pounds per annum than I was able to earn, I stand aghast at money's significance… there is no moral good which has not to be paid for in coin of the realm." Gissing does not half-starve in carefree gaiety. Nor does he identify with the half-starved proletarians he lives with. "I knew the poor, and I knew that their aims were not mine. I knew that the kind of life (such a modest life!) which I should have accepted as little short of the ideal, would have been to them… a weariness and a contempt." In his own way, Gissing is as aristocratic as Flaubert.[40]

This makes his contempt for those who sell out all the greater. He seems like one of the Society of Water-Drinkers brought to life and turned into a cynic. This is the theme of *New Grub Street*, his best-known novel, which follows the fortunes of a couple of writers who choose opposite paths. Reardon remains loyal to art, even if he is incapable of making a first-rate work, while Jasper is a sell-out whose goal is to turn his mediocrity into a fortune. The hypocritical mediocrity Jasper has nothing but ill-hidden contempt for Reardon, the true artist: "He is absurd enough to be conscientious, likes to be called an 'artist', and so on. He might possibly earn a hundred and fifty a year if his mind were at rest, and that would be enough if he married a decent little dressmaker." But Reardon cannot follow the advice of a Jasper. He marries a middle-class girl without independent fortune, and is doomed to unhappiness. He and several other intellectuals in the novel must learn the hard way that it is a disaster "to receive an intellectual training wholly incompatible with the material conditions of their life. To the relatively poor (who are so much worse off than the poor absolutely) education is in most cases a mocking cruelty." To be trained to live a life of the mind of aristocratic leisure, and discover one must be a stockbroker or starve, against all the moral instincts of a classical education, is no blessing. Reardon does not sell out in Gissing's novel, and he suffers for it.[41]

Jasper says that if the intellectual wishes to succeed in commercial society, he must learn to "supply the market…. Literature nowadays is a trade. Putting aside men of genius, who may succeed by mere cosmic force, your successful man of letters is your skillful tradesman. He thinks first and foremost of the markets; when one kind of goods begins to go off slackly, he is ready with something new and appetizing." The market needs "good, coarse, marketable stuff for the world's vulgar." Jasper has no moral qualms: "I maintain that we people of brains are justified in supplying the mob with the food it likes," and so "I shall write for the upper middle-class of intellect, the people who like to feel that what they are reading has some special cleverness, but who can't distinguish between stones and paste." Note the contempt for the "middle class," even the "upper middle class," by even so humble an intellectual aristocrat as Jasper.[42]

Jasper may be honest in private, but in public he is a hypocrite, selling paste as the real thing. Of course, the true aristocrat/intellectual is incapable of hypocrisy, and Reardon cannot do it, although his materialistic wife does not understand why he has torn up the beginnings of three potboilers. "There was no need to destroy what you had written. It was all good enough for the market." This is what Reardon cannot bear to hear, and he replies in despair, "No, that is the unpardonable sin! To make a trade of an art! I am rightly served for attempting such a brutal folly." His wife replies: "How very silly it is to talk like this!… Art must be practiced as a trade." She tells Reardon that before her marriage she didn't think money was important, but now knows that "it is the most powerful thing in the world. If I had to choose between a glorious reputation with poverty and a contemptible popularity with wealth, I should choose the latter." But Reardon is a failure, and eventually a suicide. Jasper's attitude is very different. "Never in my life shall I do anything of solid literary value; I shall always despise the people I write for. But my path will be that of success." And it is. He goes so far as to tell the woman he wishes to marry, "I shall never write for writing's sake, only to make money." The sum of his desires is "to have easy command of all the pleasures desired by a cultivated man."[43]

In real life Gissing played the part of Reardon, although he bitterly recommends that of Jasper. Gissing wrote as an impoverished intellectual living an isolated life among the poor of London. He sees no possibility for change, he is no revolutionary. But he sees commerce and art as black and white, with no reconciliation possible. If his life as a bohemian was untypical (if only in its isolation from others), the conclusion he drew from it was not.

The final bohemian critic of the middle-class lifestyle we shall consider may at first seem surprising. Yet the author of "The Soul of Man under Socialism" was Oscar Wilde. Wilde is better known for his light comedies (*The Importance of Being Earnest*), his carefully planned witticisms, or his sexuality than for his social theories. A few of his bon mots and his jailing for sodomy remain notorious. But in his lifetime he was a leader of the London bohemians, and the attitudes he expressed towards capitalism are typical. Wilde, like many bohemians before and after, turned to socialism as the only way to live in the style he wanted. Not the material lifestyle, of course, but the intellectual, artistic lifestyle. We can only speculate whether his praise of individuality free from the restraints of capitalism was also a plea to be allowed to express his homosexuality in freedom as well.

Like all bohemians, Wilde loved to flaunt convention, and he had an almost French taste for paradox. "It takes a thoroughly selfish age, like our own, to deify self-sacrifice. It takes a thoroughly grasping age, such as that in which we live, to set above the fine intellectual virtues, those shallow and sentimental virtues that are an immediate practical benefit to itself." Thus self-sacrifice turns into selfishness, sentimentality becomes the product of a grasping age, and Wilde has turned bourgeois morality upside down. He goes on: "They miss their aim, too, these philanthropists and sentimentalists of our day, who are always chattering to one about one's duty to one's neighbor. For the development of the race depends on the development of the individual, and where self-culture has ceased to be the ideal, the intellectual standard is instantly lowered, and, often, ultimately lost." What matters to Wilde is not giving money to one's neighbor, it is developing one's own intellect. "It is so easy for people to have sympathy with suffering. It is so difficult for them to have sympathy with thought." Poor isolated intellectual aristocrat! Even the poor get a better press, and more sympathy too.[44]

Wilde's ideal is the development of the individual personality. The problem with private property is that it makes this doubly impossible, first by an unequal distribution of wealth, and worse, by a misguided system of values. Capitalism:

> has made gain, not growth, its aim. So that man thought that the important thing was to have, and did not know that the important thing is to be. *The true perfection of man lies, not in what man has, but in what man is....* [Private property] has debarred one part of the community from being individual by starving them. It has debarred the other part of the community from being individual by putting them on the wrong road, and encumbering them.[45]

Poor rich folk, says Wilde, their property prevents them from cultivating their intellect. "Property not merely has duties, but has so many duties that its possession to any large extent is a bore.... In the interest of the rich we must get rid of it." Wilde is quite serious. The rich will be better off without their money. Why don't they give it away then? Because in a society based on private property, people need wealth. Only a society that has abolished private property will allow individuality to flourish.[46]

Individuality, for Wilde, is another way of saying art. Only when commerce, which is based on satisfying the desires of others, no longer dictates what the artist does, will true art, Reardon's kind of art, be possible. "A work of art is the unique result of a unique temperament. Its beauty comes from the fact that the author is what he is. It has nothing to do with the fact that other people want what they want." Commerce, rather than satisfying the artist's need to develop her own personality, interferes with it by encouraging the artist to produce for someone else's needs and tastes. Producing for the sake of others could be seen as love, or altruism, but for Wilde, in one of his paradoxes, altruism is self-destructive: "The majority of people spoil their lives by an unhealthy and exaggerated altruism—are forced, indeed, so to spoil them."[47]

The purpose of life is to develop one's own individuality. For Wilde, priest of an intellectual religion, "he who would lead a Christlike life is he who is perfectly and absolutely himself." Thus a saint, a composer like Wagner, and a poet like Shelley are all equally Christlike according to Wilde. To be Christlike requires freedom and perfect autonomy. "Every man must be left quite free to choose his own work. No form of compulsion must be exercised over him," including any form of economic compulsion, such as the need to earn a living. So Wilde is a socialist.[48]

But he is an unusual kind of socialist. He rejects any socialism that transfers authority to the state. "If the Socialism is Authoritarian; if there are governments armed with economic power as they are now with political power; if, in a word, we are to have Industrial tyrannies, then the last state of man will be worse than the first." If socialism means that everyone loses freedom, then socialism is a bad thing. Fittingly for a bohemian, Wilde is more an anarchist than a socialist. In his view, "all modes of government are failures," because they are all despotisms which oppress the individual. Thus "the form of government that is most suitable to the artist is no government at all." Private property and government should both be abolished. Only then can the human being/intellectual attain the opportunity to develop her personality in complete autonomy and self-direction.[49]

However, with private property, at least some people are free: "At present, in consequence of the existence of private property, a great many people are enabled to develop a certain very limited amount of Individualism.... These are the poets, the philosophers, the men of science, the men of culture—in a word, the real men, the men who have realized themselves, and in whom all humanity gains a partial realization." There are real individuals in modern society, but only to the extent that money allows. Although there were bohemians who romanticized poverty, like the Water-Drinkers, Wilde is not one of them. If he must choose, Wilde actually prefers the rich to the poor: "Wealthy people are, as a class, better than impoverished people, more moral, more intellectual, more well-behaved. *There is only one class in the community that thinks more about money than the rich, and that is the poor.*"[50]

Wilde's preference for wealth over poverty leads him to come out strongly in favor of technology. "A great deal of nonsense is being written and talked nowadays about the dignity of manual labor. There is nothing necessarily dignified about manual labor at all, and most of it is absolutely degrading. It is mentally and morally injurious to man to do anything in which he does not find pleasure." A machine that will do a repetitive task like street sweeping liberates humanity. It performs the role of the ancient slave, and makes freedom possible for all. In the future, "Humanity will be amusing itself, or enjoying cultivated leisure—which, and not labour, is the aim of man.... The fact is that civilization requires slaves."[51]

Wilde's position in favor of technology was by no means unique among anti-capitalist writers (Marx shared it), but the nineteenth century was also the beginning of an intellectual movement that rejected technology, or at least wished to limit it. The rejection of technology as bad for the environment and bad for the character became more popular after World War I, and still more influential in the second half of the twentieth century. The precursors of the ecologists were thin on the ground in the nineteenth century, but their criticism of the bourgeois lifestyle became so important in later anti-capitalist thought that it deserves separate mention here.

The Question of Technology

William Morris (1834-1896) is a good example of nineteenth-century literary criticism of capitalism from an ecological perspective. It is a little difficult to characterize Morris as a bohemian in the narrow sense. He was more interested in lifestyle than anything else, but he preferred the countryside to the café—a more traditional aristocratic preference. He was the leading figure in the Arts & Crafts Movement, promoting a revival in fine hand-made furniture, textiles, glassware, and decorative arts. This also had aristocratic connotations—the Arts & Crafts Movement was an aristocratic rejection of the technology that brought cheap imitations of elite goods to the masses. In addition, Morris was an important early British socialist. He was also a gifted writer of fantasy fiction, publishing novels that are still in print in paperback over a hundred years after his death. But as he described himself, "apart from the desire to produce beautiful things, the leading passion of my life has been and is hatred of modern civilization."[52]

Morris expressed his hatred of modern civilization in a Utopian novel, *News from Nowhere*. The book begins with a dispirited hero trudging home from yet another pointless socialist meeting in late nineteenth-century London, at which no one can agree on what is to be done. When he falls asleep that night, he has a vision. In it he is transported to a future England in which private property has been abolished. But while no one owns anything in Nowhere, most of the novel is not about economics or politics, but lifestyle. The novel is full of reminiscences about the bad old days of the nineteenth century, when the need for cheap methods of production forced everyone, even the rich, "to live amidst sights and sounds and smells which it is in the very nature of man to abhor and flee from...," those black and purple waters of Coketown, for example. Morris is full of contempt for the shoddy, low-quality products of the assembly line. He acknowledges the skill with which machines were made, but it was all a waste: "the great achievement of the nineteenth century was the making of machines which were wonders of invention, skill and patience and which were used for the production of measureless quantities of worthless make-shifts." When the only measure of quality is whether someone will buy it if the price is low enough, then quality disappears.[53]

All this ugly stuff, both the machines and their products, is destined to disappear in the new England of *Nowhere*. London and all the large manufacturing cities are replaced by villages and scattered houses. The old urban centers "were centres of nothing but 'manufacture', and served no purpose but that of the gambling market...." After the revolution, or "Great Change," as Morris calls it, people rapidly abandon the cities for the countryside. They study machines only in order to re-learn how to do everything possible by hand: "the feeling against a mechanical life, which had begun before the Great Change among people who had leisure to think of such things, was spreading insensibly." Machinery, except the simplest and most direct kind of hand tools, separates us from nature, and prevents us from seeing that work and pleasure are meant to be the same thing. Eventually pleasure in handwork eliminates mechanical toil. Cities, railways, and factories all disappear, and England resembles one great garden.[54]

In Morris' view, capitalism and machinery are on one side, socialism and art on the other. Mass poverty "is the result of the system that has trampled down Art, and exalted commerce into a sacred religion," instead of the reverse. In this Morris is a good example of the intellectual as pseudo-clergyman. He is a priest, like many bohemians, of the god Art. But if Morris is comfortable with intellectuals as preachers, he rejects intellectuals as aristocrats. There is not a shred of aristocratic consciousness in Morris, despite his championship of handicrafts. He felt an urgent need to link himself with the masses. He mocks those who believe in an artistic aristocracy. In *Nowhere* he devotes a few lines to a small, illogical group of people, generally rich, who thought even after the revolution that the use of machines would set free the "more intelligent part of mankind… to follow the higher forms of the arts, as well as science and the study of history. It was strange, was it not, that they should thus ignore that aspiration after complete equality which we now recognize as the bond of all happy human society?"[55]

Morris was ahead of his time in his concern for the environment and his criticism of technology. His rejection of the bourgeois lifestyle, on the other hand, was a typical bohemian attitude. One way in which Morris' reaction to capitalism was typical of intellectuals, whether bohemian or not, was its incomprehension of why any honest person of average intelligence would *want* to be a businessman. This attitude was widespread among intellectuals of all kinds. Incomprehension was widespread on the other side, too, of course. Stories about businessmen without sympathy or understanding for their sons' artistic or literary inclinations were commonplace in the nineteenth (and twentieth) century. This mutual incomprehension is of fundamental importance to the history of the war between mind and money, and no discussion of nineteenth-century literary attacks on capitalism would be adequate if it did not explore it. Since this book is about the war intellectuals have waged, it will be explored from their side. And nowhere is this incomprehension more clearly expressed than in the writings of John Ruskin.

Our Mutual Incomprehension

John Ruskin (1819-1900) was a well-known critic of architecture, art, and society in his day. He was, on Morris's own account, a great influence on Morris's ideas, and it is from Ruskin that Morris took his rejection of technology. They were not clones, however. Unlike Morris, Ruskin did not think much of manual labor. Ruskin acknowledged that intellectual work was a waste of time more often than manual labor, "but when both kinds are equally well and worthily done the head's is the noble work, and the hand's the ignoble." He is thus more aristocratic in his approach than Morris.[56]

But Ruskin's individual peculiarities as a thinker are not what matters here. What matters is the way he perfectly expressed how many intellectuals had lost touch with commercial society in the nineteenth century. The way these intellectuals saw the world had become incommensurable with the way the bourgeoisie, or rather capitalism as a whole, understood reality. In their different ways, all the writers discussed above express incomprehension of capitalism and those who make it work. It may seem incredible to suggest that the novelists and writers who portrayed commercial society so vividly did not understand what they were seeing. Dickens and Mann and Zola and Howells and Gissing and their fellows were highly accurate and skilled observers. But their observations were filtered through similar moral biases. They are hard to detect because we are so used to literature written in their shadow. Ruskin lets us see them for what they are.

Ruskin, like many others, talks about life as "play." He is more careful to define the distinction between play and work than most, however. "'Play' is an exertion of body or mind, made to please ourselves, and with no determined end; and work is a thing done because it ought to be done, and with a determined end." Play may or may not be useful, but it is something we choose to do, not something we have to do. Does a businessman play or work? He plays. He plays a game: "The first of all English games is making money. That is an all-absorbing game; and we knock each other down oftener in playing at that, than at football, or any other roughest sport: and *it is absolutely without purpose; no one who engages heartily in that game ever knows why.*" The emphasis is added because it so clearly shows Ruskin's own total incomprehension of commerce. How could Ruskin know that "*no one... ever knows why*"? But certainly Ruskin himself did not. Insofar as Ruskin represents the attitude of his fellow intellectuals, the same applies to them.[57]

Ruskin and his fellows think the businessman must be as ignorant about the game he plays as they are: "Ask a great money-maker what he wants to do with his money—he never knows. He doesn't make it to do anything with it. He gets it only that he *may* get it." To play such a game is *pointless.* You must go on playing a futile match in which no matter how many times you score the game goes on. In the eyes of the intellectual, the businessman can't win. His only possible victory would be to stop playing, that is get out of business, as so many intellectuals have urged. Whether he gets out of business of his own free will, or is forced to by bankruptcy, is the difference between Mr. Gradgrind, or Silas Lapham and Thomas Buddenbrook.[58]

In thinking about this strange being, the businessman, Ruskin does not know where to begin. He cannot put his existence down to original sin, for Ruskin is a Christian, and thus knows that he himself must be a sinner. But he is no businessman. So what is it that distinguishes a Ruskin from an entrepreneur? In the final analysis, Ruskin the aristocratic intellectual can think of only one criterion weighty enough to account for the difference:

brains. Intellectuals are smart and bourgeois are stupid. Or rather, the difference is stupidity and a little immorality, since intellectuals tend to be preachers as well: "There will always be a number of men who would fain set themselves to the accumulation of wealth as the sole object of their lives. Necessarily, that class of men is an uneducated class, inferior in intellect. And, more or less, cowardly. It is physically impossible for a well-educated, intellectual, or brave man to make money the chief object of his thoughts...." Not every intellectual puts the differences between intellectuals and the bourgeoisie down to brains. But all share Ruskin's *incomprehension* for the accumulation of wealth by individuals, even sometimes by society. Only the intensity varies.[59]

Commerce and moneymaking are literally demonized in Ruskin's account. Work comes from God, but it is paid for by the Devil. "It is indeed very clear that God means all thoroughly good work and talk to be done for nothing."[60] The idea that the market could establish value is as incomprehensible to him as the rest of the money game. He is only surprised to discover that the non-intellectual world doesn't see it this way:

> ...I have found myself totally unable, as yet, by any repetition, or illustration, to force this plain thought into my readers' heads,... that the real good of all work, and of all commerce, depends on the final intrinsic worth of the thing you make.... But the English public has been so possessed by its modern school of economics with the notion that Business is always good,... and that buying and selling are always salutary, whatever the intrinsic worth of what you buy or sell, that it seems impossible to gain as much as a patient hearing for any inquiry respecting the substantial result of our eager modern labour.[61]

Ruskin, though a gifted writer and speaker, finds himself unable to communicate. The gulf between the intellectual and capitalism has grown too great. All that makes it across are insults and propaganda, and the occasional refugee. The war between mind and money is the original model of the Cold War.

Incomprehension of the dominant way of life in capitalism became increasingly typical of intellectuals as the nineteenth century wore on and became the twentieth. It is as typical of the renowned intellectual as of the unknown bohemian. Kenneth Rexroth wrote that "no literature of the past two hundred years is of the slightest importance unless it is 'disaffiliated'. Only our modern industrial and commercial civilization has produced an elite which has consistently rejected all the reigning values of society. There were no Baudelaires in Babylon." Rexroth exaggerated, a little. But what he perceived was the literary front in the war between mind and money.[62]

Whether criticizing the capitalist or capitalism, the sins of the individual or the flaws of commercial society, the writers and artists of the nineteenth century were highly effective. The contest between Alger and Howells was no contest. Dickens and Co. made their names; their opponents faded into oblivion. The capitalist's reputation became what it remains today. Can we know how many voters, politicians, and revolutionaries this disaffected, anti-commercial literature influenced? No. But without it, neither Nazism, nor communism, nor the welfare state is imaginable. The demolition of capitalism's good character played an important role in the events of the twentieth century, although just how great a role is impossible to establish.

The ways in which intellectuals directly contributed to anti-capitalist political movements in the twentieth century will be the subject of later chapters. It is important to bear in mind, however, that this literary tradition persists today. As one critic wrote: "It cannot have escaped teachers of English literature that much of their time is spent unfitting their pupils for the lives they will eventually have to lead. Most twentieth century authors, and in particular the greats... inculcate an attitude of contempt for ordinary, bread-earning citizens, which must eventually unsettle youngsters who are on the point of choosing a career, unless they are mercifully too dense to get the modernists' message at all."[63] Leading writers and artists of the twenty-first century very often continue to adopt the anti-capitalist themes of their predecessors. A glance at any list of twentieth-century winners of literary prizes makes this clear. Describing how capitalism lost the battle over character is not to describe an event that took place entirely in the past. It is an ongoing performance. There is no truce in the literary war between mind and money.

Notes

1.   Jules Vallès, "The Dead," from *Le Figaro*, 1 Nov. 1861, cited in Seigel, *Bohemian Paris*, 200.
2.   Horatio Alger, Jr., *Two Novels: Julius, or The Street Boy Out West. The Store Boy or The Fortunes of Ben Barclay* (New York: Holt, Rinehart and Winston 1967), 46.
3.   Alger, *Cast Upon the Breakers* (New York: Doubleday, 1974) 79, 169.
4.   Alger, *Cast Upon the Breakers*, 159.
5.   Alger, *Store Boy*, 98.
6.   Alger, *Store Boy*, 68.
7.   Alger, *Cast Upon the Breakers*, 77, 184.
8.   William Dean Howells, *The Rise of Silas Lapham* (New York: Prentice Hall, 1974), 132, 153.
9.   Howells, *The Rise of Silas Lapham*, 208.
10.   William Dean Howells, *A Traveler from Altruria* (New York: Sagamore Press, 1957), 142, 146.

11. Emile Zola, *Pot-Bouille* (Paris: Flammarion, 1979), 62, 135, 192, 287, 385, 396, 439.
12. Emile Zola, *L'Argent* (Paris: Gallimard, 1980), 85-6, 151.
13. Zola, *L'Argent*, 188-89, 290-91.
14. Zola, *L'Argent*, 286.
15. Zola, *L'Argent*, 293, 497.
16. André Wurmser, preface, in Zola, *L'Argent*, 7.
17. François de la Rochefoucauld, *Maxims*, in *The Oxford Book of Money* (Oxford: Oxford University Press, 1996), 332.
18. Marx, *The Communist Manifesto*, in *The Marx-Engels Reader*, ed. Tucker, 338.
19. Charles Dickens, *Hard Times* (London: Penguin, 1995), 28-29.
20. Dickens. *Hard Times*, 28-29, 31, 54-55.
21. Dickens, *Hard Times*, 68.
22. Dickens, *Hard Times*, 10, 61, 216, 284, 287-88.
23. Dickens, *Hard Times*, 21, 122, 296.
24. Thomas Mann, *Buddenbrooks: The Decline of a Family*, trans. John E. Woods (New York: Knopf, 1993), 15.
25. Mann, *Buddenbrooks*, 66, 104, 236.
26. Mann, *Buddenbrooks*, 100, 193.
27. Mann, *Buddenbrooks*, 254.
28. Mann, *Buddenbrooks*, 298, 300, 339.
29. Mann, *Buddenbrooks*, 415, 417.
30. Gustave Flaubert, 14 August 1853, *Correspondance*, ed. Bernard Masson (Paris: Gallimard, 1975), 246.
31. Flaubert, *Correspondance*, 17 August 1876, 680; 21 November 1877, 704.
32. Flaubert, *Correspondance*, ed. Masson 16 January 1866, 81; *Correspondance*, vol. 4, January 1869—December 1875, ed. Jean Bruneau (Paris: Gallimard, 1998), to George Sand, 5 July 1869.
33. Flaubert, *Correspondance*, ed. Masson, 30 April 1871, 587-88.
34. Howells, *Altruria*, 188, 190.
35. César Graña, *Modernity and Its Discontents: French Society and the French Man of Letters in the Nineteenth Century* (New York: Harper, 1967), 162, 169.
36. "Bohemian" was coined well before "intellectual." Malcolm Cowley, "The Green-wich Village Idea," *On Bohemia*, ed. Graña, 132; Thomas Craven, "A Pustule on the Organism of Paris," *On Bohemia*, ed. Graña, 330.
37. Vigny, cited in Siegel, *Bohemian Paris*, 16; Mühsam and Goncourt, cited in Helmut Kreuzer, *Die Boheme: Beiträge zu ihrer Beschreibung* (Stuttgart: J. B. Metzlersche Verlagsbuchhandlung, 1968), 15.
38. Henry Murger, *Scènes de la vie de bohème* (Paris: Gallimard, 1988), 41, 273.
39. Murger, *Scènes*, 292-93 ; Charles Baudelaire, "Les Tentations, ou Eros, Plutus et la Gloire," in *Le Spleen de Paris* (Paris: Librio, 2004), #21.
40. George Gissing, *The Private Papers of Henry Ryecroft*, cited in Kreuzer, *Die Boheme*, 264, 285.
41. George Gissing, *New Grub Street* (New York: Modern Library, 2002), 4, 38.
42. Gissing, *New Grub Street*, 5-6.
43. Gissing, *New Grub Street*, 49, 51-3, 76, 124, 350.
44. Oscar Wilde, "The Critic as Artist," in *Essays*, ed. Hesketh Pearson (London: Methuen, 1950), 160, 161.
45. Oscar Wilde, "The Soul of Man Under Socialism," *Essays*, 234.
46. Wilde, "The Soul of Man Under Socialism," 230.
47. Wilde, "The Soul of Man Under Socialism," 227-28, 246.
48. Wilde, "The Soul of Man Under Socialism," 233, 241.

49. Wilde, "The Soul of Man Under Socialism," 240-41.
50. Wilde, "The Soul of Man Under Socialism," 229, 238.
51. Wilde, "The Soul of Man Under Socialism," 244-45.
52. William Morris, "How I Became a Socialist (1894)," in Morris, *News From Nowhere*, ed. Stephen Arata (Peterborough, CA: Broadview Press, 2003), 15.
53. Morris, *News From Nowhere*, 139, 141.
54. Morris, *News From Nowhere*, 116, 119, 217, 271-72.
55. Morris, "Art and Socialism," in *News From Nowhere*, 253; *News From Nowhere*, 218.
56. John Ruskin, "Work," in *The Crown of Wild Olive* (London: George Allen, 1905), 50.
57. Ruskin, "Work," 31-32.
58. Ruskin, "Work," 31-32.
59. Ruskin, "Work," 41.
60. Ruskin, "Work," 43-44, 58.
61. Ruskin, "Introduction," *The Crown of Wild Olive*, 11.
62. Kenneth Rexroth, "San Francisco Letter," 1957, cited in Kreuzer, *Die Boheme,* 278. But there *was* a Baudelaire in Babylon reading the writing on the wall—the prophet Daniel. When he told King Nebuchadnezzar the meaning of what the moving finger wrote, it spelled doom for his kingdom. Intellectuals have often predicted the doom of capitalism, and even more often coveted the role of prophet.
63. John Carey, *The Listener*, 1974.

5

Academic Alternatives to Capitalism

The Babel Project: Building Alternatives to Capitalism

Nineteenth-century literature left the moral reputation of capitalism in shreds. "Capitalism" and "capitalist" became dirty words, or at least synonyms for evil people and an immoral economic system, machines were new ways to enslave and degrade humankind, and the middle-class virtues were so many different forms of hypocrisy. Novelists and artists made reputations, and livings, by blackening the businessman's character. According to those who supervise morality, every society is immoral to some extent. But as anti-capitalist intellectuals saw it, the sins of capitalism were not accidents of individual behavior or the result of flaws inherent in human nature, they were society's fault. It was the reigning socio-economic system which was to blame.

In the end, Mr. Smith the merchant looked more like a beast than a human being. In many a novel, who could tell the difference? There was a reason Dickens' characters were made out of cardboard—there was no humanity in them, or in the society they represented. The conclusions of the writers discussed in the last chapter add up to this: capitalism is not merely immoral, it is inhuman.

But literary works rarely did the addition themselves. They presented a part of the picture, often in passing. It was not their purpose to be system-atic. Characters might prophesy an end to capitalism, but those prophecies tended to be vague, and usually came at the end of the book.

For systematic attacks on capitalism, and above all for alternatives to it, we must turn our attention from Bohemia proper to Academia, although even there the criticism is usually more systematic than the alternative. Nevertheless, the alternatives social theorists proposed had a direct impact on modern politics. Literature influenced an ever more literate society on a broad scale, but its political influence was usually indirect. Social and political theories influenced fewer people, but often influenced policy and political movements directly (as well as influencing many novelists). Dickens did more damage to Mr. Smith's reputation than Marx, but it was Marx who presented an alternative to the merchant's existence. However many people became revolutionaries because of Dickens, the name inscribed on the red banner was not Dickens, but Marx.

The alternatives to capitalism constructed by intellectuals share a certain resemblance. They replace the chaotic, inhuman world of commerce with something more structured, more human. Humanity's need for visible structures is, after all, very old, and not restricted to intellectuals:

> And they said, "come, let us build us a city, and a tower with its top in the sky, to make a name for ourselves, else we shall be scattered all over the world." The Lord came down to look at the city and tower that man had built, and the Lord said, "If, as one people with one language for all, this is how they have begun to act, then nothing that they propose to do shall be out of their reach. Let us, then, go down and confound their speech there, so that they shall not understand one another's speech." Thus the Lord scattered them from there over the face of the whole earth; and they stopped building the city. That is why it was called Babel, because there the Lord confounded the speech of the whole earth...
>
> Genesis, 11:4-9

Intellectuals, because of their identity and social situation, have a special need for visible structures, towers with their tops in the sky, to build up and to tear down. As members of a permanently alienated elite, some of them are always searching for a way out of their alienation, even if they can never be satisfied for long with any construction. As a pseudo-aristocracy, intellectuals long for a structure in which they can find a place, even if it is only a pulpit from which to criticize. The chaos and creative destruction of capitalism provokes even more fear and hatred among intellectuals than among the population at large—even if they do more to foment it. They try to wall out capitalism's anarchy and contain its inhabitants' materialism by constructing Utopias.

But unlike the people of Babel, intellectuals have rarely come close to succeeding. It does not need divine intervention to send Ivory Towers tumbling to the ground. Perhaps this is because intellectuals' language is sometimes unintelligible even to other intellectuals. But intellectuals share with all the people of Babel the desire to build a structure with its top in the sky. They want something visible to hold society together, to keep it from being "scattered all over the world" in alienation, anomie, and unbridled competition. It is a very human desire, and one that has always been connected with religion, the most powerful human technique for giving meaning to the world. As secular clergy, intellectuals have taken up the task of giving meaning to life. Traditionally, the "tower with its top in the sky" has been understood as one of the step-pyramid temples common in ancient Babylonia. Academic intellectuals create their constructions out of careful critical discourse, rather than well-laid mud bricks. But they too want to build a temple, a structure that, whether imaginary or institutional, theoretical or real, can be seen for miles around. Even the most individualist intellectuals want a temple in which to preach and issue the oracles of reason. They wish to construct systems, and then tear them down, to alternately play the role of the people of Babel and the avenging Lord, building up structures, and chasing the moneylenders out of their new temple.[1] Adam Smith's "Invisible Hand" is a metaphor for a socio-economic system that works well without good intentions or rational planning. It has no moral or institutional focus other than the marketplace which replaced the temple. But for intellectuals this does not work. The market square is not a satisfactory substitute for the Temple.

George Orwell noticed intellectuals' longing for vanished Babel: "The underlying motive of many socialists, I believe, is simply a hypertrophied sense of order. The present state of affairs offends them not because it causes misery,... but because it is untidy." Intellectuals' disenchantment with untidy reality had begun long before Orwell wrote. As Tocqueville described it, in the eighteenth century, "above the real society there was slowly built an imaginary society in which everything seemed simple and coordinated, uniform, simple, equitable, and in accord with reason," the heavenly city of the philosophes. Intellectuals want a visible hand, preferably one that can be rationally directed. Often the new Tower takes the form of a community, a city on a hill. The Babel Project of the intellectuals is to build a visible community in a world broken apart and scattered, not by the Lord, but by capitalism.[2]

The alternatives to capitalism proposed by nineteenth-century social theorists usually proposed a community as an alternative to capitalism. A few nineteenth-century theorists, however, concentrated less on the community and more on the individuals who had once been able to build Babel. These theorists' alternatives to capitalism aimed to encourage the kind of individual who would be capable of such a feat. They emphasized a better kind of person, rather than a better kind of society. Naturally there is much overlap between the two.

Marx, Toennies, and Veblen are among those who fought capitalism on behalf of the community, Arnold, Nietzsche, and to some extent Tocqueville among those who fought it in the name of the individual. These six hardly exhaust the forms anti-capitalist theory has taken, in the nineteenth century or since. But their attacks on capitalism, and their alternatives to it, shed special light on the ways in which the war between mind and money has been fought, and have exercised especially great influence.

Of all the modern intellectuals who systematically criticized capitalism and proposed an alternative, the most famous was Karl Marx.

In the Beginning There Was Marx

In the early twenty-first century, it is obvious that Marx and Marxism must be central to a book about the struggle of mind vs. money. This would not have been obvious in 1848, when Marx first published the *Communist Manifesto*. Marx was then only one of a number of socialist writers. The words "socialist" and "socialism" had only recently been invented (they were first used in the1830s, a sign that the honeymoon between mind and money was over). In the 1860s and 1870s Marx became the guru of the socialist movement, and remained so until his death in 1883. But by 1900, Western socialism had largely ceased to be revolutionary, and Marx's ideas were beginning to lose influence. It was by no means clear they would matter to the twentieth century.

They might not have, if World War I and above all the Bolshevik Revolution in Russia, which created a government of self-professed Marxists, had not given them enormous prestige. Since then they have slipped towards oblivion on numerous occasions, only to be revived by events like the Great Depression of the 1930s or the upheavals of the 1960s. Given the ongoing conflict between mind and money, Marx may again return from the abyss into which the collapse of the Soviet Union flung him.

Why is it that "no other perspective on modern society has persuaded so many people of its ability to find meaning in the chaos of experience"? What has made Marx's influence last is not his brilliance, no greater than that of many less important figures. It is certainly not his originality. He himself acknowledged that some of his most central ideas were borrowed. As for his scientific theories about economics, a now almost forgotten twentieth-century economist described him as a "second-rate neo-Ricardian." Whatever it means to be a "second-rate neo-Ricardian," it is nothing to make one immortal. Marx's historical predictions were also, Max Weber long ago pointed out, almost always wrong.[3]

Yet Marx's influence is not just an enormous mistake. There are powerful reasons for Marx's periodic resurrections. He appeals to intellectuals in part because he exemplifies ALL their classic characteristics and prejudices—he offers something to everyone. In every way, he embodies the intellectual described in the preceding chapters. His works resonate with all the "Don'ts" of the Western intellectual tradition. They use many of the insights of the honeymoon period, too. Above all, they mimic the sinuous, torturous curves of the intellectual psyche, playing on all the different aspects of the intellectual's identity, both social and psychological, described in chapter one.

This is true of Marx's theories, and it is also visible in his writing style and his life. As a pseudo-cleric Marx wrote with a pen dipped in anger, in the tone of moral outrage. It is not for nothing that Marx has been compared to an Old Testament prophet. As a pseudo-aristocrat his contempt for money was not only theoretical: He treated it with a disdain worthy of a duke. His wife Jenny (herself from an aristocratic family) told this story: "Jenny's mother had given them some money for their honeymoon and they took it with them, in a chest. They had it with them in the coach during their journey and took it into the different hotels. When they had visits from needy friends they left it open on the table in their room and anyone could take as much as he pleased. Needless to say, it was soon empty."[4] Throughout his life, Marx aristocratically refused to take up any kind of regular employment or live within his means, means aristocratically acquired largely by gift, inheritance, or subsidy from his wealthy friend and collaborator, Friedrich Engels. As a bohemian, Marx's life would not have been out of place in Murger's *Scenes de la vie de Bohème*. A Prussian government spy, reporting on his lifestyle in London, wrote:

> He leads a real gypsy existence. Washing, grooming and changing his linen are things he does rarely, and he is often drunk. Though he is often idle for days on end, he will work day and night with tireless endurance when he has a great deal of work to do. He has no fixed times for going to sleep and waking up. He often stays up all night, and then lies down fully clothed on the sofa at midday and sleeps till evening, untroubled by the whole world coming and going through the room.[5]

Marx also incarnated the latest form of intellectual life. He had a Ph.D. in philosophy from the University of Jena, and studied at the University of Berlin, the leading educational institution in Germany.

By themselves these traits would not have been enough to make Marx the leading figure of a century of Western thought and politics. At most, they would have made him popular with a few intellectuals. Why was he so important?

Marx was the greatest over-simplifier of modern times. This is what made the mixture so attractive, and still appeals. The ability to make the complex simple is the mark of genius. It is also a religious trait. It is the clergy's job to explain the divine to humanity; it is the job of the secular clergy to explain the world. Marx did that. Marx's ability to oversimplify at many levels, to present concepts easily digestible by both intellectuals and proletarians, gave his attacks on capitalism tremendous force.[6]

Because Marx and Marxism are so important, they require extended consideration. We will concentrate on three particular aspects of Marx's thought: his view of capitalism, his theory of revolution, and his conception of post-revolutionary society. We will start by examining Marx's attitude towards something at once fundamental to capitalism and less central to the usual picture of Marx: money.

"Money is the jealous god of Israel, beside which no other god may exist. Money abases all the gods of mankind and changes them into commodities.... Money is the alienated essence of man's work and existence; this essence dominates him and he worships it."[7] Marx hated money. He hated it with religious fervor. Money destroyed God, all gods, and made people into devil-worshipers. Money destroyed all real value, everything human and natural that ought to be valued. Money turned truth into lies, and black into white:

> *money* transforms the *real essential powers of man and nature* into what are merely abstract concepts and therefore *imperfections*—into tormenting chimeras- just as it transforms *real imperfections and chimeras...* into *real powers* and *faculties...* .[money] transforms fidelity into infidelity, love into hate, hate into love, virtue into vice, vice into virtue, servant into master, master into servant, idiocy into intelligence and intelligence into idiocy.[8]

Money can do anything, yet it is an illusion, a chimera. Money gets this power because we give it to it. We do things not to satisfy our needs, but just to get more money. Money makes us think our needs are less important than our bank balance. The more money you do not spend on your needs, the more you have. Invented to make the satisfaction of needs easier, money becomes a reason not to satisfy them: "The less you eat, drink, buy books... the more you will be able to save and the greater will become your... capital. The less you are, the less you express your life, the more [money] you have...." This is what Aristotle called chrematistic—the pursuit of money for its own sake (see chapter 2). Why do we produce things? Not because we or others need them, but in order to get more money. When that is why we produce, buy and sell, we become slaves of the market.[9]

Once people produce commodities only to get money, the commodities become what Marx calls "fetishes," because like magical objects

(Marx had the anthropological, not sexual meaning of "fetish" in mind) they are human creations that people endow with life and powers. "Commodity fetishism" means that human beings make handbags and then worship Gucci. Brands are magic. But before (and after) people made brand-names into fetishes, they had already made money into a fetish, indeed a god.[10]

Because of money, the economic system and the individuals who make it work have ceased to be fully human, in Marx's view. Money is the great dehumanizer. At the origin of commercial society is the dehumanization of what ought to be under human control—all because of money. We have replaced the community that built Babel with the marketplace. The building of a tower to reach Heaven was a project under the control of human beings. By contrast, the market is controlled by no one, rather, it controls us all. By setting commerce free, the community has become enslaved to the market. Money has destroyed the community. We will need a revolution to put commerce back in its subordinate place.[11]

One aspect of Marx's discussion of money merits a special digression. This is the link Marx makes between money and Jews. Marx, born of parents who converted from Judaism to Christianity and baptized as a child, strongly identified Jews and money. "What is the worldly cult of the Jew? *Huckstering.* What is his worldly god? *Money.*" In Marx's view the Christian world has taken over and spread this Jewish cult, but if Christianity has become the carrier of this Jewish disease, the Jews have not been slow to help it along: "We discern in Judaism,… a universal *antisocial* element of the *present* time, whose historical development, zealously aided in its harmful aspects by the Jews, has now attained its culminating point,…." As those most devoted to money, it is only appropriate that the Jews have no state, no political community, since cash and community are natural opposites.[12]

The connections between Jews and money made by Marx were also made by other anti-capitalist intellectuals, and furthermore had deep Christian roots. They were not invented by Marx, or necessarily typical of later Marxists. Marx's essay "On the Jewish Question" was not his most famous work. The point is not to convict Marx or Marxists of anti-Semitism. It is to show how anti-Semitism could gain strength from anti-capitalist ideas, and become an episode in the struggle of mind vs. money. The German Socialist leader August Bebel, one of Marx's correspondents, remarked that "anti-Semitism is the socialism of fools." However Bebel, who wrote before the Nazis, missed the point of his own remark. He thought what mattered was that anti-Semites were fools. What really mattered, in hindsight, was that anti-Semitism *could* be a form of socialism. Anti-capitalism is the anti-Semitism of foolish intellectuals.

Marx blamed Judaism, and its heir, Christianity, for spreading the gospel of wealth. But where a medieval priest would have called on his congregation to give up the worship of Mammon and return to God, Marx calls on humanity to give up both God and Mammon as illusions and make a revolution. Furthermore, Marx the prophet, or Marx the scientist, tells us why revolution is inevitable, how it will be made, and who will make it. There is something for everyone.

Paradoxically (or dialectically), the revolution will be based on capitalism's accomplishments. What makes Marx stand out from most anti-capitalist thinkers, before or since, is his *approval* of capitalism *as a means* of getting humanity to where he wants it to go, a place it has never been before. His view is akin to St. Augustine's exclamation "felix culpa," "lucky mistake," when speaking of Adam and Eve eating the apple and being expelled from Paradise. Because they fell, Christ came and redeemed us. Because capitalism has revolutionized the world, the Revolution will come and we will be redeemed. Part of Marx's genius is his partial acceptance of the pro-commercial arguments of the eighteenth century. He believes in material progress, a notion foreign to Aristotle, inherited from the honeymoon between mind and money. By creating material abundance, capitalism prepares the way for the future. "There'll be pie in the sky, bye and bye, it's a lie," sang an American anarchist group of the late nineteenth century, the International Workers of the World. They were denying that the meek would inherit the earth after they died, as the Christian preachers said. But Marx said just that, although turned upside down and secularized. There will be pie for the poor. Pie made by capitalism, but delivered by the revolution. Marx sees capitalism as the springboard to heaven. It is only because we have created money, private property, steam-engines and all the rest that we possess the "inexhaustible productive powers of modern industry" which alone make possible a decent society.[13]

But Marx rejects capitalism[14] on both moral and economic grounds. Although it is impossible for any reader to ignore the moral tone of Marx's argument, Marx himself, at least the later Marx, always denied that he made moral arguments. He was a scientist, explaining the laws of history using careful critical discourse, not a clergyman demanding justice. It just so happened that justice was what the laws of history entailed, in the form of the scientifically inevitable proletarian revolution. This coincidence was very fortunate for his appeal, of course. Had Marx's laws of history predicted permanent oppression, very few people would have wanted to be Marxists.

We need a revolution, *and* we know one is coming, because the capitalist economic system makes it inevitable. In the end, it is the economic situation that determines the outcome of everything for Marx. Politics, religion, ideas, art, it all comes down to the way in which production is structured. Capitalism won't disappear because it is inhuman. It will disappear because in the long run its economic consequences are disastrous. Ultimately, falling rates of profit due to ever-increasing competition will make it impossible to keep production going on a commercial basis. We shall have to abolish capitalism or starve to death. Marx is an economic determinist. He believes that economic facts in the end determine the results of all social, political and even intellectual questions. It is the capitalist economy which will make its own revolutionary destruction inevitable.

Before describing Marx's theory of revolution and revolutionaries, however, a word about how intellectuals respond to its economic basis is in order. Economic determinism has always made many intellectuals uncomfortable, while at the same time providing them with psychological reassurance. It makes them uncomfortable because of the limits it places on their autonomy. It reassures them because they know that with the help of Marx's economic theories they can prove not only that they are morally right, but that they will win. Marx's economics proved that capitalism cannot survive. The proof was no proof, and it is not worth repeating. But it had power in its time—and still does.

"What the bourgeoisie, therefore, produces, above all, is its own gravediggers. Its fall and the victory of the proletariat are equally inevitable." Marx's economics do not merely predict revolution, they predict who will make it, and against whom. Marx thinks that history is the history of class struggles between different economic interest groups. In the modern world, the struggle is between the bourgeoisie and the proletariat. The bourgeois, of course, are the villains. The revolutionary heroes are the proletarians, the factory workers.[15]

After Marx, the proletariat will become the heroes of much anti-capitalist theory and literature. The proletarians are the new Chosen People. They replace the old one. In many ways the Jews for Marx are not the Antichrist, but the Antiproletariat. Like the proletariat, the Jews are exclusively concerned with material things, the Jews by choice, the proletariat out of necessity. Like the proletariat in Marx's view, the Jews have no nation. As the proletariat will one day, the Jews have taken over the world. The proletariat is to the bourgeoisie as Christianity is to Juda-ism. Except, of course, that the proletariat changes things for the better instead of spreading the commercial disease. The proletariat is a universal class, one which virtually everyone, Jew and Gentile, will eventually be forced to join by capitalism. They are the new bearers of a universal message of good tidings—the revolution is coming.

Marx's choice of the proletariat as heroes seems less inevitable than his choice of the bourgeoisie as villain. In some of his earliest writings he gave the heroic role to the press, praising journalists in terms later transferred to factory workers. An early description of the proletariat looks like a description of the intellectuals described in chapter one: "A class must be formed which has radical chains, a class in civil society which is not a class of civil society [the intellectuals!], a class which is the dis-solution of all classes [ditto], a sphere of society which has a universal character because its sufferings are universal [less true, but intellectuals like to think so], and which does not claim a particular redress because the wrong which is done to it is not a particular wrong but wrong in general [a typical intellectual's moral claim]." Marx is only one of many intellectuals, bohemians and academics alike, to project the intellectual's traits, and griefs, onto the proletariat—and thus find a way out of their isolation. The need to overcome isolation by joining the masses might have been strengthened in Marx's case by his situation as an ethnic Jew and a political exile.[16]

The nineteenth-century proletariat certainly had reason to be unhappy, and capitalism was then making more people into factory workers ev-ery year. Thus the inevitable revolution had more and more inevitable revolutionaries around to make revolutions. The economy is what matters—yet according to Marx, the way to the workers' paradise lies through their heads as much as their hands. For the revolution to occur, workers need to unite. Union struggles for better pay will bring them together, but this is not enough. Workers should fight for pay raises, but they must understand them as a step towards the revolution, not an end in themselves. This is a matter of consciousness, not material fact—the pay raise is the same either way. Marx is an economic determinist, but he is still an intellectual. In order for the proletariat to make their revo-lution, they have to become *conscious* that a revolution is needed, and that they are the ones to make it. Capitalism will create the conditions necessary for the proletariat to become conscious of its revolutionary role. But consciousness is something that must be created by people. It is not automatic. If you don't want the revolution, it doesn't happen. In the meantime, Marx's political advice, like that of any professor, is more often to raise consciousness than to raise barricades.[17]

He is also a Protestant preacher. The class-consciousness of the revolutionary is Marx's equivalent for the faith of a Christian. It is Marx's equivalent of Luther's doctrine of salvation by faith alone. Marx, however, is more optimistic than Luther. Luther does not think that everyone will attain faith, and not everyone will be saved. Marx thinks that in the long run the proletariat will become conscious of its situation, and then the revolution will occur and everyone will enter paradise.

Who then is to play the role of consciousness-raiser for the proletariat? Who will lead the revolutionaries? Leninist theorizing about a "vanguard party" and the creation of Communism with a capital "C" is a response to this question (see chapter 6). Other answers have led to everything from Anarchism to Syndicalism and even Surrealism. From the perspective of this book, the answer to the question is obvious, or ought to be—the intellectuals should to be the Guardians of the proletariat's conscience, to mix Greek and Christian metaphors in a manner wholly appropriate for Marx. Marx's own response is more complicated and less explicit. In his early works he claims a guiding role for himself and other left-wing intellectuals. "In [the Reformation] the revolution originated in the brain of a monk, today in the brain of the philosopher... our status quo—will be shattered by philosophy." A nice example of the intellectual stepping into the clergyman's shoes! The proletariat will be the material base of the revolution, but also its "passive element," directed by the intellectuals.[18]

However, the mature Marx does not think that philosophers, or intellectuals in general, are an independent class. Since, in his over-simplifying way, he defines class exclusively by relationship to the means of production, he cannot see intellectuals as anything but a kind of bourgeois. They must serve the ruling class. Intellectuals are the "ideologists, who make the perfecting of the illusion of the class about itself their chief source of livelihood...." So there is no room for intellectuals to play any role except that of sycophants.[19]

But not all intellectuals. Marx, after all, needs a way of explaining himself:

> Finally, in times when the class struggle nears the decisive hour,... a small section of the ruling class cuts itself adrift, and joins the revolutionary class.... a portion of the bourgeoisie goes over to the proletariat, and in particular, a portion of the bourgeois ideologists, who have raised themselves to the level of comprehending theoretically the historical movement as a whole.[20]

For Marx, the struggle of mind vs. money is waged by "a portion of the bourgeois ideologists," along with the proletariat. The communists are the leaders of the proletariat. But are these communists intellectuals? In his later work Marx claims that "the emancipation of the working class must be the work of the working class itself." They cannot be freed by "philanthropic bourgeois," e.g., well-disposed intellectuals. But this does not really answer the question either, since in Marx's terms a philosopher-elite would have gone over to the proletariat, and ceased to be bourgeois. All we can say is that Marx, unlike Mao, never told intellectuals to go work in factories to learn from the workers. Rather, he told workers to read. He left the way open for his fellow intellectuals either to assume the leadership of the proletariat, or to subordinate themselves to the new ruling class that would abolish all classes, or some combination of the above. He allowed intellectuals to act as a pseudo-aristocracy, *and* to wholly identify themselves with the masses—another way in which he appealed to intellectuals of every stripe.[21]

Marx's theories show why capitalism is bad, why it will end in revolution, why the proletariat will make that revolution. And how will things work afterwards? Marx's vision of the future communist society stresses its rationality. The capitalist economy is irrational, guided by an Invisible Hand. We cannot see how it works. Supply and demand are never constant, they are always changing, always variable. They represent chaos. For Smith, the mechanism of the market is there to providentially bring order out of chaos. But for Marx, such an invisible, unpredictable God is not acceptable. This "all-round dependence, this natural form of the world-historical cooperation of individuals, will be transformed by [the] communist revolution into the control and conscious mastery of these powers,...." Reason, controlled by people, must replace an irrational market which people create but do not control. Marx wanted to see his God. Reason compelled a market made flesh and put under human control. Marx was a Christian despite himself, one might say. In his hatred of the irrational, Marx was seamlessly united with many of his fellow intellectuals. His combination of rationalism and anti-capitalism was an important source of his influence.[22]

Reason would be made flesh and turned into action through the community, that is through politics and association. For Marx, the political community is the equivalent of heaven—almost literally. "The political state, in relation to civil society, is as spiritual as heaven in relation to earth." The individual human being for Marx is always a political animal, who can thrive only in association with others. "Only in community [with others has each] individual the means of cultivating his gifts in all directions; only in the community, therefore, is personal freedom possible." Politics is not just a means to private ends. It is the essence of being human.[23]

For Marx, the ideal form of politics is not the state, which he famously predicted would wither away, but free association. In emphasizing association, as in so many things, Marx was hardly original. Many nineteenth-century intellectuals saw associations as the salvation of modern democratic society. The obvious example is Tocqueville, who saw in American associations the democratic replacement for a vanished aristocracy. Like Tocqueville, and in contrast to most of his followers, Marx praises the decentralized state, a state with "few but important functions," in which "the old centralized government would in the provinces, too, have to give way to the self-government of the producers." These producers would form "united co-operative societies" which would rationally "regulate national production under a common plan."[24]

In this politicized world, what shall we do, besides go to political meetings? Work!

Marx identifies work with creativity. Before the revolution, work is bad. Capitalism degrades work into a means to an end, a way to make money. Because working is not the worker's free choice, he is unhappy and coerced, and he hates work, for "it belongs to another, it is the loss of his self." Thus his work is alien to him and he is an alienated worker. This "alienation" is independent from how much the worker is paid. Even if all wages were equal, and high, the worker would still be alienated. You cannot buy someone's time without creating alienation. Work, to be meaningful, to be human, to be free, must be completely autonomous. Hired labor, working *for* someone else, is not autonomous, so it is a bad thing. All labor under capitalism is alienated labor for Marx. This applies equally to executives, even if they do not suffer from the physical effects of low wages or unemployment. Everyone has "become more and more enslaved under a power alien to them… a power which has become more and more enormous and, in the last instance, turns out to be the *world market*." If the word "globalization" had been invented, Marx would have used it. *Everyone* is enslaved to its demands. Commerce, globalization, destroys everyone's work autonomy. It makes it impossible to be a free worker or a free intellectual, or even a free entrepreneur.[25]

Work in capitalism is not only alienated, it is highly specialized, ever more so as the world becomes more industrialized. Specialization is inevitable. Marx praises the improved production, but condemns its effect on the producers. Rather than producing freedom, machinery restricts the worker to an ever-narrowing set of skills and tasks. Instead of increased production along with increased efficiency leading to increased freedom and free time, in capitalism there is "that remarkable phenomenon in the history of Modern Industry, that machinery sweeps away every moral and natural restraint on the length of the working-day."[26]

But work itself is good. And after the revolution it will be very good. In *Capital* Marx praises child labor. Not the 12-14 hour a day drudgery of the cotton mills, of course, but Robert Owen's suggestion that in future the education "of every child over a given age" will "combine productive labor with instruction and gymnastics, not only as one of the methods of adding to the efficiency of production, but as the only method of producing fully developed human beings." Life's purpose is work, but only work produced without any outside pressure, even the need to eat: "In fact, the realm of freedom actually begins only where labor which is determined by necessity and mundane considerations ceases...." What makes the human species unique is that "man produces even when he is free from physical need and only truly produces in freedom therefrom."[27] After the Revolution all work will be, in effect, a kind of art, and everyone will be free to do every kind of art, without having to become a professional at it. A Bohemian paradise!

> In communist society, where nobody has one exclusive sphere of activity but each can become accomplished in any branch he wishes, society regulates the general production and thus makes it possible for me to do one thing today and another tomorrow, to hunt in the morning, fish in the afternoon, rear cattle in the evening, criticise after dinner, just as I have a mind, without ever becoming hunter, fisherman, shepherd or critic.[28]

Marx thus universalizes the intellectual's bohemian attitude, with its insistence on autonomy. Indeed, it is hard to imagine a more intellectual or aristocratic attitude towards work. "In aristocracies it is not exactly work itself which is despised, but work with an idea to profit. Work is glorious when inspired by ambition or pure virtue," wrote Tocqueville.[29]

This new kind of work will only be possible when the community, the "associated producers," rationally control production in order to give people time for work that does not produce anything material. For this "true realm of freedom," "the shortening of the working day is its basic prerequisite." Thus the demand for the 8-hour day is theoretically grounded in Bohemia's demand for individual autonomy. Can one imagine a program better suited to appeal to both intellectuals and proletarians?[30]

And appeal it certainly did. To speak only of the intellectuals, by appealing to so many facets of their identity, by suggesting so many appealing strategies, Marx made himself an indispensable reference in intellectuals' struggle against capitalism. His vision of proletarian revolution as the alternative to capitalism became the pre-eminent anti-capitalist vision of the world. His ideas became the most widely-used weapons in the war between mind and money. The word "Marxist," despite Marx's own declaration "I am not a Marxist," became shorthand for anti-capitalist. Those who wanted to oppose capitalism without adopting a Marxist viewpoint had to explain why they were NOT Marxists.

But Marx and Marxists were by no means the only anti-capitalist theorists of the nineteenth century who defended the community against the ravages of commerce. One author who emphasized the moral roots of his rejection of capitalism was Ferdinand Toennies.

The Moral Community: Toennies

Ferdinand Toennies (1855-1936) is the first genuine academic discussed in this book (Marx had a Ph.D., but never taught at a university). Toennies' enormous influence on Western political thought has never been adequately acknowledged. Perhaps this is because he taught at the not-very-renowned University of Kiel, near the farm where he had been brought up. He was known for a single book, and essentially for the contrast that appears in the title. In German the work is called *Gemeinschaft und Gesellschaft*, and it has been translated as *Community and Civil Society* or simply *Community and Society*. The translations of the title are accurate, but need explanation. *Gemeinschaft* means community. But *Gesellschaft* does not only mean "civil society," which in its broadest sense is everything outside the state. *Gesellschaft* also means a company, or more strictly a corporation owned by stockholders. It thus is strongly associated with commerce. Toennies' book is based on the existence of a fundamental opposition between *Gemeinschaft* and *Gesellschaft*, and the idea that Western society is evolving away from community towards commercial society. This contrast has been taken up by a host of people since, on every part of the political spectrum. Toennies' influence on twentieth-century thought is probably second only to that of Marx, but he is much less well-known.[31]

What is the difference between community and society? Community is based on the family, the village and the town. It is idyllic. "Family life = concord," according to Toennies, and the household is founded on "nurturing, creating and preserving," its members. The community's economy is agricultural and follows a routine that requires cooperation. Work there is based on a combination of tradition and innovation. Toennies associates all the cuddly, warm, fuzzy feelings with community.[32]

The big city, on the other hand, epitomizes Toennies' vision of "society." Urban life is centered on "the individual human being with all his ambitions. Its core is competitive market society...." "In the big city,... family life is in decline. What remains of it must appear increasingly incidental the more the influence of the cities is brought to bear. In this context, few people will confine their energies to so narrow a circle as the family. Everyone is drawn to the outside, and away from each other, by business, private interests, and amusements." The city's economy is capitalist. In capitalism, contracts replace morality. Societies produce more goods, but less happiness, than communities.[33]

Toennies' book is devoted to exploring the contrasts between community and society. Community is genuine, society is superficial. Community is a living thing, society is a mechanical artifact. In communities, guilds and all other forms of economic life form "a religious community," and thus spirit and flesh are happily combined. Toennies always stresses that the community, which is humanity's original state, is naturally harmonious, while society is full of strife.[34]

For Toennies, commerce is completely incompatible with community. "It would sound quite revolting to make the linguistic compound 'joint-stock community.'" His view of commerce is that it is a zero-sum game, in which for every winner there is a loser, and in the end the community is destroyed and replaced by competitive individualism. Competition, not cooperation, is the essence of commerce: "Harm to one means profit to another.... This is the essence of general competition...." Commerce destroys the community's values and replaces them with wealth. This can be seen in what it does to art: "All creative, productive activity of mankind is a kind of art.... When this serves to maintain, promote, or give pleasure to the community,... it can be understood as an intrinsic function of the community.... *Commerce*, the skill of making a profit, is the opposite of all such art. Profit is not value [*Wert*], it is just an alteration in the distribution of wealth: a plus for one means a minus for the other." Commerce is what causes the transition from community to society.[35]

If commerce is incompatible with community, this means it is incompatible with happiness. Again and again Toennies comes back to the point that society transforms us all into isolated individuals at war with one another. For Toennies, individualism means pure selfishness: "everyone is out for himself alone and living in a state of tensions against everyone else...." Like Marx, who influenced him, Toennies sees the first merchant as the first free man, autonomous from the community. Like Marx, he thinks this development is a disaster: "The merchant is the first reflective and *free* human being.... He is free from the ties of community life, and the freer he is, the better it is for him," but the worse for the community he no longer serves or belongs to. The merchant's gain is the community's loss (once again Adam Smith is turned upside down).[36]

What distinguishes Toennies from Marx is that he has almost nothing positive to say about capitalism. Despite the academic compulsion to evenhandedness, capitalism rarely benefited from it after 1870 or so. Another way in which Toennies is a typical figure is his attitude to his own class, intellectuals. Marx is ambivalent about intellectuals; he expresses his self-contempt in other directions. Toennies despises them. According to Toennies, intellectuals have all the vices of society and none of the morality and warmth of the community. The search for knowledge "even in its purest form is still an offshoot of and a type of vanity." The "educated, enlightened classes" don't feel shame, and they lack a conscience.[37] Intellectuals stand apart, and the democratic Toennies cannot accept their aristocratic behavior. As a result, he offers them the supreme insult. He compares them to merchants:

> Among the *educated*,...the family becomes an accidental form for the satisfaction of natural needs, while neighbors and friends are replaced by special interest groups and conventional socialising. The life of the common people finds its fulfillment in home, village and town [i.e., community]; whereas educated people are metropolitan, national, international [i.e., society]. To expand these contrasts more fully, only one point needs to be stressed. In any autochthonous home-based culture, *commerce* is an alien phenomenon not much liked. The trader combines all the typical characteristics of the man with an education...."[38]

The parallels continue for some time, rubbing in the insult—educated people are like merchants in many ways.[39]

What then is Toennies' solution to the problems of modern life? The alternative to society is obviously community. But Toennies does not tell us how to attain community. He has no program and no Utopian plan. He is a pessimist. The development of the community leads naturally to market society, which naturally destroys community and replaces it with society. Socialism is coming, but represents no improvement, because the proletarians have "become active members of competitive market society, and settle for the same ways of thinking and behaving." Indeed the world as we know it is coming to an end, which may be its only salvation: "The entire culture has been overturned by a civilization dominated by market and civil Society, and in this transformation civilization itself is coming to an end; unless it be that some of its scattered seeds remain alive, so that the essential concepts of Community may be encouraged once again and a new civilization can develop secretly within the one that is dying."[40]

There are a few optimistic notes like this here and there. Toennies was a partisan of the cooperative movement, and in a footnote added in 1912 wrote "it is clear that a principle of communitarian-style economy has acquired a new lease of life…. it is capable of development of the highest significance." In 1922, after World War I, he added that the demand for "Community has grown louder and louder, very often with explicit or (as in the case of British Guild Socialism) tacit reference to this book." Toennies' work is particularly important because of the influence it has had on both left- and right-wing anti-capitalists.

Toennies opposed the Nazis. He joined the German Socialist party in 1932 in order to express his opposition. As a result, he was stripped of his pension and title of professor emeritus when Hitler took power in 1933. Nevertheless, in 1935 the Nazis allowed a conference devoted to his work to be held in honor of his 80th birthday—many Nazis saw the Third Reich as a revival of Community (see chapter 6).[41]

The idea that modern society is dying, and that something new and better, but still hidden, is coming soon, was widespread in late nineteenth and early twentieth-century Europe. It had optimistic variations, such as Marxism, for which the future was already more than half born, and hardly hidden. Thinkers more romantic or less sure of themselves than Marx were less clear about what was coming—but they hoped devoutly that it was coming soon. These thinkers, like Toennies, appealed for something, anything, to bring capitalism to an end. Toennies' contrast between Community and Society was taken up by others in many forms (one common form in Germany was to contrast "Culture," i.e., community, with "Civilisation," i.e., society). Toennies' disciples varied between outright pessimism and occasional optimism. The optimism often had esoteric, aristocratic elements, based on knowledge of the future reserved for an intellectual or spiritual elite. The one thing they all had in common was rejection of capitalism. They were all convinced that there *must* be an alternative to capitalism, and we *must* find a way to get there. The intellectuals' imperative is categorical.

Toennies, in contrast to Marx, emphasizes the moral limitations on production necessary to preserve community. But Marx was not the only nineteenth-century communitarian to believe that increased productivity was a necessity both economic and moral. Thorstein Veblen joined Marx in opposing capitalism not because it produced too much too quickly, but because it worked too slowly and inefficiently.

The Protestant Critique of Capitalism: Veblen

Veblen (1857-1929) was morally repelled by capitalism, but on very different grounds than Toennies. He was not looking for ways to limit materialism. Like Marx, for whom he displayed a mixture of admiration and contempt, Veblen criticized capitalism for limiting production, not for encouraging it. The son of Norwegian immigrants to America, he translated Norse sagas and maintained a life-long interest in Protestant theology despite personal agnosticism. By profession he was an economist who taught at a number of American universities. There is no better example of Protestant critique of capitalism than Veblen's *The Theory of the Leisure Class*, published in 1899. In it Veblen gave the world the phrase "conspicuous consumption."[42]

Veblen loved productive work, and hated waste. He appealed to what he called "the instinct of workmanship," which "disposes men to look with favor upon productive efficiency and on whatever is of human use. It disposes them to deprecate waste of substance or effort." Under modern conditions, an economy based on trade and commerce was inherently wasteful. People competed for status not by producing more, but by showing off their ability to consume—hence conspicuous consumption "a conspicuous waste of time and substance and a withdrawal from the industrial process." The upper classes in capitalism used conspicuous consumption to show off their wealth. They did not work as hard as others, and they produced less. Nothing could be more contemptible from Veblen's perspective.[43]

But it was not just through individual wastefulness that capitalism incurred Veblen's ire. Capitalism prevented, indeed "sabotaged," the efficient organization of production, because profit, not production, was its purpose. Like Marx, Veblen suggested that full production and employment are impossible to combine with profits in a developed industrial economy under capitalism. But Veblen insisted that maximum production of needed goods was the only proper economic goal. He criticized Ruskin and Morris for preferring inefficient archaic technologies, just as he criticized factory-owners for not fully utilizing their machinery. Veblen was a productivity-minded Calvinist, smiting the lazy and the inefficient right and left.[44]

Capitalist immorality was directly related to capitalist inefficiency. As Veblen put it:

The collective interests of any modern community center in industrial efficiency....
This collective interest is best served by honesty, diligence, peacefulness, goodwill, an
absence of self-seeking.... On the other hand the immediate interest of the individual
under the competitive regime is best served by shrewd trading and unscrupulous management. The characteristics named above as serving the interest of the community
are disserviceable to the individual, rather than otherwise.[45]

Veblen concludes that "the greater the number and the higher the profi-
ciency of the community's businessmen, other things equal, the worse
must the rest of the community come off...." The basic problem is that
"business is occupied with the competitive acquisition of wealth, not
with its production," and the same is true of the businessman as an
individual.[46]

What was Veblen's alternative? For Veblen, as his admirer, the distinguished American sociologist David Riesman, put it, "good could never
come from evil"—so much for Adam Smith and the Invisible Hand.
Veblen's Protestant critique of capitalism rejected commercial society on individual *and* communitarian, moral *and* utilitarian grounds.
Any alternative to it had to be based on a different kind of individual,
someone with good intentions, living in a different economic system,
which was more concerned with production than profit. Veblen found
the people he needed to run the new world in those whom he called
the "general staff of industry," the "production engineers." Industry
ought to be controlled by "suitably trained technological experts...
without a commercial interest." Only in this way would production,
not profit, be the goal of the economic system, pursued by engineers
whose prowess was demonstrated by their ability to produce, not to
consume.[47]

Veblen was one of the early proponents of technocracy as an alternative to capitalism. On the other hand, Veblen's faith was not always
placed in technocrats. In a deviation from his Calvinist norm, his book
on American higher education placed "idle curiosity" alongside the
"instinct of workmanship" as a useful human trait. Provided universities had nothing to do with commerce or business, provided they were
strictly research institutions, they met with Veblen's approval. The separation of commerce and learning ought to be absolute. The only proper
response to someone who wanted to find a commercially useful purpose
for a university was Benjamin Franklin's remark, "What is the use of
a baby?" Indeed, remarked Veblen, "work that has a commercial value
does not belong in the university." This gesture towards the scholar as
cloistered monk, cut off from the sinful concerns of commerce, seems
to contradict Veblen's emphasis on productivity, but the contradiction is

apparent, not real. Veblen's academics, like his engineers, do work that is not oriented towards profit.[48]

Veblen's revolution is to be made by a general strike of the engineers, backed up by the skilled laborers. His revolution is one that is made in the name of the community's production, and for its benefit. But technocracy is cold comfort. Perhaps that is why his Protestant criticism of the leisure class is what has usually appealed to readers. Veblen is the Viking turned moralist. Once his work of destruction is done, he is ready to sail on.

Sweetness and Light, Sturm und Drang: Arnold and Nietzsche

The alternatives to capitalism proposed by Matthew Arnold and Friedrich Nietzsche were based less on creating a new community than on encouraging a certain kind of personality. Arnold's and Nietzsche's hostility to capitalism emphasizes the damage it does to the individual, the crippling restraints it imposes on autonomy and creativity. Capitalism cripples individuals who often look suspiciously like intellectuals.

In examining the writings of Arnold and Nietzsche, we are turning to writers who are less academic and more literary. Their attitude to capitalism is also more strictly bohemian. It places more emphasis on the autonomous individual, and on intellectual and cultural repugnance for the businessman, than we have seen since the last chapter. This is one reason to treat Arnold, the apostle of "sweetness and light," and Nietzsche, the champion of the "superman" who embodies storm and thunder, (*Sturm und Drang*) together. Their ideals are both highly aristocratic. At first glance, Arnold appears less radical than Nietzsche, but appearances can be deceiving.

Matthew Arnold (1822-1888) was a social theorist, but his academic position was not a university one. This was largely due to the nature of the contemporary British university system, which would have been able to find a place for him only as a poet, which he also was. He demonstrates in his person the essential unity of bohemia and academia. But his career is also significant because his livelihood came from a source that did not exist a few decades previously. He was an inspector of schools, charged with evaluating the success of publicly-funded educational establishments in England. This was the kind of job which enabled the intellectual class to grow in numbers and autonomy.

Arnold's major theoretical work, *Culture and Anarchy*, was published in 1869. In it he divides society into three groups, the "Barbarians," the "Philistines," and the "Populace," his equivalents for the more familiar aristocracy, middle class, and working class. The Philistines of the Bible are the great heathen nation that contends with the Jews for the domination of Canaan. German university students, in their town vs. gown confrontations, applied the word to the non-academic population of university towns. It was a synonym for bourgeois, with the usual negative connotations.

In Arnold's view, nineteenth-century Britain is dominated by philistines. Only the "residuum," the very poor, are outside the Pale of philistinism. Philistine attitudes lead to a world in which "trade, business, and population,—are mechanically pursued by us as ends in themselves, and are worshiped as what we call fetishes;...." Marx and Arnold both talk about fetishes when it comes to capitalism. Perhaps it is an example of what Freud called projection, when we see in others or in the outside world what we have repressed in ourselves. Intellectuals see the religious/magical element in others' pursuit of money, while refusing to recognize the religious element in their condemnation of commerce. Arnold, however, does dimly recognize the religious nature of his adoration of sweetness and light (see below).[49]

What Arnold objects to in the philistines is not their economic methods, but their goals. Arnold wonders why "we fix on some object, which in this case is the production of wealth, and the increase of manufactures, population, and commerce through free-trade, as a kind of one thing needful, or end in itself." Trade, business, etc., become ends instead of means. Arnold does not reject commerce entirely, but it should not be our purpose in life. "Now, culture admits the necessity of the movement towards fortune-making and exaggerated industrialism, readily allows that the future may derive benefit from it; but insists, at the same time, that the passing generations of industrialists,—forming, for the most part, the stout main body of Philistinism,—are sacrificed to it."[50]

Arnold's alternative to commerce is "culture." Culture and commerce, under various synonyms such as "anarchy," are the great opposites in Arnold's thought, as mind and money are in this book. For Arnold, philistines want to get rich, but "culture...helps us...to regard wealth as but machinery...." Culture says most wealthy people are not the kind of people we should be: "Would any amount of wealth be worth having with the condition that one was to become just like these people by having it? And thus culture begets a dissatisfaction which is of the highest possible value in stemming the common tide of men's thoughts in a wealthy and industrial community...." Perfection is an "inward condition." How do we attain perfection? By cultivating "sweetness and light," which Arnold identifies as beauty and intelligence, through culture. "If it were not for this purging effect wrought upon our minds by culture, the whole world, the future as well as the present, would inevitably belong to the Philistines."[51]

Any definition of perfection is based on a value judgment. Who should make it? According to Arnold, we need to find "a source of authority" for the ranking of values—as we will see below, he comes very close to Nietzsche here. Who will this source be? Arnold is too modest to say, but clearly it is the intellectuals. He knows that he and his fellows are not philistines, and not barbarians or populace either. They are something else, something alien to all the traditional classes. "Therefore, when we speak of ourselves as divided into Barbarians, Philistines and Populace, we must be understood always to imply that within each of these classes there are a certain number of *aliens*, if we may so call them,—persons who are mainly led, not by their class spirit, but by a general *humane* spirit, by the love of human perfection...." The aliens who love perfection are the intellectuals, the permanently alienated elite.[52]

In typical intellectual fashion, Arnold is willing to impose his alien judgment on the philistines. That is why he cautiously criticizes the idea of freedom as it is understood in contemporary England: "the very absence of any powerful authority amongst us, and the prevalent doctrine of the duty and happiness of doing as one likes, and asserting our personal liberty, must tend to prevent the erection of any very strict standard of excellence...." Arnold's position in favor of sweetness and light is aristocratic. His rejection of freedom is based on a desire to impose a hierarchy of values. One of the ways intellectuals come to conservatism is to protect intellectual values and hierarchies which they see capitalism undermining. Commerce replaces such hierarchies with the anarchy of the market.[53]

But as opponents of commerce, intellectuals usually share the egalitarian feelings that surround them. Arnold is no exception. He feels both the pseudo-aristocrat's need to connect with the masses, and the democratic shame of being embarrassed by his own elitism. Rather than stand up for his "aliens," he claims to be on the side of the common man—almost. "[Culture] is not satisfied till we *all* come to a perfect man; it knows that the sweetness and light of the few must be imperfect until the raw and unkindled masses of humanity are touched with sweetness and light. If I have not shrunk from saying that we must work for sweetness and light, so neither have I shrunk from saying that we must have a broad basis, must have sweetness and light for as many as possible." But how many are "as many as possible"?[54]

Arnold's search for sweetness and light has a religious ring to it. His critics accused him of proposing a new "religion of culture," but he preferred to present culture as Christianity's co-worker, not its replacement. He suggests that "religion comes to a conclusion identical with that which culture... likewise reaches. Religion says: *The kingdom of God is within you*; and culture, in like manner, places human perfection in an *internal* condition." Arnold forbears to point out that he is replacing perfection as the imitation of Christ with perfection as the pursuit of Reason and Beauty. Instead, he emphasizes their potential cooperation against the philistines. When Arnold has to respond to attacks made on him for promoting a religion of culture, he in turn attacks a society which does not value culture. He upholds his new faith, and passes over the old one in silence. But his real attitude is clear: "how generally, with how many of us, are the main concerns of life limited to these two: the concern for making money, and the concern for saving our souls! And how entirely does the narrow and mechanical conception of our secular business proceed from a narrow and mechanical conception of our religious business!" Arnold couples capitalism with Methodism. There is no salvation from either outside sweetness and light.[55]

Arnold's defense of culture against capitalism was aristocratic, but embarrassed. He was reluctant to proclaim his distaste for either democracy or Christianity. By contrast, Nietzsche's defense of the intellectual was uninhibited. He was openly aristocratic, upholding the superiority of the "philosopher" to the "herd." His criticism of capitalism owed nothing to the Democratic or Christian Don'ts, too egalitarian for him. Nietzsche was a class-conscious intellectual. His alternative to capitalism, insofar as he had one, was to paint a picture not of an alternative society or economic system, but an alternative individual. More than any other thinker of the nineteenth or twentieth century, Nietzsche describes the intellectual, the intellectual's characteristics, social role, and psychology, in ways analogous to those of this work. But Nietzsche's rejection of equality leads him to repulsive views about ordinary people, about women, about "inferiors" of all sorts, the kind of views likely to be expressed by an aristocrat who feels threatened. It also leads him astray in discussing the relation between intellectuals and the rest of society.

For Nietzsche, the problem is not so much that capitalism dehumanizes people, as that capitalism is appropriate for the stupid sots who make up the majority. Nietzsche's criticism of capitalism repeats themes already covered. He didn't like commerce or people who devoted their lives to making money. What did he prefer?

Beauty and brains, like Arnold. Nietzsche's emphasis shifts between them, depending on whether he is talking about art or morals or science. In his view, most people can create neither beautiful new objects nor beautiful new ideas. They can't think, and they don't even care. Nietzsche retains just enough democratic sensibility to be slightly embarrassed by this judgment. "I keep having the same experience and keep resisting it anew each time; I do not want to believe it although I can grasp it as with my hands: *the great majority lacks an intellectual conscience*...." It is hard to believe that most people don't engage in careful critical discourse, in other words, hard to believe that most people can't or won't be intellectuals: "I mean: *to the great majority* it is not contemptible to believe this or that and to live accordingly *without* first becoming aware of the final and most certain reasons pro and con, and without even troubling themselves about such reasons afterwards...."[56]

Nietzsche has only aristocratic contempt for those who lack an intellectual conscience. His problem is that his fellow intellectuals *don't* feel this way. They do not share his contempt, they do not share his willingness to proclaim their class superior. "It is very rare that a higher nature has enough reason left over to understand and treat commonplace people as what they are; above all it believes in its own passion as something that is present in everyone but concealed." How frustrating it must have been for Nietzsche when he met fellow aristocrats who insisted they were commoners just like everyone else. But this is part of the democratic imperative to presume that everyone is equal, Tocqueville would have told Nietzsche. Democratic intellectuals think everyone must have some talent hidden somewhere. Democratic intellectuals often value their own superior knowledge and CCD only as a means to something more democratic, like virtue, or the revolution. For Nietzsche, however, the chief interest the average man has for the "philosopher"—the intellectual, in our terms—is as an object of study.[57]

Nietzsche recognizes the novelty of his position. He knows that "it is something new in history that knowledge wants to be more than a means." Arnold described his call for sweetness and light as a return to an old balance. Nietzsche has no desire for balance, and no desire to conceal that the independent class of intellectuals is new.[58]

What are the values of Nietzsche's new intellectual aristocracy? "The three great slogans of the ascetic ideal are familiar: poverty, humility, chastity." How can these Christian, democratic traits be aristocratic? Because intellectuals have transformed them from Christian virtues into their own tools: "you will always encounter all three to a certain degree.... as the most appropriate and natural conditions of their *best* existence, their *fairest* fruitfulness." Intellectuals judge ideals by what is necessary to their own existence: "They think of what *they* can least do without: freedom from compulsion, disturbance, noise, from tasks, duties, worries...." Then intellectuals must impose their values on the masses. How? With words, of course. *"What things are called* is unspeakably more important than what they are.... But let us not forget that in the long run it is enough to create new names and valuations and appearances of truth in order to create new 'things.'" This is what intellectuals do with CCD. This is the work of supermen. Nietzsche, of course, is known as the apostle of the *Ubermensch*, the superman. The Nazis thought that when he talked about the ruthless strength of such men he was praising physical violence and blond hair. But for Nietzsche the real "blond beast" of modern society is not the tall man with the gun, it is the man with the extraordinary pen and tongue.[59]

Not that Nietzsche wanted the world to be run by German or Swiss professors. Nietzsche had a Ph.D., and taught at the University of Basel. But he did not like the specialization of modern academic life, and he ultimately took a true bohemian's superior attitude to the professors. Here we find an early example of a phenomenon more prominent in the twentieth century than the nineteenth—the family quarrel between academia and bohemia proper. As a good aristocrat, Nietzsche believes in a hierarchy of ranks, even among the aristocrats themselves, and in this order, philosophers and poets rank above scholars. They are related but different. "We are different from scholars, although we are inevitably, among other things, scholarly. We have different needs.... There is no formula for how much a mind needs for its nourishment; but if it has a taste for independence, for quick coming and going, for wandering [the bohemian]... it would rather live free with little food than unfree and stuffed." This is a description of bohemia, written by an academic tired of the business-like obligations of academia. This ultra-bohemian perspective led Nietzsche to rank scholars lower than creative spirits like himself. He goes so far as to say that "a preponderance of mandarins always means something is wrong; so do the advent of democracy, international courts in place of war, equal rights for women, the religion of pity, and whatever other symptoms of declining life there are." Here we see a repulsive side of Nietzsche's rejection of democracy.[60]

Nietzsche is not sure, however, if he wants the world to be run by intellectual aristocrats, or even by bohemian philosophers. He defends the aristocratic individual against the herd. He cannot do this while wanting to be its bull. Nietzsche vacillates on the subject of the role of the super class, the intellectuals. Rulers or recluses? On the whole, Nietzsche prefers to position himself on the outside. In this mood he rejects the idea of a conquering aristocracy in favor of a cloistered, contemplative one. He wants a place for his kind, but it need not, even should not, be a dominant one. *"We others are the exception and the danger*—we stand eternally in need of defense!—Now there is certainly something to be said for the exception, *provided it never wants to become the rule."* Nietzsche does *not* (at least not always) want the supermen to conquer. They just need a safe place, defended from the world, as the world is defended from them. Can mind and money be penned separately?[61]

Schumpeter would later say this is impossible—Money will always end up producing Mind in its midst, because it needs it. Nietzsche says the same thing: "The age loves the mind, it loves and needs us." But Nietzsche does not give the age any credit for this. He does not like to see any connection between intellectuals and democratic society. Only once does he glimpse it: "In Europe the scholar grows out of all kinds of classes and social conditions... thus he belongs, essentially and involuntarily, to the bearers of the democratic idea." But he immediately turns his eyes away from this, to him, unpleasant truth.[62]

For Nietzsche, whether philosopher-kings or philosopher-hermits, the intelligentsia can only establish its position as an aristocracy by overthrowing the current rulers. By the late nineteenth century the remaining obstacles to intellectual hegemony were democracy and the Church. In order to affirm the new secular clergy's pre-eminence, Nietzsche does openly what Arnold does covertly: He declares God dead.

For Nietzsche, religion may be useful, but only if it recognizes its secondary role. "In the end... one always pays dearly and terribly when religions do *not* want to be a means of education and cultivation [the servants of sweetness and light!]... when they themselves want to be ultimate ends and not means...." It is bold of Nietzsche to criticize religion for making God an end and not a means. But Nietzsche is nothing if not bold, and he sees the old clergy as the rival of the new: "The time is past when the Church had a monopoly on contemplation, when the *vita contemplativa* always had to be first and foremost a *vita religiosa."* Nietzsche wants to physically knock down churches and replace them with buildings designed for thinking secular thoughts. Universities, perhaps? Addressing the "seekers of knowledge," he says: "Soon the time will be past in which you had to be content living hidden in forests like shy deer! Finally the search for knowledge will reach for its due; it will want to rule and possess...!"[63]

This is the motivation behind Nietzsche's famous claim that "God is dead." It is the statement of a wish, something intellectuals want and *need* to be true. It is also the statement of a historical fact. The educated classes of late nineteenth-century Europe lived in a secular world in which reference to religion was by courtesy or hypocrisy only. Nietzsche was one of the first to state an open secret—that many intellectuals no longer took traditional religion seriously. "The practical indifference toward religious matters into which he [the scholar] has been born and brought up is generally sublimated in him into caution and cleanliness that shun contact with religious men and matters...."[64]

"God is dead" is a striking way of saying that the modern world is disenchanted, Max Weber's famous argument. What separates Nietzsche from Weber is that Nietzsche is overjoyed that God is dead, because now the intellectuals can inherit His and His ministers' functions: "at hearing the news that 'the old God is dead', we philosophers and 'free spirits' feel illuminated by a new dawn; our heart overflows with gratitude,... every daring of the lover of knowledge is allowed again; the sea, *our* sea, lies open again; maybe there has never been such an 'open sea.'" There are no longer any limits on CCD, any boundaries of authority it must respect.[65]

But Nietzsche does not content himself with saying God is dead. He says that God was murdered. "Where is God?... I'll tell you! *We have killed him*—you and I! We are all his murderers." God has been killed by the secular intellectuals who have expelled him from their world. But in Nietzsche's story no one will listen to the "madman" who says this, and the madman concludes that the news of God's death has still not reached his audience. Society is unaware of it. Even dead, God is a formidable adversary. "After Buddha was dead, they still showed his shadow in a cave for centuries—a tremendous gruesome shadow. God is dead; but given the way people are, there may still for millennia be caves in which they show his shadow. And we—we must still defeat his shadow as well!" This then is the intelligentsia's task—to defeat the shadow of God, and the clergy who display it.[66]

Even Nietzsche was sometimes afraid of this new situation. Most people are *not* intellectuals. They want faith, not CCD. "Christianity, it seems to me, is still needed by most people... hence it still finds believers," he wrote. Nietzsche's "Gay Science" is not for everyone, it is for the spiritually "homeless," the intellectuals. But here is where Nietzsche's work breaks down. His contempt for the world around him shows how far he is from a real aristocratic position, in which each rank acknowledges not just the necessity, but the merit of the others. He cannot discover a satisfactory relation between intellectuals and democracy, or intellectuals and capitalism.[67]

Nietzsche is torn, torn between aristocracy and democracy, torn between religion and atheism, torn between fear and joy. Nietzsche recognizes this internal battle as typical of the intellectual soul: "... today there is perhaps no more decisive mark of a *'higher nature,'* a more spiritual nature, than that of being divided in this sense and a genuine battleground of these opposed values." Intellectuals less class-conscious than Nietzsche—the great majority—frequently turned their conflicting attitudes into a form of self-hatred, as can be seen in the history of intellectuals' relationship with Fascism and Communism (see chapter 6).[68]

Because he is so torn, Nietzsche cannot create a blueprint for an alternative society. All he offered was a moral appeal: "*All* the sciences have from now on to prepare the way for the future task of the philosophers: this task understood as the solution of the *problem of value,* the determination of the *order of rank among values.*" The new clergy must create a new morality; the new aristocracy must find a way to impose it. Nietzsche does not show us how this might happen. What he does say sheds light on what would happen in the next century, when many intellectuals would try and impose a new order of values on a sometimes recalcitrant society. But the desire to replace capitalism's values was already widespread in the nineteenth. Even Alexis de Tocqueville, in many respects a friend of capitalism, felt it.[69]

With a Friend Like This, Who Needs Enemies?—Tocqueville

Alexis de Tocqueville was not a professor, did not possess a Ph.D., and was not fond of bohemians. Was he an intellectual? A French aristocrat, he would have been embarrassed by the question. He was born in 1805, when the intellectual class was barely formed, and died in 1859, when it was just making its presence obvious. He fits most of the criteria of chapter one, however. As in much else, Tocqueville is a borderline figure with regard to membership in the intelligentsia.

If Tocqueville had been asked if he opposed capitalism, he would have said "no." He was a well-known opponent of socialism, and as a member of the French National Assembly gave a speech against including a "right to work" in the French constitution of 1848. He believed private property was "the basis of civilization." Even more importantly, from his point of view, capitalism and freedom were linked. No commercial nation, Tocqueville thought, had ever been anything but free. There was "a hidden relationship between these two words: *freedom* and *commerce*" (emphasis original).[70]

But Tocqueville's support for capitalism was accompanied by disdain for capitalists, and a deep suspicion of capitalism's social and moral consequences. Tocqueville's objections to a large extent repeated the themes covered in the last chapter. Despite the support Tocqueville voiced for capitalism as the mother of freedom, it is easy to imagine one of Dickens' heroes in *Hard Times* uttering this sentiment from *Democracy in America*: "I believe that the manufacturing aristocracy that we see rising before our eyes is one of the harshest that has ever existed on earth." It would have made a good motto for Dickens' novel. Tocqueville's chapter on "How Industry Could Give Rise to an Aristocracy," both frightening and contemptuous, has been cited many times by commentators who wanted to bring Marx and Tocqueville together. Besides raising the specter of a new industrial aristocracy, it pointed out the dark side of the division of labor in language that Marx could not have bettered: "As the principle of the division of labor is more thoroughly applied, the worker becomes weaker, more limited, and more dependent. The art progresses, the artisan regresses."[71]

Tocqueville was not really afraid of a new capitalist aristocracy. He did not believe it would happen, and if it did happen, the new capitalist aristocracy would be "one of the most limited and least dangerous" in history. What he was afraid of was a capitalist society in which everyone, not just the proletarian, was a willing participant in their own degradation. The prime source of this degradation would be the "taste for material well-being." This passion was natural in democratic societies. But if it was natural to everyone, it originated with one class: "The passion for material well-being is essentially a middle-class passion. It grows and spreads with that class; it becomes preponderant when the class does."[72]

For all the benefits it brought (and Tocqueville noted them), the passion for well-being led people to become obsessed with making money. It did not necessarily impel them to try and become millionaires. Instead, "the goal is to add a few acres to one's fields…to enlarge a home, to make life constantly more comfortable and more convenient…. Such goals are small, but the soul invests in them…. Ultimately they block its view of the rest of the world and sometimes come between the soul and God." In the workings of capitalism Tocqueville sees a permanent temptation for individuals to devote themselves to making money for their families at the expense of taking any interest at all in the wider community. People indulge in petty material passions rather than what Tocqueville sees as more elevated goals. As he put it, "I reproach equality not for leading men into the pursuit of forbidden pleasures but for absorbing them entirely in the search for permitted ones…. the world might well come to see the establishment of a kind of respectable materialism, which rather than corrupt souls would soften them and in the end silently loosen the tension in all their springs." What a marvelous image: capitalism, the pursuit of material well-being, loosens the tension in our springs. Our minds and souls can no longer be projected into the higher realms intellectuals wish them to inhabit, and fall back from the heights.[73]

This is what Tocqueville fears will happen to people in a commercial culture. They will become petty, absorbed in petty goals, "lapse into limpness rather than debauchery." Absorbed in buying a summer place, they forget about the rest of society. They lose interest in politics, except when their direct material interests are threatened, and ultimately they are willing to trade their political freedom to anyone who will let them make money in peace. Tocqueville does not think that despotism is good for business in the long run, but he is afraid that many people will not look that far ahead.[74]

Tocqueville does not equate capitalism with despotism. Indeed, one of the many reasons he chose to write about America was to show that capitalism could be reconciled with freedom. He even reassures his readers that the great commercial nations of the world have always been free. Nevertheless, the greed encouraged in such societies is so absorbing to the average human mind that it threatens to crowd out all other values. America was a prime example of this, in Tocqueville's eyes. In America, "the possibilities open to greed are endlessly breathtaking, and the human mind, constantly distracted from the pleasures of the imagination and the works of the intellect, is engaged solely by the pursuit of wealth." When people rapidly develop a taste for material pleasures—as Tocqueville saw in America, foresaw for Europe, and has happened in many places since, notably twenty-first century China—"there is no need to strip such citizens of their rights; they let those rights slip away voluntarily." "The love of public tranquility is often the only political passion that these people retain, and in them it becomes more active and more powerful as all the others dwindle and die."[75]

Like many other intellectuals, Tocqueville saw capitalism as a threat to what he most valued in the human personality, even if he did not reject it outright. His criticism of capitalism was sharp, and not necessarily constructive. Capitalism cannot be improved merely by telling capitalists they are petty-minded. Their petty-minded pursuit of material well-being is essential to the workings of capitalism, including those Tocqueville acknowledged as positive. Tocqueville's criticism of the passion for material well-being is associated with attacks on the middle class, and his analysis of this aspect of democratic society becomes practically indistinguishable from a critique of bourgeois society. In this respect he comes very close to being an opponent of capitalism. Tocqueville is in this respect typical of many social and political writers and thinkers since, who have undermined the legitimacy of capitalism *without* attacking it frontally. Indeed, where he is atypical is in the extent to which he explicitly supports capitalism.

In the long run, Tocqueville thought that the remedy for capitalism's failings was essentially the same as his remedy for all other problems—freedom, above all political freedom. It was a remedy which left the source of the problem, capitalism itself, intact. But Tocqueville's "friendship" for capitalism is not very useful to it. If capitalism's friends quote him, it is for his criticism of socialism, not for his praise of the free market. His criticism of capitalism has been more useful to its enemies, who quote him more often on such questions. His attitudes are typical of many intellectuals whose relationship to the struggle between mind and money is ambiguous.

In the calmer periods of the last 150 years, Tocqueville's kind of attitude has been more widespread among intellectuals than Marx's. The ambiguous class status of intellectuals, and their hazy class consciousness, has helped make this a comfortable position for intellectuals. But even when on balance positive, as Tocqueville was, such attitudes were (and are) a reservoir of potential opposition to capitalism, and weaken the legitimacy of capitalist society.

In the end, Tocqueville is not that far from Arnold and Nietzsche, who took an overtly anticapitalist position just on the other side of the border from his. He had a lot of company in the frontier zone he occupied. In the right circumstances, it was easy to change sides. But for most intellectuals, that time did not come in the nineteenth century. Neither Nietzsche's thunder and lightning, nor Arnold's sweetness and light, nor Tocqueville's hand-wringing, nor all the jeremiads of Marx and Dickens and Co. were enough to seriously challenge capitalism during the nineteenth century. This turned out to be the task of the twentieth.

***

Throughout the twentieth century, intellectuals' criticism of capitalism was a continuous bass line beneath the ever-changing treble of events. After World War I, the bass swelled, and sometimes overtook the treble. Many had been disappointed by their old gods and their old elites in the course of the Great War and its aftermath. Many were willing to listen to a new message of good tidings, preached by a new clergy, and for which a new class was available to provide ideas and leadership. Writers and artists had been blackening the reputation of capitalism for decades, and social theorists had been proposing alternative schemes for almost as long. There had been little obvious effect, outside a little educational and social reform, and a lot of books. But in post-War circumstances, anti-capitalist alternatives to a system discredited by the War and later by the Great Depression suddenly seemed reasonable. What was morally questionable might be tolerable when it put money in your pocket, but when it took it out? Where economic and political success had reinforced the attractions of capitalism, failure reinforced the argument that it was morally repulsive. Much of what took place in World War I was inhuman on a previously unknown scale. As a result, the argument that capitalism had dehumanized people gained strength.

Demands for a visible hand to put money back in people's pockets, and morality back in their lives, took many forms. A bohemian minority of the intelligentsia sought refuge from war and Depression by dropping out, but that alternative was more popular in the 1950s and 1960s. Many intellectuals became communists or fascists. Others returned to their religious roots, and found them refreshingly anti-capitalist. Still others found the remedy for capitalist chaos in expert planning, and helped create the New Deal.

After World War I, the alternatives to capitalism were longer merely academic, as history and the next chapter make clear.

Notes

1. And tearing down the imperfect structures built by their colleagues. After all, in Genesis 11 God is a deconstructionist—he destroys Babel by making people use unintelligible language, like a late twentieth-century critical theorist.
2. Orwell, *The Road to Wigan Pier*, cited in Paul Hollander, *Political Pilgrims: Travels of Western Intellectuals to the Soviet Union, China, and Cuba* (New York: Oxford University Press, 1981), 502; Tocqueville, *The Old Regime and the Revolution*, trans. Alan S. Kahan (Chicago: University of Chicago Press, 1998), 1:200-01.
3. Jerrold Siegel, *Marx's Fate: The Shape of a Life* (Princeton, Princeton University Press, 1978), 391.
4. David McClellan, *Karl Marx, His Life and Thought* (New York: Harper & Row, 1973), 66.

5.   Cited in McLellan, *Karl Marx*, 280.
6.   When Jacob Burckhardt wrote of the *"terribles simplificateurs"* who would dominate Europe, he probably had Marx in mind. See Burckhardt, 24 July 1889, *Briefe*, ed. Max Burckhardt (Basel/Stuttgart: Klett-Cotta, 1980), 9:203.
7.   Marx, "On the Jewish Question," *Marx-Engels Reader*, 26. Despite the Biblical tone, this passage is based on Aristotle, with whose writings Marx was familiar. See Berthoud, *Aristote et l'argent*, 100.
8.   Marx, "Economic and Philosophic Manuscripts of 1844", *Marx-Engels Reader*, 82.
9.   Marx, "Economic and Philosophic Manuscripts of 1844," 7, 58, and cited in Avineri, *The Social and Political Thought of Karl Marx* (Cambridge: Cambridge University Press, 1970), 110.
10.   Marx, *Capital*, *Marx-Engels Reader*, 217, 224.
11.   Marx, "On the Jewish Question," 48.
12.   Marx, "On the Jewish Question," 46.
13.   Marx to the Chartist Congress, cited in Avineri, *Social and Political Thought*, 117.
14.   Although tradition makes it difficult to talk about Marx without using the word "capitalism," Marx himself never used it, although he did talk about "capital" and "capitalists."
15.   Marx, *Communist Manifesto*, 345.
16.   Siegel, *Marx's Fate*, 109; Marx, "Contribution to the Critique of Hegel's "Philosophy of Right," *Marx-Engels Reader*, 22.
17.   Marx, "On the German Ideology," *Marx-Engels Reader,* 118-19, 133; "Address to the Communist League," *Marx-Engels Reader,* 371.
18.   Marx, "Critique of Hegel's 'Philosophy of Right'," 18-19, 23.
19.   Marx, "On the German Ideology," 136-37.
20.   Marx, *Communist Manifesto*, 343.
21.   Marx, Letter to Bebel, Liebknecht, Bracke and Others, *Marx-Engels Reader,* 405.
22.   Marx, *The German Ideology*, 128.
23.   Marx, "On the Jewish Question," 32; "The German Ideology," 161.
24.   Marx, "The Civil War in France," *Marx-Engels Reader*, 555-56.
25.   Marx, "Economic and Philosophic Manuscripts of 1844," 60, see also 58-59; *Capital*, 273, 319; "The German Ideology," 127.
26.   Marx, *Capital*, 287, 294, 296-98; *Communist Manifesto*, 341.
27.   Marx, *Capital*, 300; "Economic and Philosophic Manuscripts of 1844, 62-63.
28.   Marx, "The German Ideology," 124. See also "Critique of the Gotha Program," 388.
29.   Marx, "Inaugural Address of the Working Men's International," *Marx-Engels Reader,* 380; "On the Realm of Necessity and the Realm of Freedom," *Marx-Engels Reader,* 319; "Early Writings," cited in Avineri, *The Social and Political Thought of Karl Marx*, 106; Tocqueville, *Democracy*, 550. Marx actually criticizes capitalism for making work so unattractive that people begin to prefer leisure! "Its alien character is clearly shown by the fact that as soon as there is no physical or other compulsion [work] is avoided like the plague."
30.   Marx, *Capital*, 319; "On the Realm of Necessity and the Realm of Freedom," 320. On work as art in Marx, see Avineri, *The Social and Political Thought of Karl Marx*, 228.
31.   Toennies' contrast is similar to Maine's contrast of "status" and "contract," to which Toennies pays homage while criticizing it. Toennies see this evolution much more negatively than Maine. In fact, the contrast can be traced back to Aristotle.

32.   Ferdinand Toennies, *Community and Civil Society*, ed. Jose Harris, trans. Jose Harris and Margaret Hollis (Cambridge, Cambridge University Press, 2001), 257-58.
33.   Toennies, *Community and Civil Society*, 251, 255, 257-58.
34.   Toennies, *Community and Civil Society*, 19, 22, 50, 248.
35.   Toennies, *Community and Civil Society*, 18, 65, 68.
36.   Toennies, *Community and Civil Society*, 52, 65, 168, 249.
37.   Toennies, *Community and Civil Society*, 164-65.
38.   Toennies, *Community and Civil Society*, 173.
39.   Toennies, *Community and Civil Society*, 123, 164-65, 257-58. Toennies leaves a small loophole for the "genius." See *Community and Civil Society*, 156, 161.
40.   Toennies, *Community and Civil Society*, 174, 257-58, 260.
41.   Toennies, *Community and Civil Society*, 210.
42.   David Riesman, *Thorstein Veblen: A Critical Interpretation* (New York: Continuum, 1960), 1-44.
43.   Thorstein Veblen, *The Theory of the Leisure Class* (New York: Viking, 1953) 75, 218.
44.   Thorstein Veblen, *The Engineers and the Price System* (New York Viking: 1933), 9; *Theory of the Leisure Class*, 114.
45.   Veblen, *Theory of the Leisure Class*, 154.
46.   Thorstein Veblen, *The Higher Learning in America: A Memorandum on the Conduct of Universities by Business Men* (New York: Augustus M. Kelley, 1965), 208-09.
47.   Riesman, *Thorstein Veblen*, 105; Veblen, *The Engineers and the Price System*, 52-53, 55, 58.
48.   Veblen, *The Higher Learning in America*, 151, 200.
49.   Matthew Arnold, *Culture and Anarchy*, in *Selected Prose*, ed. P. J. Keating, (London: Penguin, 1970), 251, 254; Arnold, *Culture and Anarchy* (Indianapolis: Bobbs-Merrill, 1969), 156.
50.   Arnold, *Culture and Anarchy*, 156, 159; Arnold, *Culture and Anarchy*, in *Selected Prose*, 211.
51.   Arnold takes the equation of sweetness and light with beauty and intelligence from Jonathan Swift's *Battle of the Books*. See Arnold, *Culture and Anarchy*, in *Selected Prose*, 213; Arnold, *Culture and Anarchy*, in *Selected Prose*, 134, 213, 218-19.
52.   Arnold, *Culture and Anarchy*, in *Selected Prose*, 257. Arnold distinguishes himself by contrasting the "unsatisfied seeker," himself, with the "perfect self-satisfaction current in my class, the middle class." See *Culture and Anarchy*, in *Selected Prose*, 250.
53.   Arnold, *Culture and Anarchy*, in *Selected Prose*, 258.
54.   Arnold, *Culture and Anarchy*, 225, 272.
55.   Arnold, *Culture and Anarchy*, 205-07, 286.
56.   Friedrich Nietzsche, *The Gay Science*, ed. Bernard Williams, trans. Josefine Nauckhoff (Cambridge: Cambridge University Press, 2001), 29-30.
57.   Nietzsche, *The Gay Science*, 31, 41, 64, 243; *Beyond Good and Evil*, trans. Walter Kaufmann (New York: Vintage, 1966), 37-38. Nietzsche sometimes searches for a word to describe what he here calls "philosophers," and I call "intellectuals," a term he would have rejected as too academic. See *The Gay Science*, 203.
58.   Nietzsche, *The Gay Science*, 119.
59.   Nietzsche, *Beyond Good and Evil*, 74; *On the Genealogy of Morals*, trans. by Walter Kaufmann and R. J. Hollingdale (New York: Vintage, 1969), 108; *The Gay Science*, 69. I have taken the liberty of substituting "minds" for "spirits" in the

translation, in order to get closer to what I think Nietzsche meant by the ambiguous German word *Geist*.

60. Nietzsche, *The Gay Science*, 189, 246, *Beyond Good and Evil*, 121-22, 125, 134, 140; *On the Genealogy of Morals*, 154.
61. Nietzsche, *The Gay Science*, 77.
62. Nietzsche, *The Gay Science*, 136, 206, 244.
63. Nietzsche, *The Gay Science*, 119, 159-60; *Beyond Good and Evil*, 74.
64. Nietzsche, *Beyond Good and Evil*, 70.
65. Nietzsche, *The Gay Science*, 159-60; *On the Genealogy of Morals*, 115.
66. Nietzsche, *The Gay Science*, 109-110, 119-120.
67. Nietzsche, *The Gay Science*, 205.
68. Nietzsche, *On the Genealogy of Morals*, 52.
69. Nietzsche, *On the Genealogy of Morals*, 56.
70. Alexis de Tocqueville, *The Old Regime and the Revolution*, 2:91; Tocqueville, "Voyage to England and Ireland in 1835," in *Oeuvres complètes* (Paris: Gallimard, 1958), 5:90-91.
71. Tocqueville, *Democracy in America*, 651-52.
72. Tocqueville, *Democracy in America*, 507, 618, 652.
73. Tocqueville, *Democracy in America*, 621-22.
74. Tocqueville, *Democracy in America*, 621.
75. Tocqueville, *Democracy in America*, 516, 630, 793-94.

Part III

Triumphs and Tragedies of the Anti-Capitalist Spirit: The Twentieth Century (1914-2001)

6

War

Why Great Revolutions Did Not Become Rare

Tocqueville's analysis of democratic society has been central to this book. Even his mistakes can be illuminating. One such mistake is crucial to understanding the role intellectuals have played in the twentieth century. He wrote that "great revolutions will become rare." The twentieth century experienced more great revolutions than any other in history. Why was he wrong?

Tocqueville thought great revolutions would become rare because "almost all the revolutions that have changed the face of nations were made to consecrate or destroy inequality." In societies that were already egalitarian, like America or increasingly Europe, this motive would disappear. Once everyone had something to lose, no one would be a revolutionary. The spread of capitalism would also serve to discourage revolutions, in Tocqueville's view: "...I know of nothing more opposed to revolutionary mores than commercial mores. Commerce is naturally the enemy of all violent passions. It likes moderation, delights in compromise, and is careful to avoid anger. It is patient, supple, and insinuating, and resorts to extreme measures only when obliged to do so by the most absolute necessity." Therefore, Tocqueville thought great revolutions would become rare, which was his cautious way of saying they would not happen. The outcome of the revolutions of 1848 seemed to prove Tocqueville right. In the end, the revolutions of 1848 were all failures. None succeeded in maintaining power.[1]

But the same cannot be said of the revolutions of the twentieth century. Tocqueville reckoned without the intellectuals in *Democracy in America*. He would partly repair this omission in *The Old Regime and the Revolution*, his study of the French Revolution, where he devoted a chapter to the revolutionary characteristics of the eighteenth-century French intelligentsia, but he never had occasion to consider the long-term consequences.

When we consider the nature of the intellectual class in democratic society, it goes a long way towards explaining Tocqueville's mistake. If Tocqueville was right to suggest that "men in democracies not only have no natural desire for revolutions, they also fear them" on account of their property, this consideration weighs much less with intellectuals. If Tocqueville was right that "in democratic societies it is generally only small minorities that desire revolutions, but a minority is sometimes enough to bring a revolution about," then intellectuals are such a minority. If Tocqueville was right that people in democratic societies "change, alter and replace things of secondary importance every day but are extremely careful not to tamper with things of primary importance. They like change but dread revolutions," then intellectuals are the people in democratic society most prepared to challenge fundamental assumptions, and most accustomed to doing so.[2]

There is another phenomenon Tocqueville described as natural to democratic society that helps explain both why many intellectuals would be inclined to make revolutions, and more importantly why they might find enough followers to succeed. Tocqueville recognized that capitalism was destined to flourish in a democratic world. However, he expected that a minority would react strongly against this: "I would be surprised if, in a nation preoccupied solely with its well-being, mysticism did not make some progress before long." And then "it can no longer find its bearings and often hastens without stopping beyond the limits of common sense." In other words, those who reject capitalism may well fling caution to the winds and join a New Age religion or the local Communist Party—and make a revolution.[3]

But neither the nature of democratic society, nor the nature of the intellectual class is enough to explain the wave of revolution that broke over the Western world after World War I. Events matter, and cannot be predicted. Without World War I, many intellectuals would still have rejected capitalism. But without World War I, it would have been much less likely that the struggle between mind and money would have turned into a bloody war.

Continuity and Change after World War I

World War I changed everything, and nothing. That was its tragedy. Afterwards, everything was the same as before, except for the 15 million dead and 22 million wounded. Except for the dead and wounded, in many respects the postwar period merely amplified the trends of the prewar period. Nevertheless World War I was a turning point in world history, and it was a turning point in the struggle between mind and money.

World War leaves little room for moderation, and the habits of the War were ingrained in every nation. Whether people found the war experience horrible, or admirable, or both, it shaped their ideas and served as a model. But what the model looked like varied. For some, it was the creation of a centralized, planned wartime economy that was the essence of what the war had to teach. For others it was the camaraderie of the front line, or the unity behind it, or the worship or hatred of technology. For many intellectuals, the War represented the revival of community they longed for. It made urgent the necessity of creating such a community in peacetime.

It is difficult to tell if more intellectuals were opposed to capitalism after the war than before, but their dissatisfaction took on new meaning in the post-war political context. As pseudo-clergy with a moral mission, intellectuals had always sought to find meaning and moral structure in historical events. World War I left many ordinary people looking to find meaning as well. Intellectuals wanted to see a visible temple, a visible hand at work in the world. They sought to re-enchant the world, to find new sources of morality and meaning in the nation or the proletariat or anti-capitalist variations of traditional Christianity. So did many others. The characteristics of the intelligentsia suddenly had a great deal of resonance in society at large.

Disillusion with capitalist democracy was widespread after World War I. Tocqueville wrote that "the preference one shows for absolute government is in direct proportion to the contempt that one has for one's country." After World War I contempt for democratic government was widespread throughout society. This led to increased sympathy, especially among intellectuals, for violence, revolution, and totalitarian government. It meant support for communism, fascism, or for some revolutionary "Third Way." The conflict between mind and money was already old in 1914, at the outbreak of World War I. But it was only after World War I that intellectuals who had thrown the household china at their adversaries put down their remaining teacups and picked up their guns. The end of World War I marked the outbreak of war between mind and money.[4]

The arrival of the Great Depression in 1929 convinced even more people, both intellectuals and others, to reject capitalism, and to join one or more movements to replace it with something better. Ideas once confined to learned publications, found in the occasional novel, or even scrawled on banners carried tamely through the streets on May Day had come to power in St. Petersburg, and Rome, and soon in Berlin. Americans wondered if "it could really happen here?" However, it would be a mistake to over-emphasize the Depression, and give in to the temptation of looking for a purely economic explanation of the success of anti-capitalist movements after World War I. Lenin and Mussolini came to power before the Depression, and the social Catholic "Third Way" critique of capitalism flourished before serious unemployment came to Europe. It was not just capitalism's economic failures that made it anathema to so many intellectuals on both left and right.

After World War I, four anti-capitalist movements were especially significant: communism, fascism, social Catholicism, and, with some caveats, the New Deal. All four shared the goal of creating a new kind of community. Three of them, communism, fascism, and social Catholicism, embraced revolution. The fourth, the New Deal, was not revolutionary in intentions or results, although its opponents often accused it of being so. The four differed considerably among themselves. They sometimes detested each other as much or more than the bourgeoisie. Communists and fascists usually saw each other as the Antichrist, and just as devotees often hate heretics more than unbelievers, communists sometimes hated socialists even more than fascists. On the other hand, individual intellectuals might change denominations while never leaving the anti-capitalist faith. Hitler thought that ex-Communists made excellent Nazis. A surprising number of intellectuals showed sympathy for both communism *and* fascism, even if they were themselves neither communist nor fascists. It is hard to tell whether intellectuals' dissatisfaction with capitalism in the '20s and '30s was greater on one flank or the other. Calls for the end of capitalism came from both sides, and were meant and taken seriously. As individuals and as a class, intellectuals helped create all these anti-capitalist movements and greatly influenced their reception. We will begin with what is hardest to understand, intellectuals' relationship to the great tragedies of the twentieth century, communism and fascism.

Communism: The Red and the Pink

The Russian Revolution's impact was enormous. Something that had hitherto been a fantasy, a successful anti-capitalist revolution, had suddenly come to pass. It transformed intellectual opposition to capitalism from a pastime into a deadly form of roulette. It showed that what intellectuals said about capitalism mattered.

The romance of revolution had always been attractive to intellectuals. The Russian Revolution doubled its pull. Nadezhda Mandelstam (1899-1980), a Russian poet during the communist period, tells this story: "My brother…used to say that the decisive part in the subjugation of the intelligentsia was played… by the word 'Revolution', which none of them could bear to give up. It is a word to which whole nations have succumbed, and its force was such that one wonders why our rulers still needed prisons and capital punishment." Revolution was indeed the opium of the intelligentsia.[5]

Intellectuals had never needed Utopia, e.g., the Soviet Union, to exist in real life in order to criticize society. The Kingdom of Heaven, the realm of ideas, was always available as a model. But the existence of what appeared to be a real Utopia in Russia made rejecting capitalism seem more practical and more attractive. Many intellectuals who harbored anti-capitalist attitudes were radicalized by World War I and converted to outright rejection of capitalism by the Russian example. By 1890, Marx's writings seemed outdated to reformist socialist thinkers. After 1919, it was reformism that seemed outdated, and the works of Marx and Lenin were the relevant ones. When Russian democrats overthrew the czar in 1917, it was an important but not earth-shattering event. People had long expected an end to autocratic rule in Russia. When the Bolsheviks overthrew the Kerensky government in 1919, the Western world immediately saw the event as one of extraordinary importance, as indeed it proved to be. Russia was suddenly transformed, in the imagination of Western intellectuals, from a backward nation into a beacon pointing the way to the future. Nothing like this had been seen since the American Revolution transformed thirteen far-away colonies into the beacon of democracy.

The Russian Revolution provided intellectuals with both a fact and a myth. They preached both—the Soviet Union as economic paradise and the Revolution as myth. In many ways, what was important to Western intellectuals was that Russia had had a Revolution, rather than what was really going on in Russia. As early as 1919, some of the revolution's friends were defending it not for what it had done, but for what it *intended* to do. They could thus support the revolution for what it *meant* and for what it *intended*, rather than for what it did, and judge it in moral rather than political or economic terms. They separated its *meaning* from its *results*, and thus "eliminated politics in favor of morality. This is an old habit with intellectuals."[6]

For other friends of the Russian Revolution what mattered were its enemies. The bourgeoisie and the reactionaries hated it, so it must be good. At bottom, the two reasons were one: intellectuals supported the Russian Revolution because it was made against capitalism. Hatred of the bourgeoisie, rather than any commitment to Marxism, was enough to make intellectuals support it. Russia had abolished capitalism, and intended to create an egalitarian society, and that put the communist regime on the side of the angels.

But there were other reasons that made communism especially attractive to intellectuals. The Bolsheviks, known after taking power as the Communist Party, were a party that had been shaped and formed by intellectuals, in accord with Lenin's theory of a vanguard party. Lenin's vision of the communist party was the embodiment of a very old idea, and one that held great attraction for intellectuals.

Alvin Gouldner suggests that there is a "Plato complex" among Western intellectuals. He referred to Plato's argument in the *Republic* that philosophers, specially educated for the task (and forbidden to own private property), ought to be the ones to rule the state. For a long time this argument had little impact. However, as the idea of meritocracy and careers open to talent spread after the French Revolution (and incidentally as the intellectual class took shape), it seemed more plausible, at least to a few intellectuals, that political power might be reserved for those with intellectual talents, as opposed to those born or elected to it. In the nineteenth century, Coleridge and his successors in England spoke of the new intellectual elite as the "clerisy," and in France the Saint-Simonians and Auguste Comte and his followers, known as Positivists, made their own arguments for why intellectuals should rule.

These claims never attracted the support of more than a small minority, even among intellectuals. In the twentieth century, however, the idea took on a new form. Inspired by Marx, who spoke of bourgeois ideologists going over to the proletariat, Marxist intellectuals began to carve out a special role for themselves as political leaders. In 1901 the German socialist leader Karl Kautsky justified the role intellectuals played, or ought to play, within socialist parties:

> Modern socialist consciousness can only arise on the basis of profound scientific knowledge.... The vehicles of science are not the proletariat, but the *bourgeois intelligentsia* [emphasis original]: it was in the minds of some members of this stratum that modern socialism originated, and it was they who communicated it to the more intellectually developed proletarians.... Thus, socialist consciousness is something introduced into the proletarian class struggle from without, and not something that arose within it spontaneously.[7]

In other words, it is the proletariat that creates the class struggle, but the intellectuals who create socialism.

Kautsky recognized the fundamental role intellectuals played in socialism's struggle against capitalism. What is significant, however, is not that Kautsky dimly recognized the fundamental importance of the struggle between mind and money, but that this quotation is to be found in Lenin's "What is to be Done?." "What is to be Done?" was the bible of Bolshevik organization before the Russian Revolution, and thereafter of the communist movement generally.

The ascendance of intellectuals among the Bolsheviks was unique. Lenin notoriously called for the dictatorship of the proletariat. That dictatorship was to be the dictatorship of the communist party in the proletariat's name. And the communist party was to be a party of intellectuals. Lenin endorsed Kautsky's view that socialism had to come to the workers from the intellectuals. The communists were to be a "vanguard party," the leaders of the working class, not merely their representatives. Without the leadership of a small, highly trained and educated group of professional revolutionaries, no revolution would be possible. This training would need to be practical, of course, but even more so it would have to be theoretical. *"The role of vanguard can be fulfilled only by a party that is guided by an advanced theory"* (emphasis original). "Without a revolutionary theory there can be no revolutionary movement." Lenin even imagined a communist party in which workers, at least those who aspired to join the vanguard, would have to become intellectuals: "our very first and most imperative duty is to help train working class revolutionaries who will be on the same level *in regard to Party activity* as intellectual revolutionaries (we emphasize the words 'in regard to Party activity', because although it is necessary it is not so easy to bring the workers up to the level of intellectuals in other respects)."[8]

Lenin's conception appealed to intellectuals. As communists, intellectuals were members of the vanguard whose theoretical knowledge was their patent of nobility. They were the acknowledged leaders of the proletariat, attached to but apart from the mass of workers, like aristocrats. Many Western intellectuals acknowledged that they saw the Bolsheviks as an intellectual aristocracy, and were attracted to them for that reason.

Even before World War I, this had been part of the attraction of Marxist socialism for intellectuals—or sometimes a motive to oppose it. Marx's leading rival, Mikhail Bakunin, warned that a revolutionary ruling class of intellectuals would treat people like rabbits. He perceived that in modern society *"savants* [i.e., intellectuals] form a separate caste, in many respects analogous to the priesthood. Scientific abstraction is their God, living and real individuals are their victims, and they are the consecrated and licensed sacrificers." Bakunin was right. No better description could be given of Leninists, Stalinists, Maoists, and the followers of Pol Pot, massacring millions in order to establish "scientific socialism." Bakunin warned that "Mr. Marx's People's State" would mean "the reign of the *scientific mind*, the most aristocratic, despotic, arrogant and contemptuous of all regimes."[9]

Despite this prescient criticism, Bakunin, who played a founding role in the anarchist movement, also appealed to a dedicated elite to form a secret headquarters for his version of the coming revolution. This organization "should be composed of the strongest people, *the cleverest*....[who] renounced once and for all... everything that entices men, all the material pleasures and comforts of society.... they must be people who would refuse personal historical importance during their lives and even a name in history after their death."

If Marxists emphasized the aristocratic aspect of the professional revolutionary, Bakunin called for what can best be described as a monastic order. Already in the nineteenth century Gustave Le Bon had recognized that "socialism is becoming a belief of a religious character." After World War I Communism, the most rigorous socialist sect, received many intellectuals' devotion after their conversion. Lenin's party appealed to intellectuals both as pseudo-aristocrats and as pseudo-clergy.[10]

Conversion is not too strong a word to describe how intellectuals felt when they joined the communist party. "For me to join the Party of Proletarian Revolution," wrote the great Italian novelist, Ignazio Silone, "was not just a simple matter of signing up with a political organization; it meant a conversion, a complete dedication.... Life, death, love, good, evil, truth, all changed their meaning or lost it altogether." Silone's words bear out the truth of another ex-communist's statement: "From the psychologist's point of view, there is little difference between a revolutionary and a traditionalist faith."[11]

In the disenchanted post-World War I world, intellectuals were ripe for revelation. To turn to Arthur Koestler, describing his reaction after his first reading of Marx and Lenin: "To say that one had 'seen the light' is a poor description of the mental rapture which only the convert knows.... The new light seems to pour from all directions across the skull, the whole universe falls into pattern like the stray pieces of a jigsaw puzzle assembled by magic at one stroke. There is now an answer to every question...." Reading Marx and Lenin did for Koestler precisely what reading the New Testament did for St. Augustine. It made him a believer.[12]

But communism was not only based on the Book of Marx. For some believers the religion of revolution owed little to any scripture. Marxism was not necessarily a requirement for sympathizers with communism. The spiritual rejection of capitalism often counted more. As one American supporter, Malcolm Cowley, wrote, "Communism... seemed capable of supplying the moral qualities that writers had missed in bourgeois society: the comradeship in struggle, the self-imposed discipline, the ultimate purpose." Lenin would not have approved, but he profited nonetheless.[13]

Both the aristocratic and the religious appeal of communism were effective after World War I, and both the science and religion of communism were the basis for mass murder. From the first months of the Bolshevik Revolution and the Russian Civil War that followed, communists showed little regard for human freedom or human life. A handful of radical intellectuals, like Rosa Luxemburg, immediately recognized them for what they were (as early as 1904, Luxemburg criticized Lenin for creating a party run by an oligarchy of intellectuals, dedicated to power at any price).[14] But for many intellectuals, neither the dismissal of the Russian Constituent Assembly in 1918, nor the massacre of the Kronstadt sailors and the banning of other political parties in the 1920s, nor the death of millions by starvation in the Ukraine, nor the Moscow Trials of the 1930s, when dozens of leading revolutionaries were sentenced to death on trumped-up charges and tortured into confessions, were enough to shake their reasoning or their faith. Why? There were many reasons why intellectuals persisted in their error (see below), but there is one that is particularly applicable to their attraction to communism and their willingness to accept its atrocities.

Communist intellectuals belonged to what Max Weber, discussing the sociology of religion, calls a "salvation aristocracy." Weber describes their attitude:

> Every organization of salvation... feels responsible before God for the souls of everyone, or at least of all the men entrusted to it. Such an institution [e.g., the Communist Party] will therefore feel entitled, and in duty bound, to oppose with ruthless force any danger through misguidance in faith.... When salvation aristocracies are charged by the command of their God [or history] to tame the world of sin... they give birth to the 'crusader'.[15]

For the sake of salvation, theirs and yours, such crusaders kill mercilessly, and die selflessly. Modern Western intellectuals are a kind of multivalent salvation aristocracy, capable of attaching themselves to various vehicles of salvation from capitalism—communism being one. The salvation they seek for themselves and their faithful is the Revolution, the new paradise.

This is a glorious and very attractive role. Few if any intellectuals joined anti-capitalist movements or became communists for the sake of becoming mass murderers. But once committed to the cause, revolutionary jihad became a possibility.

What was the nature of the new Marxist-Leninist religion? It was the religion of history—a religion that had the added benefit, from an intellectual's critical perspective, that it claimed to be a science. Marx taught that history had a predictable end. The Last Days were here, and the end of the bourgeoisie, indeed of all classes, was nigh. After World War I, this claim seemed plausible. The way to paradise was through revolution, and victory and paradise were assured, in the not too distant future. The Communists were the Party of the God of Historical Necessity, a God who combined many Christian features, for example radical equality, a Last Judgment and a coming messianic age, with radical secularization and careful critical discourse. Communism was a religion that was also a science.

During the Depression, when communists claimed to understand the economy and capitalists clearly did not, the communist claim to scientific certainty was as attractive as its quasi-religious claim to truth. Marx's "labor theory of value" was not what interested people in communist economics. What attracted intellectuals and many other people to communism during the Depression was the idea of a science of economic planning. Actually communists, fascists, social Catholics, and many of those most influential in the American New Deal were all fascinated by the idea of a planned economy replacing the economic and spiritual anarchy of capitalism. The general interest in planning among anti-capitalist movements will be discussed under the heading of the New Deal, but it gave added "scientific" appeal to communism.

For many intellectuals, the aristocratic, religious and scientific appeal of communism made a perfect combination. They gave their souls to the revolution while giving their minds to science, and since Marxism-Leninism was a science, it was much the same thing. Intellectuals could be priests, continue to engage in careful critical discourse (CCD), and rule the world, all at the same time. The Communist Party appealed to all facets of intellectuals' social and moral identity. Just as Marx had appealed to all aspects of intellectuals' rejection of capitalism, so communism gave intellectuals scope to exercise the moral voice and priestly function as well as CCD. The ability to preach while doing science, combined with the sense of being part of a revolutionary aristocracy, produced a pleasant feeling of wholeness in intellectuals, and strengthened their commitment.

Not all intellectuals were attracted by both science and religion. But singly or together, both pulls strongly attracted intellectuals to communism. It was a match made in Hell.

Intellectuals had to be willing to take a lot of abuse in order to be communists—and not just from their opponents. It may seem strange that Lenin's vanguard party, which appealed to intellectuals by calling on them to assume a leadership role in the revolution, could also treat intellectuals with contempt. However, there had always been tension within the socialist movement between workers and intellectuals. It was partly to address this tension that Lenin had written "What is to be Done?" After the Russian Revolution, and especially after Lenin's death in 1924, the tension increased, and intellectuals proved remarkably willing to accept their dual status as aristocratic theorists and bourgeois pigs. It is striking how much abuse intellectuals were willing to accept, and even to inflict upon themselves, while serving the anti-capitalist movement of their choice. It demonstrates both the depth of many intellectuals' hatred for capitalism and the intellectual class's ambivalent feelings about itself.

Communist intellectuals wanted to be one with the people. "We craved to become single- and simple-minded. Intellectual castration was a small price to pay for achieving some likeness to Comrade Ivan Ivanovich." When they couldn't achieve the correct appearance of ignorance, they were ashamed. Furet notes that among intellectuals "the masochistic pleasure of losing oneself in the service of a cause finds its most complete expression." Self-inflicted pain in the service of a higher cause has often been a priest's role. Is not self-mortification, both physical and psychological, common among the clergy of many religions? The revolution's priests were happy to bear witness to their devotion by bearing pain in the revolution's name. When Stalin and his minions condemned them, it only reinforced their revolutionary fervor, and even their support for Stalin.[16]

If all this was too much, intellectuals could stay outside the Party as "fellow travelers," and retain at least an illusion of independence. Fellow travelers were "pinks," not "reds." There were always many more pinks than reds, and their importance was no less and perhaps greater in contributing to the struggle of mind vs. money. It was typical of intellectuals' relation with all the anti-capitalist movements, but especially with communism.

Fellow-traveling involved "commitment *at a distance* which is not only geographical but also emotional and intellectual." It provided more scope for the bohemian spirit of autonomy than did the monastic discipline of

Party membership. Fellow-traveling allowed pinks to feel they were revolutionaries, without feeling a duty to commit themselves to the doctrines of Marxism-Leninism. Most fellow travelers did not regard themselves as Marxists, much less Leninists, but they believed in the revolution. Many took their position from Christian motives. As André Gide put it, "what leads me to communism is not Marx, it is the gospel." A leading American Protestant theologian, Paul Tillich, wrote that "any serious Christian must be a socialist" and that "socialism is the economics of which Christianity is the religion." David Caute, author of the most comprehensive study of communist fellow travelers, argues that it was Protestants who were most likely to be fellow travelers because of their faith. However, the enormous extent of the social Catholic movement among European intellectuals suggests that if there was a difference between Catholic and Protestant fellow-traveling with anti-capitalist movements, it was only that Catholic (Thomist) theology provided a better way to be militantly anti-capitalist within a traditional religious context. Indeed, many social Catholics in the 1930s were able to sympathize and travel much of the way with both communists *and* fascists. The Second, Christian, Don't, "Don't Have or Make Money, Give it Away," exercised influence throughout the anti-capitalist movements of the mid-twentieth century.[17]

The relative numbers of Western communists and their fellow travelers rose and fell according to circumstances. Their heroes also might vary. Following the Soviet suppression of the Hungarian uprising in 1956, the focus of Western fellow-traveling shifted to the Third World, and intellectuals substituted figures as diverse as Mao, Pol Pot, Castro, or even Envher Hoxha (of Albania) for Stalin and the Soviet Union. What remained constant was their rejection of capitalism. The history of fellow-traveling shows, better than any other, the way in which intellectuals' support for any particular anti-capitalist movement was subordinate to their desire to destroy capitalism. Stephen Spender, writing about his disillusionment with communism, found it necessary to remark, "In writing this essay I have always been aware that no criticism of the Communists removes the arguments against capitalism."[18] Spender was typical. It was always easier for a European intellectual to be pro-communist, no matter what the latest news from the Gulag, than to support capitalism. Simone de Beauvoir knew this milieu perfectly. In her 1954 novel *The Mandarins*, the character Henri represents Camus. He insists on publishing articles about the Gulag, despite the arguments of the character who represents Sartre. Nevertheless, when Henri encounters the American Cold War liberal Bennet, the following exchange takes place:

Bennet: "In sum, between America and the USSR, you would choose the Soviet Union?

Henri: "Yes, and I have never made a secret of it."[19]

Furet's analysis of the situation was correct:

> If they had to pay for defending freedom against Stalin with a blessing for the American cult of free enterprise, how could they easily accept the choice? It was less costly for them to be anti-American than to be anti-Soviet—or rather to retain the intellectual comfort of a double critique that rejected both.... The philocommunism of the Cold War was less and less protected by antifascism. But it retained the alibi of anti-capitalism more than ever....[20]

Anti-capitalism is the key to understanding why intellectuals persisted in their communism. In this regard, things have not changed, although appearances have. Thus the following report from 2000: "At a conference I attended recently, a friend with impeccable left-wing credentials who until communism's recent collapse had been an ardent champion of the proletarian cause, jumped on the pan-Arab bandwagon, reciting the names of obscure Muslim intellectuals who he claimed, offered a promising political alternative to the debilities of Western liberalism. Plus ça change...." It took a lot to disenchant intellectuals with communism. The stories of their ostrich-like illusions about the Soviet Union and other communist countries have filled books. Everyone has illusions about their beloved, even those who use careful critical discourse.[21]

Many intellectuals became communists after World War I, and many more became fellow travelers. Dissatisfaction with capitalism reached such a pitch that if more intellectuals did not become communists, it was only because there were many other movements appealing for their devotion. Communism's leading competitor was the era's other great revolutionary movement, fascism.

Fascism

Some may object to describing fascism as a revolutionary movement. Others will object to describing fascism as an anti-capitalist movement. There has even been scholarly debate about whether any such thing as "fascism" existed at all. Those who deny the existence of fascism claim that Hitler's Nazism, Mussolini's Fascism, and the various French, Spanish, English, etc. movements that have been labeled "fascist" were so different that it is misleading to give them the same name. They were all nationalists, but there the similarity ends, in this view.[22]

However, it is more misleading to describe them all as nationalists than to call them fascists. "Nationalism" is used to describe everything from the independence or unification movements of the nineteenth century to the anti-colonial movements of the late twentieth, which differ from each other far more than Italian and French fascists. Fascists were nationalists, but fascism was much more than extreme nationalism. There were ideological and political traits particular to fascist movements. Among the similarities of fascist movements were their claims to be revolutionary and their anti-capitalism. The romantic appeal of revolution was as much a part of fascism as of communism. Fascists often described themselves as "conservative revolutionaries." Like all twentieth-century revolutionaries, their revolution included rejecting capitalism.[23]

Later intellectuals, including historians, have been reluctant to recognize that fascism, for which they have no sympathy, shared many features of socialist and communist criticism of capitalism, with which they do sympathize. But in the 1920s and 1930s fascism was "just one of the competing movements which shared a common hatred of the money, the values and the life of the bourgeois." The same historian of French fascism continues: "Not all anti-materialism is fascism, but fascism constitutes a variety of anti-materialism and channels all the essential currents of twentieth-century anti-materialism. In this sense fascism constitutes an authentic revolutionary movement." Like other anti-capitalist movements, fascism was an authentic search for community. This is why fascism was a mainstream political movement in its day. So many intellectuals (and other people) were looking for a way out of commercial society that fascists seemed much like everyone else.[24]

Just as with communism, the ideas of fascism were a combination of old and new. Before World War I, conservative anti-capitalism usually rejected modern technology. But most fascists did not. Jeffrey Herf has used the phrase "reactionary modernism" for this phenomenon. Reactionary modernists were:

> nationalists who turned... romantic anticapitalism... away from a backward-looking pastoralism, pointing instead to the outlines of a beautiful new order replacing the formless chaos due to capitalism in a united, technologically advanced nation.... They called for a revolution from the Right that would restore the primacy of politics and the state over economics and the market....[25]

Herf is talking about Germany, but his description is valid for other fascists, especially in Italy, where the "Futurist" artistic and literary movement loved speed, airplanes and Mussolini. During the Depression, many anti-capitalist intellectuals, whether fascists, communists, or New Dealers "viewed themselves as liberators of technology's slumbering powers, which were being repressed and misused by a capitalist economy," as Herf says of his reactionary modernists. Fascists (and communists) linked technology's slumber not just to technical incompetence encouraged by a narrow concentration on short-term profits, as an American New Dealer might, but to the nature of capitalism. Unlike the communists, however, fascists associated the revival of technology with the revival of a spiritual community: the nation.[26]

Fascists combined their nationalism with corporativism. They liked to use the community vs. society distinction developed by Toennies (see chapter 5), and they linked modern technology with older visions of a non-commercial society based around people's work and occupation, organized into "corporations." Thus Mussolini: "Corporativism is animated by the possibility of morally and technically unifying social life; it believes in the joy of giving and of sacrifice. It is opposed to every uniquely private goal in life and precisely for that reason, corporativism is not an economic notion, but the unique political, moral, religious, essence of the Fascist revolution." The corporation gave priority to the community, the nation, rather than to the individual businessman. Fascists saw themselves as re-establishing a traditional economic hierarchy, one in which the community took priority over commerce. In support of this, they could invoke Aristotle's condemnation of chrematistic, (see chapter 2), as well as Marx. Both Hitler and Mussolini appealed directly to the working class, with some success. They wanted to reclaim them from "international Communism," and claim their allegiance for the nation. It was no accident that the Nazis were formally the NSDAP, the "National Socialist German Worker's Party." They were national *and* socialist. It was part of fascist ideology that the national community must include the proletariat, and that restoring the proletariat to the nation meant freeing it from the oppression of the bourgeoisie.[27]

The economic problem fascists were trying to overcome, one familiar to Aristotle and Marx, was that "in proportion as economic life grew to be the dominant mistress of the state, money became the god whom all had to serve and to whom each man had to bow down. More and more, the gods of heaven were put into the corner as obsolete and outmoded, and in their stead incense was burned to the idol Mammon," as Hitler put it in *Mein Kampf*. The fascist economy was meant to be subordinate to higher ends—those of the nation, embodied in the state. The Fascist Don't was "Don't Have or Make Money for Yourself—Do It for the Nation." Fascism made the state the focus of society. It appealed to intellectuals to become priests of the nation. Many intellectuals responded. The nation was a community, and embracing it a way to find the sense of belonging intellectuals craved. Before World War II, perhaps as many intellectuals were attracted to fascism as to communism.[28]

However, there was a barrier to prevent intellectuals from becoming fascists: Fascists frequently claimed to hate intellectuals. There is a famous saying, probably apocryphal, attributed to Hitler's henchman Goering: "When I hear the word 'culture', I reach for my gun!" Italian and Spanish fascists liked to shout "Long Live Barbarism." But a large number of German, Italian, and other intellectuals proved receptive to those who proclaimed their contempt for reason. Why?

In part, the answer is parallel to why communist intellectuals accepted abuse. Intellectuals abased themselves in order to feel less like alienated individuals, and more a part of the People. But there were other reasons at work too. Fascists might attack reason, but always in the name of "higher spiritual ideals." This appealed to many intellectuals. The French novelist Jules Romain supported fascism because, unlike Marxism, fascism restored "a genuine and natural hierarchy of values." Fascists attacked only "decadent" culture, the culture of commerce, not the true culture of the people—or of the people's real intellectuals. Thus Italian fascism's semi-official philosopher (and sometime minister of education), Giovanni Gentile: "Fascism... disdains culture that is only ornament.... Fascism seeks a culture in which the spirit is armed and reinforced in order to prevail in ever-new battles. That is, and must be, our barbarism—a barbarity of intellectuals." For Gentile, fascism only attacked intellectuals when they cut themselves off from the nation.[29]

If fascists attacked the intellectual as an isolated aristocrat, they praised him as the priest of nationalism—and invited him in by the back door to exercise a leading role, as the spokesperson for spiritual/intellectual ideals against capitalist society. Hitler argued that "our intellectual classes, especially in Germany, are so segregated and ossified that they lack a living connection with the people below them. We suffer from this...." This is the classic intellectual's lament at being separated from the people, a lament also to be found in Mussolini's writings. Yet once in contact with the people, intellectuals, at least properly educated ones, were their natural leaders, according to Hitler. A properly organized community *must itself be an embodiment of the endeavor to place thinking individuals above the masses, thus subordinating the latter to the former"* (emphasis original). Intellectuals must be educated to fight capitalism on behalf of the nation. "A sharp difference should exist between general education and specialized knowledge. As particularly today the latter threatens more and more to sink into the service of pure Mammon, general education, at least in its more ideal attitude, must be retained as a counterweight." These attitudes were, and are, typical of intellectuals—which helped many sympathize with fascism as fellow travelers, even if they did not join fascist parties.[30]

Hitler himself was an intellectual (as was Mussolini). However he was not, like Lenin and many communists, by inclination an academic. Rather, Hitler was a classic bohemian, as his early years as a starving artist demonstrate. Like most bohemians, he had aristocratic pretentions: "*A philosophy of life which endeavors to reject the democratic mass idea and give this earth to the best people—that is, the highest humanity—must logically obey the same aristocratic principle within this people and make sure that the leadership and the highest influence in this people fall to the best minds*" (emphasis original). A very aristocratic attitude, which either Nietzsche or Flaubert would have endorsed.[31]

Hitler was not a systematic thinker, and his ideas, taken individually, possess little or no originality. He was the stupid man's Marx. Both took others' ideas and oversimplified and impoverished them, but Hitler started out with vastly less intellectual capital than Marx. Hitler never displays brilliance, although he is a less muddled writer than often portrayed. He was not very good at careful critical discourse, although he tried very hard in his autobiography, *Mein Kampf* (being an intellectual does not guarantee being good at it). His writings therefore serve all the better to show the role anti-capitalist commonplaces played in fascist ideology.

An example is Hitler's particular horror of the stock exchange. In *Mein Kampf* he wrote: "*A grave economic symptom of decay was the slow disappearance of the right of private property, and the gradual transference of the entire economy to the ownership of stock companies*" (emphasis original). Just like Aristotle or Aquinas, Hitler thought private property was good, but transformed into money (Marx's bête noire) and shares of stock, it became an end in itself rather than a tool for satisfying needs, and thus bad. With the stock market Hitler associated another age-old complaint, the evil of interest. The Nazi Party Program included the "abolition of unearned (by work and labor) incomes." Interest and dividends were part and parcel of the stock exchange and the international (Jewish) banking conspiracy.[32]

But Hitler was living in historical circumstances different from those of Aristotle and Marx, and his ideas were directed against a somewhat different set of adversaries, e.g., Jews and communists, along with the usual suspects, the bourgeoisie: "This bourgeois world... worships a view of life which in general is distinguished from the Marxists only by degrees and personalities. The bourgeois world is Marxist, but believes in the possibility of the rule of certain groups of men (bourgeoisie) while Marxism itself systematically plans to hand the world over to the Jews." For Hitler, both the bourgeoisie and the Marxists are materialists who reject spiritual, national, and racial values. His struggle is to fight their materialism in the name of those values. "It may be that today gold has become the exclusive ruler of life, but the time will come when man will again bow down before a higher god. Many things today owe their existence solely to the longing for money and wealth, but there is very little among them whose non-existence would leave humanity any the poorer." If only those words weren't Hitler's, how many readers would want to agree? Words like them led many intellectuals to sympathize with fascism.[33]

Hitler's struggle against materialism meant fighting the group that in his view incarnated both communism and materialism, the Jews. The relationship between anti-capitalist attitudes and anti-Semitism was discussed in chapter 5, in regard to Marx's essay "On the Jewish Question." Nazi anti-Semitism "fetishized anti-capitalism." The Jew became a fetish, a magical symbol of the evils of commerce. Nazi anti-Semitism transformed protest against capitalism into protest against a "race."[34]

It is hard to imagine an anti-Semitic Hitler, or any other twentieth-century anti-Semite, who did not appeal to anti-capitalist attitudes as part of his anti-Semitism. As in so many other things, the Jews serve as the canary in the mine. When anti-Semitism rises in the Western world, capitalism is in trouble. To a large extent the reverse has also been true: when anti-capitalist attitudes are spreading, things get worse for the Jews. Widespread anti-capitalist attitudes help make anti-Semitism acceptable. Nevertheless, anti-Semitism was hardly the leading factor in most post-World War I anti-capitalist movements. It was not even necessarily part of fascism. It was central to Nazism, but not to most fascist movements.[35]

Fascism was well positioned to attract many intellectuals as an anti-capitalist movement, and it did, both as members of fascist parties and as fellow travelers. As with communism, intellectuals' anti-capitalist attitudes contributed greatly to fascism's influence. To ask whether intellectuals as a class were responsible for Hitler and Mussolini is like asking whether they were responsible for Lenin and Stalin. A historian of German academia has summed up the responsibility of the German intelligentsia neatly, and his words are equally valid for intellectuals in other anti-capitalist movements:

[They] did not actively desire the triumph of the Third Reich; nor were they to blame for the actual propositions of National Socialist propaganda. Their responsibility was more indirect than that, more negative than positive. It was more a matter of ideological affinities and mental habits than one of formal theories. But their responsibility was great nonetheless.... They fostered chaos, without regard for the consequences.[36]

In other words, "they sapped the moral legitimacy of an entire civilisation," that is, the legitimacy of capitalism. Much the same can be said for anti-capitalist intellectuals in general.[37]

Social Catholicism

Not every intellectual who sought refuge from capitalism, or to make a revolution against it, turned to fascism or communism. There was a more traditional way of rejecting the world—religion. For those who looked to Christian tradition, Catholicism offered an alternative anti-capitalist community. These anti-capitalist social Catholic movements are, outside Catholic circles, mostly obscure today, especially to Americans, but they exercised considerable influence in the 1930s and still do in the twenty-first century.

These movements, here called "social Catholicism," could look to both a recent and a more distant past for inspiration. There was the New Testament, the monastic tradition, and the philosophy of St. Thomas Aquinas (see chapter 2). And there was a modern history of Catholic intervention in favor of the poor. From the 1870s, leading representatives of the Catholic clergy, such as Cardinal Manning of London, Bishop Ketteler in the Rhineland, and Cardinal Gibbons of Baltimore had taken the side of striking labor unions. In 1890, London dockworkers honored Cardinal Manning by carrying his portrait next to that of Karl Marx in their May Day parade. The pre-World War I climax of this movement was the 1891 papal encyclical of Pope Leo XIII, *Rerum Novarum*. In it the pope reminded the wealthy that being rich was an obstacle to salvation, and cited Aquinas that ideally everyone should give away all they had beyond what was "reasonably required to keep up becomingly his station in life." The pope supported unions as a modern form of the traditional guild or worker's corporation.[38]

Before World War I, however, Catholic anti-capitalist sentiment had limited effect, like anti-commercial thought generally. After World War I, new social Catholic movements exerted widespread influence. In England and the US the "Distributionists," led by the popular Catholic writers Hilaire Belloc and G. K. Chesterton, were influential. In America, Father Coughlin, initially a supporter of the New Deal, tried and failed to create a new party that would "eradicate the cancerous growths from decadent capitalism and avoid the treacherous pitfalls of red communism." His radio program was among the most popular in the country. On the American left, the Catholic Worker movement was founded in 1933 by Doris Day and Pierre Maurin, a "personalist."[39]

The most influential Catholic anti-capitalist movement among intellectuals was "personalism," founded by the Frenchman Emmanuel Mounier. Many of personalism's ideas were typical of social Catholicism in general. They were also often similar to those of fascists or communists. As Mounier wrote, "there is almost no one today, from the extreme right to the extreme left, who does not profess anti-capitalism." The anti-capitalism of Mounier and the personalist movement was profound—and commonplace in the 1930s. Personalists liked to talk about the "established disorder," that is, the economic anarchy of capitalism. Even more than most intellectuals, they were appalled by an invisible hand. Mounier's economic remedies were an appeal from disorder to order. Like many fascists, he wanted to return to a corporate organization of economic life.[40]

What distinguished personalists from their competitors for the anti-commercial vote? Personalists often referred to their movement as a "Third Force," or "Third Way," to distinguish themselves from the alternatives of capitalism or communism, or sometimes from communism and fascism. "We are a new force, the Third Force, beyond dying capitalism and reconsidered Marxism," wrote Mounier. When it came to politics, the followers of the Third Way took pains to stress that they were revolutionaries, too, as the title of Mounier's collected works, "The Communitarian and Personalist Revolution," emphasized. Revolution there must be, but it must be a spiritual revolution, not one made by or for the state. Personalism was, above all, spiritual. From the personalist perspective capitalism and communism were both forms of materialism, while Hitler and Mussolini (and Roosevelt) placed too much emphasis on the state. "We put human values at the summit: they put the state, we the person." It was personalism's emphasis on the individual, on their "personality," that gave the movement its name and made it different.[41]

Personalism emphasized criticizing the bourgeois lifestyle over criticizing the economic results of capitalism, although it practiced both. Mounier was very clear about the lifestyle he advocated. The good life was incarnated in two forms: the artist and the saint (the aristocratic and clerical aspects of the intellectual identity). Since Mounier was a Catholic, he began by talking about the artist's suffering, his link to Christ: "Besides the condition the modern world imposes on the proletarian, there is no other condition more miserable than that it imposes on the artist. It rejects the unemployed like waste from its mechanized body, it rejects the artist like waste from the mechanization of its soul...." Real art must revolt against capitalism. If one was not an artist, at least one could be a saint. This sounds strange, because we think it is harder to be a saint than an artist. But that was not Mounier's view. "Sainthood is not an extraordinary vocation, it is the natural vocation, although not the habitual vocation, of the Christian." Mounier's Christian is a spiritual being, the opposite of the bourgeois in every way. But the Christian is human, and must struggle against bourgeois original sin. "Each of us is half, a quarter, an eighth, or a twelfth bourgeois, and the bourgeois is angered by hearing his name the same way a demon who has possessed someone is." The bourgeois is the very devil. To fight him, we must be heroes, saints, poets.[42]

This saintly, heroic individual should desire a simple life, the precondition for spiritual growth. There ought to be both a minimum of material well-being, and a maximum: *"The ideal of life for which we ought to struggle is an ideal of living poverty or, if one prefers, a generous simplicity; against two enemies: wealth and misery"* (emphasis original). Personalism rejected the idea that needs ought to be always increasing, that as one desire is satisfied, let us say for a refrigerator, another should take its place, for example for air conditioning. The indefinite expansion of material needs and desires destroys all prospects for a spiritual life. "One of the leading flaws of capitalism is to have made spiritual life submit to consumption, consumption to production and production to profit, while the natural hierarchy is the opposite one."[43]

Mounier rejected the bourgeois lifestyle because it encouraged a type of personality he despised. Being bourgeois was *not*, according to Mounier, about how much money one had or one's relationship to the means of production. It was a matter of values and attitudes:

> A rich man is not just one someone who has a lot of money.... The typist who accepts the world as it is because his boss is nice to him, the salesgirl who takes the side of the luxury goods she sells, the proletarian who devours the cast-off ideals of the bank clerk, the young antimilitarist who secretly dreams of being a reserve second lieutenant, they are rich too.[44]

The bourgeois only cares about what is useful. His ideal of happiness is gilded mediocrity: "The bourgeois lifestyle is based on order and happiness.... Gilded mediocrity.... The Christian's desire is to *be*, his is only to *have*." This bourgeois is one of the characters nineteenth-century novelists poked fun at. But Mounier is writing after World War I, and he is in earnest: "The bourgeois is not only curious or amusing. He represents, for what we are concerned with here, a good-natured form of the Antichrist; and not the least odious one."[45]

Mounier's discussion of the good life is a classic example of a phenomenon found throughout the revolutionary anti-capitalist movements intellectuals supported. It is an archetypal demonstration of intellectuals' tendency (a tendency found in every class) to see their personal situation and the situation of their class as representative of society at large. It is easy to read Mounier's discussion of artists, saints, and heroes, indeed his whole vision of human spirituality, as an unconscious commentary on the situation of the intellectual in democratic society. When Mounier wrote that "the Christian's desire is to *be*, [the bourgeois'] is only to *have*," he unwittingly echoed William James' contrast of businessmen and intellectuals as "men who *have*" and "men who *are*" (see chapter 1). James' intellectuals are Mounier's Christians. Unable to speak openly on behalf of his class, Mounier identified their cause, not with that of the proletariat or the nation, but with Christianity. In personalism intellectuals could once again become priests, guides to salvation, exercising their moral voice.[46]

All anti-capitalist movements that appealed to intellectuals allowed the intellectual to attach her personal or class grievances to them, or else they would not have appealed. But in this respect personalism's appeal was stronger than communism and fascism, at least to intellectuals disposed to Christian values. It was less closely linked to a different class, to a particular nation, or even to a particular religion, despite its ties to Catholicism, and thus allowed the intellectual maximum autonomy. Personalism was a generalized protest of the intellectual class against capitalism, revolutionary yet still inchoate, like the intellectual class itself.

Unlike communism and fascism, personalism was not a mass movement—another way in which it showed its affinity with the intelligentsia. Its influence was broad, but indirect: it never founded a political party. Personalism was an attempt to make a revolution in values. So were communism and fascism, but for them a political or political/economic revolution came first. Rejecting the prevailing political and economic system was part of personalism, and part of its appeal, but taking over the government was not its main focus.

"Community" was a key word when personalists discussed politics. Like so many other post-World War I anti-capitalist intellectuals, they leaned heavily on Toennies' community vs. society distinction. Personalists used the word "community" with a particular purpose, however.

They wanted to avoid talking about the fascist "state," the communist "class," or the bourgeois "individual" (hence their use of "personality"). Like all third parties, the personalist defenders of their Third Way constantly struggled to maintain their own identity. Personalism emphasized the community and the person against capitalism, independently of any particular political form. While this made it difficult for personalism to take power, it enabled it to influence widely disparate figures who were attracted by its spiritual rejection of capitalism. Personalists could find something good to say about everybody as long as they rejected capitalism. In the 1930s, Mounier wrote of the communists that "we also want to underline, before examining anything else, our profound sympathy for motives whose intellectual superstructure we do not always accept." At the same time he could visit Italy and Germany and speak of these "countries which have rediscovered the meaning of dignity" and "the authentic spiritual élan present in men violently torn away from bourgeois decadence." The influence of personalism was multivalent. Before World War II figures associated to one degree or another with the personalist movement in France include de Gaulle, Mitterrand, and Maritain, along with Mounier. Mitterrand and Mounier initially collaborated with Vichy. De Gaulle and Maritain did not.[47]

In the 1930s, however, social Catholics were more often sympathetic to fascism than to communism. Spanish fascism had strong links to social Catholic movements like *Opus Dei,* which was influenced by personalist ideas. *Opus Dei* and its very conservative influence spread well beyond Spain after World War II. In France, on the other hand, in the late 1930s, "a remarkable contingent of what we would call militant 'greens',... became one of the most significant spin-offs...." After World War II, of course, this changed. Father Le Bret, a personalist and founder of the worker-priest movement, whose writings of the early 1940s sound fascist, became more and more Marxist after World War II. Mounier himself was much friendlier to the fascists in the 1930s than to the communists. But in 1946, after first supporting and then breaking with the Vichy regime, Mounier wrote that "everyone [should] remember that every arrow directed against the Communist Party strikes the very flesh of the hope of the desperate, and saps the force of their silent army."[48]

After World War II, personalism's influence was widespread, but hard to characterize. In post-World War II France, people associated with the movement were key actors in the French Socialist party, in the Ecole National d'Administration founded to train France's business and political elite, in the newspaper *Le Monde,* etc. Its influence rivaled that of existentialism. Mounier's journal, *Esprit,* still survives, and prominent personalists like Denis de Rougemont played a leading role in French intellectual life for decades after World War II. Personalists were also involved in the creation of Liberation Theology, so influential among Latin American leftists in the 1960s. The Liberation Theologians' critique of capitalism could have come straight out of Mounier—and sometimes it did. The Jesuit Henri de Lubac, another personalist, went on to become a prominent theologian at Vatican II and later a Cardinal. On the other hand, Pope John Paul II, who crushed the liberation theologians, had long-held ties with several personalists. *His* anti-capitalist feelings were better expressed by the Polish Solidarity movement.[49]

Because it was a Third Way, personalist ideas were consistently anti-capitalist, but not consistently associated with the left or the right. They inspired Catholic movements, but also non-Catholic and even non-Christian rejections of capitalism. Personalist ideas and language reappeared in the counter-culture and in New Age religious movements, as will be seen in the next chapter. Many "communitarian" movements have replayed its themes. For all their separate disagreements, they share personalism's revolutionary rejection of the bourgeois lifestyle.

Communism, fascism, and social Catholicism were all revolutionary anti-capitalist movements. But not all intellectuals who rejected capitalism were revolutionaries. Even among critics of capitalism, not all wanted to reject it entirely. Among the anti-capitalist movements that arose after World War I were a number that were more reformist than revolutionary. Among these perhaps the most successful was the American New Deal.

The New Deal

Anti-capitalist attitudes were slower to take root in the United States than in Europe (see chapter 3). But by the late nineteenth century, they were prominent in American literature, and by World War I all the characteristic anti-capitalist rhetoric had American spokespersons. In the 1920s, criticizing the bourgeois lifestyle, making fun of the "yahoos" and the "booboisie," as H. L. Mencken called them, was the dominant form of anti-capitalist expression in America, although there were also "Progressive" and agrarian traditions that criticized the anarchy of capitalism from an economic perspective.

The Depression had a greater effect on the attitudes of American intellectuals than it had on European ones. The philosopher John Dewey noted that after World War I there had been much discussion of American intellectuals moving to the left. After the Depression, "there is no longer such a discussion; the intellectuals *are* left.... The only question is how far left they have gone." The tone of their criticism changed, and, as in Europe after World War I, it began to matter more. Before the Depression, when American intellectuals criticized their society for being dominated by a bunch of money-grubbing barbarians, they never made much headway. During the Depression and the New Deal, their criticism of a society with 25 percent unemployment and no idea what to do about it proved more influential.[50]

The New Deal, of course, is the name given to Franklin D. Roosevelt's social and economic policies in 1932-40, and to the era in American politics he dominated. American intellectuals' reaction to the Depression and the New Deal took many forms. Some became communists or fellow travelers, some fascists or their fellow travelers, and some social Catholics. But the economic remedies that exercised the most influence in America, and were the most distinctively American, were not revolutionary but technocratic solutions to capitalism. It was above all the idea of economic planning and regulation that appealed to American intellectuals. Similar attitudes on the part of anti-capitalist intellectuals produced different results in the differing circumstances of Europe and America: in Europe, frequently, government ownership, in the United States, government regulation.

Is advocating economic regulation and planning equivalent to rejecting capitalism? Historians of the New Deal have been reluctant to say so. Just as there are those who deny that fascism was an anti-capitalist movement, because they insist on equating opposition to capitalism with abolishing private property, so there are those who deny that the New Deal was opposed to capitalism. Left-wing historians, who wish the New Deal had been more radical, refuse to admit that it was radical at all. The most widespread view sees the New Dealers as working for the preservation of capitalism, not its destruction. Its proponents argue that support for welfare-state measures is not sufficient to make an anti-capitalist, even if some capitalists see it that way. As a representative historian writes, "Even the most precedent-breaking New Deal projects reflected capitalist thinking and deferred to business sensibilities.... Roosevelt's program rested on the assumption that a just society could be secured by imposing a welfare state on a capitalist foundation." The author concludes that the intellectuals most deeply involved in creating and administering the New Deal "...rejected laissez-faire, yet shrank from embracing socialism."[51]

What matters from the point of view of the struggle of mind and money is not whether a given measure is incompatible with capitalism—the New Deal evidently was not. What matters is the intention of its authors, and the way in which it is perceived. The latter changes over time, making judgment tricky.

It is true that most New Deal intellectuals were not socialists, even if they did not like laissez-faire, but it is not the whole truth, and not enough of the truth as it was understood at the time. When Roosevelt was elected in 1932, the business community did not see regulators as its friends, even if the regulators thought they were. No matter how much the regulators may have approved of capitalism in the abstract, they were acting, and were perceived to be acting, in the name of the community against capitalism. The fact that they "rejected laissez-faire" was enough to make them enemies of capitalism in the eyes of the average capitalist. Even if they didn't "embrace socialism," they were called socialists, communists, and worse. Their own language gave businessmen reason to think they were on opposite sides. Rexford Tugwell, a member of Roosevelt's five-man "Brains Trust" during the presidential campaign, and later an influential member of the administration, wrote in December 1931 that "this... is literally meant. Business will be logically required to disappear. The essence of business is its free venture for profits in an unregulated economy." Adolf Berle, another member of the Brains Trust and, like Tugwell, a professor at Columbia University, claimed he wanted to save capitalism, not destroy it. But he also declared himself ready to jettison it if it could not feed the nation.[52]

Yet it would be an exaggeration to describe the New Deal as fundamentally anti-capitalist. New Deal technocrats were not primarily interested in destroying capitalism, but in *limiting* it. There is a spectrum of anti-capitalist visions of community whose edges are defined not by right and left, but by degrees of hostility, and the New Deal is on the moderate edge of the anti-capitalist spectrum in the twentieth century. There is such a thing as fruitful conflict, and in some respects the New Deal is a model of it.

The New Dealers preferred to reform capitalism, but they were prepared to treat its existence as provisional. This did not mean the end of private profit. It meant the replacement of the invisible hand by the long arm of the state, an arm directed by planners, that is by expert intellectuals. The New Dealers were "especially disturbed by the *chaos* of private capitalism." They wanted to replace chaos with order, like so many other anti-capitalist intellectuals. But whereas in Europe this tended to result in government ownership of certain industries, in America it led to government regulation. The anti-capitalist motivation was the same, but the New Dealers were reformers, not revolutionaries. They were *liberals*, in the meaning that term had in the 1930s, that is, they were opposed to those who were *orthodox* in their economics. The orthodox supported the free market and the Invisible Hand. The liberals favored planning and government intervention in the name of the community.[53]

Being liberal was not revolutionary. "The idea of planning tended increasingly to stand for administrative experience and managerial efficiency in the interest not of social revolution but of social control." This was not enough to satisfy some more radical American intellectuals (or historians), whose vocal dissatisfaction has had a wide echo. The radicals wanted revolution. The idea of planning attracted intellectuals by presenting them with an aristocratic role to play as planners, but it did not much appeal to intellectuals' bohemian side, and gave only limited scope to their moral or clerical voice. Nevertheless, from the perspective of the struggle between mind and money, there is no doubt that planners and revolutionaries were, if not precisely on the same side, at least on the same wavelength. Both saw the community as independent from and superior to commerce, and at least to some extent opposed to it.[54]

Although the first Soviet Five-Year Plan dated to 1928, it was not until 1930 that it attracted widespread attention and enthusiasm. After the great crash of 1929, many intellectuals and politicians, including conservatives, were fascinated by the Soviet Union's blueprint for economic development, and its fascist analogues. The idea that economic planning could create full employment and encourage the efficient use of technology and resources was widely attractive. A former president of General Electric called for the creation of government-sponsored cartels that would guarantee workers minimum standards of pay, health care, and pensions. David Lilienthal, an intellectual who became a leading New Deal administrator, wrote that "there is almost nothing, however fantastic, that (given competent organization) a team of engineers, scientists, and administrators cannot do today." In the circumstances it was easy for American intellectuals like Dewey to conclude that "the only form of enduring social organization that is now possible is one in which the new forces of productivity are cooperatively controlled.... Such a social order cannot be established by an unplanned and external convergence of the actions of separate individuals,...bent on personal private advantage.[55]

The New Dealers rejected the old American economic ideal of a world of independent small businessmen. There were moments when a populist campaign of anti-trust lawsuits was too tempting to pass up, but on the whole the New Dealers argued for accepting big corporations, big business, and even cartels. However, these corporations would need government supervision and government oversight, government planning, to insure they functioned efficiently and in the community's interest. Tugwell thought government had the right and power to make sure prices were reasonable, production met people's needs, and profits were subordinate to the public interest. Berle, on the other hand, was more inclined to talk to businessmen than to issue them orders. Both saw a role for government in the distribution of income, to make sure that there was sufficient economic demand. Later in the 1930s, in what historians sometimes call the "second" New Deal, the balance of government intervention shifted somewhat from planning to regulation. The differences, whatever they may be, were secondary to the continued belief that government "must exercise an increased level of authority over the structure and behavior of private capitalist institutions."[56]

Instead of appealing to revolution to save civilization from capitalism, the New Dealers appealed to planning and regulation. But if the New Dealers did not make the proletariat their heroes, they did see themselves on the same side as the struggling farmer or worker. This itself was a change from the 1920s and the days of Mencken, when intellectuals in America were often as alienated from the yahoo lower classes as from bourgeois philistines. The new ideal of economic planning entailed a new attitude on the part of democratic society towards its intellectual class and the role they would henceforth play.

Thurman Arnold, who was an assistant attorney-general during the New Deal, complained that while the public respected judges, it despised bureaucrats. America needed to allow its administrators "to come out of the disreputable cellars in which they have been forced to work." Arnold wanted America to find a place for a new bureaucratic aristocracy. America needed "a religion of government which permits us to face frankly the psychological factors inherent in the development of organizations with public responsibility." In other words, to turn the bureaucracy into a secular priesthood, an ideal well suited to an intellectual class in a democratic society. Rexford Tugwell went even further on the road towards creating a new intellectual aristocracy. In an argument reminiscent of John Stuart Mill's desire for a chamber of experts to draw up legislation for parliamentary approval, Tugwell wanted to create a "fourth power" of government, alongside the executive, legislative and judicial powers, for the purpose of expert planning. Plans would be drawn up by the experts, subject to approval by the legislative branch. The experts themselves would be recruited from the most intelligent ½ of 1 percent of the population. Such planning would make the abolition of capitalism superfluous. Along with many New Dealers, Tugwell believed in a "planned capitalism," which was perhaps another way of saying a capitalism in which intellectual bureaucrats and professors, not entrepreneurs, were the aristocrats.[57]

Some of these ideas remained pure theory, and none were universally applied. But what was truly remarkable about the New Deal was the extent to which ideas like these, their authors, and thousands of other intellectuals succeeded in influencing and even in entering government. The circumstances of America in 1932 were sufficiently novel, and sufficiently dire, for politicians to look for advice from even the most unlikely quarter—which at that time meant the university. During his campaign for President in 1931, Roosevelt created the "Brains Trust." It was a group of five men, two lawyers and three professors, including Tugwell, Berle, and Raymond Moley, whose job was partly to write FDR's speeches, but mostly to come up with economic and social policy ideas. They never had a united economic policy (the Roosevelt administration was not known for coherence), but they and the many intellectuals subsequently recruited into government service all shared the conviction that reason could and should shape the economy. As Tugwell put it, "the jig is up. The cat is out of the bag. There is no invisible hand. There never was…. Men were taught to believe that they were, paradoxically, advancing cooperation when they were defying it. That was a viciously false paradox." So much for Adam Smith. New Deal intellectuals assumed that "the nation's greatest problems were rooted in the structure of modern… capitalism and that it was the mission of government to deal somehow with the flaws in that structure." In his Second Inaugural address of 1936, Roosevelt confirmed that this vision had become his: "We refuse to leave the problems of our common welfare to be solved by the winds of chance and the hurricanes of disaster… and in so doing we are fashioning an instrument of unimagined power for the establishment of a morally better world."[58]

The New Dealers liked to combine moral language with the language of economic efficiency. Roosevelt's rhetoric in his First Inaugural Address (1932) was typical in this regard. "Plenty is at our doorstep, but a generous use of it languishes in the very sight of the supply. Primarily this is because rulers of the exchange of mankind's goods have failed through their own stubbornness and their own incompetence, have admitted their failure, and have abdicated.... the money changers have fled from their high seats in the temple of our civilization. We may now restore that temple to the ancient truths." Roosevelt's lines combined rational criticism of incompetence with biblical imagery, chasing moneylenders from the temple and restoring the "ancient truths." That truth, moral and economic both, was that the community came first, and was entitled to assert its priority. As Roosevelt put it in a 1934 speech, "The old fallacious notion of the banker on one side and the Government on the other side as being more or less equal and independent units, has passed away. Government by the necessity of things must be the leader, must be the judge of the conflicting interests of all groups in the community, including bankers."[59]

The Brains Trust itself was dissolved after the election of 1932, but its members went into government, along with a huge influx of intellectuals, and more particularly of professors. The New Dealers used their power to plan and regulate. Although their most ambitious creation, the NRA (National Reconstruction Administration), which effectively set up industry-wide cartels under government supervision, was ruled unconstitutional by the Supreme Court, many of their efforts became landmarks of the American economic system. Without going into details that can be found in any history, these include an "alphabet soup" of legislative acts and agencies, from the AAA (Agricultural Adjustment Act) and CCC (Civilian Conservation Corps) to the TVA (Tennessee Valley Authority) and WPA (Works Progress Administration). They had a vast effect on American society.

For the first time since the mid-nineteenth century, American intellectuals felt good about their role. In FDR's government, "intellectuals took on an importance in the White House that they had not enjoyed since the days before Jackson.... Even Woodrow Wilson, himself a professor, had not given intellectuals the prominence they had in the New Deal." Intellectuals naturally welcomed the change. Edmund Wilson observed that the Depression made intellectuals feel "exhilarated.... It gave us a new sense of freedom; and a new sense of power...."[60]

The New Deal was by no means the rule of experts Tugwell imagined, but it was a period of unprecedented influence for them. It was a brief renewal of the alliance of property and education, even if few people perceived it that way. If mind and money remained divorced, at least they could be civil on the telephone and recognize common interests. The New Deal planners and regulators criticized the bourgeoisie and capitalism from a stance that allowed their opposition to occasionally concede a point, with fruitful results. The New Deal was an important moment in the struggle between mind and money because it ended in reform, rather than revolution. It "created the welfare state. Never again would it be seriously argued that society had no responsibility for the unemployed, the aged, and the infirm." Without the human sacrifices demanded by communists and fascists, without the spiritual revolution demanded by the personalists, the New Dealers succeeded in changing capitalism. They attained more of their goals, without revolution, than those who made revolutions, or tried to. Even though the New Deal did not fully bring the American economy out of decline until World War II, one can hardly say that the American intelligentsia were wildly mistaken in supporting it—which is much more than one can say for their communist, fascist, and even social Catholic colleagues.[61]

The New Deal may have been America's most anti-capitalist moment, and the moment in which its intellectuals had the most influence, but it by no means satisfied all America's anti-capitalist intellectuals. Alphabet soup was not necessarily a good substitute for the red meat of revolution. In 1932, there were more prominent writers supporting Norman Thomas, the Socialist candidate for president, or even William Foster, the communist, than Roosevelt. However, after 1932 American intellectuals gave massive support to the New Deal, and to a considerable extent abandoned groups to its left. Support for the American Communist Party, never very strong to begin with, peaked in the early 30s. Most of the New Dealers were not interested in creating a new kind of human being. They did not, by and large, reject the bourgeois lifestyle. This further differentiated them from communists, fascists, and social Catholics, all of whom did.[62]

Success never reads as well as failure. Catastrophes make much more exciting stories. Nevertheless, it is striking that among intellectuals, at least, catastrophe has often had a better reputation. Despite the failure of revolutionary anti-capitalism, many intellectuals continued to support it, to varying degrees, well after that failure was apparent. The New Deal has always retained a certain nostalgic appeal, but communism has far outdistanced it in the intellectual imagination. Why?

Why Smart People Persist with Dumb Mistakes

During a debate in 1866 in the British Parliament, John Stuart Mill was asked by a Conservative MP of considerable intellectual accomplishment if he thought that all Conservatives were stupid, since he had written that the Conservatives were the party of the stupid. Unembarrassed, Mill replied that he didn't think that all Conservatives were stupid, but rather that stupid people were generally Conservative. Looking at the political choices made by so many intellectuals in the twentieth century, one can only conclude that it might be smarter to be stupid than it is lucky to be smart. Intellectuals were far from the only people to be attracted to communism, fascism, etc.—but they were supposed to be smart enough to avoid such mistakes. Communism and fascism would have existed whatever intellectuals thought about capitalism, but neither would have been as strong without the participation, support, or benevolent neutrality of much of the Western intelligentsia. Whether they were revolutionaries or only fellow travelers, intellectuals played a significant role in the political disasters of the twentieth century.[63]

Many intellectuals could and did reject capitalism without supporting mass murder or the abolition of democratic government. But it is intellectuals' support for Hitler, Lenin, Stalin, Mussolini, and later Mao, Pol Pot, Castro, etc. which strikes the eye. How and why did so many smart, well-educated people make such big mistakes? And once they had made them, why did they persist in them for so long? The initial mistake was often plausible. The persistence appears incredible. The American novelist Saul Bellow remarked of left-wing intellectuals that "a great deal of intelligence can be invested in ignorance when the need for illusion is deep." The statement is just as true of right-wing intellectuals, as Heidegger's refusal to acknowledge the importance of the Holocaust shows. However, to understand why so many intellectuals were committed to ignorance about capitalism's enemies, we will take their infatuation with communism as the example.[64]

Illusion, a deliberate suspension of disbelief and critical discourse, is central to intellectuals' political behavior in the twentieth century. Everything bad about the Soviet Union was known, or knowable, very early on. Yet even in 1992, after everything about Lenin, Stalin, Mao, the Chinese Cultural Revolution was common knowledge, one ex-communist titled an article on the end of the Soviet Union "The End of Communism: The Winter of Souls." Why was it a winter of souls? Was it summer when Stalin ruled? Even when intellectuals did give up their illusions about communism, they found it heart-rending. Another ex-communist agreed that communist intellectuals were imbeciles, but at least they were imbeciles with "a generosity and an altruism that no longer exists at the end of the twentieth century." In this view, evidently, one ought to admire mass murderers provided they show altruism and generosity. Intellectuals' desire for illusion was obviously very strong.

The question is "under what circumstances and for what motives do 'critical intellectuals' become uncritical ones?" The long history of intellectuals visiting Stalin's Russia, Mao's China, Castro's Cuba, even Pol Pot's Cambodia (or for that matter Hitler's Germany or Mussolini's Italy) and coming back with laudatory accounts, is testimony to their selective perception—often with their eyes wide open. They knew they were being fooled, and they didn't care.[65]

Intellectuals' desire to remain ignorant owes much to what Jean-François Revel refers to as "the omnipresence of an almost unconscious layer of anti-commercial culture" in their minds, a layer explored in chapters 2-5. The influence of the Three Don'ts, and of the literary and theoretical images so broadly diffused in the nineteenth century, helped polish the slippery slope on which many intellectuals found themselves after World War I. But this hardly seems a sufficient explanation. How can we improve upon it?[66]

Intellectuals fall in love with revolution. Once they have identified themselves with the revolutionary cause, intellectuals are as subject to the blindness of love as any. Even when they have given up loving, in their disillusion they love the idea of being in love—hence their nostalgia for communism. Stephen Spender, who flirted with communism in the 1930s, remarked of some renowned British scientists who remained in the party that "it is wrong to think that scientists show the same qualities of detachment and considerateness in their social attitudes as they do in the laboratory. They are as liable as anyone else to be carried away by their emotions; and planned societies offer them special temptations." Intellectuals are pseudo-aristocrats and pseudo-clerics but not, *pace* Nietzsche, superhuman. Therefore they are just as capable of self-deception as other human beings. Their love for the revolution is a strong emotional reason for it.[67]

Along with love, another human need, a need to which intellectuals are peculiarly subject, is to identify with a group. Because they are a permanently alienated elite, with ambivalent feelings about their own status, many intellectuals experience a strong desire to overcome their separation from society (see chapter 1). When a group to identify with exists, it encourages a complete loss of critical distance and a complete abandonment of CCD where it is concerned. Closing ones' eyes is easy. "The need for identification may result in an almost unbelievable loss of critical reasoning, as has been confirmed by all the well-known intellectuals who identified themselves with Stalinism, Nazism, Maoism, and various fanatic sects." This is all the more true when a real, tangible

Utopia exists. Anti-capitalist illusions were incomparably stronger and more widespread in the twentieth century than in the nineteenth, because the Soviet Union made the word flesh. Even intellectuals somewhat critical of the actually existing Soviet Union, Maoist China, fascist Italy, etc. were encouraged to suspend disbelief in the possibility of a similar, better, not-yet existing alternative to capitalism. By way of compensation and bad conscience, one cultivates CCD all the more sharply where capitalism is concerned. That a flawed Utopia is a contradiction in terms escapes the defenders of the beloved regime. It is still Utopia. When given the choice of "socialism or barbarism," as the German radical Rosa Luxemburg put it, what intellectual could choose capitalist barbarism? Even if the reality of socialism turned out to be worse, the illusion was incomparably more beautiful.[68]

This leads us to another contributing factor in the ability of intellectuals to maintain illusions, their need for an enchanted world. Intellectuals have been leading agents in disenchanting the world, destroying religious and political illusions with glee. To displace the traditional clergy and emancipate themselves from the authority of the Church, to have scope for careful critical discourse, intellectuals had to disenchant the world. But with the pulpit discredited, where is a preacher to preach? The university doubtless, or even the new marketplace of commercial publishing. But there must be something to preach about. There must be a new dogma to explicate and debate, and a new moral language, built on new foundations that give an ultimate meaning to life. The revolutionary anti-capitalist movements of the twentieth century, especially communism, provided a means for investing daily life, and ordinary political choices, with ultimate meaning. Intellectuals were looking for a religion. Capitalism could not provide that. Revolutionary faith could.

It is only natural for an unfrocked clergy to search desperately for a religion, perhaps even more desperately when it is their own criticism that has cost them their priestly robes. Deep religious commitment can lead to tunnel vision. *This* is a miracle, *that* is a fraud. *These* are the accomplishments of socialism, e.g., free medical care for the poor. Socialist poverty is a *lie*, or the fault of the old system. This attitude is why, as the Mexican writer Octavio Paz said, "Marxism… is the *superstition* of the twentieth century" (emphasis added).[69]

But it is not only their identity as pseudo-clergy that encourages intellectuals to political blindness, it is also their situation as a pseudo-aristocracy. This is why intellectuals always have a soft spot for what Benjamin Constant called the ancient as opposed to the modern idea of freedom. Modern freedom is the freedom of a democratic capitalist society. It is based on private individuals pursuing their own individual happiness in the way that seems best to them, without interference so long as they do not hurt others. The ancient world identified freedom not with private life, but with political participation. The free man must identify himself fully with his community. Ancient freedom means participation in community life, in politics, rather than pursuing private pleasures. Intellectuals are attracted to this ancient political definition of freedom. It is a political means of overcoming their alienation, and of ascribing to themselves an aristocratic function as the architects of community. This is one reason why the notion of community is so attractive to intellectuals, who otherwise tend to cultivate their independence.

In itself, there is nothing necessarily sinister about this attitude. However, in the twentieth century, many intellectuals found the ultimate justification for political illusions and self-deception in their commitment to the ancient idea of freedom. Committed to politics, deriving their identity as human beings, that is, as intellectuals, from it, they were willing to ignore anything that was harmful to the private sphere, provided it was done in the community's name.

Love, religion and politics—all these reasons have served to blind anti-capitalist intellectuals to reality. Some explain the actions of certain individuals, some of others. Some intellectuals were motivated by all of them. But more important than all else was a different motivation for intellectuals' persistent blindness to the faults of communism, fascism, and other alternatives to capitalism. This reason is the most simple of all: hatred. Many intellectuals hate capitalism. A large fraction of the intelligentsia will always hate capitalism, even if they have no alternative to love. Hatred is even more effective in short-circuiting critical discourse than love.

This hatred was in part a necessary consequence of the intellectual's identity and social situation (see chapter 1). It was reinforced by the historical traditions embodied in the Three Don'ts (see chapter 2). Hatred had briefly turned into love for commercial society during the honeymoon period between mind and money (see chapter 3), but the antipathy was reinforced by their divorce. Then Dickens, Marx, and Co. stoked hatred for Mr. Smith the merchant for most of the nineteenth century (see chapters 4 and 5). World War I and its aftermath loosed all restraints on expressing it. Violent antipathy to capitalism led very smart people to make very dumb mistakes, and to keep on making them.

From some errors, history discouraged intellectuals. There were very few fascists left after 1945. Other mistakes persisted longer. But in the decade or two after 1945 most anti-capitalist Western intellectuals slowly withdrew from direct political challenges to capitalism, at least in the Western world (they were more inclined to support them when they were far away). Ex-communists repented, while avowing their good intentions. Ex-nazis concealed the fact. Personalists continued to look for community, but on a smaller scale. After World War II, the war between mind and money saw mind stage a tactical retreat. But mind kept up its fire on money even while withdrawing towards the Ivory Tower. During lulls in the fighting, intellectuals wrote books and got stoned, which, after all, was another way to demonstrate their disdain for capitalism.

Notes

1.   Tocqueville, *Democracy in America*, 747-50.
2.   Tocqueville, *Democracy in America*, 748-52, 756n.1.
3.   Tocqueville, *Democracy in America*, 624.
4.   Tocqueville, *The Old Regime*, 1:88-89.
5.   Nadezhda Mandelstam, *Hope Against Hope* (New York: Athenaeum, 1976), 126.
6.   Vincent Descombes, *Philosophie par gros temps* (Paris: Minuit, 1989), 41.
7.   Kautsky cited by Lenin, "What is to be Done?," in *The Essential Works of Lenin*, ed. Henry M. Christman (New York: Dover Books, 1987), 81-82.
8.   Furet, *Le passé d'une illusion: essai sur l'idée communiste au XXe siècle* (Paris: Robert Laffont/Calmann-Lévy, 1996), 310; Lenin, "What is to be Done?," *Essential Works*, 69-70, 74, 145, 153.
9.   Michael Bakunin, *Selected Writings,* ed. Arthur Lehning (New York: Grove Press, 1973), 160, 266.
10. Bakunin, *Selected Writings,* 194; Le Bon, cited in Hollander, *Political Pilgrims*, 400.
11. Silone and Koestler's accounts of becoming and ceasing to be Communists are in *The God that Failed*, 12, 87.
12. Koestler, *The God that Failed*, 19.
13. Cowley, in Hollander, *Political Pilgrims*, 83.
14. Furet *Le passé*, 142-151, which also discusses Kautsky's similar position.
15. Weber, "Religious Rejections of the World and Their Directions," *From Max Weber*, 336-37.
16. Koestler, *The God that Failed*, 42-43; Hollander, *Political Pilgrims*, 63; David Caute, *The Fellow-Travellers: Intellectual Friends of Communism* (New Haven: Yale University Press, 1988), 219; Furet, *Le passé*, 197.
17. Caute, *The Fellow-Travellers*, 4, 238, 256, 335, 337; Tillich, in cited in Richard John Neuhaus, "Wealth and Whimsy," in *The Capitalist Spirit: Toward a Religious Ethic of Wealth Creation*, ed. Peter L. Berger (San Francisco: ICS, 1990), 138. Neuhaus cites Karl Barth in the same sense. Gide, *The God that Failed*, 151; Furet, *Le passé*, 358, 496, 581.
18. Spender, *The God that Failed*, 241.
19. Simone de Beauvoir, *Les Mandarins* (Paris: Gallimard, 1954), 2:157.
20. Furet, *Le passé*, 696. See chapter 8 for the relationship between anti-Americanism and anti-capitalism.

21. Richard Wolin, *The Seduction of Unreason: The Intellectual Romance with Fascism from Nietzsche to Postmodernism* (Princeton: Princeton University Press, 2004), 308.

22   For a good discussion of the issues involved, see Stanley Payne, *A History of Fascism 1914-1945* (Madison: University of Wisconsin Press, 1995), Part II.

23   A. James Gregor, *Mussolini's Intellectuals: Fascist Social and Political Thought* (Princeton: Princeton University Press, 2005), 4, 15, 17; Michel Ostenc, *Intellectuels Italiens et Fascisme (1915-1929)* (Paris: Payot, 1983), 19. See also the 1930s analysis of fascism as an anti-capitalist revolutionary movement discussed in Martin Jay, *The Dialectical Imagination: A History of the Frankfurt School for Social Research, 1923-1950* (Boston: Little Brown, 1973), 154-55.

24   Zeev Sternhell, *Ni droite, ni gauche: l'ideologie fasciste en France* (Paris: Seuil, 1983), 313, 347, 362.

25   Jeffrey Herf, *Reactionary Modernism: Technology, Culture, and Politics in Weimar and the Third Reich* (Cambridge: Cambridge University Press, 1984), 2.

26   George L. Mosse, *The Crisis of German Ideology: Intellectual Origins of the Third Reich* (New York: Grosset & Dunlap, 1964), 313; Herf, *Reactionary Modernism*, 12.

27   Mussolini, cited in Gregor, *Mussolini's Intellectuals*, 129. See also Adolf Hitler, *Mein Kampf*, tr. Ralph Manheim (Boston: Houghton Mifflin, 1943), 602.

28   Hitler, *Mein Kampf*, 234.

29   Romain, cited in Alastair Hamilton, *The Appeal of Fascism: A Study of Intellectuals and Fascism, 1919-1945* (London: Anthony Blond, 1971), xxviii, 207; Giovanni Gentile, *Origins and Doctrine of Fascism, with selections from other works*, trans. and ed. A. James Gregor (New Brunswick: Transaction, 2002), 23, 66, 67.

30. Hitler, *Mein Kampf*, 423, 431, 446.

31. Hitler, *Mein Kampf*, 442.

32. Hitler, *Mein Kampf*, 210, 214, 235.

33. Hitler, *Mein Kampf*, 234, 382, 436.

34. Moishe Postone, cited in Herf, *Reactionary Modernism*, 225. See also Herf, 231.

35. Henry Ford is the exception who proves the rule about anti-Semitism and anti-capitalism. As late as 1937 Italian Fascists were publishing articles in the official press describing Nazi racism as idiocy. See Mosse, *The Crisis of German Ideology*, 315.

36. Fritz K. Ringer, *The Decline of the German Mandarins: The German Academic Community, 1890-1933* (Boston: University Press of New England, 1990), 446.

37. Sternhell, *Ni droite, ni gauche*, 365.

38. Jay P. Corrin *Catholic Intellectuals and the Challenge of Democracy* (Notre Dame, IN: University of Notre Dame Press, 2002), 2, 50, 54-54; Leo XIII, *Rerum Novarum*, http://www.papalencyclicals.net/Leo13/l13rerum.htm, 22, 36, 49. Other prominent pre-war social Catholics included Charles Maurras and Péguy, whose vitriolic 1913 essay, "Money," makes Marx sound moderate.

39. Father Coughlin, cited in William E. Leuchtenberg, ed., *The New Deal: A Documentary History* (Columbia, SC: University of South Carolina Press, 1968), 190.

40. Emmanuel Mounier, *Révolution Personnaliste et Communautaire* (Paris: Aubier, 1935), 270.

41. Mounier, *Révolution Personnaliste et Communautaire*, 687-89; Mounier, cited in Sternhell, *Ni droite, ni gauche*, 312.

42. Mounier, *Révolution Personnaliste et Communautaire*, 255-56, 389-90.

43. Mounier, *Révolution Personnaliste et Communautaire*, 453, 455-57, 493.

44. Mounier, *Révolution Personnaliste et Communautaire*, 241. See also 390.

45. Mounier, *Révolution Personnaliste et Communautaire*, 390-92.

46.   For American parallels, see David E. Shi, *The Simple Life: Plain Living and High Thinking in American Culture* (New York: Oxford University Press, 1985).

47.   Mounier, cited in André Mandouze, "Mounier et les communistes," in *Le personnalisme d'Emannuel Mounier: Hier et Demain*, ed. Bertrand d'Astorg (Paris: Seuil, 1985), 100; Mounier, cited in Sternhell, *Ni droite, ni gauche*, 326.

48.   Hellman, *The Communitarian Third Way* (Montreal: McGill-Queen's University Press, 2002), 2, 83, 148; Mounier, cited in Sternhell, *Ni droite, ni gauche*, 318, 326; Hellman, "Personalisme et fascisme," in *Le personnalisme d'Emannuel Mounier*, 123; Daniel Lindenberg, *Les années souterraines (1937-1947)* (Paris: Editions de la découverte, 1990), 239; Mounier, cited in André Mandouze, "Mounier et les communistes," *Le personnalisme d'Emmanuel Mounier*, 100.

49.   Lindenberg, *Les années souterraines*, 11-12; Hellman, *The Communitarian Third Way*, 2, 182-83, 202, 204.

50.   Dewey, cited in Ekirch, *Ideologies and Utopias*, 128; Richard H. Pells, *Radical Visions and American Dreams: Culture and Social Thought in the Depression Years* (New York: Harper & Row, 1973), 23; Aaron, *Writers on the Left*, 199.

51.   William E. Leuchtenberg, *Franklin D. Roosevelt and the New Deal, 1932-1940* (New York: Harper & Row, 1963), 57, 165.

52.   Tugwell, cited in Bernard Sternsher, *Rexford Guy Tugwell and the New Deal* (New Brunswick, NJ: Rutgers University Press, 1957), 99; Berle, cited in Leuchtenberg, *The New Deal: A Documentary History*, 42.

53.   Pells, *Radical Visions*, 69.

54.   Pells, *Radical Visions*, 79, 367.

55.   Hollander, *Political Pilgrims*, 77, 121; Alan Brinkley *The End of Reform: New Deal Liberalism in Recession and War* (New York: Knopf, 1995), 37; David Lilienthal, cited in Leuchtenberg, *Franklin D. Roosevelt and the New Deal*, 342; Dewey, cited in Ekirch, *Ideologies and Utopias*, 128.

56.   Brinkley, *The End of Reform*, 56.

57.   Thurman Arnold, cited in Brinkley *The End of Reform*, 109-110; Tugwell, cited in Sternsher, *Rexford Guy Tugwell*, 102-05, and see also 377.

58.   Sternsher, *Rexford Guy Tugwell*, 13, 17-18, 92, 377, 395; Leuchtenberg, *Franklin D. Roosevelt and the New Deal*, 33-35; Brinkley *The End of Reform*, 5, 16.

59.   Cited in Leuchtenberg, *Franklin D. Roosevelt and the New Deal*, 41, 89.

60.   Robert S. McElvaine, *The Great Depression: America, 1929-1941* (New York: Three Rivers Press, 1993), 326; Wilson, cited in Ekirch, *Ideologies and Utopias*, 35, 94.

61.   McElvaine, *The Great Depression*, 336.

62.   Cited by Ekirch, *Ideologies and Utopias*, 71, 87-88, 103. For the "moral syphilis" remark by Waldo Frank, see Aaron, *Writers on the Left*, 193, and 180-185 for other examples.

63.   Mill, speech of 30 May 1866, in *Public and Parliamentary Speeches*, ed. John M. Robson and Bruce Kinzer, *Collected Works* (Toronto: University of Toronto Press, 1988), 28:85-86. Mill also notes that the half-educated tend to be Liberals, but can't be counted on, because they are too likely to be influenced by the last book they have read. Mill originally remarked on stupid people being Conservative in *On Representative Government*.

64.   Bellow, cited in Hollander, *Political Pilgrims*, 3.

65.   Furet, *Le passé*, 245; Revel, *La grande parade: essai sur la survie de l'utopie socialiste*, (Paris: Plon, 2000), 23, 25; Hollander, *Political Pilgrims*, 6-7.

66.   Revel, *La grande parade*, 253.

67.   Spender, *The God that Failed*, 235.

68.   Kolakowski, *Modernity on Endless Trial*, 40.

69.   Paz, Cited in Paul Hollander, *Political Pilgrims*, 419.

7

Retreat

Let Ares doze, that other war
Is instantly declared once more
'Twixt those who follow
Precocious Hermes all the way
And those who without qualms obey
Pompous Apollo.[1]

Brutal like all Olympic games,
Though fought with smiles and Christian names
And less dramatic,
This dialectic strife between
The civil gods is just as mean,
And more fanatic.

W. H. Auden, 1946

The Culture Wars

After World War II, Western intellectuals slowly retreated from direct political confrontation with capitalism. In a world where the only political choice was between communism and commerce, they were largely reduced to political impotence. Intellectuals who did not want to be called communists had to either withdraw from politics or seek some non-political way to oppose capitalism. In Western Europe, Communist parties and their fellow-travelers continued to exercise some influence, but they were on the defensive and excluded from power. Revolution, at least at home, was far down their agenda. In the second half of the twentieth century, Western intellectuals supported many revolutions but made none. If circumstances after World War I multiplied the political significance of the struggle between mind and money, circumstances after World War II decreased it. The Cold War between the Soviet Union and the capitalist West inhibited political struggle between mind and money.

The new battleground was culture. Intellectuals had always despised bourgeois culture and the bourgeois lifestyle. But broadly speaking, in the first half of the twentieth century intellectuals emphasized political and economic criticism over lifestyle criticism. In the second half, this emphasis was reversed. In a period when Western capitalism was experiencing enormous economic growth and declining economic inequality, intellectuals stressed the area in which a plausible argument could be made that there had been decline: culture.

Even before World War I, when everyone expected prosperity and no one had nightmares, the German sociologist Georg Simmel had shown the way. He lamented that in the last 100 years "individual culture, at least in the higher strata, has not progressed at all… indeed, it has even frequently declined."[2] This essentially aristocratic, even reactionary line of criticism became increasingly significant after World War II. Before World War II, criticism of the bourgeois lifestyle was generally directed at the middle classes. After World War II, it was often directed at a working class whose increasing consumption of hitherto bourgeois goods and values made them newly vulnerable to attacks once reserved for their social betters. John Dewey, writing in 1939 when an economic boom was being enjoyed by an America still at peace, wrote:

> What gain has been made in the matter of establishing conditions that give the mass of workers… constructive interest in the work that they do? What gain has been made in giving individuals… an opportunity to find themselves and then to educate themselves for what they can best do in work which is socially useful and such as to give free play in development of themselves?[3]

Matthew Arnold had directed this kind of criticism at the Philistine middle classes. Dewey directed it at everyone—except intellectuals..

Dewey criticized workers' lives, but not the workers themselves. This is typical of the more democratic post-World War II intellectuals. When they criticize mass culture, they avoid blaming the masses. Mass culture is imposed on the masses, hence not their fault. One typical line is to suggest that with greater material progress comes greater "alienation," imposed on people by capitalism. The average man is going to the dogs, and what is worse, he is often too deluded by capitalism, by its advertising, its media, by the thought of a week in Vegas, to realize it. This form of cultural criticism, essentially aristocratic in its rejection of popular culture, is not new, but only becomes central to the war between mind and money after World War II. It is practiced by two groups: a new generation of academic theorists, fond of abstruse and radical language; and a counterculture, fond of radical clothing and behavior.

Aristocratic attitudes are prominent in the academic theorizing variously described as postmodern, poststructuralist, post-Marxist, etc. In these movements, which take their inspiration from thinkers like Heidegger, the Frankfurt School, and Foucault, capitalism is taken to task for reasons that have little to do with unemployment or declining productivity, and everything to do with having the wrong attitude. This aristocratic critique is typically conducted in an exceptionally vague vocabulary. Marx's genius for simplification was not shared by his late-twentieth-century followers.

This aristocratic cultural critique was paralleled by a more democratic cultural criticism, whose words and message were simpler to understand. The "counterculture" of the 1960s and 1970s was a mass movement (in many respects it was the mass movement the personalists of the 1930s never created). Like the academic critique of commercial culture, the counterculture was based in the universities, but it overflowed them and formed its own bohemian bases, in "communes" and neighborhoods scattered across America, Europe, and even the Third World. The counterculture did its best to live without structures, or rather with temporary ones, like the rock concert which might extend for several days, as at Woodstock, or the political demonstration. The purest embodiments of the counterculture were the "Hippies," long-haired pacifists whose lifestyle and music became emblematic of the era. Hippies spread throughout the Western world and beyond, but they were especially characteristic of America. Although the Hippy era was brief, it had profoundly anti-capitalist implications, and some lasting effects.

Cultural criticism, aristocratic and democratic, took on more importance as the revolutionary significance of communism, fascism, and even the New Deal faded. However, the old word "alienation" is central to much of this new cultural critique. It became a staple term after World War II, and its use spread well beyond academia. It is an important word, and an important concept. Before we can understand the anti-capitalist culture-criticism of the late twentieth century, we must understand what is meant by alienation. What is alienation? It is a myth.

The Myth of Alienation

A myth is a legend, a fairy tale, a story that may not be literally true, but nevertheless expresses an important truth. Like most myths, the myth of alienation is a little fuzzy about the details. What does the word "alienation" mean? One dictionary admits that "in none of the established usages is the notion very clear, but in all of them it expresses the search for a theory that will describe the condition of the modern self, and also explain the sense of being 'separated' from some truly human way of being." The myth of alienation expresses the idea that there is something fundamentally wrong with our life, and in particular something wrong with life in a capitalist society.[4]

According to myths of alienation, all societies, but especially capitalist societies, produce alienation. This alienation is all around us. Normally it merely produces a moderate amount of misery, but when the misery becomes sufficiently great, our alienation either as individuals, or a class, or a whole society results in madness, revolt, or both. In optimistic versions of the theory of alienation, like Marx's, after the revolution we cease to be alienated and can become fully human beings. In moderate versions, like Freud's, when we finish psychotherapy we achieve a merely average amount of unhappiness and alienation, since some repression of our instincts is necessary to civilized life. In pessimistic versions, like that of the late Frankfurt School, we are too alienated from our real selves to even know we are oppressed, and things are hopeless.

All versions of the myth of alienation have a few features in common. In all of them, there is something wrong with the lifestyle of the alienated person. Of course, in order to know what is wrong, we have to know what an unalienated lifestyle looks like. In other words alienation is a concept which claims to be descriptive, but is actually based on a decision about what is a good or bad life. Further, in all or almost all concepts of alienation, a distinction is drawn between "real" needs and "artificial" needs. This distinction is arbitrary. The "distinction between real needs and false (or 'artificial') needs cannot be anything but arbitrary, unless if here too the bearers of superior reason [the intellectuals!] decree that, from their position of superiority, they have the right to decide what the rest of humanity really needs and what they only imagine they need." The myth of alienation is fundamentally a story about values. It is a natural subject for the sermons of the modern intelligentsia. The alienation of the masses is also a fit topic for the aristocratic contempt of an elite. Only intellectuals know what really matters, because only they can justify their choices by CCD. Others can't, and don't.[5]

Twentieth-century versions of the myth, found in the works of Freud, Fromm, Marcuse and others, emphasize the moral and psychological meaning of alienation. They define alienation as the result of the repression of our natural instincts and our inability to satisfy them. The alienated individual is powerless: Powerless to satisfy her real needs, powerless to relate to others, powerless to satisfy her desires, politically powerless to effect meaningful change. Therapeutic action, whether individual, social, or more rarely political, is needed to restore the individual's sense of control and power, and give meaning to life.

In the most radical forms of the myth of alienation, as preached in the latter part of the twentieth century, alienation is everywhere. This is a negative version of pantheism, the belief that the divine is everywhere. In panalienation, instead of the divine being everywhere, alienation is present in every new electronic toy, in every job offer, even in every marriage proposal, because in capitalist society they lack truly human meaning. The myth of alienation explains everything, or at least everything bad. The failures of any individual or any group, psychologically or politically, can be explained as a result of their own alienation or that of other people.

The myth of alienation is a secular theodicy, a way of explaining the existence of evil. The world would be good, if only we could overcome the alienation/sin we are born into. In the doctrine of panalienation, intellectuals found all the advantages of Original Sin and none of its disadvantages. It was not the fault of our ancestors Adam and Eve, it was capitalism's fault. Capitalism was no one's ancestor, no one's child, no one's religion. The myth of alienation attributed the origin of evil to capitalism, and located it in every individual—we are all more or less alienated—while leaving the individuals themselves blameless.

It is noteworthy that the growing acceptance of myths of panalienation in the 1960s occurred simultaneously with the spread of pantheism. Pantheist ideas were widespread in the counterculture, and in New Age spiritualism in the late twentieth century. Evidently, what Tocqueville said of pantheism is true of panalienation as well: "Among the various systems that philosophy employs to explain the universe, pantheism seems to me one of the most apt to seduce the human mind in democratic centuries."[6]

The myth of alienation is a religious story, the kind that pseudo-clergy ought to tell. But in the modern world, such tales often take on scientific form—they become theories. Marx's discussion of alienation is strictly scientific. But when alienation becomes a "scientific" concept, it becomes one of those words which "obscure more than they explain and whose essential function consists of creating a semblance of explanation where there isn't any." However, alienation has nonetheless become a scientific theory, or at least a theory of people who describe themselves as social scientists. In these scientific theodicies, alienation plays the role that the mythical "phlogiston" once played in chemistry.[7]

In the early days of modern chemistry, one of the problems chemists set out to solve was why things burned and stopped burning. The answer, before the role of oxygen was understood, was phlogiston. According to the phlogiston theory, all combustible substances contain phlogiston. Phlogiston is released into the air when something burns, but air has a limited ability to absorb phlogiston. A flame goes out either when the burning substance has used up all its phlogiston (it becomes "dephlogisticated") or when the air around it is saturated with phlogiston. A nice touch to the theory was that phlogiston cannot be detected by the senses. It cannot be touched, seen, or smelled—and it is very hard to measure, which eventually proved the downfall of the theory. Like phlogiston, alienation is something almost omnipresent. It plays an important role in society, however, rather than combustion. It is present wherever things are going wrong, just as phlogiston is crucial for burning. Of course, now we know there is no such thing as phlogiston.

The discovery of oxygen was an alternative solution to the problem of combustion. But late-twentieth century intellectuals lacked alternative means to solve their problem, that is, of attacking capitalism in the absence of a convincing alternative. When he was still a Marxist, the Polish philosopher Leszek Kolakowski wrote that "it would be useful to exclude the concept of alienation from socialist thought.... The word alienation lets it be understood that we others who use it, we have a general solution ready-made for all human problems, whereas such a solution does not exist and will never exist." He did not realize that post-World War II anti-capitalist thought could not give up the myth of alienation without something to put in its place, something Kolakowski could not provide. He eventually abandoned Marxism.[8]

Interestingly, while intellectuals have always associated alienation and capitalism, they did not always see this as a bad thing. The myth of alienation was originally not a theodicy, an explanation of evil, but a story of progress. Back when Mr. Smith the merchant was the good guy, some intellectuals thought alienation was good, too. Treating one's customers as a means to the end of making money, rather than seeing them as human beings with souls to be saved, if necessary at the cost of their lives, seemed wonderful. Nothing could be more alien to human nature than an Invisible Hand, which might arrive at the best result without regard for human intentions—which were too often evil or counterproductive. None of the later theorists of alienation, from Marx to Marcuse, realized how wonderful a little alienation had seemed to people a century or two before, when Europe was emerging from a long period of religious wars.[9]

Opposing alienation has been part of anti-capitalist rhetoric since Marx's time, but originally it played a relatively minor role in anti-capitalist theory. As late as 1930 the *Encyclopedia of the Social Sciences* contained no entry for "alienation." Marx's own use of the concept of alienation was most extensive in his 1844 philosophical manuscripts, which were only published in the 1930s. For Marx, we are alienated when capitalism forces us to see ourselves and other people as means rather than ends. Our own products, especially money, become ends in themselves, rather than means to satisfy our real needs. This concept of alienation was analogous to the theological idea that alienation meant separation from God. In Marx's secular version, alienation meant that capitalism separated us from what made us truly human.

It would be convenient for the argument if the discussion of alienation only took on special prominence after World War II. But alienation, partly because of the psychotherapeutic use of the term, began to be used more prominently even before Marx's early writings became known. However, the myth of alienation became an especially useful weapon in the struggle between mind and money when mind was in retreat after World War II. Myths or theories of alienation, and especially of panalienation, were useful then because they emphasized the self. They attacked capitalism not on political or economic grounds, where the Western intelligentsia was relatively weak after World War II, but on cultural and moral grounds, their strength. After the trauma of fascism and communism, the fight to overcome alienation turned attention away from economics and turned it inward, towards the individual. By the late 1960s all the standard English-language dictionaries of social concepts had long articles on alienation. In the process some intellectuals turned against the Enlightenment, largely because of its honeymoon with capitalism. In their view the Enlightenment was an introduction to bondage and domination, in which human beings were turned into things. Enlightenment meant alienation, and the enlightenment and disenchantment of the world meant panalienation.[10]

After World War II the idea that everyone was alienated gradually made its way into popular culture. Existentialism, popular after World War II, had something to do with this, but the process accelerated greatly in the 1960s. In the '60s, many intellectuals stopped complaining that people were too conformist and began to complain that they were cut off and alienated. Others blamed conformism on alienation. All emphasized alienation in their criticism of the middle classes. This was especially true of "Western Marxism," which was largely a critique of alienation and relied heavily on Marx's 1844 manuscripts.[11] But the critique of alienation was not limited to academia. Late twentieth-century best-sellers urged people to "get in touch with themselves" and "get in touch with their feelings" to overcome their alienation. The myth of alienation may have been, like phlogiston, a weak tool for scientific analysis, but it was, and is, a superb text on which to base a sermon.

However, the myth of alienation is not just an anti-capitalist tool. The myth does express a truth, not a truth about capitalism, but a truth about intellectuals. Intellectuals *are* a permanently alienated elite. They know about alienation from their own experience as a class and as individuals. They are prevented from realizing their own ends. Democratic capitalism prevents intellectuals from building their Towers of Babel up to heaven, prevents them from fulfilling their aristocratic and clerical identity. *Intellectuals* are alienated.

There is a democratic aspect to intellectuals' insistence that their problem is everyone's problem. Intellectuals need autonomy and need to practice careful critical discourse. When they see that other people lack these things, they make the democratic assumption that others have, or ought to have, the same needs and desires they do. They project their own feelings onto others, whether the others are the proletariat, the nation, or humanity as whole. These others must be alienated, because they lack the autonomy that intellectuals need and want. Intellectuals, the makers of meaning, find capitalism meaningless. Therefore, others must think so too, unless they are deceived.

But even if produced by democratic motives, intellectuals' projection of their own alienation onto society as a whole is an aristocratic act. Intellectuals are attempting to take on the aristocratic (and clerical) role of imposing their values on society at large. But since this act takes place in a democratic society, and since intellectuals themselves usually accept democratic values, the aristocratic basis of their claim is masked by its democratic, universal forms, such as demands for cultural revolution and liberation. Nevertheless, the myth of alienation is essentially an aristocratic reaction against capitalism. It became the background, and often the foreground, of a series of reactions by intellectuals against capitalism after World War II. These reactions took many forms, all of which criticized the bourgeoisie for their alienated attitude and their poor choice of moral values. In retreat, however, mind no longer usually directed its diatribes against capitalism to a mass audience. Post-World War II intellectuals preferred to talk to themselves. Of course they lamented the disappearance of their audience—and blamed it on capitalism.

Aristocratic Reactions: Heidegger, the Frankfurt School, and Foucault

In the culture wars of the late twentieth century, a rapidly expanding capitalist society provided new social bases for the intelligentsia. Academia expanded enormously after World War II. New universities were created and old ones expanded, especially in the United States. Retreating from politics, intellectuals took refuge in the ivory towers that were emerging like mushrooms. They provided vastly increased opportunities for employing and training intellectuals, even if they were intended to breed accountants and engineers. Before World War II, professors made up a small if growing portion of the intelligentsia. After World War II, academia became much more important, in both numbers and significance. The new university faculties were not immediately filled with fire-breathing revolutionaries, however—there were too many World War II veterans among them who never wanted to breathe fire again. Opposition to the bourgeoisie was more often whispered than shouted in America in the 1950s, and mostly ignored by society at large, even in Europe. But academia provided intellectuals with refuge in periods when they lacked mass support or a mass audience.

After World War II intellectuals were faced with a considerable loss of influence. Since the masses were no longer revolutionary (except in the Third World), and rarely looked to revolutionary intellectuals for leadership, intellectuals responded to the rejection of their leadership by rejecting their former followers. For the first time since Marx, the proletariat left center stage. This process took decades, but by the 1970s Michel Foucault could, with little contradiction, deny the special role of the proletariat: "there is no single locus of great Refusal, no soul of revolt, source of all rebellions, or pure law of the revolutionary. Instead there is a plurality of resistances, each of them a special case...."[12]

Some intellectuals continued to try to break out of their isolation in the old ways, by supporting anti-colonial Third World movements, or racial minorities, or inventing other democratic links. But a large number accepted their caste-like situation, at least for the moment. They retreated to the ivory tower and pulled up the drawbridge. Their proud isolation was marked by the increasing obscurity of their language, which put a new gulf between them and capitalism. No longer concerned with reaching a mass audience that was in any event beyond reach, intellectuals' language, their critical discourse, was increasingly intended for a narrow circle. It became, consciously or not, more refined, more complicated, more based on internal conventions not easily accessible to outsiders—more aristocratic. Or rather more pseudo-aristocratic, the language of a caste cut off in their ivory towers, rather than an aristocracy acting as society's leaders.

This process had been going on since the nineteenth century, but in the twentieth the worship of language became widespread among intellectuals. The German philosopher Martin Heidegger was typical: "Language is the house of Being. In its home man dwells. Those who think and those who create with words are the guardians of this home. Their guardianship accomplishes the manifestation of Being insofar as they bring the manifestation to language." For Heidegger, thinking and creating with words is better than doing.[13]

This kind of obscure and self-referential language became increasingly popular among intellectuals in the late twentieth century. Indeed, among intellectuals obscurity became a sign of political correctness and insider status. Using complicated forms of critical discourse identified the speaker as an intellectual *and* as an opponent of capitalism. This is why conservatives typically write so much better than leftists in this period—they don't feel compelled to be obscure in order to signal they oppose capitalism, because they don't oppose capitalism. The crucial importance of foggy language as a weapon against capitalism was announced in a book that contained in germ much of the intellectual history of the next fifty years, Max Horkheimer and Theodor Adorno's *Dialectic of Enlightenment*, published in 1947. Horkheimer and Adorno argued that the bourgeoisie is only interested in facts (this was Dickens' complaint too, see pp. 109-10). Likewise, the bourgeoisie demands "clarity in language." The natural corollary is that to oppose the bourgeoisie we must avoid clarity: "Even the most honorable reformer who recommends renewal in threadbare language reinforces the existing order he seeks to break by taking over its worn-out categorial apparatus and the pernicious power-philosophy lying behind it." In other words, if your meaning is clear, if you use "threadbare language," you are objectively a bourgeois and a supporter of capitalism. Clarity is a bourgeois plot to make us accept the world the way it is, it is "false clarity." Reacting against such false clarity, intellectuals created new forms of Gnosticism. Their secret languages revealed the evils of capitalism to the cognoscenti, and sometimes promised them salvation. Nothing could better illustrate Tocqueville's point that "should members of the lettered class fall into the habit of frequenting only themselves and writing only for one another, they may lose sight of the rest of the world entirely and thereby lapse into affectation and falsity.... gradually alienating themselves from common sense...."[14]

In post-World War II anti-capitalist gnostic theories, the source of salvation was usually left vague. By refusing to name a "locus of resistance," by refusing to give any specific content to "Being" or to "the Other," intellectuals left the heroic role open. It would be filled in the future. A future, perhaps, when intellectuals would no longer be afraid to proclaim their class a new source of aristocratic values. In the present, their gnostic language gave intellectuals access to privileged knowledge which justified their clerical role and their use of the moral voice in their classrooms or in public pronouncements. It also reinforced their aristocratic identity. If this meant that fewer people read intellectuals' books, listened to their music, or liked their art, this was another sin to lay to capitalism's account.[15]

The intelligentsia's aristocratic reaction against capitalism after World War II took many forms, but a few, found in Heidegger, the Frankfurt School, and Foucault, were especially influential. Heidegger's reputation and influence predate the Second World War, but notwithstanding his Nazism, hushed-up until the 1990s, Heidegger was most significant after World War II, influencing existentialists and postmodernists alike. Outside of moments of ecstatic fascist exaltation, Heidegger was an aristocratic pessimist who preferred contemplation to action. After World War II, his pessimism spread to many Marxists, especially the "Western" Marxists who by the 1970s mostly changed their name and became "Critical Theorists." Their attitude is represented by the Frankfurt School for Social Research, and embodied in the work of Horkheimer and Adorno. The influence of the Frankfurt School and other critical theorists melded with Heidegger's in the work of writers like Michel Foucault, a French intellectual whose influence was stronger in the United States than at home. Politically less important than Heidegger or the Frankfurt School, Foucault was even more successful in influencing many academic disciplines.

Heidegger was hardly the first German philosopher to write in difficult language, but he was perhaps the first to glorify it and make it the "House of Being." He was part of a wave of anti-capitalist gnosticism in the Germany of the 1920s and 1930s, with roots dating back to the fin-de-siècle. These semi-mystical attitudes were often linked to fascism or social Catholicism (or neither, as with Walter Benjamin), but Heidegger's version was uniquely successful.

Heidegger was susceptible to spiritual/religious rhapsodies about "Being." For example: "what is Being? It is It itself. The thinking that is to come must learn to experience that and to say it. 'Being'—that is not God and not a cosmic ground. Being is farther than all beings and is yet nearer to man than every being, be it a rock, a beast, a work of art, a machine, be it an angel or God. Being is the nearest. Yet the near remains farthest from man." At least this has the merit of avoiding the threadbare clarity of bourgeois language. But as it has no direct connection to the struggle between mind and money, we can put Heidegger's meditations on Being aside.[16]

More relevant to the aristocratic reaction of the intelligentsia against capitalism after World War II are Heidegger's comments on technology. He expressed, for an intellectual audience, many ideas that took popular form in the counterculture and the ecology movement. For example, Heidegger argues that modern technology "…puts to nature the unreasonable demand that it supply energy that can be extracted and stored as such. But does this not hold true for the old windmill as well? No. Its sails do indeed turn in the wind… but the windmill does not unlock energy from the air currents in order to store it." The problem with modern technology, with having power plants instead of windmills, is that power plants do not use energy to fulfill an immediate need, as windmills were used to grind grain. They store energy, they treat it like money in the bank, like an end in itself. On the one hand, in accord with the modern gospel of alienation, this describes the power plant as alienated, while the wind mill is authentic. This idea is recycled Aristotle. Power stations engage in chrematistic, in Aristotle's terms, storing power/money for its own sake.[17]

Once the Rhine was a beautiful river with wooden bridges. Now it is a source of power for electric plants, and ugly. It has been, in Heidegger's aristocratically complicated terminology, "enframed." In Heidegger's version of the myth of alienation, the Rhine has been cut off from its true nature by technology, which turns everything into a "standing-reserve" of power or utility. When man treats nature as an object in this way, he runs the danger that "he himself will have to be taken as standing-reserve," in other words that he will treat himself and others as objects. When we treat ourselves and others as things, it means we are alienated. Modern technology means human alienation. This is the modern aristocratic complaint of mind against money.[18]

Does Heidegger have a remedy? After World War II, at any rate, Heidegger did not endorse any political solutions. Instead he preached salvation by contemplation, for the elite. There is a "saving power." Not Christ—Heidegger is not a social Catholic—and not bourgeois rationality, too linked to the dark side of technology. But "…technology harbors in itself what we least suspect, the possible upsurgence of the saving power. Everything, then, depends on this: that we ponder this arising and that we, recollecting, watch over it." Contemplation of the saving power, that is, contemplation of the fact that human beings are not standing-reserves of power, but the makers of art, will save us. Art and "questioning," that is applying careful critical discourse to technology and capitalism, these are the saving power. In this Heidegger (like Marx!) appealed to both the academic and bohemian fractions of the intelligentsia, to artists and critics both. He put it all together in a vague religious formula: "questioning is the piety of thought." Or, as the Deconstructionists would put it, "Problematize!"[19]

Heidegger's search for salvation in aristocratic art and contemplation appealed to many members of an intellectual class in retreat. Despite its right-wing origins, it was highly influential on the left, especially in France. The Frankfurt School, on the other hand, probably exercised more influence in America than Heidegger did. It represented on the left what Heidegger did on the right—a retreat from political confrontation into aristocratic language games and criticism of the bourgeois lifestyle.

Founded by an independent group of Marxist social thinkers in Frankfurt, Germany in 1923, its members fled in the 1930s. Some occupied academic positions in America, where several, such as the sociologist Herbert Marcuse and the psychologist Erich Fromm, remained and became highly influential. However, the Institute's two founders, Horkheimer and Adorno, returned to Frankfurt and reopened the Institute. Although they were largely unknown outside Germany in the 1950s, by 1970 paperback editions of their work were found in campus bookstores all across Europe and America.

The Frankfurt School put forth a particularly powerful version of the myth of alienation. Panalienation dominates their analysis. For example, in modern society people consume much more than in the past, but we derive less real satisfaction from our greater consumption, because we have become alienated consuming machines, rather than human beings. In a sense, "consumption tends to vanish today, or should I say, eating, drinking, looking, loving, sleeping become 'consumption', for consumption already means that man has become a machine outside as well as inside of the workshop…." The consumer society is the alienated society. There is nothing the individual can do to stop this, no effective resistance she can make. Individuals become "a degree more powerless with each prescribed increase in their standard of living."[20]

The Frankfurt School's criticism of alienation, while unusually thorough, was not unusual. What was striking was the historical context they put it in. They blamed it on capitalism, of course, but they located the essence of capitalism as much in the realm of ideas as in economics, and the ideas they blamed were the Enlightenment's. Their criticism of the Enlightenment was a landmark in intellectual history. It was the first serious left-wing criticism of the Enlightenment for having gone too far, rather than not far enough. Previously, criticism of the Enlightenment was hard to disassociate from support for the intelligentsia's rivals, the old clergy and aristocracy. But after World War II the old aristocracy and clergy were no longer serious foes, and intellectuals were free to attack the Enlightenment as the symbol of capitalism and the beginning of panalienation.

Horkheimer and Adorno agreed that the Enlightenment had replaced myths with science, superstition and ignorance with a real understanding of nature. But this was not the liberation it seemed. "What human beings seek to learn from nature is how to use it to dominate wholly both it and human beings." The promised liberation thus becomes a greater tyranny. The root problem with the Enlightenment's scientific ideal is that "on their way toward modern science human beings have discarded meaning," that is discarded the very thing intellectuals claim the monopoly on producing. Anti-Enlightenment intellectuals of the Frankfurt type reject the Enlightenment because, in their view, it has diminished them. This is why Adorno and Horkheimer, like Heidegger, conclude that the Enlightenment's embrace of science and technology alienates us from "Being." They sum up: "Animism had endowed things with souls; industrialism makes souls into things." And once we see people as things, we are free to dictate to them like things. The Enlightenment ultimately destroys all values, leaving only naked power in their place. Horkheimer and Adorno's criticism of the Enlightenment repeats the old moralists' complaints against capitalism. But they identify the Enlightenment as the origin of the evil.[21]

Horkheimer and Adorno were also some of the first on the left to single out for attack science and its "objective" language, beginning a line of criticism that became increasingly popular in the late twentieth century. For them, science and its objective language stand as proxies for capitalism and bourgeois rule. The clear language and logic which the Enlightenment thought liberated humanity actually serve the bourgeoisie and existing power relations, according to Horkheimer and Adorno. Instead of criticizing the world, much less changing it, the Enlightenment ended up justifying it.[22]

The crux of the matter is that the Enlightenment turned out to be bad for intellectuals, a threat to the existence of the intellectual class. Once again, this turned conventional wisdom upside-down. Hadn't the Enlightenment created the intellectual class in the first place, allowing them to displace the clergy as the guardians of morality and helping them achieve autonomy? Yes, but at a price, a price that in the long run would end up submerging the intellectuals in an alienated, bourgeois world: "The present order of life allows the self no scope to draw intellectual or spiritual conclusions. Thought, stripped down to knowledge, is neutralized, harnessed merely to qualifying its practitioner for specific labor markets and heightening the commodity value of the personality." Capitalism turns the autonomous intellectual into a commodity like any other, and so destroys his identity.[23]

Was there a way out? Horkheimer and Adorno sometimes appealed to high art as the source of salvation: "Art, since it became autonomous, has preserved the utopia that evaporated from religion," as Critical Theory, we might add, helped intellectuals preserve utopian politics. Adorno loved Schoenberg's 12-tone music, abstract, difficult to understand and impossible to hum, because he saw it as a rejection of the bourgeoisie. But even music was threatened. Adorno lamented that classical music in the twentieth century was subject to the tyranny of the conductor, who deprived individual musicians of their autonomy. Even worse was the tyranny of the composer's score, which demanded slavish obedience, whereas nineteenth-century performers had still been left some autonomy.[24]

What is left? Not revolution—there is no heroic class left to make one. The time for revolution is over. Nothing was left but to write essays in the comfort of university offices. "Philosophy... lives on because the moment to realize it [i.e., to make a revolution] was missed.... The attempt to change the world... miscarried." Adorno was more interested in keeping the ivory tower free than reaching out to mass movements. But in the 1969 preface to a new edition of *Dialectic of Enlightenment*, Horkheimer and Adorno wrote that "critical thought... requires us to take up the cause of the remnants of freedom, of tendencies toward real humanity, even though they seem powerless in face of the great historical trend." When the trend seemed to change in their favor, during the late 60s, such intellectuals were ready to lend it their support.[25]

Neither Heidegger nor Horkheimer and Adorno saw any safe ground from which to contest the victory of capitalism beyond the ivory tower's walls. Michel Foucault adopted much of their analysis and equaled or surpassed their obscurity of language. He became a leading Western intellectual. Important in his native France and in Europe, he was a still more important figure in American academic thought from the 1970s through the turn of the century. Why?

There are many reasons, but the most important is this: When a new way of looking at things, what Kuhn calls a new paradigm, is invented, it is often worse at solving many little questions than the old way of looking at things. For example, Foucault's books often got some facts wrong. But the new paradigm must solve one big problem better than the old one. The big problem Foucault solved better than anyone else, at least in the judgment of much of American academia, was how to oppose capitalism without using Marxist language. The Frankfurt School and their followers still claimed a connection to Marx, and Heidegger's language of Being had little resonance in America. Foucault invented a new language, one that exalted language itself (under the aristocratic name of "discourse"), as all the aristocratic reactions did, but that used an appealing new vocabulary. He talked about *power*.

With Foucault, everything is about discourse, and every discourse is about power. Neither discourse nor power derive primarily from economics. The power that surrounds us is created by discourse, and must be fought by new discourses, by new words. What could delight an intellectual more? We will destroy the bourgeoisie by talking about them in ways they are too stupid to understand! Some of Foucault's arguments were anticipated by Horkheimer and Adorno. They too saw language as linked to the exercise of power and domination, and rejected the idea of neutral language. That is why they rejected clarity, a prescription Foucault followed to the letter. They, however, were still loosely tied to Marx's idea that the economy, or at least the bourgeoisie, was what counted in the final analysis, and that language or discourse was fundamentally a reflection of society's class structure. Foucault was a much more free-floating intellectual, a bohemian in spite of his academic position. He rejected the idea that either class or the state dictated language, or that power flowed from the top down or the center outward. For Foucault, "Power is everywhere, not because it embraces everything, but because it comes from everywhere."[26]

Power is also not just repressive, in Foucault's view. It does not just forbid. It creates, even when it seems to do the opposite. His view of the history of sexuality is an example of this. Before the seventeenth century, Foucault suggests, only monks were obsessed with sex. Then sexuality became a common obsession, and discussions of sex multiplied. Power, in Foucault's universe, like Victorian sexuality, is everywhere, ceaselessly multiplying its assaults—and just as constantly being resisted.[27]

The popularity of the word "power" and the language games Foucault played with it owed something to the history of the 1960s. Foucault's writings were read in an atmosphere that was saturated with "power" of all kinds. After the "Black Power" movement in the United States, the term "power" was attached to the most unlikely objects, from the "Flower Power" of the hippies to the "psychedelic power" of the drug culture. Power was democratized in the 60s, and Foucault's conception of power was nothing if not democratic: "...let us not look for the headquarters that presides over its [power's] rationality; neither the caste which governs, nor the groups which control the state apparatus, nor those who make the most important economic decisions direct the entire network of power...." Rather, "power comes from below, that is, there is no binary and all-encompassing opposition between rulers and ruled at the root of power relations...."[28]

Perhaps even more important, resistance to power was equally democratic in Foucault's theory, even if only intellectuals could understand Foucault: "Where there is power, there is resistance, and yet, or rather consequently, this resistance is never in a position of exteriority in relation to power." Foucault's doctrine combined panalienation with pantheism. Power and resistance are everywhere. Both the good and the bad are omnipresent. Neither the good nor the bad, neither power nor resistance, can ever eliminate the other: "...No matter how terrifying a given system may be, there always remain the possibilities of resistance, disobedience, and oppositional groupings. On the other hand, I do not think that there is anything that is functionally—by its very nature—absolutely liberating."[29]

What matters to Foucault are the classic concerns of the intellectual: "I would more or less agree with the idea that in fact what interests me is much more morals than politics or, in any case, politics as ethics." What kind of new ethic did Foucault have to propose? "We have to promote new forms of subjectivity through refusal of this kind of individuality which has been imposed on us for several centuries." What kind of individuality should we substitute? Foucault, like Horkheimer and Adorno, or Nietzsche, turns to art, and the bohemian ideal of the individual life as a unique work of art: "What strikes me is the fact that in our society,... art is something which is specialized or which is done by experts who are artists. But couldn't everyone's life become a work of art? Why should the lamp or the house be an art object, but not our life?" In other words, we must overcome our alienation. This sounds like existentialism, but Foucault distinguishes himself from existentialism by saying that we should devote ourselves not to being "authentic" Sartre's old existentialist slogan, but to being "creative." By espousing creativity, Foucault claims to be closer to Nietzsche than to Sartre. The choice shows Foucault's more aristocratic, late-twentieth-century intellectual taste.[30]

Foucault cast about somewhat wildly on occasion for political alternatives. He supported the Iranian Revolution in 1978, and in particular its religious content. The Iranians, he wrote, were looking for what the West had lost since the Renaissance and the great crises of Christianity, "a *political spirituality*. I can already hear some French people laughing, but I know they are wrong." Foucault's odd enthusiasm for a regime that would have stoned him for his flamboyant homosexuality shows how desperate anti-capitalist intellectuals can be to find some weapon with which to attack capitalism.[31]

The odd burst of pro-Iranian enthusiasm aside, however, Foucault was a typical intellectual of his period, a pessimistic pseudo-aristocrat. He was frequently accused of preaching apathy, since power could not be overcome, but this is not quite correct. "My point is not that everything is bad, but that everything is dangerous, which is not exactly the same as bad. If everything is dangerous, then we always have something to do [there's always a job for a preacher!]. So my position leads not to apathy but to a hyper- and pessimistic activism." In other words, intellectuals should keep shouting while retreating to their towers.[32]

The aristocratic reactions of intellectuals like Heidegger, the Frankfurt School, and Foucault were widely popular in academic circles, but had no direct connection to political movements. Most of the time, such intellectuals didn't mind. Their ideas weren't intended for everyone, but rather the opposite, "we might say that the less comprehensible it is, the better, because it shuts the poet off from the wrong people," wrote Czeslaw Milosz of postmodern poetry, and this applies equally well to postmodern "Critical Theory." Nevertheless, mind's withdrawal from direct political engagement after World War II was temporary. That the antagonism was as strong as ever, and potentially as important as ever, became clear in the late 1960s.[33]

Make Love, Not Money: The Counterculture

The second half of the twentieth century was generally characterized by social and political stability in the West. One exception is the period loosely known as the "60s," although it ran from the early 1960s to 1975 or so. The '60s saw the arrival of sex, drugs, rock 'n' roll, and youth culture. They were the coming of age, or at least adolescence, of the baby boom generation. There were three related but distinct socio-political phenomena; the American civil rights movement, climaxing with the assassination of Martin Luther King in 1968; the Vietnam War and the anti-war movement that opposed it; and the counterculture. All three were often lumped together under the name of "The Movement."

Many people were part of all three, but not all. American President Lyndon B. Johnson was a partisan of the civil rights movement, but obviously no supporter of the anti-war movement or the counterculture. Many so-called "Old-Left" figures, notably the communist parties, were in favor of civil rights and against the Vietnam War, but were hostile to the counterculture. The counterculture was not dependent on either Vietnam or the civil rights movement for its existence, although both contributed to its energy. In Europe, there was no civil rights movement, and little direct involvement in the Vietnam War, and yet the counterculture flourished, despite the hostility of the old left. Political action was essentially only a by-product of the counterculture, which was chiefly interested in cultural revolution. Where the civil rights movement and the anti-war movement were always political, but not necessarily opposed to capitalism, the counterculture was sometimes political, but always opposed to capitalism.

The counterculture emerged when the Western world had been immersed for a generation in recovering from the material deprivations of the Depression and World War II. For 20 years, making money had been almost everyone's chief preoccupation. The counterculture was a reaction against this. It was the democratic counterpart to the aristocratic reaction of Heidegger, the Frankfurt School, Foucault, and their ilk. The counterculture's emergence within capitalism, amidst its frantic pursuit of prosperity, had been predicted by Tocqueville:

> If ever the vast majority of the human race were to concentrate its thoughts on the quest for material goods alone, we may expect a powerful reaction to take place in certain souls. These would plunge headlong into the world of the spirits lest they find themselves trammeled unduly by the fetters the body would impose on them.[34]

America was the most capitalist society in the democratic world, and it was no accident that the counterculture began there.

The counterculture was the most original aspect of the 1960s, and the most significant from the perspective of the war between mind and money. The counterculture attempted to make everyone under 30 into a bohemian, a project in which it was surprisingly successful. In the hippie movement the counterculture created a democratized bohemia in America, the democratic country par excellence, and took it all over the world. The counterculture spread an ideology of universal love and mystic pantheism, and created a nomadic culture of love, sex, drugs, and rock 'n roll. It has been called a form of "romantic anticapitalism," and it clearly had analogies with both traditional bohemian life and with the longing for community expressed by Toennies and others. In its call for the creation of a new kind of human being it had much in common with Personalism. But the transformation of these old longings into a mass movement for cultural change was new.

The counterculture was the antithesis of aristocratic intellectuals like Heidegger or Horkheimer. Where they were pessimistic, the counterculture was wildly optimistic. Where they bemoaned panalienation, the counterculture practiced spontaneity. Instead of lectures, the counterculture preferred "Happenings" and "Be-Ins." If both used religious language, the academics used it to give consolation in defeat, whereas the counterculture made it into triumphant credos. Old elements of mind's struggle against money were tumbled together in new circumstances with results that were, briefly, astonishing.

The embodiment of the counterculture was the "hippie." "Hippie" derived from the Beatnik term "hip," used for someone who was part of their group. It continued to have this connotation in the late 1960s, but added other meanings. Looking at the hippie phenomenon from the outside, an Indian sociologist, Tribhuwan Kapur, compiled a list of nine traits for identifying hippies, many of whom made trips to his country (Western hippies frequently traveled to India in search of enlightenment). According to Kapur, a hippie:

1.   Is presently using, and has been using, for more than three years at least, drugs synthetic and natural.
2.   Has a drug of preference...
3.   Has sexual mores and norms overtly apart from the mainstream of society...
4.   Sees in sexual experimentation and diversification evidence of a superiority to the member-in-society.
5.   Has not suffered economic deprivation, or has developed an apathy to it, and to all forms of work that binds one to a regular salary, promotions and similar bureaucratic procedures.
6.   Is itinerant.
7.   Is obsessed with the concept of freedom and orders his or her life with it as a central focus of motivating action.
8.   Has acquired an indifference to the body, which leads to chronic disease, torn clothes, and bodily dirt.

9.   Who sees in religion a way of negating his or her own religion and
      transferring allegiance to another...[35]

Kapur gives a good picture of the "soldiers" of the counterculture. However, his definition ignores music. Rock music was an essential part of
the counterculture. Its revolution was fueled by music as much or more
than by drugs. As one unusually politically conscious musician put it:
"MUSIC IS REVOLUTION. Rock and roll music is one of the most
vital revolutionary forces in the West—it blows people all the way back
to their senses and makes them feel good, like they're *alive* again in the
middle of this monstrous funeral parlor of western civilization."[36]

This was enough to make many intellectuals adopt the counterculture
as their own. Of course, most hippies were not intellectuals, even if they
did resemble them in certain ways. Careful critical discourse was hardly
their distinguishing mark. But intellectuals shared with hippies the view
that one must choose one's lifestyle, create one's own life and make it
a work of art, as Foucault put it. The hippies had more in common with
the intelligentsia than the proletariat ever did.

The hippie movement gave intellectuals a lever with which to move
capitalism. The counterculture aimed to change people first, and institutions second. Charles A. Reich, in his 1970 best-seller, *The Greening of
America*, proclaimed that the new revolution was about the coming of
better people, with a better consciousness. The new generation possessed
"Consciousness III," which is to say they were not alienated they way
their elders were. Unlike their elders, they would not be enslaved by
their jobs, turned into "lifeless and selfless" creatures by the "Corporate
State." Reich, a law professor and typical intellectual, claimed that the
majority of American adults hated their work, but lacked the necessary
vision to do anything. The younger generation was superior. Reich praised
the counterculture's search for community, its communes and hippie
"tribes." The new Consciousness III generation managed the neat trick
of combining community with autonomy, creating insider groups while
maintaining outsider status towards society at large. A hippie could be
both a completely autonomous individual and a completely integrated
community member at the same time—thus realizing an old dream of
the intelligentsia.[37]

The counterculture was a fun, democratic, anti-capitalist cultural
revolution. It brought intellectuals into contact with the people. As Abbie
Hoffman, a figure who was a leader in both the counterculture and the
antiwar movement, put it: "That was the difference between the Yippies[38]

and the straight Left with its language of anti-hedonism and austerity. I thought it was extremely counterproductive. I couldn't stand it. You see, I accept American culture, its demand for entertainment. Europeans who observed the period of the Sixties tell me that my contribution to revolutionary theory was to come up with the idea that revolution could be fun."[39]

The counterculture dominated the political events of the 1960s. This was especially true in America, where political movements tended to gain leverage only to the extent that they were also counterculture events. The 1968 sit-ins at Columbia University were one example of this. Another was the testimony of Jerry Rubin before the House Un-American Activities Committee in 1968. To get maximum attention for his testimony against the Vietnam War, he dressed up in the uniform of an American Revolutionary War soldier. It was politics as theater—Rubin was saying that in Vietnam, America was violating the ideals of its own Revolution. It was wonderfully effective, and became even more so when the committee refused to let him testify. Whereas when Rubin made a traditional political speech at the San Francisco Be-In, it fell flat, by his own admission. "I became very influenced by this. I thought maybe the real battle of America is not politics, it's lifestyle. And lifestyle determines politics."[40]

The hippies deliberately rejected the "American way of life." "For them, as for Oscar Wilde, it is not the average American who is disgusting; it is the ideal American," that is the hard-working individual striving to better his family's material situation. American society in the 1960s was not rejected by poor people who thought it denied them economic opportunities. It was rejected by middle-class adolescents who thought it condemned them to lives spent successfully pursuing wealth. Susan Sontag stated the counterculture's case against America: "The quality of American life is an insult to the possibilities of human growth; and the pollution of American space, with gadgetry and cars and TV and box architecture, brutalizes the senses, making gray neurotics of most of us…." Jerry Rubin put it more simply: The counterculture "signifies the total end of the Protestant ethic: screw work, we want to know ourselves." The counterculture totally rejected money-making. "The idea of making money or becoming successful in the economic sense was just odious to me. It struck me that the only way to make money was to sell your soul," wrote Rubin. The old bohemian expression "selling out" became part of American popular culture in this period. Virtue was identified with poverty in a manner reminiscent of the early Christians, who were held up as models by many hippies. The Christian Don't, "Don't Have Money (Give It to the Poor)," was embraced by many who had little interest in traditional Christianity, but who accepted voluntary poverty. As one ex-hippie later put it, "I was willing to embrace poverty if it meant building a new way of life. I was convinced we were fated to slay the dragon of American imperialism and greed."[41]

There were strong affinities between the theatrical/spiritual/lifestyle emphasis of the counterculture and intellectuals' desire to enforce a moral dimension on a recalcitrant capitalist society. This affinity encouraged widespread sympathy among intellectuals for the counterculture. The counterculture, however, was essentially democratic and thus in some respects hostile to intellectuals. It was not really likely that it would ever accept their leadership, no matter how much intellectuals kowtowed to its superior spirituality. As a movement, it did not last very long, and by 1975 had lost much of its importance. It had enduring influence on some areas of culture, e.g., sex, drugs, and music, but these proved to be perfectly compatible with capitalism. The counterculture did, however, provoke another kind of aristocratic reaction among a minority of intellectuals, a reaction that is of interest in its own right. The counterculture created the neoconservatives.

The Neoconservatives—A Contradiction within the Intellectual Class?

The counterculture was a mass movement, but it never represented the majority, either in America or elsewhere. Indeed, it provoked a strong conservative reaction. Richard Nixon defeated Hubert Humphrey as a direct result of the Chicago riots during the Democratic National Convention of 1968, one of the counterculture's intersections with the anti-war and civil rights movements. In France, the nation's response to the student movement of 1968 was to elect a conservative, Georges Pompidou, president in 1969. Similar political reactions took place elsewhere.

Less predictable, perhaps, was the reaction of a number of American intellectuals who became known as "neoconservatives." They were so horrified by the counterculture that they became outspoken supporters of capitalism. Of course, at no time were all intellectuals ever opposed to capitalism, but the neocons, as they became known, are a special case that demands attention.

A small group, the neoconservatives nevertheless rapidly developed a considerable readership and a significant influence on American policy, domestic and foreign. Gaining a public identity in the 1960s, they quickly achieved prominence. They were certainly intellectuals as defined here. A few were academics, many entered government for a period of time, most made their livings as writers or later in think tanks. Yet their attitudes seem to be a contradiction of everything that prominent Western intellectuals usually stand for. Against the dominant intellectual trends of their time, the neoconservatives saw capitalism as a positive development in Western culture. When most of their fellows were moving left, aligning themselves with the counterculture, the student movement, and other anti-capitalist forces, they did the opposite. By examining their views, we can learn a great deal about the intelligentsia in general.

The neoconservative movement was in many respects typical of the intellectual class in its attitudes, even if atypical in its pro-capitalist conclusions. In their own way, the neocons were as aristocratic and moralistic as any Heideggerian, although they expressed themselves in plainer language. Indeed, there were ways in which the neoconservative analysis of American society more or less unconsciously mirrored the anti-capitalist views more common among intellectuals. At first glance, however, this does not seem to be the case.

The neoconservative movement of the 1960s and 1970s was first and foremost a reaction against the counterculture (the second generation of neoconservatives, active in the 1990s, were in a different situation, and will be left out of this account). Many neocons supported the civil rights movement, at least in its early phases. They rejected legal discrimination against black people, although most opposed "affirmative action," that is legal preferences for racial minorities. Most of the neocons, despite being fiercely anti-communist, also opposed the Vietnam War. What differentiated them so strongly from their fellow intellectuals was that "The founding generation of neo-cons never overcame their shock that many of America's privileged children turned against their country on the 1960s. Many neo-cons found the antiwar movement more repulsive than America's incineration of Vietnam."[42]

It was not the fact that the counterculture opposed the Vietnam War that upset the neoconservatives. They did, too. It was the counterculture's open rejection of American values that upset them. Their quarrel with the counterculture and their fellow intellectuals was fundamentally a quarrel about morals and culture. America in their view was a success story, and they rejected the counterculture's interpretation of America as evil. The neoconservatives could neither accept nor understand the counterculture's contempt for an America identified with materialism.

Partly this incomprehension was generational—the neoconservatives, reared in the Depression and World War II, had no objection to material prosperity. Partly it was intellectual. Many of the original neocons had been Marxists in their student years in the 1930s, and they often knew their Marx a great deal better than the radical students of the 1960s. This was, if anything, a disadvantage to them in understanding the counterculture. The neocons' juvenile Marxism was of the "vulgar," 1930s-style variety. It was the unreconstructed economic-determinism popular among American communists and fellow travelers during the Depression. Neocons could understand the Old Left who claimed that capitalism could not provide economic well-being. By their own admission, they could not understand the New Left of the 1960s because its concerns were different. It was largely uninterested in economics, as the neocons recognized. The hippies didn't want more money or more things, they wanted less. This made no sense to the neocons. They could not understand why America's middle class youth was rejecting the life of economic privilege and opportunity that lay open to them, in the name of some nebulous spiritual utopia.[43]

The neocons had left Marxism behind before the critique of alienation was developed by Western Marxists after World War II. They had no sympathy for it. The democratic bohemianism of the counterculture was equally alien and unwelcome to them. Although most neocons did not have formal academic positions, and made their living as independent writers (at least early in their careers), they were not bohemians. They wanted to assimilate with bourgeois society, not flee it. In 1975, after experiencing all the turmoil of the 1960s, Midge Decter wrote an anti-bohemian rant titled "A Letter to the Young (and their parents)." She condemned the counterculture for its bad manners, bad dress, and self-absorption, in short for its refusal to join the middle-class world of its parents. This was typical of the neoconservative attitude to the counterculture. Yet her essay was also typical of the neocons in another, unintended way. It was not free from classic anti-capitalist sentiment. After talking about the kinds of jobs hippies took, and above all the small businesses they created to sell tie-dyed T-shirts, handicrafts, etc., Decter proclaimed that "In purely personal terms, all these unexpected occupations of yours have one large feature in common: they are the work of private, and largely unregulated, entrepreneurs... free of all that patient overcoming and hard-won new attainment that attend the conquest of a professional career." Her contempt for the small businessman, and her respect for getting good grades at university, could hardly be more clear.[44]

In opposition to the counterculture, the neocons called for a return to traditional moral values. In the nineteenth century, this had been common among anti-capitalist conservative intellectuals, who blamed capitalism for disturbing traditional social hierarchies. What differentiated the neoconservatives from old-fashioned conservatives was that they identified traditional moral values with capitalism. But like them, they were committed to the idea of a morally virtuous economic system. This distinguished them from conservatives whose views were rooted in the political economy descended from the honeymoon period's disassociation of economics and moral intentions. The neocons did not wish to limit the sphere of moral judgment as Smith or Hume did, they wanted to preserve it. Irving Kristol criticized the conservative economist and political thinker Friedrich von Hayek for saying that capitalism was amoral. If the neoconservatives had thought capitalism was amoral, they would have opposed it.[45]

The neoconservatives found their moral ideals embodied in the professional middle classes. For them, capitalism was identified with certain bourgeois virtues which they wished to uphold against all comers, whether on the right, like Hayek, or on the left, like the counterculture. They rejected anyone who attacked commerce as immoral or amoral. In Kristol's view, "capitalism at its apogee saw itself as the most just social order the world has ever witnessed, because it replaced all arbitrary (e.g., inherited) distributions... with a distribution that was... linked to personal merit—this latter term being inclusive of both personal abilities and personal virtues." For George Gilder, another neoconservative defender of bourgeois morality, capitalism "calls forth, propagates, and relies upon the best and most generous of human qualities." Capitalism has material virtues, but its moral virtue is what makes it legitimate.[46]

The neoconservatives' emphasis on morality, natural to intellectuals, is found in their rejection of the counterculture, and also in their explanation of why the counterculture had come to exist in the first place. For Kristol, the reason capitalism had run into trouble in the late twentieth century was because it had lost its *moral* legitimacy. For Michael Novak, the neoconservative movement was in part defined by adherence to the idea that "Culture is even more fundamental than politics or economics." The neocons wished to reclaim the moral/cultural high ground for capitalism. They recognized they were fighting an uphill struggle, but all the neocons were characterized by a liking for a good fight.[47]

The neocons had an explanation of why capitalism had lost its moral legitimacy: success. "The dynamics of capitalism itself" had subverted the idea of virtue. Capitalism's economic and political success had made virtue unnecessary or even counterproductive. This argument is sketched in Kristol's writing, and made at length in Daniel Bell's *Cultural Contradictions of Capitalism* (echoed on the left in Christopher Lasch's *Culture of Narcissism*). Effectively, there were two forms of neoconservative moral critique of contemporary culture: an optimistic version, which proclaimed capitalism morally superior to its rivals and capable of happily propagating its virtues, and a pessimistic one, which agreed that capitalism was a morally superior system, but saw capitalist virtue in decline, perhaps terminal. In making the latter arguments, neoconservatives could use much of the literary critique of capitalism while defending it. They could thus both praise capitalism's virtues and attack it for its sins—twice over, if they thought the moral decline was reversible with the right intellectual moral (and aristocratic) leadership.

There were thus ways in which the neoconservatives were closer to the anti-capitalist commonplaces of their time than they liked to admit. Their critiques of contemporary moral decay echoed those of many anti-capitalist thinkers. Overall they were, like the rest of the intellectual class, in retreat from the broad sociopolitical claims intellectuals had made between World War I and World War II. Instead of seeking refuge in the ivory tower, the neoconservatives asked shelter of the middle class, and in return offered to preach it sermons on its once-great virtues. In the end, however, many of them were as pessimistic as Heidegger, Adorno, and Foucault. Kristol, Bell and some other neoconservatives were left speculating that capitalism would be its own gravedigger, as Marx predicted. Not because it could no longer feed the proletariat, but because it could not preserve the bourgeois virtues. This argument also had parallels in nineteenth-century anti-capitalist thought—the new twist was that the neocons emphasized the virtue the bourgeoisie had once possessed.[48] Insofar as they took this attitude, the neoconservatives furnish another example of aristocratic pessimism from an intellectual class in retreat. But many remained resolutely optimistic. Whether or not capitalism's moral decline could be reversed, and how, was a subject which neoconservatives loved to debate. All of them rejected the "inner spiritual chaos of the times," a phrase reminiscent of Personalism. The intelligentsia is inevitably a pseudo-clergy, no matter what religion it embraces.[49]

The neoconservatives had another explanation for the counterculture's assault on capitalism besides cultural decline, one more in line with an intellectual aristocracy's distrust of possible rivals. They never forgot the lessons of their Marxist youth. Why had so many people revived dying anti-capitalist ideas? It must be because it was in their class interest to do so. The neocons did not usually blame the intelligentsia for this, however. After all, they were intellectuals themselves, and proud of it. They blamed the "new class," whom they defined more or less as government bureaucrats and those professions that benefited most from an expanded government. These people profited from capitalism's loss of moral legitimacy, because it increased the moral standing, and power, of the noncommercial, "nonprofit" institutions they were associated with. The intellectuals were the "ancestors" of this new class, but "very few" of the new class were intellectuals themselves. The neoconservatives' attack on the new class allowed them to take on an identity dear to all intellectuals in democratic societies, that of defender of the common man against the elite—the bureaucrats and professionals of the new class. The attraction of "new class" theory for many (though by no means all—many stuck to preaching moral decay) neoconservatives lay in the way it allowed them to clothe their aristocratic reaction to the counterculture in democratic language.[50]

The neoconservatives of the 1960s and 1970s were thus typical intellectuals who took atypical positions—not in itself unusual, as the intelligentsia has never found it easy to agree on anything. They offered an olive branch to capitalism, in return for police protection for their offices during student riots, and recognition of their moral/clerical role. But even when aligning themselves with capitalism, they could not forebear from criticizing it, and lamenting its moral decay.

* * *

In the 1960s the struggle between mind and money took on new forms, as was only to be expected after the catastrophes that preceded it. None, fortunately, were as disastrous as fascism or communism, and by 1992 both fascism and communism were history. The aristocratic reactions of Heidegger, The Frankfurt School, Foucault and their fellows made academic discourse dreary, but that was a small price to pay compared to what the war between mind and money had exacted in the past. The counterculture brightened some lives, and blighted not a few. If in the judgment of some neoconservatives it represented a period of moral decline, well, clergy of one sort or another had been saying much the same thing for a long time. The drug culture might threaten individuals, but it did not challenge capitalism. One might think that the struggle between mind and money had finally passed its crisis point, that the fever of anti-capitalism was broken, and that this conflict was no longer significant in the history of Western society.

But this would be a mistake. The counterculture was not the intelligentsia's creation, just as communism wasn't, but the role intellectuals played in the counterculture showed their ability to lead and participate in new and innovative challenges to capitalism. If capitalism proved equally adept at turning the Summer of Love into an opportunity to make money for the music industry, and if hippie slogans would one day become part of advertising campaigns, this was only a sign that neither side was giving up. The neoconservative presence on the American intellectual scene endured into the twenty-first century, but it hardly became the dominant intellectual trend, and it had little resonance in Europe. Anti-capitalist attitudes were as strong in art, literature, and social theory at the end of the twentieth century as they had been at the beginning, even if Marxism was seemingly in its death throes. Meanwhile, the intellectual class continued to grow in absolute numbers, although the pace of that growth slowed as the century ended and the boom in university growth came to a close.

Still, on the whole, capitalism seemed in a strong position at the end of the twentieth century—as it had in 1900. But the conflict between mind and money continued to burn under the surface, every now and then sending up a wisp of smoke. Once in a while, some new idea or movement would catch fire, flare up, and a brushfire would break out. The most recent transformations of the ongoing struggle between mind and money are the subject of the next chapter.

Notes

1. Ares is the Greek god of war, Hermes the god of commerce, and Apollo the patron of artists and intellectuals.
2. Georg Simmel, *The Philosophy of Money*, tr. Tom Bottomore and David Frisby (London: Routledge & Kegan Paul, 1978), 448.
3. Dewey, "The Economic Basis of the New Society," cited in Charles A. Reich, *The Greening of America* (New York: Random House, 1970), 54.
4. Roger Scruton, *A Dictionary of Political Thought* (London: Macmillan, 1982), 12.
5. Leszek Kolakowski, "Ce qu'on appelle 'aliénation'," in *Le village introuvable* (Brussels: Complexe, 1986), 76, 85-86. Simmel, *Philosophy of Money*, 236.
6. Tocqueville, *Democracy in America*, 513.
7. Kolakowski, "Ce qu'on appelle 'aliénation'," in *Le village introuvable*, 85-86. Along with alienation, Kolakowski includes "dialectically," "structure," "humanism," "reification," and "liberation" as words to avoid.
8. Kolakowski, "Ce qu'on appelle 'aliénation'," in *Le village introuvable*, 85-86.
9. This point is made by Hirschman, *The Passions and the Interests*, 133.
10. "Alienation," *Dictionary of Concepts in History*, ed. Harry Ritter (Westport, CT: Greenwood Press, 1986).
11. See Howard Brick, *Age of Contradiction: American Thought and Culture in the 1960s* (New York: Twayne, 1998), 14, 16-17.

12. Michel Foucault, *The Will to Knowledge. The History of Sexuality,* vol. 1, trans. Robert Hurley (New York: Penguin, 1990), 95-96.
13. Martin Heidegger, "Letter on Humanism," in *Basic Writings*, ed. David Farrell Krell (New York: Harper & Row, 1977), 193, 239.
14. Max Horkheimer and Theodor W. Adorno, *Dialectic of Enlightenment*, trans. Edmund Jephcott (Stanford, CA: Stanford University Press, 2002), xvi-xvii; Tocqeville, *Democracy in America*, 540-41.
15. Horkheimer and Adorno, *Dialectic of Enlightenment*, 106; Horkheimer, cited in Jay, *The Dialectical Imagination*, 262, 277-78.
16. Heidegger, "Letter on Humanism," in *Basic Writings*, 210.
17. Heidegger, "The Question Concerning Technology," *Basic Writings*, 296.
18. Heidegger, "The Question Concerning Technology," *Basic Writings*, 296-97, 300-02, 308. Note that for Heidegger the business enterprise is the opposite of creativity. See "The Word of Nietzsche: God is Dead" in *The Essay Concerning Technology and Other Essays*, tr. and ed. William Lovitt (New York: Harper, 1977), 64.
19. Heidegger, "The Question Concerning Technology," *Basic Writings*, 314, 317.
20. Horkheimer, cited in Jay: *The Dialectical Imagination*, 214. Horkheimer and Adorno, *Dialectic of Enlightenment*, 30.
21. Horkheimer and Adorno, *Dialectic of Enlightenment*, 1-3, 6, 21.
22. Horkheimer and Adorno, *Dialectic of Enlightenment*, 17, 20.
23. Horkheimer and Adorno, *Dialectic of Enlightenment*, xiv, 21, 163.
24. Horkheimer and Adorno, *Dialectic of Enlightenment*, 179; Jay, *The Dialectical Imagination*, 179, 182-85.
25. Horkheimer and Adorno, *Dialectic of Enlightenment*, xi; Rolf Wiggershaus, *The Frankfurt School: Its History, Theories, and Political Significance*, tr. Michael Robertson (Cambridge, MA: MIT Press, 1994), 599, 621.
26. Foucault, *History of* Sexuality, 1:93.
27. Foucault, *History of Sexuality,* 1:12, 20, 24-25.
28. Foucault, *History of Sexuality,* 1:95.
29. Foucault, "Space, Knowledge, Power," in *The Foucault Reader*, ed. Paul Rabinow (London: Penguin, 1991), 245.
30. Foucault, "Politics and Ethics," *The Foucault Reader*, 375; "On the Genealogy of Ethics," *The Foucault* Reader, 350-51; "The Subject and Power," in *Michel Foucault: Beyond Structuralism and Hermeneutics*, ed. Hubert Dreyfus and Paul Rabinow (Chicago: University of Chicago Press, 1982), 216.
31. Foucault, *Dits et Ecrits, 1954-1988*, (Paris: Gallimard, 1994), 3:694.
32. Foucault, "On the Genealogy of Ethics," *The Foucault Reader*, 343.
33. Milosz, "Against Incomprehensible Poetry," in Czeslaw Milosz, *To Begin Where I Am: Selected Essays* (New York: Farrar, Strauss and Giroux, 2001), 375.
34. Tocqueville, *Democracy in America,* 623-24.
35. *The Counterculture Reader*, ed. E. A. Swingrover, (London: Longman, 2003), 40-41.
36. John Sinclair, in *The Counterculture Reader*, ed. E. A. Swingrover, (London: Longman, 2003), 43.
37. Charles A. Reich, *The Greening of America* (New York: Random House, 1970), 2, 16, 90, 141, 158, 165, 245, 272-73, 276, 385.
38. The Yippies, or "Youth International Party," were an anti-war counterculture political organization.
39. Hoffman, *The Portable Sixties Reader*, ed. Ann Charters (London: Penguin, 2002), 259; and Joan and Robert K. Morrison, *From Camelot to Kent State: The Sixties Experience in the Words of Those Who Lived It* (New York: Oxford University Press, 1987), 294.
40. Rubin, *The Portable Sixties Reader*, 283.

41. Irving Kristol, "'When Virtue Loses All Her Loveliness'—Some Reflections on Capitalism and 'The Free Society'," in *The Essential Neo-Conservative Reader,* ed. Mark Gerson (Reading MA: Addison Wesley, 1996), 104; Susan Sontag, "What's Happening In America," *The Portable Sixties Reader,* 120; Jerry Rubin, cited in Shi, *The Simple Life,* 251-52; Rubin, *From Camelot to Kent State,* 290; Iris Keltz, *The Counterculture Reader,* 53.

42. Gary Dorrien, *The Neoconservative Mind: Politics, Culture and the War of Ideology* (Philadelphia: Temple University Press, 1993), 356.

43. Mark Gerson, introduction, *The Essential Neo-Conservative Reader,* xvi; Irving Kristol, *Two Cheers for Capitalism* (New York: Basic Books, 1978), 58, 62-63.

44. Midge Decter, "A Letter to the Young (and to their parents)," *The Essential Neo-Conservative Reader,* 70-73.

45. Kristol "'When Virtue Loses All Her Loveliness'," *The Essential Neo-Conservative Reader,* 107.

46. Kristol, "'When Virtue Loses All Her Loveliness'," *The Essential Neo-Conservative Reader,* 107-09; George Gilder, "Moral Sources of Capitalism," in *The Essential Neo-Conservative Reader,* 153; Michael Novak, "What is a Neoconservative?," article posted 11/18/2005, http://www.michaelnovak.net/.

47. Kristol, "'Some Reflections on Capitalism and 'The Free Society'," *The Essential Neo-Conservative Reader,* 106; *Two Cheers for Capitalism,* x.

48. See the masterful summary in Albert Hirschman, "Rival Interpretations of Market Society: Civilizing, Destructive or Feeble?," *Journal of Economic Literature,* Dec. 1982, 1463-84.

49. Kristol, "Some Reflections on Capitalism and 'The Free Society'," *The Essential Neo-Conservative Reader,* 115.

50. Kristol, *Two Cheers for Capitalism,* 27-29.

8

Recent Battles

Anti-Americanism as an Anti-Capitalist Movement

Many people thought the collapse of Soviet communism in 1989 would be a decisive blow to mind's struggle against capitalism. Certainly, the decades afterwards saw a decline in the number of people killed in socialism's name. Was this just a trough in a wave, or the beginning of something more permanent? It will take a few generations for the answer to become clear. The long-term reaction to the stock market panic of 2008 may provide clues.

Among intellectuals the effects of communism's collapse were marginal. Academic Marxism suffered a little, but "bourgeois" remained an epithet. There was, in fact, no reason to expect the end of the Soviet Union to make much difference. Many intellectuals rejected capitalism. Eliminating one of capitalism's enemies, communism, did nothing to change that. In the twenty-first century, three battlefronts between mind and money still regularly make headlines: anti-Americanism, the anti-globalization movement, and ecologism. Let us begin with anti-Americanism, a subject often murky to Americans. In the year 2000, all over the world, many people hated America. Why?

There are many reasons for people, and in particular for intellectuals to hate America (or love it, but we are not concerned with that here). One is that America is identified with capitalism—and that's reason enough for many intellectuals to despise America. Most Americans see America as a beacon of freedom and prosperity. They do not understand that when America is identified with capitalism, America is transformed from a moral beacon into the Great Satan, not just in the eyes of Iranian fundamentalists, but in the eyes of many European and even American intellectuals. For many Western intellectuals, to identify America with Coca-Cola is to brand it with the mark of Cain.

Another reason for intellectuals' anti-Americanism has to do with their role as a pseudo-aristocracy. Because America, as Tocqueville tells us, is the world's most democratic society, it is the least friendly to a pseudo-aristocracy, and perhaps especially to intellectuals. Intellectuals have always perceived America as particularly hostile. As one British intellectual put it, "the things that rubbed into me in this country are 1) that the future of the world lies with America, and 2) that radically and essentially America is a barbarous country. The life of the spirit…is, not accidentally or temporarily, but inevitably and eternally killed in this country." The combination is intolerable to intellectuals. Thus, just as many intellectuals have a class interest in fighting capitalism, some think they have a class interest in fighting America. Because America is identified as the world's pre-eminent capitalist society, and because it rejects intellectuals' claim to aristocratic status, intellectuals are the social class most likely to hold anti-American attitudes.[1]

These are not the only reasons many intellectuals have anti-American attitudes. The question is complex, and needs to be broken down into parts. In discussing anti-Americanism as an anti-capitalist movement, three separate questions must be addressed:

1) Is America considered a capitalist society?
2) Does being anti-American mean opposing capitalism?
3) Is opposition to capitalism the chief cause of anti-Americanism?

The answers to these questions are Yes, Usually, and Sometimes. From a very early period, European intellectuals identified the United States with commercial society. When Tocqueville published *Democracy in America* in 1835, he wrote at length about Americans' passion for making money. Of course, Tocqueville was more subtle than most who came later, and he was making a larger point about democratic societies in general. In his view, all democratic societies encourage people to make money and keep on making money. They allow no one to feel secure, and encourage everyone, rich and poor alike, to aspire to better their position. Trade and industry respond to this need to make money far more quickly than agriculture. Insofar as America, in Tocqueville's view, was the world's most democratic country, this meant that America was also the country most devoted to commerce and industry, and to making money.[2]

If we contrast Tocqueville's description of the American attitude to work with how intellectuals look at work, we can see why many intel-

lectuals have always been estranged from America. It is not that intellectuals don't like to work. On the contrary, it is because Americans and
intellectuals both make work central to their lives that their differences
result in mutual contempt. "In the United States professions are more or
less unpleasant, but they are never high or low. Every honest profession
is honorable." Intellectuals find it hard to look fondly on a society that
does not recognize the special nature of their calling. It calls into question
their patent of nobility, denies the basis of their aristocratic self-image.
Insofar as America is the world's most wholly democratic society, it is
the society from which intellectuals feel most alienated.[3]

By Tocqueville's time, the fundamental identification of America with
capitalism was established, and being anti-American almost always meant
opposing capitalism. "The basic cultural critique of America prevalent
in twentieth and twenty-first century [indeed, in nineteenth-century]
Europe was already in place.... Materialism plus democracy made for a
spiritual emptiness. The United States was a mass culture based on the
lowest common denominator." Nothing was less likely to make anti-
capitalist intellectuals admirers of American society, no matter how
much they admired Thomas Jefferson. There were national variations
on anti-Americanism. The British emphasized excessive equality, the
French America's intellectual and cultural poverty, and the Germans
stressed spiritual barrenness, but intellectuals everywhere had got their
lines down pat.[4]

Lines learned, "discourse" created, rejecting American culture as a
form of capitalism was a minor theater of operations in the wars between
mind and money in the nineteenth century. Examples can be found in
a number of novels of the period. Dickens, much preoccupied with
America's refusal to honor the copyright of his novels, visited America
for five months in 1842, and published an unflattering account in his
American Notes. More importantly, he devoted a considerable section
of his next major novel, *Martin Chuzzlewit* (published 1843-44), to his
hero's misadventures in the United States. Martin, the English hero,
flees to America hoping to make his fortune as an architect. When his
ship docks, he meets an American who owns a newspaper that suppos-
edly is directed at the aristocracy of America. Much surprised to hear
that America has an aristocracy, our hero inquires about its nature, only
to be told that it is composed "of intelligence and virtue. And of their
necessary consequence in this republic. Dollars, sir."[5]

Martin soon discovers that in America, "all their cares, hopes, joys,
affections, virtues, and associations, seemed to be melted down into

dollars.... Men were weighed by their dollars, measures gauged by their dollars; life was auctioneered, appraised, put up, and knocked down for its dollars." The American businessman is typically a swindler, happy to "make commerce one huge lie and mighty theft." There is no room left for any interest in literature or the arts, and when Martin asks, he is told that American literature consists of tabloid newspapers. In their perpetual chase for money, Americans end up seeming much alike to Martin, "strangely devoid of individual traits of character." All in all, enough to make anyone, but especially an intellectual, cringe at the thought of the United States.[6]

Dickens had a personal ax to grind, but even relatively friendly observers like Oscar Wilde echoed Dickens' identification of America with capitalism in its grossest form. Wilde, like Dickens, visited America on a lecture tour, and he reported on his impressions in a lecture he gave on his return to England in 1883. His first impression was favorable. Whereas Martin Chuzzlewit was struck by the low-brow nature of American society before he ever got off the boat, the first thing that strikes Oscar Wilde when he gets off the boat is that Americans all have decent clothing. If there is not much in the way of high fashion, there are no rags to be seen either. Wilde echoes Tocqueville by praising how politically well-educated the average American is. Moreover, Wilde gushes enthusiastically about the beauty of American machinery. Wilde *likes* America. But Wilde, too, identifies American culture with commerce. "The men are entirely given to business," everyone is in a hurry, and when the Americans deliberately try to create beautiful things, they have "signally failed" (the beauty of their machines is an unintended by-product).[7]

Even many intellectuals who like America feel this way, and have from Wilde's time to the present. Czeslaw Milosz (1911-2004), a pro-American Pole much taken by American literature, still described America as "millions of people who care about money." The impression left by Dickens and Wilde and Milosz is that America is a not-quite fully human society, a society whose devotion to commerce has destroyed something important. America is capitalism writ large, and for many intellectuals capitalism and humanism are naturally incompatible.[8]

Wilde and Dickens and Milosz were, after all, foreigners to America. The extent to which such criticism of America can be found in the writings of American intellectuals is, however, striking. American intellectuals tended to become anti-American a little later than Europeans, since the American intellectual class coalesced later and adopted anti-capitalist attitudes later. But their criticism was often identical, in its broad lines, with European criticism of America. It is a rare event in history when class proves more important than nationality.[9]

We have already seen William Dean Howells and Thorstein Veblen writing in this vein. Perhaps an even better example is the great American novelist Henry James, because he deliberately contrasted America and Europe. James was a Boston Brahmin who early abandoned residence on his native shores for England. He wrote several novels about the adventures of Americans in Europe, and one account of the adventures of an expatriate American on a tour home—himself. James went back to the United States for an extended visit in 1904. He was horrified. Some of his horror was for modernity, and some for the uncouth accents of New York immigrants, but much of it was for America as a capitalist society.

New York City, where James had spent much time as a child, epitomized American capitalism. The skyscrapers of New York were testimony to an unlimited desire to make money, and only money. James wished Emile Zola had known New York instead of Paris—then he would have been able to describe a truly commercial society in his novels, rather than its pale French imitation. In France, things besides business still matter, but "'Business' plays a part in the US that other interests dispute much less showily than they sometimes dispute it in the life of European countries; in consequence of which the typical American figure is above all that 'business man'...." In *The American Scene* James concluded that America was a "great commercial democracy seeking to abound supremely in its own sense and having none to gainsay it."[10]

Of course, no one claimed that America was the *only* capitalist society. Dickens set *Hard Times* in England and based it on Manchester, not Pittsburgh. Most anti-capitalist literature and theory was produced by Europeans, for Europeans, and was about Europe. Americans and Europeans knew very well that Europe was a capitalist society. The difference intellectuals perceived between Europe and America was that Europe was also something besides capitalism. In America, commerce had "none to gainsay it." In Europe, that was not the case. Nineteenth-century intellectuals perceived European capitalism as less mass-oriented, more friendly to intellectuals, less alienated from them and their ideals. They still think so. The fall of the Soviet Union did nothing to change this attitude. America is "untamed capitalism," "*le capitalisme sauvage*" as the French call it. Europe represents a kindle, gentler, tamer (leashed!) market. European intellectuals are alienated, but they have an easier time imagining what it would be to live in a world in which they were not, in which they felt at home—one reason so many American intellectuals have preferred to live in Europe.

Before World War I, people like James were in the minority among American intellectuals. Most had not yet turned against capitalism. Woodrow Wilson, President of the United States and of Princeton University, intellectual, could still say, in a speech to American businessmen: "with the inspiration of the thought that you are Americans and are meant to carry liberty and justice and the principles of humanity wherever you go, go out and sell goods that will make the world more comfortable and more happy, and convert them to the principles of America." In Wilson's view, commerce and "the principles of humanity" went hand in hand, as they had in the Honeymoon Period. After World War II, one could imagine President Eisenhower saying the same thing, but not many professors.[11]

The Cold War strengthened the identification between America and capitalism, because America was communism's leading opponent. Since then the identification of America with capitalism has become commonplace. One American historian described America's rise to superpower as "the rise of a great imperium with the outlook of a great emporium." Anti-Americanism is the natural result among intellectuals. For example, a 2005 study comparing American and European models of commercial culture concludes by suggesting that the end of socialism in eastern Europe after 1989 "raised new questions about the viability of the American model of consumer society: Could there not be an alternative that was less devastating in its free-market megalomania and claims on global resources...?" "Free-market megalomania"—just the kind of thing that Dickens or James might have said about America. Intellectuals' tendency to anti-Americanism has been as constant in the modern Western world as their hostility to capitalism. It is possible for people to say that America is the world's pre-eminent capitalist society—and love it. But not for intellectuals.[12]

How anti-capitalism and anti-Americanism have operated naturally varies according to circumstances, but it is useful to examine what may be the most famous case: France.

The French Case

France has generally been the European nation where opinion is most hostile to America. French anti-Americanism is characterized by certain images that are recognizable from the early nineteenth century. As one French commentator put it, "we know the themes on which hatred of

America is nourished... puritan idiocy, barbarian arrogance, unchained capitalism, and drive for hegemony." Tocqueville was partly an exception, but partly also an example. When the French read Tocqueville, it is often to selectively borrow tidbits designed to fit anti-American attitudes. "Even America's great admirer Tocqueville recognized that...," is often the way such quotations are framed. There is a well-established set of ideas to follow. French intellectuals have been playing the anti-American game for a very long time. In 1878, after being exhibited in Paris, the head of the Stature of Liberty, France's gift to America, was shipped to New York. A Paris newspaper cartoon depicted the head in tears as it contemplated leaving.[13]

By the late nineteenth century, the conventions of anti-Americanism had taken form in French literature—as had the conventional grounds on which French intellectuals rejected capitalism. The formation of anti-American attitudes among European intellectuals largely tracks the formation of anti-capitalist attitudes. By the interwar period, French anti-American attitudes became disconnected from any particular facts about the United States—a mirror image of the way they had become disconnected from the facts about the Soviet Union. One no longer needed the authority of first-hand experience of the United States to describe it as a cultural wasteland, the image was established. Anti-Americanism became a sort of "anti-American culture, produced by a limited milieu, but broadly diffused beyond it." Even if most French intellectuals did not write anti-American things, they nodded when they read them. Intellectuals are not the only ones in France (or the world) who enjoy anti-American discourse. Still, they are disproportionately fond of it. A 2000 poll found that while only 10 percent of the French felt "antipathy" towards America, that figure rose to 15 percent among those who had completed university. It would have been even higher in academia.[14]

In the 1930s, all six of the leading French commentators on the United States, left, right and center, were anti-American to one degree or another. They all borrowed from the same set of established stereotypes. They published widely read works with titles like *The American Cancer*, *The Crisis of American Capitalism* or *Who will be the Master, Europe or America?* (many of the most pro-European writers in France in the 1920s and 1930s were also the most anti-American). Many of the leading spirits of anti-Americanism in France were Personalists (see chapter 6), concerned about the kind of person capitalism created. By writing books about *The American Cancer* (the authors were Personalists), they were calling on the French to exorcize this cancer from themselves, to create a new kind of human being who would be different from and better than the crass capitalist denizens of America—and France.[15]

French anti-Americans in the 1930s often identified America not merely with capitalism, but with the traditional incarnation of all things monetary—the Jews. French anti-Semitism mingles with French anti-Americanism in these years. Widespread was the theme of America as Uncle Shylock, rather than Uncle Sam. America was the evil Jewish banker demanding the repayment of World War I debts from a France already bled white. This paved the way for the combination of anti-Semitic and anti-American language used by the authorities of Vichy France during World War II—a combination absent from post-World War II French anti-Americanism, but common in Arab anti-Americanism after the creation of Israel in 1948—which indirectly led to its return to the French political scene after the North African immigration of the 1960s—1980s.[16]

What is notable about French anti-Americanism in the 1930s is its defensive character. The 1930s were a period of revolutionary general offensive by French intellectuals against capitalism, but when it came to America, French intellectuals were on the defensive. They identified the United States with capitalism run wild, and held it up as a scarecrow with which to frighten their compatriots, attempting to frighten people into revolutionary change by brandishing the specter of America—if you do not change course, you will end up looking like this! They were not altogether successful in this endeavor, just as intellectuals in general failed to mobilize the masses against capitalism. But they had some effect. They complicated relations between de Gaulle and the Americans during World War II. In May 1944, a month before D-Day, Hubert Beuve-Méry, once associated with the Personalists, later with de Gaulle, still later founder of *Le Monde*, France's leading newspaper, wrote the following:

> The Americans represent a real danger for France. A danger very different from what the Germans threaten us with or which the Russians might threaten us with one day... The American can prevent us from making a necessary revolution and their materialism doesn't even have the tragic grandeur of the totalitarian states. If they preserve a real cult for the idea of Liberty, they do not feel the need to liberate themselves from the bondage their capitalism entails.[17]

Beuve-Méry, even in the midst of World War II, would not abandon the struggle between mind and money. He saw America as France's enemy in that fight.

Beuve-Méry was a Socialist, but there was no part of the French intellectual spectrum exempt from anti-Americanism. Even the old

Gaullist Etiemble, in a 1964 best-seller, *Do You Speak Franglais?* (Do you mix English with your French?), denounced America as a cultural menace worse than the Nazis. This was a manifestation of a particularly French linguistic inferiority complex, but it was also a symptom of a more general problem that contributed to anti-Americanism elsewhere. The triumph of English represented a leveling of cultural differences. French intellectuals feared that capitalism, embodied in America, would bring with it a leveling that would wipe out the intellectual class along with all other non-commercial aspects of culture. In France, "from the nonconformists [Personalists] of the 30s to the Communists of the 50s to the leftist radicals of the 70s, it is the same revolt against the 'American way of life.'"[18]

For many French intellectuals, America is the scapegoat for the sins of capitalism. Attacking America helps them either to rouse their nation to resistance, or to reluctantly accept what the ugly American forces on them, like the Marshall Plan (which at the time most French opposed). By blaming these things on America, France is exonerated from blame, since she had been forced against her will to conform to a foreign, American model of capitalism. The special merit of France is that it resists capitalism—thus the great French historian Fernand Braudel: "it seems to me that France... was never consumed by the necessary passions for the capitalist model, by that unbridled thirst for profits without which the capitalist engine cannot get started." French resistance to capitalism is often equated with resistance to America. In this French anti-Americanism is typical of anti-Americanism worldwide.[19]

Another way in which French anti-Americanism is typical is that is has often acted to unite the French when they are otherwise divided. At the height of the Dreyfus Affair, the one thing pro- and anti-Dreyfusards could agree on was support for Spain against America in the Spanish-American War of 1898. In 2005, both those for and against France ratifying the proposed European Constitution often cast their positions in anti-American terms. Anti-Americanism's function of uniting those opposed to capitalism has become more important since the collapse of the Soviet Union. If it is harder to attack capitalism directly, for lack of an alternative, it can be indirectly attacked through the United States. Anything capitalist can be identified with the United States and so discredited. This can be taken to absurd lengths. In May, 2001 the French newspaper *Le Monde Diplomatique* (a left-wing publication of some influence, but not to be confused with *Le Monde*) published an article on "Sects, the American Trojan Horse in Europe." The author argued that the American government was plotting to introduce its version of capitalism and free markets into Europe by promoting the spread of Scientology and fundamentalist Protestant sects. He recounted how American efforts to protect religious freedom worldwide were led by people close to conservative American economic organizations. By forcing European countries to extend legal protections to religious sects that supported untrammeled capitalism, America was following a devious strategy intended to achieve "the globalization of the world market." In this task the American government was aided by "the links which tie ABC, CNN and their consorts to the American fundamentalist lobbies," and their "total adhesion to the dominant ideology" (i.e., capitalism).[20]

Before finally leaving the French case, there is one particular explanation for French anti-Americanism yet to be considered, and which sheds light on anti-Americanism in general. Both America and France have historically claimed to be a light unto the other nations of the world, a chosen people who wish to make their special blessings the basis for universal happiness and imitation. In the American version, this means free elections, a free press, freedom for religions, free enterprise, and learning English. In the French version, this means free elections, a free press, freedom from religion, a state free to intervene, and learning French. The French count on high culture and the language of Molière, the Americans on mass culture and McDonalds' advertising. Since both cultures claim universal validity, and only one can be universal, it is natural they are opposed. This is the "two universalisms" argument.[21]

But this argument does not explain why so many intellectuals from other European countries, not to mention the United States, are also anti-American. Although there is some truth in the "two universalisms" thesis, it leaves out the third, and most important, universalism at work: the universal detestation of capitalism by many Western intellectuals.

The Anti-Globalization Movement

Nowhere is this third universalism better demonstrated than in the anti-globalization movement. The anti-globalization movement is frequently lightly disguised anti-Americanism. "Behind the struggle against globalization,… there hides another older and more fundamental struggle against liberalism [e.g., capitalism] and therefore against the United States, its chief representative and its most powerful planetary vehicle." In the late twentieth and early twenty-first century, attacks against multinational corporations, against America, against globalization or against all three rolled into one were new ways for mind to attack money. Since the anti-globalization movement borrows so much of its language from anti-Americanism, its needs relatively brief treatment, but this does not mean it is any less important as a twenty-first century battlefront between mind and money.[22]

Does anti-globalization matter? Anti-Americanism has a history, but attacks on globalization have usually had little concrete effect—though not always. In November 1999 the Seattle meeting of the World Trade Organization collapsed as anti-globalization protesters from all over the world rioted in the streets. Their argument was a slightly updated version of Marx's old prediction about capitalism: that globalization would make the rich richer and the poor both poorer and more numerous. A new wrinkle was the prediction that globalization would destroy the planet ecologically. Later meetings of the WTO have often been accompanied by similar demonstrations, making similar claims. "While claiming to attack globalization, the Genoa rioters [at another international meeting, this time of the G-8] in reality were attacking capitalism in itself." Some anti-globalization, like some anti-Americanism, is not directed against capitalism except incidentally. But most is. Its effects largely remain to be seen, but it has already started to create institutions.[23]

This new attack on capitalism was institutionalized by the creation of the World Social Forum at Porto Allegre, Brazil, in 2001, a global organization to oppose globalization. This is not really a contradiction in terms. The opponents of globalization do not object to political globalization nearly as much as they do to economic or even cultural globalization. Careful critical discourse (CCD), after all, does not acknowledge national boundaries to its applicability. The World Social Forum's "Charter of Principles" defines the WSF as a "movement of ideas that prompts reflection... on the mechanisms and instruments of domination by capital, on means and actions to resist and overcome that domination, and the alternatives proposed to solve the problems of exclusion and social inequality that the process of capitalist globalization with its racist, sexist and environmentally destructive dimensions is creating internationally and within countries." The only thing that betrays the collapse of communism in this proclamation (which would certainly have qualified its authors as "fellow-travelers" in the 1930s or 1950s) is the avoidance of any mention of the word "socialism." By contrast, the anti-globalization movement is not shy of using the word capitalism to describe its enemy. However, it does sometimes use a substitute. The latest name for commercial society is "neoliberalism." The very first point of the WSF charter defines it as an open forum for "groups and movements of civil society that are opposed to neoliberalism and to domination of the world by capital...." "Neoliberalism" may or may not be destined for a long life, but some form of anti-capitalist language certainly is.[24]

While the anti-globalization movement's goals are not very clearly identified, their opposition to capitalism is clear. In its stead the WSF supports "social justice, equality and the sovereignty of peoples." Who doesn't? If we want to get a clearer grasp on the nature of the anti-globalization movement's rejection of capitalism, we will have to examine specific examples. ATTAC is a reasonably representative one.[25]

At its height, ATTAC had over 30,000 dues-paying members. It was founded in France in 1998 in support of the so-called Tobin Tax, named after Nobel laureate in economics Prof. James Tobin, who first proposed it. The Tobin tax was a tax on all international currency transfers, to be used for humanitarian purposes. ATTAC, however, never limited itself to support for the Tobin tax, and has always been an integral part of the anti-globalization movement. It favors a "Universal Declaration of a Right to Fiscal Justice, Social Justice, and a Better Distribution of Wealth," very much in line with the Democratic Don't (Don't Have or Make More Money Than I Do—It's Not Fair). Its "Manifesto for a Different World" blames "neoliberalism" for unemployment, inequality, and war. It declares that the seven pillars of neoliberalism must be sawn off. The seven pillars of evil are: 1) Free trade; 2) Disregard for the environment; 3) Limiting democracy; 4) Putting government at the service of capitalism; 5) Giving shareholders everything, workers nothing; 6) Permanent readiness for War; and 7) Persuading everyone of the virtues of 1-6. In ATTAC's view, the "ideal human being" of neoliberalism "is a consumer enjoying himself in a Disneyland identically reproduced everywhere on the planet." ATTAC's support for the Tobin tax is merely one example of its view that "the economy must be subject to political choice, thus to democratic decision." In other words, an end to the Invisible Hand.[26]

The anti-globalization movement is obviously another incarnation of the struggle between mind and money. It is true that anti-globalization and to a lesser extent anti-Americanism have been relatively powerless to effect political decisions in recent years, if potent in fomenting riots. They have exerted some influence at the margins, but rarely, if ever, been decisive factors in events. Of the two, anti-American attitudes have been the more potent. Indeed, one wonders if the anti-globalization movement could survive without anti-Americanism to give it backbone. It is rare that any speech against globalization does not include some anti-American references, if only to Disneyland.

But if anti-globalization movements and even anti-Americanism have had relatively little concrete effect, the same cannot be said about the other major form which anti-capitalist attitudes among intellectuals have taken in the late twentieth century, ecologism. Like anti-Americanism, ecologism has roots that date well before the Second World War. Both anti-Americanism and ecologism were transformed after World War II. Anti-Americanism had an entirely different meaning and significance before America became the world's leading economic, military and cultural power. Ecologism had old roots too, but the environment, both physical and political, of the late twentieth century radically altered its significance and scope. Both ecologism and anti-Americanism gathered force as the twentieth century gave way to the twenty-first. Intellectuals were not solely responsible for either, nor was hostility to capitalism their only source. Nevertheless, the struggle between mind and money made a mighty contribution to both, and thus remained a constant influence on the course of Western, and increasingly world, history.

Green vs. Gold

Anti-Americanism is by its very nature a negative movement. It can be a weapon to attack capitalism, but it does not provide a substitute. It is therefore not wholly satisfying either intellectually or morally. Ecologism, the most recent opium of the intellectuals, does provide, to a certain extent, a real alternative to capitalism. It has alternative values, alternative means to achieve them, and presents both a different moral and an alternative economic perspective on the world. Much of the idealism once embodied in socialism has found its way into the environmental movement. For these reasons it has been much more successful in influencing events. Since the 1960s, no rejection of capitalism has had as much impact on the West as ecologism.

Of course, this statement is open to challenge on the ground that many environmentalists have nothing against capitalism. Many multinational corporations make big profits on "green" technology, and many small entrepreneurs attempt to do likewise. Enlisting capitalism in the service of the environment is a widely practiced strategy in the environmental movement, even if more than one environmentalist has to hold his nose while doing so. Furthermore, the twenty-first century faces environmental challenges, some extremely serious, which would have to be faced even if there were no such creatures as intellectuals and everyone loved the market. But ecologism is not about the state of the environment, it is about an attitude towards the environment independent of any given set of environmental facts.

The attitude is what separate environmentalists from ecologists. Environmentalists are reformers, only some of whom hold anti-capitalist attitudes. Ecologists, however gentle their tactics, are revolutionaries, and almost all of them reject capitalism. Environmentalists want to manage environmental problems, "secure in the belief that they can be solved without fundamental changes in present values or patterns of production and consumption, while ecologism holds that a sustainable and fulfilling existence presupposes radical changes in our relationship with the non-human natural world, and in our mode of social and political life." Environmentalists agitate for their governments to set environment-friendly policies. Ecologists create Green parties in the hope of one day becoming the government. The two groups are often found next to each other at rallies and their voting behavior may sometimes be similar, but they are profoundly different. While it may be the reformist environmentalists who have had the most direct influence on events, it has largely been ecologists who have done the most to create environmentalism in the first place.[27]

The origins of both movements can be traced to the nineteenth century. The Romantic poets inaugurated one of Western culture's recurrent infatuations with nature early in the century. The word "ecology" was first used in the late nineteenth century by the German biologist and social Darwinist Ernst Haeckel. American President Teddy Roosevelt (president, 1901-09) is a good example of a nineteenth-century environmentalist, creating national parks and nature reserves. The Englishman William Morris (see chapter 4) and the American Henry David Thoreau (1817-62) on the left, and a number of now obscure Germans on the right are examples of nineteenth-century ecologists. They demanded the rejection of machinery, and the establishment or re-establishment of a new relationship between human beings and nature, far from the big cities created by commerce—Toennies (see chapter 5) had something in common with this school. Ecologism has always been linked with communitarian attitudes. It is no accident that its first stirrings were simultaneous with the development of the struggle between mind and money in the mid to late nineteenth century. Early ecologism was a form of that struggle, although not the most prominent.

But twentieth-century ecologism differs in significant ways from the Romantics and Morris and the German back-to-nature youth movements of the fin-de-siècle. It endorses scientific research. It is not necessarily hostile to new technology—the ecology movement has nothing bad to say about solar power, for example. Above all it takes a far more comprehensive view of ecology than William Morris or Ferdinand Toennies dreamed of. But this does not mean it was without a nineteenth-century theory-hero. No twentieth-century ideology can do without one. In the case of ecologism, that hero has been insufficiently recognized. The founders of "Earth Day" did not know it, but they were often retracing the footsteps of John Stuart Mill (1806-73). The "limits to growth" that are central to ecologism found in Mill one of their earliest champions.[28]

Mill is not important to the ecology movement for anything he said about the environment. Environmental science was in its infancy during his lifetime. But one short chapter in his *Principles of Political Economy*, the standard economics textbook of his time, develops almost all the fundamental ideas of ecologism. It is called "Of the Stationary State." An understanding of it is crucial to understanding the relationship between ecologism and the struggle between mind and money.

Mill was perhaps the first, and certainly the most important economist to question the goal of economic growth. What was the point of annually increasing the GDP, he asked? Merely by raising the question Mill was going against the grain of conventional economics. Since Adam Smith it had been accepted that without economic growth the vast mass of mankind was doomed to eternal poverty. For the ordinary economist, in Mill's time and ours, the idea of a stationary state, in which the economy neither grows nor contracts, is an evil to be avoided. For Mill, it is inevitable. For the ecologists of today, the inevitable has arrived. For both Mill and the ecologists, this deserves more celebration than tears.

In Mill's view, a stationary economic state would be, "on the whole, a very considerable improvement on our present condition. I confess I am not charmed with the ideal of life held out by those who think that the normal state of human beings is that of struggling to get on; that the trampling, crushing, elbowing, and treading on each other's heels, which form the existing type of social life, are the most desirable lot of human kind, or anything but the disagreeable symptoms of one of the phases of industrial progress." Mill even uses America as proof that economic progress always comes at a moral price, even in the most favorable circumstances. In America they have political democracy, a highly educated people, "and they have no poverty; and all that these advantages seem to have done for them is that the life of the whole of one sex is devoted to dollar-hunting, and of the other to breeding dollar hunters." Mill links economic growth with a contemptible lifestyle, and concludes that when growth ceases, humanity will be the better for it.[29]

Anti-Americanism aside, Mill does not want the world to be poor, but neither is he interested in its becoming rich. Like the ecologists, his rejection of economic growth is grounded in a moral criticism of capitalism, overlaid by an economic argument that an end to growth, and limits on population, will eventually be necessary:

> I know not why it should be matter of congratulation that persons who are already richer than any one needs to be, should have doubled their means of consuming things which give little or no pleasure except as representative of wealth; or that numbers of individuals should pass over, every year, from the middle classes into a richer class.... It is only in backward countries of the world that increased production is still an important object: in those most advanced, what is economically needed is a better distribution, of which one indispensable means is a stricter restraint on population.[30]

Advanced societies should aim at a state "in which, while no one is poor, no one desires to be richer, nor has any reason to fear being thrust back, by the efforts of others to push themselves forward." When we remember that Mill is writing this in England in the late 1840s, we see that the level of per capita GDP he thought "advanced" was far below that of any developed country today.[31]

Mill thus announces the revolutionary program of twenty-first century ecologism. Limits on economic growth and population, combined with greater economic equality and some slack for the Third World, all to save the planet and make us better people at the same time. Mill is more skeptical than the average ecologist of the ability of what he calls "leveling institutions" to achieve this, but his goals are very similar. For both, it is in a stationary economic state that humanity is most likely to make spiritual and intellectual progress.

There is however one fundamental difference of economic opinion between Mill and modern ecologists, although it reveals much about their similarities as well. As will be seen below, the ecologists believe that achieving economic growth without bringing about the ecological collapse of the planet is impossible. Mill believes it might be possible, but that it is not desirable, for reasons that any ecologist, or even environmentalist, would find familiar. Mill did not want to see a world "with nothing left to the spontaneous activity of nature; with every rood of land brought into cultivation,... every flowery waste or natural pasture ploughed up, all quadrupeds or birds which are not domesticated for man's use exterminated as his rivals for food, every hedgerow or superfluous tree rooted out, and scarcely a place left where a wild shrub or flower could grow without being eradicated as a weed in the name of improved agriculture." But this is the world that must come to pass if humanity insists on the indefinite growth of its population and economy. The ecologists' nightmare is Mill's nightmare too.[32]

Mill also anticipates the criticism sometimes leveled at ecologists—that a stationary state means stagnation. Growth would continue in the stationary state, according to Mill, but it would be a different *kind* of growth, growth more in tune with the ideals and lifestyles favored by intellectuals. Mill favors improved technology, not for the sake of increasing production, but so that improved productivity will allow increased leisure. Whereas "hitherto it is questionable if all the mechanical inventions yet made have lightened the day's toil of any human being," in a stationary state of production inventions will enable all to enjoy more free time and create "a much larger body of persons than at present, not only exempt from the coarser toils, but with sufficient leisure, both physical and mental,... to cultivate freely the graces of life." Human improvement will no longer be equated with increased wealth. "There would be as much scope as ever for all kinds of mental culture, and moral and social progress; as much room for improving the Art of Living, and much more likelihood of its being improved, when minds ceased to be engrossed by the art of getting on." The stationary state of economic production will do much to enforce this point of view.[33]

Capitalism is built for economic growth. This is what the Invisible Hand does best. In a stationary state, what will be needed is a Visible Hand. Mill concludes his chapter on the stationary state in this vein: "Only when, in addition to just institutions, the increase of mankind shall be under the deliberate guidance of judicious foresight, can the conquests made from the powers of nature by the intellect and energy of scientific discoverers, become the common property of the species, and the means of improving and elevating the universal lot." The stationary state begins to sound a lot like the rule of the intellectuals, or at least of those who possess the "judicious foresight" to be guided by them. In one short chapter of economic fantasy Mill anticipates some of the best-selling ecologists of the 1970s.[34]

In the twentieth century, ideas about a stationary economic state, about the "no-growth society," are fundamental to ecologism. Ecologism argues that there are natural limits on the growth of economies and populations, that these have been or will soon be exceeded, and that we must learn to accept them. Consumption in the developed world, at least in its most voracious regions (e.g., America—yet another reason for anti-Americanism), must be reduced. This is not as great a hardship as it might seem to the average, alienated consumer (a touch of the old myth of alienation here), because true human needs cannot be satisfied by economic growth anyway. Less consumption will bring us more opportunity for spiritual growth. We must learn that true progress "may consist of finding ways of reducing GNP," not increasing it. The market is therefore usually seen by ecologists (as opposed to environmentalists) as an enemy, since it encourages people to have more and more material needs, and fulfills them. The (sometimes) unspoken corollary is that progress may well mean less profits, but so what? By ending the exploitation of the planet, we will bring about an end to the exploitation of people. By accepting limits on the "needs" that will be satisfied, we will be able to insure that everyone's "real" needs will be satisfied. Often the sustainable society that ecologists promote stresses material equality.[35]

All this is merely a repetition, more or less unconscious, of Mill's message. But there is more than a century between ecologism and "Of the Stationary State," and there are issues ecologists have to grapple which were not of concern to Mill. Mill retained the nineteenth-century faith in the benefits of technology. Ecologists are ambivalent about them. Ecologists often attack the Enlightenment faith in technology, which they link to its pro-growth attitude, its alleged view that nature is the enemy, and naturally its embrace of commercial society. But ecologists adopt the Enlightenment's critical thinking (after all, ecologists are intellectuals who practice CCD), they support scientific research into environmental problems, and many ecologists are happy to turn to technology as part of the solution to the ecological challenges facing humanity.

Nevertheless, the differences between Mill and ecologism are important. Ecologists are willing (as an ordinary environmentalist is usually not) to put the interests of trees and insects above the interests of people, unlike Mill. Where Mill talked about a "Religion of Humanity," twenty-first century ecologists substitute a "Religion of Nature." They stress nature's intrinsic value, not just its utility to human beings. They sometimes go so far as to deify it. The "Gaia hypothesis," the idea that the planet Earth is a living creature is one example of this. So is the return to Nature-worship. More broadly, the apocalyptic tone often adopted by ecologists is one that preachers have long been familiar with. Ecologism has become a successor-religion to Marxism among intellectuals. It allows them to fulfill their role as priests and priestesses while providing access to a large congregation in the environmental movement and beyond. The German ecologist Rudolf Bahro went so far as to proclaim the need for a "new Benedictine order" of ecological communes to show the world the way. Petra Kelly, a founder of the German Green party, was also fond of proclaiming that "politics needs spirituality." The more Bohemian ecologist intellectuals are willing to go a long way in their search for spirituality. Thus Kelly: "Green politics must address the spiritual vacuum of industrial society, the alienation that is pervasive in a society where people have grown isolated from nature and from themselves.... We have forgotten our historical rootedness in an integrated way of life. We must learn from those cultures that have maintained their traditions of wisdom and harmony with nature—Australian Aborigines, American Indians, and others." New Age religion is linked to intellectuals' perennial need to find a pseudo-clerical role to play.[36]

Kelly's appeal to the value of "historical rootedness" is significant. On the one hand it is a reference to the idea that capitalism uproots people, and to the myth of alienation. On the other hand it shows why the apostles of the stationary state have often been accused of preaching stagnation. There is a strong conservative streak in ecologism, a form of conservative rejection of capitalism that dislikes the bourgeoisie precisely because they are the revolutionary class Marx said they were. This aspect of ecologism is epitomized by "the principle of precaution." The precaution principle has no single generally recognized definition, but this is one example: "Where an activity raises threats of harm to the environment or human health, precautionary measures should be taken even if some cause and effect relationships are not fully established scientifically. In this context the proponent of an activity, rather than the public bears the burden of proof." In other words, change is wrong until proven otherwise. The ecological revolution, despite the massive changes it proposes, is framed in conservative terms. In ecologists' view, their bias is towards low risk in human affairs, whereas capitalists are wild-eyed revolutionaries, blinded to the dangers of change by their focus on profit. One of the reasons for ecologism's success is, paradoxically, its appeal to the conservative instinct to resist change.[37]

In the war between mind and money, intellectuals have always been ready to ally with either the left or the right. "Revolution" and "stability" are words that have different moral connotations for intellectuals depending on circumstances. It is the "stable ecosystem" that ecologism seeks to preserve or create. The "stable ecosystem" is by definition one that is not changing. To ecologists, change, even growth, is a sign that the ecosystem has not yet attained stability. "An ecosystem that is subject to fluctuation has not reached the 'climax' stage and is therefore characterized as immature." Ecologists think it is time for humanity to leave behind its destructive childhood, full of change and immature behavior, and accept their limits.[38]

Beginning in the 1970s, intellectuals produced a flood of works preaching ecologism. Two with broad influence are E. F. Schumacher's *Small is Beautiful*, published in 1973, and *The Limits to Growth*, first published in 1971, to much fanfare, and here discussed in its updated 1991 edition. Both have become cult classics. American President Jimmy Carter, often inclined to take a pessimistic view of things, was so impressed by Schumacher's work that he invited him to dinner at the White House in 1977. Schumacher translated the old Christian or Buddhist ideal of living a simple life into the language of ecology and gave it new life. In so doing he defined ecologism as part of the long struggle between mind and money.[39]

Schumacher begins his book with two chapters that alternately argue the necessity for limiting economic growth and attack the moral justifications of capitalism touted by eighteenth-century writers like Hume and Montesquieu. Schumacher completely rejects the *doux commerce* view of economic growth. He denounces the idea that "the soundest foundation of peace would be universal prosperity." The notion that wealth and trade make men peaceful "completely bypasses the whole question of ethics." It also presumes rich traders are less likely to fight than poor farmers. But for Schumacher, "people satisfying their needs by means of a modest use of resources are obviously less likely to be at each other's throats than people depending on a high rate of use. Equally, people who live in self-sufficient local communities are less likely to get involved in large-scale violence than people whose existence depends on world-wide systems of trade."[40]

Schumacher insists on the close relationship between economics and morality. He rejects the idea of an amoral marketplace, and insists that moral limits be set on the production, consumption and accumulation of wealth. What makes his attitude ecological is that his morality is based on the idea of both limited needs and limited resources. In order to conserve our limited natural resources we must limit our needs. Any attempt, for example through advertising, to make people's perceived needs grow, any attempt to encourage economic growth not absolutely necessary, is evil. "The cultivation and expansion of needs is the antithesis of wisdom." If only we were content with a more Spartan lifestyle, we'd never need to fight, in Schumacher's view. This is not how it actually worked for the Spartans, the most aggressive warriors of ancient Greece. But Schumacher is not an historian.[41]

Schumacher is more a preacher than an economist—a good intellectual, in other words. What really upsets him about a market-based economic system is the idea that the road to heaven is paved with bad intentions. Any form of economic thinking based on the market is immoral because "to the extent that economic thinking is based on the market, it takes the sacredness out of life, because there can be nothing sacred in something that has a price." Because, in a capitalist society, people take a benign view of greed, because they regard foul intentions as the path to prosperity, they end up being demoralized and dehumanized. "Economically, our wrong living consists primarily in systematically cultivating greed and envy and thus building up a vast array of totally unwarrantable wants. It is the sin of greed that has delivered us into the power of the machine." Schumacher adds an original twist to this old argument, which sheds light on one of its often-overlooked origins. For him, one reason greed is bad is because when we are greedy, we can't be intellectuals. This is not how he puts it, of course. What he says is that "if human vices such as greed or envy are systematically cultivated, the inevitable result is nothing less than a collapse of intelligence. A man driven by the power of greed or envy loses the power of seeing things as they really are...." In other words, the greedy become incapable of careful critical discourse. They lose their intellectual autonomy and independence, and they can't be intellectuals. This argument at least has the merit of plausibility, unlike Schumacher's claim that greed makes men stupid.[42]

If this were all Schumacher said, it would have been neither original nor especially ecological. What made it more than a soft-core Buddhist vision of mind vs. money was the link Schumacher forged between a more moral economy and respect for nature and nature's limits. Economics, morality, and the environment are closely linked in his work. "Materialism—does not fit into this world, because it contains within itself no limiting principle, while the environment in which it is placed is strictly limited." Unlimited economic growth is impossible "on at least two counts: the availability of basic resources and, alternatively or additionally, the capacity of the environment to cope with the degree of interference implied." Capitalism does not recognize these limits. It is in a state of permanent revolution, or "permanent crisis." This situation must be ended. How? Through the intellectuals' favorite means: "If western civilisation is in a state of permanent crisis, it is not far-fetched to suggest that there may be something wrong with its education." We must relearn many old truths. For example, while both agriculture and industry are necessary, "agriculture is primary, whereas industry is secondary," just as Aristotle said (Schumacher actually quotes St. Thomas Aquinas). "The technology of *mass production* is inherently violent, ecologically damaging, and stultifying to the human person." Modern societies are like drug addicts, hooked on the consumption of ever greater amounts of stuff. Schumacher is typical of much ecologism. He throws in all the old arguments of mind against money along with specifically ecological points.[43]

Schumacher would probably have called himself a socialist had he lived earlier. But writing in the 1970s, and not being under Marx's spell, as many of his contemporary intellectuals still were, he had gone beyond the Old Testament of the anti-capitalist spirit. Socialism, in his view, was "of interest solely for its non-economic values," rather than as an economic system. Morality was what mattered. The power that would enforce morality on a recalcitrant bourgeoisie was no longer the law of history, nor the proletariat, but the law of nature and Mother Earth. The choice was not "socialism or barbarism" as Rosa Luxemburg once said, but "moral limits or ecological collapse."[44]

"Limits" is the key word of ecologism, and has been since *Limits to Growth* was first published in 1971. The argument presented in *Limits* is simple, and has already been sketched above. We are consuming the planet's resources at an unsustainable rate, and if we don't stop, catastrophe awaits, sooner or later—the precise date is always open to revision, as is usually the case for the Apocalypse. New technologies or new discoveries could push it back, new growth of population or per capita consumption bring it forward. Critics who attack *Limits to Growth* because of errors in its specific predictions therefore miss the larger point. "The human world is beyond its limits. The present way of doing things is unsustainable. The future, to be viable at all, must be one of drawing back, easing down, healing." Even if we have not yet gone beyond the limits, "*the equilibrium state may be a desirable option, wherever the limits to growth may be*" (emphasis original). This response to criticism of the 1971 edition of *Limits* gives the game away. It's about morality, as much or more than it is about the environment.[45]

The difference between ecologism's vision of the limits to growth and Christian visions of the Second Coming is that Christians look forward to the end of time, ecologists don't. Perhaps more importantly, ecologists think there is something people can do about it. If they do it soon enough, they may succeed in avoiding catastrophe. The ecologism of *Limits* is as much a call to repentance as a prophecy. "A sustainable society is still technically and economically possible. It could be much more desirable than a society that tries to solve its problems by constant expansion." Accepting the constraints the ecology imposes on economic and population growth is an opportunity for the kind of moral growth Mill had in mind. As one ecologist puts it in *Limits*, in terms borrowed from Mill, "the stationary state would make fewer demands on our environmental resources, but much greater demands on our moral resources." What could delight an intellectual more? Accepting limits on economic growth takes away one of the strongest argument in capitalism's favor, its success at fostering economic growth. It creates a new opportunity for mind to win the war against money, just when all seemed lost. The fight against global warming, irrespective of its own merits, opens up a new battlefront.[46]

Taking advantage of this opportunity means an ecological revolution, and revolution is what *Limits* calls for. Mere incremental change such as environmentalists support, like better gas mileage for cars, is worth little. We need to "acknowledge that the human socioeconomic system as currently structured is unmanageable, has overshot its limits, and is headed for collapse, and, therefore, to *change the structure of the system*." This will be a political revolution, since the market will not change its spots without political decisions to force it. But it will be a revolution lead by changes in values, first of all. The market will always overuse the available resources. Society must limit the market by imposing "long term communal values" on it. Individuals must learn to get their self-respect from sources other than material possessions. The problem with capitalism is that in it people fulfill their psychological needs with material goods, but "to try to fill these needs with material things is to set up an unquenchable appetite for false solutions to real and never-satisfied problems. The resulting psychological emptiness is one of the major forces behind the desire for material growth." Because of their materialism, people define their goals "in terms of getting *more* rather than having *enough*." This must stop if a sustainable society is to be achieved.[47]

Such a change in human desires would indeed be a revolution. What is new about the Green revolution is its ecological analysis. Instead of threatening people with Hell, or mass unemployment, ecologists can point to how hard it is to find new oil reserves or growing evidence of climate change. What is old is the role intellectuals play in ecologism. The ecological revolution will require leadership from a class expert in two things—values and information technology—in other words, intellectuals. Despite repeated calls for democratizing the distribution of information and decision-making, *Limits'* vision of an ecologically sound society clearly entails a leading role for intellectuals, whether as experts (here a more New Deal, professional, environmentalist vision emerges) or as preachers of new values. Saving the ecology is going to require a very Visible Hand, intervening politically. It will also require a new spiritual/technical aristocracy, prepared to impose its own values on the world the way Nietzsche says an aristocracy ought to. Preaching values and implementing technocratic solutions can be combined: "our purpose in publishing *Limits* was to encourage both the value change and the long-term planning processes." Paradoxically, the Green movement, born among the ultra-egalitarian flower children of 1971, seems to be sanctioning the creation of a new aristocracy. But the paradox disappears when one bears in mind the double role of intellectuals as both clergy and aristocracy—and their simultaneous acceptance of democratic values.[48]

Although ecologists often claim there is a necessary link between democracy and Green values, the link is more a matter of assertion than logic. Ecologism's argument is that humanity must attain certain results, adopt certain values, in order to survive. How those results are reached or values are spread (or imposed) is a separate question. The relationship remains sufficiently vague for intellectuals to keep their consciences clean, the more so as ecologism typically couples demands for greater equality with its demand for limits on economic growth and population.[49]

The end of growth does not mean the acceptance of today's inequalities. It only means that we will not be able to grow our way out of our problems. We will have to find better solutions to the problems of poverty within the limits imposed by the long-term, sustainable use of the world's resources. And we can! "We see no reason why a sustainable world would or could leave anyone living in poverty. Quite the contrary, we think such a world would have both the opportunity and the necessity to provide material security to all its people at higher standards than they have today." Lenin said Communism meant Soviet power and electricity. Ecologism means solar power and limits on everyone's use of electricity. But everyone will get some. "A sustainable society would not freeze into permanence the current inequitable patterns of distribution. It would certainly not permit the persistence of poverty." Ecologism is firmly committed to the Democratic Don't, "Don't Have or Make More Money Than Others—It's Not Fair." Of course, in strictly ecological terms this becomes don't have or make more garbage than others do, but in practice there is not much difference between those who make the most money and those who make the most waste.

How will ecologism eliminate poverty? *Limits* gives no answer to this question, but it surely will not be by the operations of the Invisible Hand. A no-growth society will have to make some conscious and difficult decisions about how to distribute a pie that is no longer growing, and may be shrinking. In the grand tradition of intellectual hubris, the authors of *Limits* are delighted that "physical growth cannot be forever substituted for the social resolution of difficult choices"—they are ready to help make them. The plans for yet another Tower of Babel are being drafted in accord with the results of their computer models. On the whole, however, ecologism shares one trait with Marx rather than with Marxism—it is more interested on how things are produced than how they are distributed. If ecologism were divorced from the struggle between mind and money, it might arrive at the conclusion that we can both save the planet from environmental disaster and maintain an inequitable distribution of wealth. But up to now ecologism, or at least the intellectuals who support it, have preferred not to acknowledge this possibility. At any rate, it is not what they want. Ecologism is the latest in the long line of battlegrounds between mind and money.[50]

A Digression: Feminism and Capitalism

The reader of this book would have to be forgiven for thinking that the author, suffering from no small amount of intellectual hubris himself, believes the struggle between mind and money is the basis for every important event in Western history since the Enlightenment, despite all disclaimers. To show that this is not so, it is worth saying a few words about what is probably the most important phenomenon in the history of twentieth-century Western culture: Feminism. The struggle between mind and money had little or nothing to do with it.

In the nineteenth-century, many leading feminist writers, like Flora Tristan or Clara Zetkin or John Stuart Mill, were also opponents of capitalism. But in the post-World War II period, the period of feminism's greatest influence, this has been much less the case. The flowering of feminist thought in the 1970s included some socialist feminists, and there are still a few feminist theorists who blame patriarchy (male dominance) on capitalism. But they are the minority. Most feminists are more interested in making women CEOs than abolishing multinational corporations. Many feminist issues, for example abortion, sexuality, and so on, are rarely addressed in terms relevant to the struggle between mind and money. There is somewhat more overlap between ecologism and feminism. The propensity to see nature as female has led to associating exploiting nature

with exploiting women, but this development postdates the most significant changes in Western gender relations. Most feminists recognize that
patriarchy existed long before capitalism did. While capitalism certainly
oppresses women, in this it is no different from any other economic
system. Feminist socialists learned early the dangers of subordinating
the struggle for women's rights to the struggle for socialism—Lenin had
little patience for Alexandra Kollontai after the revolution, and none for
any women's movement that didn't put socialism first. It quickly became
apparent that such subordination, if temporarily accepted, would turn out
to be anything but temporary. Communist countries were hardly known
as bastions of women's rights. However, the Communist Party was by no
means unique in this respect on the anti-capitalist left. Histories of the
American civil rights and anti-war movements of the 1960s are replete
with left-wing sexism. Feminists and anti-capitalist intellectuals have
shared some common enemies, but more by chance than anything else. It
would be interesting to examine why the struggle for women's rights has
not, for the most part, been swept up into the struggle against capitalism,
but that investigation must be left aside here.

Of course intellectuals, both men and women, have played an important role in feminism and in helping to change the roles women
play in Western society. They have employed their critical language
and their moral voice in advocating women's rights, with great effect.
The Western intelligentsia's careful critical discourse, its rejection of
the authority of precedent and history, was a prerequisite for Western
feminism's success. The intelligentsia's bohemian attitude helped too.
But the intellectual class's war against capitalism gained little or nothing from feminism, which accounts for some of the hostility so many
socialists showed "bourgeois feminism." Joy at seeing the bourgeoisie
discomfited was the only gain the intelligentsia saw from the women's
movement, if one insists on seeing it in terms of the struggle between
mind and money. Fundamentally, it is a separate question. The war
against capitalism is not, and never has been, the only issue that interests
intellectuals.[51]

The war between mind and money may be the great historical conflict
of modern Western history, but it is not the only conflict going on. The
friendly battle between the sexes has lasted longer. Nevertheless, for
the past 150 years, the war between mind and money has occupied
much of the intelligentsia much of the time. It has often concerned
the rest of the world as well. It is time to see what we can do to bring
about a truce.

Notes

1. Barry Rubin and Judith Culp Rubin, *Hating America: A History* (New York: Oxford University Press, 2004), 233. However, intellectuals sometimes have a class interest in fighting *for* America. Soviet and Eastern European intellectuals were very fond of America, with reason.
2. Tocqueville, *Democracy in America*, 617-19, 645.
3. Tocqueville, *Democracy in America*, 642. See also 617-18, 645.
4. Rubin and Rubin, *Hating America*.
5. Charles Dickens, *Martin Chuzzlewit* (London: Wordsworth Editions, 1994), 253.
6. Dickens, *Martin Chuzzlewit*, 263, 267-68, 272, 518-19.
7. Oscar Wilde, "Impressions of America," http://www.december2001.com/oscar-wilde/impressionsofamerica.html 4, 6.
8. Milosz, *To Begin Where I Am*, 147-48.
9. For an account of anti-Americanism among American intellectuals, see Hofstadter, *Anti-Intellectualism*, especially 409-12.
10. Henry James, *The American Essays of Henry James*, ed. Leon Edel (Princeton: Princeton University Press, 1956), 208; James, *The American Scene,* (Bloomington, IN: Indiana University Press, 1968), 82, 92, 94.
11. Woodrow Wilson, cited in Victoria de Grazia, *Irresistible Empire: America's Advance through Twentieth-Century Europe* (Cambridge, MA: Harvard University Press, 2005), 2.
12. de Grazia, *Irresistible Empire*, 3, 10, 458.
13. Jean Birnbaum, *Le Monde*, 25-26 November, 2001.
14. Philippe Roger, *L'ennemi américain: Généalogie de l'antiaméricanisme français* (Paris: Seuil, 2002), 296, 352-53, 357, 579; Poll data from Michel Winock, *Le Monde*, 25-26 November, 2001.
15. Roger, *L'ennemi américain*, 358-59, 361, 365, 382, 385.
16. Roger, *L'ennemi américain*, 387, 413, 465, 467.
17. Cited in Jean-François Revel, *L'obsession anti-américaine: Son fonctionnement, ses causes, ses inconséquences* (Paris: Plon, 2002), 98.
18. Roger, *L'ennemi américain*, 360, 441, 523-24.
19. Fernand Braudel, *The Identity of France*, vol. 2, *People and Production*, trans. Sian Reynolds (London: Fontana, 1991), 666.
20. Bruno Fouchereau, "Les sectes, cheval de Troie des Etats-Unis en Europe," *Le Monde Diplomatique*, May 2001.
21. For the two universalisms argument, see Sophie Meunier, "The Distinctiveness of French Anti-Americanism," in *Anti-Americanisms in World Politics*, ed. Peter J. Katzenstein and Robert O. Keohane (Ithaca, NY: Cornell University Press, 2006), 141.
22. Revel, *L'obsession anti-américaine*, 63.
23. Revel, *L'obsession anti-américaine*, 68-69.
24. World Social Forum, *Charter of Principles*, approved 10 June 2001, www.wsf2007.org/process/wsf-charter, especially point 11.
25. World Social Forum, *Charter of Principles*, www.wsf2007.org/process/wsf-charter, point 4.
26. ATTAC, *Vivent les impôts!* (Paris: Fayard, 2005), 206; *Manifeste Altermondialiste: construire un monde solidaire, écologique et démocratique* (Paris: Fayard, 2007), 8, 14-30, 84.
27. Andrew Dobson, *Green Political Thought* (London: Routledge, 1995), 1, 198.
28. On the distinction between 19th and 20th century ecologism, see Dobson, *Green Political Thought*, 11, 16. Malthus is the real source of the limits to growth argu-

ment, but Mill's more wide-ranging and Romantic arguments are the ones that resonate best with ecologism.

29. J. S. Mill, *Principles of Political Economy,* Book 4, chapter 6, "Of the Stationary State" in Mill, *Collected Works,* 3:754, 754n.24.

30. Mill, *Principles of Political Economy, CW,* 3:755.

31. Mill, *Principles of Political Economy, CW,* 3:754.

32. Mill, *Principles of Political Economy, CW,* 3:756.

33. Mill, *Principles of Political Economy, CW,* 3:756.

34. Mill, *Principles of Political Economy, CW,* 3:757.

35. Dobson, *Green Political Thought,* 16-18, 21, 85, 87, 91-92, 120.

36. Bahro, cited in Dobson, *Green Political Thought,* 137; Petra Kelly, *Thinking Green: Essays in Environmentalism, Feminism, and Non-violence* (Berkeley, CA: Parallax Press, 1993), 41-42.

37. This definition is from the "Wingspread Statement," signed by 32 academics and representatives of environmental organizations, 25 January 1998, http://www.gdrc.org/u-gov/precaution-3.html.

38. Dobson, *Green Political Thought,* 25.

39. He preferred to think of it as Buddhist. Many ecologists associate the "Judaeo-Christian tradition" with the idea that man possesses "the right to exploit for his own short-term purposes all other creatures and all resources the world has to offer." See Donnella H. Meadows, Dennis L. Meadows, Joergen Randers, William W. Behrens III, "A Response to Sussex," *Futures,* Feb 1973, 151.

40. E. F. Schumacher, *Small is Beautiful: A Study of Economics as if People Mattered* (London: Blond & Briggs, 1973), 11-12, 43.

41. Schumacher, *Small is Beautiful,* 17, 19-20.

42. Schumacher, *Small is Beautiful,* 18, 23.

43. Schumacher, *Small is Beautiful,* 60, 88-89, 122, 126-27.

44. Schumacher, *Small is Beautiful,* 214.

45. Donnella H. Meadows, Dennis C. Meadows, and Joergen Randers, *Beyond the Limits: Global Collapse or a Sustainable Future* (London: Earthscan, 1992), xv; Meadows, et al., "Response to Sussex," 144.

46. Meadows, et al, *Beyond the Limits,* xvi, 190.

47. Meadows, et al, *Beyond the Limits,* 188, 191-92, 216.

48. Meadows et al., "Response to Sussex," 144.

49. See Dobson, *Green Political Thought,* 26.

50. Meadows, et al, *Beyond the Limits,* 10, 210; "Response to Sussex," 145.

51. For an account of the battle between "bourgeois feminism" and socialism, see Marilyn J. Boxer, "Rethinking the Socialist Construction and International Career of the Concept 'Bourgeois Feminism'," *American Historical Review,* February 2001.

9

On Intellectuals in Democratic Society

The Hundred Fifty Years War

For over 150 years, Western intellectuals have trumpeted their contempt for capitalism and capitalists. Poor Mr. Smith the merchant is still reeling from the shock of coming home and discovering that someone had rechristened him Mr. Scrooge. No matter how hard he tries, he can't scrub off his door the red paint that proclaims "Workers of the world unite, you have nothing to lose but your chains!"

As we have seen, the problems between Mr. Smith and his highly educated vandals have a long history, even if they still leave the ill-educated Mr. Smith and his ilk astonished. Long before Mr. Smith existed, the New Testament was spreading the good news that it was easier for a camel to pass through the eye of a needle than for a rich man to enter the Kingdom of Heaven. But this was already old news. Long before Jesus walked the earth, Aristotle was telling his students that the pursuit of excessive wealth was chrematistic, an unnatural art, harmful to the community and unworthy of a free man. The life of a merchant was "vile and contrary to virtue." Besides, businessmen worked too hard at their businesses—they didn't understand when it was time to retire and devote oneself to studying serious things, like philosophy or religion.

The medieval world was not much kinder to Mr. Smith's ancestors than the ancient world. Whoever wrote on Mr. Smith's door would have agreed with Pope Leo the Great that "a merchant is rarely or never pleasing to God." Still, St. Omobono of Cremona managed to be a saint without ever giving up his business, and St. Thomas Aquinas was willing to consider that trade just might be a morally neutral occupation. He certainly favored hard work, and that was something Mr. Smith was fond of too. By the time the Protestant Reformation rolled around, Mr. Smith was beginning to find a few defenders, as long as he kept his nose to the grindstone and his mind on his eternal salvation. But Mr. Smith never had an easy time convincing anyone, even himself, of his good intentions.

Then came the Enlightenment, the century-long honeymoon between mind and money, when Mr. Smith finally felt at home. Those vandals who had once flung stones at his gilt windows no longer taunted him with his sins. Instead, they praised him for his actions. One day they even presented him with the shiny brass plaque that he hung proudly on his door, the one that read, "A. Smith, merchant to the nations and benefactor of humanity." True, there were still a few preachers who called on him to repent, like that perverse Genevan Rousseau, but on the whole Mr. Smith could bask in newfound respect, in those few moments when he wasn't hard at work.

Mr. Smith finally began to relax. People liked him. He much enjoyed spending his weekends in the shop, working on new labor-saving devices. He was sure that this was the way things would be forever. After all, it was a brave new enlightened world he lived in. Those vandals who used to throw stones at his windows were just a nightmare from humanity's long childhood.

But then came that dark and stormy night, the one that brought a sudden change in the weather. Then Mr. Smith found those awful words on his door, and the funny new nameplate, the one that read "Mr. Scrooge," above the knocker. The bad times were back. He could not relax by his fire with a novel without learning that he ought to be ashamed of himself. He was a hypocrite, a destroyer of families, and worse, a bore. His fiddling with labor-saving machinery was polluting the village stream and putting the villagers out of work. If he turned from fiction to fact, he could not read an essay without finding a plan to replace him and his kind with something more rational, with better intentions. Accused of destroying communities and families, Mr. Smith felt very lonesome. Fortunately, the vandals' ill will rarely affected his business. But sometimes he was afraid that it would.

The First World War and its aftermath did affect his business. One day he opened his much-defaced door to find his cousin Plodsky outside, newly made penniless by the Russian Revolution. A passer-by shouted, "you'll be next, Scrooge!" He found Mr. Plodsky a job, but times were very hard. Some people said he wasn't patriotic enough, others blamed him for all the flag-waving, still others said he would be all right if he only learned how to follow the Plan. Everyone thought there was something wrong with him. When the profits fell to near nothing, he began to wonder if they weren't right.

When the World Wars were finally over, the profits picked up, but Mr. Smith did not find himself much liked. He worked hard, and harder, and he was pleased to see things getting better. But his children started to dress like bums. They thought the world was entering a New Age, but they despised him the old-fashioned way. However, youth is nothing if not inventive, and his children found new reasons to look down on him. They told him his factory was producing too much smoke, too much waste, in fact producing too much, period. He looked at them in his usual bewilderment, and promised to invest in recycling. He had a feeling that wasn't enough. He was right. The red paint was still sprayed on his door every night, and the nameplate still read Scrooge.

Why should we care if Mr. Smith can clean his door? The bloody, tragic history of the past 150 years provides reason enough. "Our ruling attitude toward the marketplace has not changed since the time of Plato. Is it not possible that it is time to rethink the question?"[1]

The Chapter Tocqueville Never Wrote

The abyss between intellectuals and businessmen needs to be bridged. They are like "two nations; between whom there is no intercourse and no sympathy; who are as ignorant of each other's habits, thoughts, and feelings, as if they were dwellers in different zones, or inhabitants of different planets; who are formed by a different breeding, are fed by a different food, are ordered by different manners, and are not governed by the same laws." Throughout the West, intellectuals and businessmen form two nations within every country. They have fought the wars of mind against money. Like most civil wars, the war between mind and money has been exceptionally bitter and bloody.[2]

Since 1845, when Disraeli wrote about the "two nations" of the rich and the poor, the gap between rich and poor has shrunk. However, the gulf between intellectuals and the middle classes has, if anything, grown wider and deeper. There are many differences between the capitalism of the nineteenth century and the capitalism of twenty-first, but the differences haven't much changed intellectuals' opinion. The intellectual class is bigger now than it was in 1845, but this has only increased the number of alienated intellectuals. Many intellectuals have always found, and still find, capitalism and capitalists distasteful. They refuse to accept capitalism as legitimate.

In order to bring about détente between mind and money, we must find a way to persuade intellectuals to accept the role of business and businessmen in democratic society, or at least to moderate their opposition. Intellectuals are both inevitable and necessary in a capitalist society. They are needed for their new ideas, and for their help in creating many social and political improvements, from the New Deal to the environmental movement. They are even needed for their criticism. But up to now intellectuals have been both necessary and dangerous. We must find a more satisfying role for intellectuals to play in a capitalist society. Unless intellectuals have a role they like, they will never moderate their opposition. They will continue to be dangerous. And they will be less able than they otherwise might to improve capitalism.

It is important to persuade intellectuals to stop trying to destroy capitalism, not just to avoid catastrophes, but to make capitalism better. The intellectuals are the only class that can improve capitalism. It is a job they have been doing for a long time, unconsciously, unwillingly, and not very well. Intellectuals whose ideas or support were vital for improvements to capitalism, from social security to anti-pollution laws, were often more interested in replacing capitalism than in improving it. They were revolutionaries whose reforms were unintentional by-products. Intellectuals will do a better job of making capitalism better, and do it with less risk of revolutionary catastrophe, if they and everyone else recognize that it is their job. Struggle between mind and money is inevitable. War isn't.

Instead of producing rebels and guerrilla fighters against capitalism, the intelligentsia must become the source of its *loyal opposition*. It is possible to oppose the government without becoming a revolutionary. It should be possible dislike capitalists without wanting to get rid of them. The idea of a loyal opposition is the essence of stable democratic government. In the past the intelligentsia provided capitalism with its outlaws and revolutionaries. In the future, they must provide its loyal opposition.

There is a precedent for this. Lawyers once played a role similar to that which intellectuals have played for the past 150 years. Lawyers were once the revolutionaries of the Western world. Now they help make it work.

During the French Revolution, as the great conservative Edmund Burke complained at the time, the French National Assembly was full of lawyers, and thus doomed to radicalism, because lawyers were people who paid more attention to principles than to facts—just like intellectuals. Many of the leaders of the French Revolution, especially the most radical and bloodthirsty, were lawyers or men with legal training. Afterwards, throughout continental Europe, radicals were often lawyers.

But this was not true in England and especially America, where lawyers were known for their conservatism. Why were lawyers revolutionaries in continental Europe and conservatives in the Anglo-Saxon world? Because in continental Europe aristocratic regimes prevented lawyers from taking a leading role in political life. As a result, lawyers became radicalized. If you deny lawyers the political role they deserve, they will make you pay. However, "in a community in which lawyers hold without question that high rank in society which is naturally their due, their temper will be eminently conservative."[3]

Tocqueville devoted a chapter of *Democracy in America* to showing how lawyers, when allowed to play their proper role, could be a class that was necessary and useful rather than necessary and dangerous. Lawyers have "some of the tastes and habits of an aristocracy," but for just that reason they provide democratic society with many useful qualities that would otherwise be in short supply. Their revolutionary alienation in the eighteenth and nineteenth centuries was temporary, caused by unfavorable circumstances. An example is Carl Schurz (1829-1906): A revolutionary law student in Germany, he was forced to flee to America after the revolution of 1848 failed. In America, he finished his studies and became an attorney. Rather than promoting revolution, he became a senator from Nebraska.

Lawyers and intellectuals have a lot in common—people would often like to kill them both. But there is more to it than that. Capitalism needs lawyers, and intellectuals too. Intellectuals are its natural cultural leaders. Up to now, intellectuals have been necessary and dangerous, just as lawyers once were. Like lawyers, intellectuals will no longer be dangerous if they can be persuaded to leave off revolution. Can capitalism do for intellectuals what democracy did for lawyers?

It can, but not in the same way. Lawyers are an elite who may become temporarily alienated from society. Intellectuals are a permanently alienated elite. We cannot solve the problem of mind vs. money by simply rewriting Tocqueville's chapter on lawyers and replacing "lawyer" with "intellectual." The chapter we need is one Tocqueville never wrote. How do we persuade intellectuals to prefer loyal opposition to revolution? By making intellectuals responsible for capitalism's moral culture.

This idea is not new. In different forms, it has been suggested by writers as diverse as Matthew Arnold, Julien Benda, and Herman Hesse. But the merit of an idea has nothing to do with its originality.

Capitalism's Moral Culture

Democracy needs lawyers, and has found a way to make them less dangerous. Capitalism needs intellectuals, and a way needs to be found to make them less dangerous. Tocqueville wrote that "not only the qualities but also even the flaws of the legal mind suit it to the task of neutralizing the vices inherent in popular government." The intelligentsia, both by its qualities and its defects, is well adapted to neutralize the vices inherent in capitalism. Rather than trying to replace capitalism with something else, they can make capitalism better.[4]

Better at what? Better for whom? Not better at producing wealth. Capitalism is very good at that already. Better at distributing wealth? Perhaps, but attempts at that have had limited success at best, and have done little to reconcile intellectuals to capitalism. Intellectuals can and must make capitalism better in ways that are as important as either making money or distributing it. Intellectuals can improve capitalism's moral culture.

What is moral culture? Moral culture is everything that the market ignores. It is the proper complement of consumer culture.

Before World War II, when economists were more often intellectuals than is the case today, one wrote that "the chief thing which the common sense individual actually wants is not satisfaction for the wants he has, but more, and better wants.... Life is not fundamentally a striving for ends, for satisfaction, but rather for bases for further striving... true achievement is the refinement and elevation of the place of desire, the cultivation of taste."[5] But this is not what the market provides. The market measures consumers' satisfaction by how well it fulfills today's wants. The businessman makes profits by fulfilling the desires we already have, rather than by teaching people to cultivate "better" ones. The market is equally happy to provide for good taste or bad. It satisfies expressed needs, but it does not attempt to decide what is a need, or which needs are more worthy. Bread, SUVs, pornography, are all equally "product," to be paid for and consumed. Needs are ranked only by how much people are willing to pay for them.

The market has no opinion to express about whether one desire is better than another. Intellectuals do. We may not agree with intellectuals' opinions about what we should want (they don't agree with each other), and we certainly don't want to give them power to enforce their opinions. It is a good thing that the market does not discriminate between good and bad taste, or attempt to rank our needs on a moral scale, or else we might all be forced to accept someone else's taste and morals. But we need to hear debates about what is good taste and what are good morals. Such debates are the essence of moral culture, and they are central to what intellectuals do. They are an important way in which intellectuals improve capitalism.

Intellectuals can thus make capitalism better by helping people to interpret the world. If no one ever talks about the meaning of life, life will tend to become increasingly meaningless. Intellectuals can help people find meanings for their lives—a task the market is not much help with, despite all the bookstore shelves devoted to self-help books. Because the desire for a meaningful life, a life that means something more than making money, is nearly universal, it can be a democratic basis for intellectuals' role in capitalism. The proper role of the intellectual class is to help people perfect and develop themselves, help them to construct better meanings for their lives, meanings that the individuals concerned find more satisfying. The essential contribution of intellectuals to the moral culture of capitalism is to enable every individual "to give himself an account of the ultimate meaning of his own conduct." Do we really need intellectuals for this? "Innocence is indeed a glorious thing, only it is a pity that it cannot maintain itself well and is easily seduced." In these words Kant justified the need for theories of morality. The same justification applies to all forms of moral culture. Kant's moral theory is an example of what intellectuals ought to do to help people interpret the world and their place in it. Can intellectuals do a better job at this than the latest best-selling self-help book? They could hardly do worse. One best-selling self-helper follows another without any noticeable improvement in our culture.[6]

Why is offering moral culture the intelligentsia's task? Because capitalism will not do it on its own, without its permanently alienated intellectual elite. Capitalism encourages and enforces a certain level of moral behavior. Merchants learn that a reputation as a liar and cheat is not to their advantage. Marketers do their best to anticipate and fulfill the needs and desires of their customers, like good spouses do for each other. Tocqueville called this "enlightened self-interest." It is epitomized in the Rotary Club motto, "he who serves best profits most." In a democratic society, where almost everyone is interested in making money, enlightened self-interest is essential. But this is not enough. Alongside it, we need moral culture, to enable us to set ourselves goals beyond getting rich. By itself, enlightened self-interest gives us our daily moral bread—without its salt. Moral culture gives it savor.

In practice, moral culture is involved in many kinds of decisions we make, big and small, personal and political. It is involved in the question of whether abortion should be legal, and still more involved in whether an individual should have an abortion, legal or not. The abortion example shows that having moral culture is not the same thing as having the right answer to a moral question or being a moral person. Intellectuals don't necessarily have the former, may not be the latter—but they do know how to think about the issue at a high level.

Moral culture is involved in talking about all kinds of trade-offs, and what they mean. The economist can tell us how much choices will cost, but not how much a human life is worth, except in dollar terms that only tell part of the story. The rest of the story of how we should evaluate that life, or an unspoiled view, or which person to marry, or where to live, depends on things the market can only set a price on after we have decided their value by other criteria. What criteria? The many criteria involved in moral culture—truth and beauty, if you like poetry. Professors are good at talking about freedoms and rights and values. Novelists are good at talking about whether it is really important to have your own house. Novelists and poets are both good at talking about love—and the trade-offs it involves. All of these constitute moral culture. They are not so much *savoir-faire*, knowing how to do something, but *savoir-vivre*, knowing how to live—and why. Before the epistemologists took over philosophy, this was what philosophy was all about. Even before then, thinking about moral culture had long spread beyond the philosopher and the clergyman and become the common preoccupation of the intellectual class.

Intellectuals are people with expertise in moral culture, an expertise that does not respond to the ordinary laws of supply and demand, because in the capitalist marketplace the demand for moral culture is a demand people have tomorrow, not a demand they have today. Intellectuals as a class respond to a different market. Every well-functioning market needs commonly accepted weights and measures. Intellectuals are like "bureaus of standards for cultural weights and measures." They are moved by historical traditions, like the "Don'ts" that predate capitalism and are hostile to it. Their personal and social identity is not based on capitalism's categories of rich and poor. Their language of careful critical discourse respects only reason, not profitability. Their identity is tied to their use of the moral voice. Thus they naturally produce expertise in moral culture. This enables intellectuals to offer people alternative goals in life to those offered by capitalism. For the past 150 years they have attempted to persuade, or force, the West to give up capitalism and replace it with their goals. But what they ought to do is encourage people to have different goals, not *instead* of those the market satisfies, but *alongside* them. Capitalist culture is about being able to buy whatever you want whenever you want it. Intellectuals are about thinking about what you ought to want to buy: moral culture. Human beings need both market culture and moral culture. The proper role of intellectuals in a democratic capitalist society is to spread moral culture.[7]

This is what Nietzsche described as "the future task of the philosophers:… the solution of the *problem of value,* the determination of the *order of rank among values.*" But Nietzsche wanted intellectuals to *impose* a moral culture, a hopeless and bloody task. He wanted intellectuals to act like a true aristocracy. But while a true aristocracy's role is to determine their society's values, intellectuals are merely a pseudo-aristocracy. They cannot impose their rankings, but they can influence others' choices. In so doing intellectuals actively spread the moral culture capitalism needs. A good movie can cause the sales of gas-guzzling SUVs to drop significantly.[8]

Intellectuals, through the education they have received, participate in a long tradition of serious reflection about values and goals and how they affect our lives. They have practice talking about large moral issues, and they have words and concepts with which to talk about them. They can provide other people with the language and ideas with which to analyze and describe how they want to live—better than can be found in the self-help shelves. They can provide the tools for people to construct better meanings for their own lives. Without such tools, we are liable to do a poor job of making our own decisions. Intellectuals can help people think about what they should want, rather than about how to get what they already want (unlike most of the self-help books). Democratic societies need people whose job it is to raise these questions, questions that the market has no interest in bringing up because they are not profitable. Intellectuals' identity as a pseudo-aristocracy and a pseudo-clergy, their critical language, their penchant for moral preaching, all serve to make them ideal for this role. The German poet and critic Heinrich Heine said this as early as 1834: "It is no longer a matter of violently destroying the old Church, but rather of building a new one, and, far from wanting to annihilate the clergy, today we want to make ourselves priests." The role of the intellectual class is to spread moral culture, not by preaching any specific set of morals (they would never all agree on one, anyway), but by raising the issues capitalism otherwise ignores. Their pseudo-aristocratic autonomy puts them in position to do so.[9]

Why should a capitalist society care about this? Because humanity does not live by bread alone. No matter how well capitalism fills the belly, people have other appetites too—and not just sexual ones. Writing shortly after the collapse of communism in 1992, the French commentator Jean-

François Revel noted that "the world will be neither viable nor livable if it does not adopt democratic capitalism. But democratic capitalism will be neither acceptable nor accepted if it does not become moral."[10]

Making capitalism moral in a broad sense is crucial to making it more legitimate in intellectual eyes and to relaxing the tension between intellectuals and capitalism. A capitalist society that has no moral culture will always attract the moral contempt of a considerable portion of the intelligentsia. Worse, many people who are not intellectuals will share it. For example, Jihadists despise Europe and America because they see in them capitalism without moral culture. An economic system in such a situation will always suffer from doubtful legitimacy, even in the eyes of many who benefit from it. The moral culture of capitalism therefore matters to everyone. Everyone, even capitalists and shopkeepers, has a soul. Almost everyone, even capitalists and shopkeepers, needs something more than money to lead a life they find fulfilling. The intelligentsia's task of cultivating moral culture in a capitalist society extends to every individual. The intelligentsia has something to offer everyone. Whether they take it is up to them.

It is urgent that Western intellectuals take on this task. In the twentieth century Western society was threatened by anti-capitalist political fundamentalisms, movements such as communism and fascism. Today the world is threatened by diverse religious fundamentalisms. Capitalist society seems helpless to prevent millions of people from adopting such views. A capitalism without moral culture has little defense against fundamentalism on the one hand, or apathetic materialism, Tocqueville's great fear, on the other. Capitalism has been largely helpless because its intellectual class has too often been on the other side, because it has found no means of enlisting them, and because it has had no desire to do so. But in the long run, "only the advancement of the majority of people to a cultural mastery of themselves will permit democracy to survive." Otherwise one fanaticism or another, with the critical support of some intellectuals, will arise to fill the moral and spiritual vacuum which human nature abhors. Moral culture must fill the void before fanaticism does.[11]

Some might object that we don't need an intellectual class to talk about the meaning of life, because only intellectuals are interested in the question. Capitalism has a substitute for moral culture, one that makes intellectuals and their high-falutin' language superfluous. The substitute? Toys. Swimming pools, telephones and electronic knick-knacks can reconcile people to living pointless lives, or at least lives that intellectuals find pointless. This is the argument of the Frankfurt School and its heirs (see chapter 7). Sated with stuff, people are content, even if they remain unsatisfied in every sense except the material. The more stuff you have, the more stuff you want, the less you wonder why you want it. Maybe this is why intellectuals are so unhappy with capitalism. The more successful it is, the smaller the congregation for them to preach to.

However, while accumulating toys may be a better strategy for attaining happiness than intellectuals like to admit, it is ultimately not enough for most people. The T-shirt legend of the 1980s, "Whoever has the most toys when they die, wins," strikes few people as satisfying. Toys matter, and people need bread to live, but people need meaning, too—as demonstrated by all the books on "personal development" and spirituality in any bookstore. In the war between mind and money, hatred of the bourgeoisie has often come from hatred of the meaninglessness and lack of overall purpose of life engendered by capitalism. Revolution has been a way to restore meaning to the world. It has been, in effect, a brutal and clumsy effort by the intelligentsia to spread moral culture by destroying capitalism.

Restoring meaning to the world need not mean destroying capitalism. Moral culture can coexist with commercial society. Capitalist societies need to recognize that providing moral culture is the intellectuals' role, and intellectuals need to understand that revolution is not the best way of improving capitalism's moral culture. A layer of moral culture is something that needs to be added to capitalism, mixed into democratic society, and stirred among all our other interests, rather than substituted for them. The proper role of an intellectual class in democratic society is to provide moral culture, not to intoxicate themselves and others with millenarian fantasies. In a moderate, small-scale way, intellectuals *can* re-enchant the world. Not the whole of it, but a part of it, and a part of our personalities. For this to take place, it is not just capitalism that must change. It is the intellectual class itself that needs to change.

Reforming the Intelligentsia

We need a Reformation of the intellectuals as much or more than we need a reformed capitalism. We need a Reformation of the secular clergy—the intellectuals. Such a Reformation would serve several purposes. It would make intellectuals more useful, less dangerous, and perhaps happier. It would improve capitalism, and it would make the world more satisfied with capitalism.

Reformed intellectuals must give up claiming priestly knowledge of the meaning of history. When intellectuals talk about the meaning of history, they do not just mean the past, they mean the future. The philosophers and social theorists of the nineteenth century, and the great anti-capitalist "isms" of the twentieth century all claimed to know the meaning of history. Because Marx knew that history was the history of class struggle and that the proletariat was destined to inherit the earth, he called for revolution, confident that it would be worth whatever it cost.

The illusion that we know the meaning of history, at least in its vague outlines, is a secular version of the idea of a better afterlife. It is an attempt to preserve a religious meaning for life against the disenchantment of the world carried out by capitalism. The illusions of communism were nourished by the need to believe in a better world to come, a need felt all the more keenly by people no longer confident that Heaven awaited them after death. It kept believers in communist parties long after economic disasters and human massacres should have chased them out. This sort of illusion is part of all the Towers of Babel intellectuals have imagined or constructed. It has proven deadly time and again.

Intellectuals' expertise in moral culture does not give them special knowledge of the future. Intellectuals must preach—but they should learn to do so without claiming special access to the meaning of history. Reformed intellectuals need to turn from what Max Weber called an "ethic of absolute ends" to an "ethic of responsibility," and then combine the two.

An ethic of absolute ends is one concerned with intentions and final goals rather than immediate results. An ethic of absolute ends sets aside questions about means if they will advance the chosen goal, such as everlasting peace and social justice. It is an ethic for revolutionaries, like the socialists during World War I who declared they were happy for the war to continue, no matter how many people died, because its continuation would bring the revolution closer. This was the ethic of many intellectuals who chose to be communists or fellow travelers. They justified the revolution's horrors and hardships by its goals. They ignored its short-term results. From the viewpoint of an ethic of ultimate ends, capitalism will always be inferior to socialism simply because it does not have such laudable goals. Too often intellectuals, even those who have not supported violent revolutions, have criticized capitalism from the standpoint of an ethic of absolute ends.[12]

The ethic of responsibility uses a different language. An ethic of responsibility is concerned first and foremost with the results of any particular action, not its goal. Immediate consequences matter as much or more than those predicted for the long term. Whereas an ethic of absolute ends neglects consideration of the means, an ethic of responsibility tends to ignore the goal. It can be aimless, concerned with solving a problem, unconcerned with the ultimate meaning of the solution. People, including intellectuals, need to pay attention to both ethics, just as both enlightened self-interest and moral culture are necessary. "An ethic of ultimate ends and an ethic of responsibility are not absolute contrasts but rather supplements, which only in unison constitute a genuine man...."[13]

For the past 150 years intellectuals have too often focused exclusively on absolute ends, with disastrous consequences. Businessmen have too often focused exclusively on the ethic of responsibility, with no vision of any ultimate goal, which ultimately also contributed to more than one catastrophe. The capitalists who made Manchester the center of the industrial revolution were very good at foreseeing the immediate consequences of their actions. But they ignored the ultimate consequences, which were that Manchester's air and water became so polluted that a rich man in Manchester had barely the life expectancy of a poor peasant on an English farm. Absolute ends are not quite the same thing as long-term consequences, but ignoring them has the same effect. Reformed intellectuals must practice both ethics. They must concentrate on "and," not on "or." They must focus on capitalism *and* virtue, capitalism *and* equality, capitalism *and* ecology. They must combine the capitalist focus on means with the clerical vision of absolute ends. The slogan of the 1970s, "socialism with a human face" ultimately proved to be a contradiction in terms. Communism, when it became less repressive, collapsed. But capitalism with a human face, and a human soul, is possible—through moral culture. For examples, we can look at the enormous potential of harnessing capitalism to the protection of the environment, whether through trading carbon emissions or developing new and more efficient solar and wind-power technologies. Or at that quintessential capitalist tool, banking—applied to microcredit to bring people out of poverty.

By adopting an ethic of responsibility, alongside an ethic of ends, reformed intellectuals will have a new relationship to capitalism. They can become symbiotes of commercial society, rather than its predators or parasites. Instead of trying to kill capitalism, or live off it without contributing to its survival, they can prolong its lifespan while nourishing themselves. Reformed intellectuals can help make capitalism better.

In the past, moral culture was provided by chiefly by formal religion. For millennia, religions found ways to cultivate human spirituality while keeping it within bounds, helping people find meaning for their lives without (usually) going to extremes. Formal religion was once the dominant form in which people received moral culture, but with the decline of traditional religious practice in Western capitalism this is less and less the case. Today moral culture is more likely to come through intellectuals, the secular pseudo-clergy, than through the ordained, if it comes at all. For those without religion, secular intellectuals may be the only source of moral culture.

In the nineteenth century, John Stuart Mill suggested that a religion of humanity might be an alternative means for giving people something other than enlightened self-interest on which to base their lives. Today, it does not matter whether we call it the religion of humanity, or religion at all, but some form of moral culture is needed in capitalism. Traditional religion need not be displaced, although some intellectuals would doubtless be happy if it were. But there is no reason intellectuals and clergy—who indeed are sometimes identical—cannot, in many respects, work towards the same goals in capitalist society. Tocqueville suggested that "the chief business of religions is to purify, regulate, and restrain the overly ardent and exclusive desire for well-being that men feel in ages of equality, but I think it would be a mistake for them to try to subdue it completely and destroy it. They will not succeed in dissuading men from love of wealth…." Tocqueville's advice to "religions" holds good for the "religion of humanity," and for intellectuals. Rather than attempting to get rid of capitalism, reformed intellectuals can supplement capitalism's enlightened self-interest with a wider moral perspective.[14]

Such a reformed intelligentsia would be less dangerous to the world, and more likely to improve it. This would be great progress. But this is not the only benefit a Reformation of the intelligentsia might offer. A reformed intelligentsia can help reconcile all social classes to capitalism. Today the average person in Western society accepts the current order without great enthusiasm. "Welfare-state capitalism can call on a limited loyalty, but capitalism is not, in spite of some heroic recent attempts, morally very engaging." Why not?[15]

Capitalism has never had the ambition to build a perfect society or a perfect human being. It does not have a moral purpose. But most people do have such ambitions, even if ordinarily they rank low among their priorities. People want to improve themselves and their society in ways that are not simply material. Up to now intellectuals have equated morality and a moral lifestyle with rejecting capitalism. This has deprived capitalism of any defense against political and religious fanaticism except the not-always-sufficient barrier of enlightened self-interest. With intellectuals playing the role of loyal opposition, capitalism will be able to put up a better defense against extremism. A capitalist society in which more people feel that their lives have an elevated content will attract more loyalty. It would be better, and safer, for everybody. If Western capitalism were not identified chiefly with money, pornography, and McDonalds in much of the world, would jihad find so many supporters, even among immigrants to the West? If capitalism and soulessness were not synonyms for so many people, would not all kinds of fanaticism, political and religious, decline? Moral culture is not a luxury for the wealthy. It is a necessity if capitalism is to survive.

Are even "reformed" intellectuals really suited for spreading moral culture? One rather unflattering perspective is recorded in a poem by Auden: "To the Man in the Street who, I'm sorry to say/ Is a keen observer of life./ The word *intellectual* suggests right away/ A man who's untrue to his wife." However, intellectuals' ability to play an uplifting moral role is not, fortunately, dependent on their success at personally attaining the moral goals they aim at. Intellectuals are not morally better (or worse) than other people. It would be mistaken to think that they should be. An education, a language and a bohemian attitude are no guarantee of moral character. But moral perfection is not a requirement for moral culture. Intellectuals' education, language, attitude and social situation is what qualifies them to add moral culture to capitalism, not their behavior.

The Games People Play

A reformed intelligentsia must be an intelligentsia that has changed its attitudes towards capitalism in more than one respect. Asking intellectuals to limit their ambitions because otherwise we'll end up with totalitarianism may be sensible. But in the long run, it will only result in an intelligentsia bitter about a capitalism that deprives it of even the emotional consolation of revolt. If we want an intellectual class willing to be a loyal opposition, we will have to persuade it that there are positive reasons for loyalty to capitalism. We will have to persuade intellectuals that they have more in common with capitalists than they think. "Gentlemen! There is a misunderstanding between us! In every man who takes up a pen, a palette, a chisel, a pencil, whatever, the bourgeois sees a useless person; in every bourgeois, the man of letters sees an enemy. Sad prejudice, foolish opinion, unhappy antagonism. Our cause is the same, the valiant cause of the parvenus!"[16]

The idea that intellectuals and capitalists have something in common strikes many on both sides as unpleasant. For both, the other's lifestyle, attitudes and values are *incommensurable* with his or her own. Intellectuals and capitalists are apples and oranges. So are intellectuals and proletarians. Intellectuals need to believe "that writing a book... is a more genuine accomplishment than being the Queens [County] bowling champions for the third year in succession," and far more important than winning "best salesman." The intellectual and the capitalist play the game of life by different rules. Intellectuals' values and attitudes cannot be made commensurable with those of capitalism or capitalists.[17]

Intellectuals' criticism of the bourgeois lifestyle, professors' contempt for stockbrokers, is founded on the idea that their lifestyle is morally superior. "The world of business is to the intellectual one in which the values are wrong, the motivations low, the rewards misaddressed." An intellectual wouldn't dream of expressing contempt for a person based on their race, ethnicity or religion. She freely expresses it for someone who has chosen to work for a large investment bank. Even if, for the moment, it is no longer fashionable for intellectuals to be revolutionaries, a genteel anti-capitalism, equivalent to the genteel anti-Semitism of the nineteenth century, is taken for granted in intellectual circles.[18]

To ask the professor to give up entirely his contempt for the stockbroker is asking the impossible. But while the intelligentsia will always remain a class apart, it can learn greater respect and tolerance for those who prefer bowling to language games. In the seventeenth century, the idea of religious toleration seemed impossibly hard to most people. Is it so much harder for a professor to learn to tolerate a stockbroker than it was for a Protestant to tolerate a Catholic? Your lifestyle, the things which interest you, may be different from, even inferior to mine, but I may tolerate them, even if I do not approve of them—even if you will go to Hell as a result. Surely the Wars of Religion gave no more incentive for toleration than the gulag. Intellectuals must learn to tolerate those who prefer to count their gains in cash rather than more metaphorical coin.

Western intellectuals have been condemning those who worshiped Mammon instead of the preferred religion for millennia. They will never stop altogether, and certainly not at once. But they must learn to tolerate the infidels. After all, there are so many of them, and in a democratic society, there always will be. Such infidels are as likely to be found among the proletariat as among the business elite. "It seems to be empirically true," though intellectuals wish it wasn't, "that working people do not regard more interesting work as worth losing money for."[19] Even granting the questionable proposition that selling or making widgets is always less interesting than teaching English at a university, many people will do it, because they value money more than the things intellectuals value.

They may be morally better for an intellectual's sermon about it, or his lesson in aristocratic values, but intellectuals must learn to accept that the differences between intellectuals and other people are a poor justification for moral contempt, and none at all for class war. Intellectuals may succeed in giving the millionaire's or the shopkeeper's views a moderate elevation beyond the joys of entrepreneurship, and leave their audience improved. But that is all.

And perhaps intellectuals should think twice about Mammon. Some people pursue money as an end, rather than a means to other ends. Capitalism encourages this. Intellectuals do not. It is a good thing they don't, since if money were the only end people pursued, the world would be the poorer. It is intellectuals' job to remind the world of this. But this is different from saying that *no one* should pursue money as an end in itself. Apples and steaks are incommensurable, but they both have their place in a varied diet. If all millionaires retired from business as soon as they made their first millions, the world would be poorer, too. It would be deprived of their economic talents, and they themselves would cease to be able to do what they do best. It is *good* that the meaning of their lives is bound up with making money. If Bill Gates, the founder of Microsoft, had retired after making his first $10,000,000, the world would be worse off, just as it is better off because he decided to devote himself to charitable work after making his second billion. The intellectual might prefer that millionaire or billionaire entrepreneurs turn their talents to other ends, just as the English professor might prefer that his best student choose to major in English, instead of in sociology. However, the English professor will not condemn the student, much, for becoming a sociologist. He should not condemn him for becoming a banker, taking a job in an office or factory, or even for founding a major corporation.

Persuading intellectuals to alter their attitude to capitalists, to recognize them as fellow "parvenus," or at least as members of the same species, will not be easy. But it is not impossible. There are glimpses of such recognition to be found in the writings of well-known intellectuals. Max Weber recognized that "inspiration in the field of science by no means plays any greater role, as academic conceit fancies, than it does in the field of mastering problems of practical life by a modern entrepreneur." If intellectuals could be brought to see the problems faced by widget sellers and widget makers, to use those favorite terms of the economists, as intellectually interesting, as demanding of creativity and inspiration, worthy of an adult's time and interest, it would be a step in the right direction. If reformed intellectuals can learn to tolerate the games other people play, they will be in a position to be capitalism's loyal opposition. As a loyal opposition, intellectuals can provide capitalism and capitalists with what every dominant power and class needs: limits.[20]

The Intellectual Limits of Capitalism

One of the proper functions of intellectuals is to *limit* capitalism. This is a function appropriate for a pseudo-aristocratic class in a democratic society. A democratic society is based on equality. However, democratic societies always contain some aristocratic elements like lawyers or intellectuals. These aristocratic elements give democratic societies some of the advantages of aristocracies. Intellectuals do something similar for capitalism. They check some of its bad tendencies and balance some of its less elevated desires. They prevent us from completely ignoring other standards than those of the market. Capitalism is better, for example, for wondering whether a beautiful view sometimes ought not to be more valuable than a coal mine. Capitalism benefits from being supplemented, and limited, by intellectuals. Perhaps the best way to think of the proper role of an intellectual class is like a vitamin pill. If capitalism doesn't get its vitamins and trace elements, it suffers, and if it gets too much, it gets sick.

Acting as a limit on capitalism, and policing that limit like a border patrol, does not put intellectuals in capitalist society in a comfortable position. But discomfort is an appropriate situation for a permanently alienated elite, many of whose members dwell on the fringes by preference. One way of looking at the role intellectuals play on the fringe is to compare them to the "fool" of the medieval royal court. Intellectuals are the fools of capitalism. Just as the social function of the fool in the royal court was to stand outside all the usual rules of deference and provoke those in power into seeing the other side, so the function of the intellectual is to do the same for capitalism. Making fun of the bourgeoisie can be good for them. The perfect example is the great English playwright, and leading member of the socialist Fabian Society, George Bernard Shaw. Lenin once described him as a "fool for the bourgeoisie," but one who would become a serious threat to them after the Revolution. Unlike Lenin, we may think that Shaw was at his best when he was in the theater, performing for the bourgeoisie, rather than on his soapbox, performing for the socialists of the Fabian Society. The role of "fool" is hardly flattering to an intellectual's dignity, especially after she has tenure. But it is better than that of prophet, more useful, less dangerous.[21]

Amusing or serious, intellectuals' off-beat perspectives provide capitalism with alternative views and limit its domination. This is a very useful function. But the intellectual class can only carry out its task well if capitalist society becomes comfortable entrusting this job to them, and if they become comfortable carrying it out. In order to do this, intellectuals need to learn not to be embarrassed about moral culture, and not to be embarrassed by their own role. This will require an intellectual class that has come to a mature state of class consciousness, one that is not embarrassed by its aristocratic and clerical traits, one that no longer longs to submerge its identity with the proletariat or the peasantry. Such an intelligentsia does not yet exist. Intellectuals still hate to be called "elitists." Indeed, it is one of the first insults they use about each other. It is time for intellectuals to stop being uncomfortable with themselves and accept their difference. People who are embarrassed at how they differ from others too often compensate for their embarrassment by going overboard. Intellectuals' discomfort in democratic society leads them into revolutionary excess. A psychologically more comfortable intelligentsia will be a less revolutionary intelligentsia.

Intellectuals will perform their job much better if they do it intentionally, rather than unwillingly. They can only do a good job of improving capitalism, rather than aspiring to be its gravediggers, with their own consent. For the past 150 years, intellectuals have turned "their eyes away, and… refuse[d] to cooperate in rearing the structure of the future." A capitalist society can offer intellectuals a role, but it cannot make them accept it. If intellectuals insist they are revolutionaries, they will be less effective fools, and less effective, or else much too effective, limits on capitalist society.[22]

How can they be persuaded? The process of reconciling intellectuals to their proper role can most easily begin where intellectuals' role is least challenged: in education. It is in education, if anywhere, that intellectuals are most comfortable asserting their authority. It is in education, if anywhere, that intellectuals ought to be comfortable acting as capitalism's loyal opposition.

General Education

Not all forms of education are relevant to intellectuals' role as capitalism's loyal opposition. What matters might be called "general education." Recognized as providers of general education in moral culture, intellectuals can both make capitalism better and become better reconciled to their own situation.

The purpose of general education is to give people the basics, and more than the basics, of moral culture. General education begins in childhood, and lasts, ideally, throughout life. It is provided by parents, by kindergarten teachers, by professors and novelists and poets and pastors. But if everyone is involved in general education in some way (just as everyone is involved in the market in a capitalist society), not everyone is involved in it in the same way, or to the same extent. General education is the special province of the intelligentsia, of both its academic and bohemian wings. By participating in society's general education, the entire intellectual class can improve capitalism. By accepting that this is their role, they become its loyal opposition.

Up to now, in classrooms, novels or movies, such general education as was given has often been implicitly or explicitly opposed to capitalism. The image of business and the businessperson in film or TV is almost universally negative, just as it is in most of the novels taught in English classes. As one acute modern critic noted, "it cannot have escaped teachers of… literature that much of their time is spent unfitting their pupils for the lives they will eventually have to lead. Most twentieth century authors, and in particular the greats…, inculcate an attitude of contempt for ordinary, bread-earning citizens…." General education is the broadest front in the war between mind and money. As a teacher the intellectual often sees himself, and is seen by students and parents, by readers and listeners and often by the government, as fundamentally opposed to the established order. The German philosopher Immanuel Kant said that education always has two enemies: the government and the parents. Perhaps they have had good reason.[23]

This won't and can't change entirely: intellectuals are a permanently alienated elite. But it can be transformed by being carried out by a reformed intelligentsia. If respect, or at least tolerance, for "bread-earning citizens" is substituted for contempt, if intellectuals recognize that moral culture can supplement, not replace, self-interest, a significant change will take place. By recognizing capitalism's need for moral culture and the intelligentsia's role in providing it, the teacher (whether professor or poet), the parents, the students, and perhaps even the government can learn to work together.

General education speaks to both our public and our private selves. Moral culture is something that belongs to both the public and the private spheres of life. When moral culture means figuring out the meaning of an individual's life, it is essentially a private activity. But the moral culture taught by general education is also directed to our public selves. When our moral culture compels us to take positions about the environment or health care, then it matters politically. General education is thus directed at people both as private individuals and as citizens. It is necessary for both the "modern" idea of freedom, which sees freedom as something for private individuals to practice in their private lives, and the "ancient" idea of freedom, in which freedom was about political participation. In both spheres moral culture and the general education that creates it is the intellectual and spiritual complement to enlightened self-interest.

General education is a way of teaching people to combine the ethics of responsibility and the ethics of absolute ends. Individuals, i.e., teachers, writers, poets, and professors, will stress one ethic or the other, but both are necessary. General education is the modern equivalent of the old liberal arts, the arts necessary for a free human being, as a private individual and as a member of a political community.

It is hard to give a prescription for how the whole of the intelligentsia should carry out its educational function.[24] No such prescription is necessary. Intellectuals, once they agree that it is their job, will be more than happy to engage in endless debates and experiments in carrying it out. If there is one thing intellectuals love to argue about more than another, it is education. Nevertheless, if there is one place where general education could be most effective, and where it could influence the maximum number of both students and teachers, it is the university. The university is where people choose their careers and set the initial course for their lives. Preferably general education comes near the end of that period, when students are 20 or 21, rather than at the beginning when 18-year-olds are experiencing the first rush of autonomy. This is when people are beginning to tell their own story and construct meanings for their lives. This is a good time to take their moral culture to a new level.

Today college students are taught skills that will help them get a job. But they are not taught the skills of moral culture. "Your technical school should enable you to make your bargain splendidly; but your college should show you just the place of that kind of bargain—a pretty poor place, possibly—in the whole policy of mankind," was how the nineteenth-century American philosopher William James put it, with some anti-capitalist bias. Bias aside, James was right. General education should not provide a ready-made ideology or philosophy of life, but it should enable people to discuss such questions and create coherent answers for themselves. This is the moral culture that everyone needs.[25]

In America, something occasionally called "general education" already exists at many universities, but it rarely has anything to do with moral culture. Sometimes it is merely a "distribution requirement," a set of scattered courses in different fields. More rarely, a university has decided there is some particular set of facts that ought to be learned or books that ought to be read. Teaching some "great books" may have a little of the desired effect, but rarely enough, even if they are taught in the right spirit. The purpose of general education is to teach people how to reflect about how to become a better human being, and for this a very different kind of general education is necessary. Of course, this goal will not always be reached, and it will never be fully completed at the university—general education is a lifelong process, and the university is not necessarily the most important part of it. There will be many ways to devise a curriculum that might fulfill this goal.

Here is one example. Most general education curriculums currently take up about one of the four years of university. One year means eight semester-length courses, divided as follows: Two courses in the study of any literature, provided that the reading engages with values and moral choices, whether *The Iliad* or *The Color Purple*. Two courses in "moral and political thinking," which might be taught by the philosophy, religion, political science, sociology, or history departments, and would introduce students to thinking about issues of critical importance to themselves and their society. One course in modern history, that is history from the eighteenth century to the present, for the same reason. One course in statistics, because it is impossible to make sense of today's world without knowing something about statistics. One course in any foreign culture, to introduce students to a different set of values and meanings. And finally, an introductory course in economics, so that everyone gets an introduction to the ideas and ways of thinking fundamental to capitalism, of which most people remain ignorant.

This sketch of a curriculum might be debated endlessly. But the details are not important here. What is important is that intellectuals and capitalist society find a practical means of reaching détente. Education seems to be a strategic area in which détente can be put into practice. Any institution that furthers it—whether university general education courses, programming on public television, adult culture courses sponsored by public or private groups, etc., is important.

However, institutions will be insufficient for either persuading intellectuals to become a loyal opposition or for spreading moral culture in capitalist societies. Many intellectuals are not very comfortable with institutions anyway. Most education is carried out by individuals, and modern technology has not changed this. It is still individuals who write the books, poems, and movies which transmit our moral culture, and individuals who read them. There is no magic wand to sweep over the intelligentsia to change them from disgruntled revolutionaries and Cold Warriors into a disgruntled but loyal opposition. Bismarck was right when he wrote that "discontent among the educated… leads to a chronic disease whose diagnosis is difficult and cure protracted." The first step must come from intellectuals deciding they want to be cured. Détente between mind and money will come from individual intellectuals deciding to give peace a chance.[26]

Détente

Two nations, intellectuals and philistines, must learn to recognize that war between them is good for no one, and that neither side can afford their mutual incomprehension. There will be no second honeymoon, no remarriage, but there must be a truce. Capitalism will never give the intellectuals everything they might want from a socio-economic system, even if they could all agree on what that was. Intellectuals will never devote themselves to simply justifying capitalists' profits. Some mutual dissatisfaction is inevitable, and salutary. Democratic society is made for attaining the greatest good of the greatest number. That means not perfect justice, as either mind or money would define it, nor perfect peace between them. Détente and loyal opposition will have to do. It might look something like this:

> One fine day Mr. Smith went out to work, as usual. At the end of the day, when he came back home, there were a few people gathered by his front door. He was used to that. Often they were carrying signs and chanting slogans. On bad days they touched up the red paint on his door and splattered him for good measure. He sighed and kept on going, doing his best to concentrate on the latest sales figures and ignore the crowd. He resigned himself to pushing past them, as usual.

But this time, contrary to habit, the small crowd parted politely. To his astonishment, when Mr. Smith reached his door he discovered that rather than being daubed in fresh red paint, it had been scrubbed clean. While he stood and stared at the unadorned wood, his eye was caught by a sudden gleam of late-afternoon sunshine on the new brass plate. The plate no longer read Mr. Scrooge, he saw. His astonishment grew. It said "Mr. A. Smith," all right, but not "merchant to the nations and benefactor of humanity" as it once had. Now the inscription read in full: "Mr. A. Smith, Managing Partner, Smith, Dickens, Marx & Co."

Smith turned around and shook hands with the nearest fellow in a beard and scruffy coat. Someone offered him a bottle. Someone else offered him a joint. Smith politely declined both. Most astonishing of all, none of his new partners seemed to mind.

* * * * *

This is how we make the world safe for intellectuals, and safe from them.

Notes

1.   George J. Stigler, *The Intellectual and the Market Place* (Cambridge, MA: Harvard University Press, 1984), 158.
2.   Benjamin Disraeli, *Sybil, or, The Two Nations*, 1845, in *The Oxford Book of Money*, 184.
3.   Tocqueville, *Democracy in America*, 302-11.
4.   Tocqueville, *Democracy in America*, 309.
5.   Frank H. Knight, *The Ethics of Competition*, 1935, cited in Fred Hirsch, *The Social Limits to Growth* (Cambridge MA: Harvard University Press, 1976), 61.
6.   Max Weber thought this was the value of formal intellectual training. Weber, "Science as a Vocation," *From Max Weber*, 152; Immanuel Kant, "Groundwork for the Metaphysics of Morals", in *The Philosophy of Kant* (New York: Modern Library, 1977), 140.
7.   Hermann Hesse, *The Glass Bead Game* (New York: Picador, 2002), 358.
8.   Nietzsche, *On the Genealogy of Morals*, 56.
9.   Heine, cited in Charle, *Les intellectuels en Europe au 19eme siècle*, 71.
10.   Jean-François Revel, *Le regain démocratique* (Paris: Fayard, 1992), 453.
11.   Revel, *Le regain démocratique*, 474.
12.   Weber, "Politics as a Vocation," *From Max Weber*, 120-22.
13.   Weber, "Politics as a Vocation," *From Max Weber*, 127.
14.   Tocqueville, *Democracy in America*, 508.
15.   Alan Ryan, *Property and Political Theory* (Oxford: Oxford University Press, 1984), 187.
16.   Jules Vallès, "The Dead," *Le Figaro*, 1 Nov. 1861, in Seigel, *Bohemian Paris*, 200.
17.   Richard John Neuhaus, "Equality in Everyday Life," in *Capitalism and Equality in America*, ed. Peter L. Berger (Lanham, MD: IEA, 1987), 214.
18.   Bertrand de Jouvenal, "The Treatment of Capitalism by Continental Intellectuals," *Capitalism and the Historians*, 117.
19.   Ryan, *Property and Political Theory*, 182.
20.   Weber, "Science as a Vocation," *From Max Weber*, 136.
21.   See Rolf Dahrendorf, "The Intellectual and Society: The Social Function of the 'Fool' in the Twentieth Century," in *On Intellectuals*, ed. Philip Rieff (New York: Doubleday, 1969), 50-51. The Fabians, it is true, were very moderate socialists, facetiously known for chanting "What do we want? Gradual progress! When do we want it? In due course!"
22.   Weber, "Capitalism and Rural Society in Germany," *From Max Weber*, 371-72.
23.   John Carey, *The Listener*, 1974.
24.   Herman Hesse wrote a novel about it, *The Glass Bead Game*.
25.   James, "Democracy and the College-Bred," in *The Intellectuals*, ed. Huszar, 287.
26.   Otto von Bismarck, in Gouldner, *The Future of Intellectuals*, i.

Index

John Paul II, Pope, 194
Johnson, Dr. Samuel, 70
Johnson, Lyndon B., 227
Justinian, 29

Kant, Immanuel, 8, 51-2, 275, 288
Kapur, Tribuwhan, 228-9
Kautsky, Karl, 176-7
Kelly, Petra, 259
Kerensky, Alexander, 175
Ketteler, Bishop Wilhelm Emmanuel
    von, 189
King, Martin Luther, 227
Kissinger, Henry, 23
Koestler, Arthur, 21, 178
Kolakowski, Leszek, 214
Kollontai, Alexandra, 266
Kristol, Irving, 234-5
Kuhn, T. S., 224
Kundera, Milan, 16

La Bohème, 188
La Rochefoucauld, François de la, 108
Lactantius, 41
Lasch, Christopher, 235
Le Bon, Gustave, 178
Le Bret, Father Louis-Joseph, 193
Le Monde Diplomatique, 249
Lenin, Vladimir Ilyich, Leninism
    "What is to be Done?", 177, 181
    Academic, 187
    Ecologism, 264
    Fellow-travellers, 182
    Feminism, 266
    George Bernard Shaw, 286
    Intellectuals' support for, 188, 202
    Kautsky, 177
    Secular religion, 45, 178-80
    Vanguard party, 143, 176, 181
    View of intellectuals, 177-9
    World War I, 175
Leo the Great, Pope, 45-6, 269
Leo XIII, Pope, 189
Lilienthal, David, 197
Livy, 41
Locke, John, 39
Lombard, Peter, 46
Lubac, Henri de, 194
Luther, Martin, 39, 50, 63n.41, 143
Luxemburg, Rosa, 179, 204, 262
Luxury
    Aristocratic, 53

Cato denounces, 38
De-moralization, 68-9
Freedom, 72, 80
Gambling, 106
Greco-Roman, 66
Moral benefits, 70
Poor, 74
Rousseau, 55
Social Catholicism, 193

Magic Flute, 80
Mailer, Norman, 15
Mandelstam, Nadezhda, 175
Mandeville, Bernard de, 68
Mann, Thomas, 108, 111, 113-4, 128
Mannheim, Karl, 10, 87
Manning, Henry Edward Cardinal, 189
Mao, Tse-tung, 16, 45, 144, 178, 182,
    202-4
Marcuse, Herbert, 212, 214, 221
Maritain, Jacques, 193
Marx, Karl, Marxism. See also Frankfurt
    School.
    Alienation, 212, 214-5
    Alternative, 134, 136
    Anti-capitalist, 3
    Anti-Semitism, 139-40
    Aristocrat, 137
    Aristotle, 36, 140
    Association, 145
    Bakunin, 177-8
    Bohemian, 137, 146
    Bourgeoisie revolutionary class, 22
    Communism, 144
    Communist Manifesto, 108, 136
    Definition of class, 26n.2
    Ecologism, 251, 258-9, 262, 265
    Economic determinism, 141
    Economist, 60
    Fetishism, 138, 154
    Heidegger, 221
    Influence, 136, 164
    Koestler, 178
    Loss of influence, 136, 175, 237, 241
    Marxism, 17, 30, 147, 176, 179-80
    Marxism-Leninism, 182
    Money, 138-9
    Moralist, 63n.56, 140
    Neoconservatives, 233, 235
    On intellectuals, 143-4, 176-7
    Optimism, 140-1, 150
    Over-simplifier, 137-8, 211